Dearst oons
Happy Birthday
78

Four Rossettis

Four Rossettis

A Victorian Biography

Stanley Weintraub

W. H. Allen - London

A Howard and Wyndham Company 1978

Weybright and Talley
750 Third Avenue
New York, N.Y. 10017

Designed by Jacques Chazaud
Printed in the United States of America
for the publishers W. H. Allen & Co. Ltd,
44 Hill Street, London W1X 8LB

ISBN 0 491 01588 7

For Charles T. Butler
and
the late LaFayette L. Butler

Contents

List of Illustrations

1. *The Girlhood of Mary Virgin*, by Dante Gabriel Rossetti. Oil on canvas. Dated "PRB 1849." Gabriel's mother and sister sat for St. Anne and the Virgin. Tate Gallery No. 4872. *Courtesy the Tate Gallery.*

2. *Ecce Ancilla Domini* (*The Annunciation*), by Dante Gabriel Rossetti. Oil on canvas mounted on panel. Dated "March 1850." The Virgin is painted from Christina, the head of the Angel from William. Tate Gallery No. 1210. *Courtesy the Tate Gallery.*

3. Dante Gabriel Rossetti, by William Holman Hunt. Oval. Dated "1853." Birmingham City Museum and Art Gallery No. 33–61. *Courtesy the Birmingham City Museum and Art Gallery.*

4. Ford Madox Brown, by Dante Gabriel Rossetti. Pencil. Dated "Nov/52." National Portrait Gallery, London, No. 1021. *Reproduced courtesy the National Portrait Gallery.*

5. D. G. Rossetti sitting to Elizabeth Siddal, by Dante Gabriel Rossetti. Dated "Sept 1853." Birmingham City Museum and Art Gallery No. 480 '04. *Courtesy the Birmingham City Museum and Art Gallery.*

6. William Holman Hunt, by Dante Gabriel Rossetti. Oval. Pencil. Dated "12th April 1853." Once attributed erroneously to F. G. Stephens. Birmingham City Museum and Art Gallery No. 392 '04. *Courtesy the Birmingham City Museum and Art Gallery.*

7. William Rossetti in 1855, by Ford Madox Brown. Wightwick Manor. *Courtesy of Lady Mander.*

8. Gabriele Rossetti, in his familiar cap with eye-shade, by Dante Gabriel Rossetti. Pencil. Dated "April 28/53." *Courtesy of Mrs. Roderic O'Conor, Henley-on-Thames.*

9. Charles Cayley, by Dante Gabriel Rossetti. Pen and ink. Ca. 1853. Once owned by W. B. Scott and/or Alice Boyd. *Courtesy of T. R. R. O'Conor, Goring-on-Thames, Reading.*

10. *Ophelia*, by John Millais. Oil on canvas. Elizabeth Siddal posed for the drowning Ophelia. Tate Gallery No. 1506. *Courtesy the Tate Gallery.*

11. Elizabeth Siddal, by Dante Gabriel Rossetti. Pencil. 1854. Birmingham City Museum and Art Gallery No. 260 '04. *Courtesy the Birmingham City Museum and Art Gallery.*

12. Elizabeth Siddal, by Dante Gabriel Rossetti. Pencil, pen and ink. Dated "Hastings June 1854." Fitzwilliam Museum No. 2147. *Reproduced by permission of the Syndics of the Fitzwilliam Museum, Cambridge.*

13. Elizabeth Siddal, by Dante Gabriel Rossetti. Pen and brown and black ink. Dated "Feb. 6th 1855." Ashmolean Museum No. E 1152. *Courtesy the Ashmolean Museum, Oxford.*

Foreword
The Survivor

A silver thread of lunacy," Max Beerbohm thought, ran through "the rich golden fabric of 16 Cheyne Walk," where Dante Gabriel Rossetti lived in thrall to his heartbreak and his art. The atmosphere had been abnormal, too, in the places where Rossetti's two sisters yearned away their lives. Not so, however, on the edge of Primrose Hill, in the house where William Michael Rossetti lived out his last years surrounded by treasures from his past. There the family melodrama had become history. By 1919, even its most lurid scenes were a half-century old, electric lights and automobiles having long replaced candles and hansom cabs.

In his study at 3 St. Edmund's Terrace, so cluttered with memorabilia that the only place for one choice painting was in front of a bookshelf, the past was almost palpable. William Rossetti's eyes had dimmed, and his legs were failing; he could no longer climb the stairs into rooms laden, for him, with memories. Still, from his armchair by the fireplace, or from the massive beechwood sofa once owned by Shelley in Italy, and given to William by Edward Trelawny (who had burned the poet's drowned body on the beach at Viareggio), the history of an era was within arm's reach.

William Rossetti was the last of the four brothers and sisters, as well as chronicler and guardian of the family reputation. Around him bulked the evidences of its solidity. Christina's books and manuscript poems. Maria's scrupulous study of Dante. A portrait of Christina by her brother Dante Gabriel, and a drawing of the haunted-eyed young Gabriel by Holman Hunt. Gabriel's own drawings of his models and mistresses, one later his wife, another the wife of his best friend. For the bald, white-bearded patriarch in his ninetieth year, even what he could no longer see around him still glowed in recollection with an undefiled radiance.

Once William, too, had tried painting, but he could never get beyond a dogged competence. And his poetry, as Gabriel had said, was "always going back on the old track." Gabriel liked to tell the story of Longfellow's visit to Cheyne Walk, which had been warm and friendly and included, inevitably, a tour of the studio, and a glance at the drawings and unfinished canvases. There were two Rossetti brothers, Longfellow knew, and when he left he assumed that if one brother were standing before him in his shabby painter's smock, the other must be the poet. "I have been very glad to meet you, Mr. Rossetti," he thanked Gabriel, "and should have liked to have met your brother also. Pray tell him how much I admire his beautiful poem, 'The Blessed Damozel.' "

"I'll tell him," said Longfellow's host, amused. Perhaps Gabriel had remembered when, years before, William Morris had been trying to interest him in Norse legendry, which was at the time Morris's own inspiration for *Sigurd the Volsung*. When the exhortation finally reached the tale of Fafnir, Gabriel had objected. "I never cared much for all that stuff," he said. "There's something unnatural—monstrous—about it. How can one take a real interest in a man who has a dragon for a brother?"

The literal-minded Morris mulled over the advantages and disadvantages of having dragons in the family, then broke the silence. "I'd much rather have a dragon for a brother than a bloody fool!" Gabriel had laughed, and later, with unkind delight, would tell the story about his brother. But Gabriel knew better, as the contents of the serene study at St. Edmund's Terrace confirmed. William was satisfied with what he had accomplished.

The fourth and last Rossetti knew, although his own role had been modest, that he had been part of something which had shaken and shaped his times. After a prudent, unadventurous career he had lived on to inherit the lot of the survivor. Not for him the melodrama—nor the achievement— of his brother's life, nor for him the hidden desperation masked by the outward piety and serenity of his sisters' lives. His family had left an imprint upon English writing and English art which his own contributions—as well as his censorship of the family documents—could only enhance.

The family letters, diaries, pictures and manuscripts were now William's. And also his, for more than two decades, had been not only his civil service pension but the accumulated bank accounts of the long-lived Rossettis and Polidoris, Englishmen and Englishwomen despite their names, though none as tenacious of the years as he. Publishing their histories and their life-records had not been acts of personal immodesty, nor attempts to turn a profit. He was in no urgent need of funds for his children or grandchildren. He was a literary man who, as long as he remained able to use his pen, had needed an occupation for it, and the Rossetti papers were history waiting to be written, while the pictures summoned up the dramas of their creation.

The work remained unfinished. Although the house itself was destroyed by German firebombs in the Blitz, many of the documents remain, raw material for writers whose works would have overflowed the study at St. Edmund's Terrace. Yet these have been, for the most part, accounts of the triumphs and the tragedy of Gabriel. The four Rossettis, the notorious and the obscure, have not, until now, had their collective story told.

I
Charlotte Street
1826-1845

In a small house in drab Charlotte Street,* London, during the four years beginning in 1827, the four Rossettis were born. Their father had lived in England since 1824, having fled Italy as a hunted revolutionary, then turned toward London after temporary political refuge in Malta. What does a refugee do but seek out the solace of his brethren, and Gabriele Rossetti huddled within the Italian colony, breaking out of it only to teach Londoners the Italian language. Even his marriage, in 1826, kept him within the colony, for his wife, Frances, nearly seventeen years younger (he was forty-three), was a Polidori, daughter of another—and more prosperous —teacher of Italian. But her mother, once a governess as was Frances herself, was a Pierce, and from her came the only Anglo-Saxon ancestry the four Rossetti children would inherit.

The half-English Polidoris—Frances was one of four daughters and four sons—were not the marrying type, leaving the Rossetti children with handy recourse to such uncles and aunts as survived. John, a physician, had been a friend and companion of Lord Byron, and had poisoned himself in order to defer permanently his gambling debts. Henry (the only other married Polidori) was a mediocre and eccentric solicitor, and the other brothers were even less effectual. One sister, Eliza, later went to the Crimea with Florence Nightingale. Except for Eliza and the mother of the four Rossettis, the

---

* Not the present Charlotte Street, off Tottenham Court Road, but a nearby one afterwards renamed Hallam Street, between Portland Place and Great Portland Street.

other daughters were as ineffectual as the sons; but each had a small inheritance, frugally dispensed.

The names of the Rossetti children became less and less Italianate as one followed another. First there was Maria Francesca. In 1828 came Gabriel Charles Dante—for Gabriele's studies in Dante had already reached the far side of devotion. William Michael and Christina Georgina followed in the next two years, each christened at the Anglican All Souls' Church, Langham Place, and celebrated by their father in additional bathetic verses of his rhymed autobiography.

Gabriele Rossetti had become a professor of Italian at King's College, London, which brought him an income of £10 a year, plus whatever he could earn from his tutoring, and the title he translated beneath his name as *Professore nel Collegio del Re*. In a good year his income would approach £300; but this was rare. Yet supplementary income was often forthcoming unasked. Poet John Hookham Frere, whom Gabriele had met in Malta after escaping Naples, had independent means, and for years would send without warning £50 or £100. And Charles Lyell (son of the celebrated geologist), who doted on Dante, quietly subsidized several of the *Professore*'s books of commentary and analysis, in which secret conspiracies probably unknown to Dante dominated the great poet's work.

Gabriele was never at an end to his exegetical labors. His health was poor and his nerves bad, and as each grew worse he imagined more mysterious and paranoiac readings into the works of Dante which he set down in thousands of unpublishable manuscript pages. As his sight deteriorated he even imagined he saw Dante in person, once writing William, "Did I tell you that Dante has lately drawn part of his own portrait and written his name under it to oblige me?"

By the time all the children were born, Gabriele had begun to wear a cheap pair of glasses which very likely warped his sight further. Then he supplemented the spectacles with a green eye-shade. With both adjusted, he would often turn from his commentaries to his box of sovereigns, in which he kept his savings as would an Italian peasant. Some day he would have enough to return to Italy, but perhaps not unless his father-in-law and mother-in-law predeceased him and left Frances an expected £3,000.* One could live well in the old country on the income. In anticipation, he wrote to the king of Naples for permission to return from exile. He was rejected. Gabriele poured his frustrations into unraveling the occult secrets of Dante, into additions to his verse autobiography, and into hosting the clusters of curiously garbed émigrés who filled the small house at No. 38 Charlotte

---

* He did not know that she was already borrowing against her inheritance.

Street with Italian conversation and consumed bread and butter with coffee or tea.

What the visitors came for was talk, usually political but sometimes literary, and perhaps out of deference for the "Signora Francesca" or the children, who were permitted to wander in and listen, none ever smoked. There was the exiled General Michele Carrascosa (William's second godfather), Count Carlo Pepoli, the soprano Giuditta Pasta, the anti-feminist author Guido Sorelli, the cellist Dragonetti, the sculptor Sangiovanni, the lexicographer Petroni, the violinist Paganini. Yet the *Professore* had no caste or cultural prejudices, welcoming also Conte Faro, the coal merchant; Filippo Pistrucci, the engraver; Sarti, the plaster cast vendor; Rolandi, the bookseller; Cornaro, the gambler; Aspi, the piano-tuner and Parodi, the dancing-master, who gave the children lessons in return for Gabriele's teaching Italian to his son.

An unexpected legacy of £220 a year had prompted the retirement of Gaetano Polidori and his wife to a cottage in Buckinghamshire, at Holmer Green, where Frances would take their grandchildren to find country quiet after the din of Charlotte Street. "I am sorry to hear that that angelic little demon of a Christina is so fractious and miserable," Gabriele would write to his absent family; "but perhaps when her health is better she will get less restless." While it might improve, it was never good; but Gabriele was always optimistic, and often removed from reality. After Christina had been born, he had written a relative unfeelingly that Frances Rossetti had only "suffered a little" in childbirth, which prompted Christina to scribble on the margin of the letter when she discovered it many years later, "How could my dear Father have given such a report? Dearest Mamma had a fearful time with me."

It was obvious to the local physician at Holmer Green, Mr. Tallent, that the four Rossetti children were at least one too many for their mother, and he offered to adopt the younger boy, William, as he and his wife were childless. William liked the idea. The Tallents had a pony. But the idea was abhorrent to William's parents, and he saw less of Holmer Green thereafter.

Old Polidori—he was seventy-two in 1836—worked at literary pursuits in the morning and country matters in the afternoon, translating Milton into Italian and fashioning tables and cabinets while checking regularly for wood-pigeons or other eatable birds from the open window. As opportunity afforded, he would lay down his tools, point a shotgun out the window, and bag a morsel for the dinner table. His wife, Anna, was always nearly invisible, anticipating the female ailments which kept Victorian ladies confined interminably to bed or bedroom; and their son, Philip, who was weak-minded and "odd," kept to himself, leaving the household to be run by the managerial Eliza.

Sometimes Frances Rossetti would visit Holmer Green alone, leaving the four children with the reluctant Gabriele, who would pen long reports, in microscopic hand, on their condition, and appeal vigorously for their mother's return. Not trusting him, Aunt Eliza would come in a carriage to check, confusing young Gabriel with Christina and then wondering how Christina could have grown so. She also thought, Gabriele wrote, "that Maria's appearance had improved a great deal; and at the mixture of amazement and satisfaction she betrayed, I judged how hideous she must have thought that poor child before."

From the beginning Maria Francesca was the ugly duckling, moon-faced and swarthy, but sweet-tempered and intelligent. By the time she was seven she was turning out verse which her father would show to his friends, one of them writing from Rome in 1835, *"Bacia per me la tua figlia poetessa"* ("Give your poet-daughter a kiss from me"). The other children were more rebellious, especially Gabriel, who was regularly ejected from the drawing room for his obstinacy, and Christina, who once, on being rebuked by her mother, took a scissors and dramatically slashed at her own arm. The *Professore* decided that a more spacious house was needed, to better separate the children. They moved down the street to No. 50, where the rent was a steep £60/year.

No sooner was the move contemplated than Mrs. Rossetti fell ill. Gabriele was frantic throughout 1836, imagining imminent widowerhood. Removal to Holmer Green, and frequent dosages of port and sherry, restored her health, the two daily glasses of brown sherry even making possible her having Gabriel and Christina with her, while the quieter Maria and William remained at home—*"saggio Guglielmo,"* as he called him, in contrast to *"ingegnoso Gabriele"* or *"vivace Christina."* * "If you would like to exchange two storms for two calms," Gabriele bravely wrote his wife, "I would leave you William and Maria, and would take Gabriel and Christina back with me." The exchange was not made, and the *Professore* was able to continue his placid communion with Dante's shade until August, when all four were again under his roof.

By November Mrs. Rossetti was back at Charlotte Street, recovered, and her children demonstrated all they had done and learned since she had left London. Maria, at nine, wrote English and Italian in a flawless hand; Gabriel and Christina were writing as well as drawing; and William, just seven, was reading so well that he had been promised a six-volume

* *saggio:* wise; *ingegnoso:* ingenious; *vivace:* lively.

Shakespeare for his birthday. But Gabriele was delighted to be able to relinquish their education to their aunts and their mother, who now had added a new austerity to her ideas of religious instruction. All four children were regularly taken to Trinity Church, Marylebone Road; after 1838 they accompanied Mrs. Rossetti to St. Katherine's Chapel, Regent's Park, and then to Christ Church, Albany Street. The boys were more dutiful than devotional, William the first to drift away from regularity, reacting with hostility to the ritual at Albany Street, which was so High Church that the minister and his three curates soon turned altogether to Rome, leaving a Keble-like legacy that the ardent Maria found even more attractive than did Christina. Religion was a friend when they had no others.

So close together in age, the four Rossetti children saw little need for other playmates, and there was no parental encouragement to seek out friends. At home they read and wrote, played blindman's buff and puss in the corner, spun tops or rode a rocking horse. Despite Mrs. Rossetti's religious bent, cards were approved for play—first for such simple games as *Patience*, *Beggar My Neighbor* and the *Duchess of Rutland's Whim*, and then for *Whist* and *Tre Sette*—a favorite of Gabriel and William. There was even a recognized identification with card suits. Maria, the masterful, chose clubs; Gabriel picked hearts; Christina diamonds; William spades. Although one can read too much into the childhood choices, none now seems without a future implication.

Out of doors meant walks in newly opened Regent's Park, often as far as Primrose Hill, but always accompanied by an adult. Frances Rossetti would also take the children to the new National Gallery in Trafalgar Square, which opened in 1838, where Gabriel—at ten—quickly announced his admiration for Benjamin West's showy *Christ Healing the Sick*. His mother, though having no technical training in art, at once put him straight by condemning it as "commonplace and expressionless." It may have been Gabriel's first lesson in art criticism.

In whatever the children did when unshepherded by adults, Maria dominated and the boys and Christina followed—until the boys began going to school early in 1837. First it was a small school in Foley Street, near Portland Place, run by a Rev. Mr. Paul; then after the summer holiday they were ready for King's College School, in a basement corner of Somerset House, in the Strand, where the *Professore* had the privilege of sending the first son free, the other at a reduced tuition.

Only the charges were a bargain. School had nothing of the romantic mystery of Sir Walter Scott or "Monk Lewis," or a thriller Gabriel remembered as *Anselemo the Accursed, or, the Skeleton Hand.* And Latin, which was first as fascinating as a fairy tale, turned into drudgery. The moral atmosphere of the classroom, William later complained, "reeked . . . of unveracity, slipperiness, and shirking." At home Gabriel had been "our Dantuccio," as his father took pleasure in his unspoiled boyhood joy of learning. School worked a change.

At home Mrs. Rossetti instructed the girls from the Bible, the *Confessions* of St. Augustine, *Pilgrim's Progress*, and edifying Victorian stories for children. For a special treat there was *The Arabian Nights*. Later they, too, discovered the reading matter which first thrilled the boys, but they also quickly acquired their mother's High Anglican piety. William and Gabriel, like their father, were "avowed non-believers in Christianity," and schooling only intensified their resistance. Nor did they participate in team sports and games, or make close friends. They had each other, and William was the youngest boy at school, at first under the regulation nine. Each day they looked forward most to going home.

The one room in the house the whole family used was the front parlor. It was also the dining room as well as the *Professore*'s writing room, where, after four o'clock dinner, if he were home early enough from his walking rounds to private lessons, Gabriele would return to his Dante studies. There, too, one could find *Bell's Weekly Messenger*, Tory in politics and evangelical in religion. Daily newspapers were too expensive. Household conversation was in English when the children talked with their mother, in Italian when the *Professore* was involved. He chose English only when absolutely necessary, and he never considered it necessary *in la famiglia*.

When the room was otherwise unoccupied, young Gabriel was transfixed by the emanations from the mysterious books his father found so fascinating. The details did not interest him, but the study then seemed a "haunted room," where "the very books had a conscious and external life of their own." Alone there, his imagination racing, he would often grow afraid, sensing another presence beside him, while a copy of the *Vita Nuova* appeared to give off a faint light, which filled him "with a happy terror." On the staircase he would rush past the second landing at times when the light was bad, for a dark corner seemed sometimes to contain a spectral Dante.

There was a back parlor, too, with a lidded sink close to the single window. It was William's favorite seat for reading, and for watching his caged squirrel race fruitlessly in its treadmill. Above the back parlor was Gabriel's room, still, like the rest of the house, without pictures on the walls, but with his own small animals in cages, a dormouse and a hedgehog. The first two pictures arrived in 1837 when painter Gabriele Smargiassi, a fellow Vastese, visited and presented the family with two small oils—scenes of Capri and Vasto. Then came, from an aunt, a framed engraving of the new queen, Victoria, and—from another Italian friend—a painting of *The*

Marriage Feast of Tobias, purportedly by Veronese. But the house was also full of books, and pictures in books, from the Dutch-language *Metamorphosis Naturalis*, with Goedaerdt's realistic and sometimes repellent color prints of insects and their transformations, to Martin and Westall's imaginative *Illustrations of the Bible*, which Gabriel considered a work of power and genius. And where there were no pictures, Gabriel supplied them, drawing illustrations of Falstaff or Macbeth or Hamlet, and coloring sheets of theatrical prints. He was already talking of a career in art, but the art he produced demonstrated more enthusiasm than genius.

Money worries now obsessed the *Professore* as much as did Dante. An Irish carpenter named Mullins stole £30 from the hoard in Gabriele's box. The *Professore* asked the authorities for mercy, as it was probably a first offense, and Mullins might have stolen the entire contents but did not. Besides, he was a father of four children. The appeal was fruitless. Mullins was sentenced to ten years' transportation to Australia. There were other financial losses too, from thefts as well as from nonpayment of tutorial bills. Then the family convalescent home in Holmer Green was lost just as it was most needed, after a year's continuous family illness, when scarlet fever, then measles, coursed through the children. Gaetano Polidori had tired of the country, and found a cottage with a garden near the Regent's Park canal, just off the road to the Zoological Gardens. It was a fifteen minutes' walk from Charlotte Street, and more than compensated for the loss of country air. Mrs. Rossetti could visit her mother nearly every day, taking one or more of her children with her; and Polidori's library was more varied than the *Professore*'s collection of Dante and related material. Most exciting of all, Polidori had set up a small printing press in a shed in the back garden, and imported a Sicilian compositor named Privitera, who to the delight of the children and disgust of Aunt Eliza made soup from the garden snails.

By 1839 the children thought they were ready to publish on the Polidori press. They had long been constructing their own tales with their own illustrations, William writing from school to his mother just before the closing of the Holmer Green residence that he and Gabriel "have made a new volume of the Brigands as well as the dramatics. We have given them to Byers telling him to bind the former like 'Tales' and the latter in calf." Christina, too, was writing poetry at home, but the real prodigy was Maria, who seemed destined to be the scholar of the family. When Gabriel and William began learning Greek in school, she insisted on being taught it at home, and learned more rapidly than did the schoolboys. By twelve she was reading Euripides' plays in Italian, and—in Greek—the *Theogony* of Hesiod, and Homer. Gabriel—in February 1840, when he was eleven—did a series of pen-and-ink drawings for each book of the *Iliad* to please her.

The *Professore* wrote proudly to Charles Lyell, who was Gabriel Charles Dante's godfather, "My two boys . . . are making considerable progress in Latin and Greek, and in the other branches of instruction. But I am particularly pleased with my oldest girl Maria Francesca, who has been gifted by nature with a quite uncommon intelligence. She is a comfort to us. . . ."

In appearance Maria was much less of a comfort. Always stocky and swarthy, she recalled her dark Vastese ancestors, a resemblance which inspired her father's effusive friend, Count Pepoli, to announce, "Look what an Italian face that girl has! And what perfect and unusual beauty!" Rossetti replied quietly that it was sufficient for him that there was nothing wrong with her, and that he hoped she would be good. It was not enough for Pepoli, who thought Maria resembled a Raphael model; but Maria herself knew better. "Papa," she told her father when Pepoli was out of earshot, "I don't believe what that gentleman said. Christina is much prettier than I, everybody says so." Diplomatically, Gabriele told her that she was right, but that the Count was not wrong.

The three younger Rossettis had more obvious traces of English blood than Maria. Christina had hazel eyes set in an oval face, and light-brown hair; and the boys were also handsome. All but William were capricious in behavior, given to tantrums as well as to amiability. William was somewhat cowed by the others, but at school both he and Gabriel—although two years apart—had entered the Lower First together, and although Gabriel at times spurted ahead, by the time William reached the Lower Fourth he was again reunited with his brother, who had shown little interest in Latin, French or Greek, all drearily taught as dead languages.

The boys walked to school, tramping through most of central London in order to vary their paths and examine whatever interesting sights there were off the main streets which eventually flowed into the Strand. Writing "Jenny" years later, Gabriel recalled in it having had a sleeping woman identified as a streetwalker—a discovery he kept from his decorous parents, although he never forgot

> . . . the wise, unchildish elf,
> To schoolmate lesser than himself,
> Pointing you out, what thing you are. . . .

When the sights were uninteresting, Gabriel would create a diversion, pretending to be lame or deformed and hobbling along until a passerby demonstrated sympathy. Then he would run off, laughing, having lightened his day in advance.

Although Gaetano Polidori took fewer books with him when he moved back to London than when he departed for Holmer Green, his library still magnetized his grandchildren, improving on· school for the boys and substituting for it for the girls, who were at their grandfather's home nearly daily with their mother. Regent's Park was not a satisfactory equivalent for the country, but was still wild and wooded enough to suffice, although the opportunities for the boys to catch frogs diminished. Christina could continue her lifelong fascination with small animals, although she confined herself to observation, especially after discovering a dead mouse in the garden at Holmer Green, and burying it; for when she returned to the grave a few days later and removed the covering of moss, she saw a black insect emerge from the corpse. "I fled in horror," she recalled, "and for long years ensuing I never mentioned this ghastly incident to anyone." But birds, insects and small animals always were part of her poetic imagination, one incident involving them becoming an unrecognized epiphany for her, although it was only a dream she confided to Gabriel. She was walking in Regent's Park at dawn, and just as the sun rose she saw a wave of yellow light surge from the trees and become a multitude of canaries, which rose into the sky, circled, and scattered. All the canaries in London, she imagined, had met in the park before daybreak, and were returning to their cages. She made no effort to interpret her vision.

One of the children's favorite books was Peter Parley's illustrated *Natural History*, for plants and flowers meant almost as much to them as did small animals. For Christina the morbid or the demonic appeared in everything she loved, even the lowly plant. "I remember," she wrote, "a certain wild strawberry growing on a hedgerow bank, watched day by day while it ripened." Maria had instructed her "not to pluck it prematurely," and she complied, returning every day with her sister to watch it grow. Which one was to eat it, or whether they were to halve and share it, Christina could not recall, but "it turned out we watched in vain; for a snail or some such marauder must have forestalled us at a happy moment. One fatal day we found it half-eaten, and good for nothing." The irony in *happy* was clear; nor was the word *fatal* haphazardly chosen. It was a lesson in pessimism to complement her memory of the mouse.

On some afternoons, school began for the girls when the boys came home, for their father would barter his own expertise for lessons, just as with the dancing-master Parodi. When the German-Jewish émigré Dr. Adolph Heimann, a professor at University College, offered to teach the young Rossettis in return for Italian lessons for himself, all four were put to Schiller and the *Sagen und Marchen* under his genial direction, which flowered into one of the closest family friendships, especially after he married in 1843 and began having children of his own. For Gabriel the impact of German literature would be profound, until put to flight by Dante and the early Italian poets; but before he would reach twenty he would do a translation of Bürger's *Lenore*, begin, ambitiously, another of the *Nibelungenlied*, and complete a translation (the only one of the three which survives) of the *Arme Heinrich* of the twelfth-century poet Hartmann von Aue.

At home in the evenings all four Rossettis experimented with writing. In 1840 each of the children began a tale for a collection to be printed on their grandfather's press. William began a "romance of chivalry" to be called *Raimond and Matilda*. Gabriel contributed *Roderick and Rosalba*, which began, "It was a dark and stormy night. . . ." Enthusiastically, Gabriel also produced pen-and-ink designs for the title pages of the projected novels, circles dominated by the figures of knights in armor, each bearing the title of one of the novels: *Sir Aubrey de Metford: a Romance of the Fourteenth Century*; *Roderick and Rosalba: a Story of the Round Table*; *Raimond and Matilda*; and *Retribution*. But the ambitious writing project was never completed; nor was Gabriel's *Faust*-like novel, *Sorrentino*, with the devil as hero, which was abandoned after four or five chapters. When Gabriel had read it aloud to the family his sisters denounced it as "horrible" and "indecent," and left the room. Their reaction was unpromising if the author had hoped for a larger audience. Wearily, he destroyed the manuscript, and only William mourned the loss. Maria then became the first to supply a finished work, a blank-verse rendering of an Italian elegy for Gwendalina Talbot, Princesse Borghese. Polidori had promised "publication," and duly had it printed in 1841, although it demonstrated more persistence than poetic promise. Little better was Gabriel's first published effusion, *Sir Hugh the Heron*, which grandfather Polidori dutifully printed in 1843, labeling it "for private circulation only." But "publication" briefly inspired William, who began—and never finished—*Ulfred the Saxon, a Tale of the Conquest.*

As soon as Christina began writing verses she felt were worth keeping, she had them copied by Maria, with date of composition, into a small black notebook, for her sister's handwriting was firm and less childish; and from April 27, 1842, until November 17, 1847, the handwriting remained Maria's although the poems were by Christina. They were imitations of Herbert, Crabbe, Blake, Tennyson, and the Italian poets beloved by her father, and showed no signs of genius, but Polidori promised that if she produced enough of them for a volume, he would set Privitera to printing them. The notebook took five years to fill.

The children also collaborated on a family journal called *The Hodge Podge*, and another, *The Illustrated Scrapbook*, which Gabriel called successor to "the fallen *Hodge Podge*," and for which he conceived his first version of

"The Blessed Damozel." At thirteen Christina managed two "poetic effusions," "Rosalind" and "Corydon's Resolution," which Gabriel thought good enough to draw from her notebook for *The Hodge Podge*, but which William as her posthumous editor many decades later labeled "indisputably bad." So did Grandfather Polidori, who omitted them from the 1847 *Verses*.

If Polidori had aimed at stimulating the poetic faculty in Gabriel through his press, the stratagem failed. It took the indolent Gabriel two years to complete *Sir Hugh*, for what he really wanted was to leave school to study art. At thirteen he was showing little interest in anything else, and the old *Professore*, ailing and worried about reducing his expenses, gave in. In the summer of 1841 his eldest son's formal education ended. "Not wanting to thwart his inclination," Gabriele wrote, though hardly with conviction, "I have started him on pursuing the profession he covets. If he succeeds, he will aid my old age. A hundred times do I thank God that my four children are all studious and all good. If I can leave them a good education, leading them to an honourable path in life, I shall die contented in the fogs of England, without regretting the sun of Italy."

That he would die soon, he was sure. In 1842 he thought he was suffering from bronchitis. By the summer of the next year he had to give up all work and go to France, and milder weather, while his friend Ciciloni took Gabriele's pupils. Paris worked wonders, and his bronchitis, which was more likely tuberculosis, appeared under control. He went home, but before the year was out the *Professore* suddenly lost the sight of one eye, and his vision in the other eye grew dim. Living in fear of imminent and complete blindness, he had to greatly reduce his activity, especially his going to the homes of pupils to give lessons. Aside from tutoring pupils in his own home, his occupation was gone, and with it the family income. Only in 1847 did he resign his professorship, which meant less the relinquishing of an empty title than the acknowledgement of an empty future.

Young Gabriel was already at "Sass's Academy," an art school in Bloomsbury directed by F. S. Cary, who by no coincidence was the son of a translator of Dante known to the *Professore*. Cary was rigorous in his teaching of technique, and had among his credits the training of John Millais, who had entered as a nine-year-old prodigy and was already at the school of the Royal Academy. But Gabriel failed to flourish under discipline. He saw no purpose in highly technical representations of human anatomy, and at school was content to sketch the lower human leg with one bone. He was deliberately disobedient, and often absent, although he never indicated where he had been. He wrote poetry when he should have been drawing, played practical jokes on his classmates, and failed—out of fear of inadequacy—to present his work for criticism. The pattern would be duplicated all his life. "I believe at my birth," he told a friend ruefully, late in his life, "I must have had my hands in my pockets."

More interesting to him than art school were his two visits across the Channel to Boulogne in 1843–44, where he stayed with the Italian artist Giuseppe Maenza and his English wife, friends of his father. The old town charmed him and he charmed the Maenzas, even though they had to nurse him during one visit through a luckily mild attack of smallpox. Young Gabriel did not mind being in bed. "His imagination promises much," Maenza wrote the *Professore* on the eve of Gabriel's second leave-taking, "and I am persuaded that he will reach the goal all right." But he also saw through Gabriel's indolence, and recommended to his father that he should push him into some physical activity like fencing or gymnastics, "to check the sedentary habits to which he is greatly inclined."

By the time Gabriel qualified to enter the Antique School of the Royal Academy in December, 1845, much later than he had hoped, there had been great changes at home, some of them intended to make it possible for him to continue his art training. In 1844 Maria was seventeen. She had been helping Lyell with his translations of Dante, and acting as reader and amanuensis for her father, whose remaining eye was too weak for correspondence. She had also become his translator. A notebook dated 1842 contains her Englishing of Gabriele's monograph, "Rome, toward the middle of the XIX century." But the young girl who earlier had been able to read Hesiod in the original Greek, and translate Dante, had been educated by her mother entirely with the goal of her becoming a governess, and her help was now needed. The Marchioness of Bath, in whose household Maria's aunt Charlotte Polidori served, had a brother-in-law, Lord Charles Thynne, who was suddenly in need of a governess. The situation was claimed for Maria, who went off into what she considered exile.

William was fifteen and Christina fourteen. They had to assist in earning the family living too. Mrs. Rossetti, who had once been a governess herself, and could teach Italian and French, began seeking outside pupils, and training Christina to assist her. She also continued seeking advances on her inheritance from more comfortable members of the family, primarily her sister Charlotte, for the remaining £2000 she would have on the death of her perpetually ailing but tenacious mother had to come due some day. But William had to be found a respectable job. He had completed the Sixth Form and had shown no signs of genius. He was low in wearable clothing, and remembered daubing the worn elbows of a blue cloth jacket with Prussian blue watercolor paint in order to be presentable enough to visit a friend in opulent Cleveland Row, and his father—unaware of the experiment—saying to him expansively that if he only had the means William would be sent *"vestito come un principino"* ("dressed like a princeling").

No princeling, however, William would soon have his future urgently discussed by the *Professore* with an old and valued acquaintance, Sir Isaac Lyon Goldsmid, a wealthy stockbroker whose children Gabriele had taught Italian. William had sometimes accompanied his father to the Goldsmid home, to act as his eyes and to steer him out of the way of omnibuses and cart-horses; and there he had read from Sir Isaac's books while his father gave lessons in an adjoining room. Once, William had wanted to go to sea, but that childish fancy had been replaced by the desire to become a doctor. Yet a career in medicine meant a course of study that would have cost the family money in tuition and in lost wages, and the *Professore* did not go to Goldsmid to seek funds. An acquaintance of Sir Isaac's was Sir John Wood, Chairman of the Board of Excise. Early in February, 1845, a summons came for William to be interviewed for a clerkship in the Excise Office in Old Broad Street, east of the Royal Exchange. On February 6 he put in his first day's work. By day, at least, a quiet descended on No. 50 Charlotte Street.

II

Occupations
1845-1848

Rising early from the bed the brothers shared, William would leave for the long walk to the Excise Office in Old Broad Street, east of St. Paul's, before his brother was even awake. Gabriel could sleep the sleep of the reprieved, understanding what the job meant to William's hopes, and how it kept his own alive. With what was probably unconscious callousness he had made the point in a letter to William from Boulogne, where he was staying with the Maenzas when he first heard the news. "I was rejoiced to hear of the prospect of employment which has opened for you. Let us hope that it will be permanent." William could have been forgiven for privately hoping otherwise.

His beginning annual salary was £80—substantial for a fifteen-year-old "extra clerk." * For it he filled in appropriate places in printed forms relating to requests for sick and personal leave among employees in the far-flung Excise Service. It was dull, quasi-mechanical activity, but he performed it as if he were going to make it his life's work. Later in the year Gabriel entered the Antique School of the Royal Academy in part because William was earning a salary and in part because he had finally submitted to the Academy's board of examiners, in June, 1845, the required three drawings—an antique figure, an anatomical figure and a skeleton. The Antique School might have been so called because its venerable Keeper,

---

* The nineteen-year-old Anthony Trollope, who had gone to Harrow, began as a junior clerk at the Post Office at £90 a year.

George Jones, R.A., bore a feeble resemblance to the aged Duke of Wellington, but in actuality the name came from the first stage of Academy training—copying old statuary and casts, from which the student progressed to drawing from living models in the Life School and, finally, the Painting School.

Gabriel arrived in December, shabby in an ill-fitting, unfashionable old swallowtail coat which probably belonged to his father and complemented his unkempt, unbarbered, curly dark hair. He announced himself as Gabriel Charles Dante Rossetti. "Dear me, Sir," stammered George Jones, "you *have* a fine name." It was almost his last compliment from the Keeper, for Gabriel was put off by the obligatory exercises in technique. Instead he dashed off verses and sketches, unseen by Jones but admired by the other students. And he read, having found a new poet to replace Dante and Goethe and Shakespeare in his affections. To the public the young Robert Browning was incomprehensible; to Gabriel (in his brother's words), "Here were passion, observation, aspiration, mediaevalism, the dramatic perception of character, act, and incident. In short, if at this date Rossetti had been accomplished in the art of painting, he would have carried out in that art very much the same range of subject and treatment which he found in Browning's poetry; and it speaks something for his originality and self-respecting independence that, when it came to verse-writing, he never based himself upon Browning to any appreciable extent, and for the most part pursued a wholly diverse path."

All the energy which might have gone into the Antique School seemed applied to Italian translation, or to the reading of Shelley and Browning, and Gabriel even discovered, at the British Museum, an anonymously published poem, *Pauline* (1833), which he was sure had been written by his hero. Screwing up his courage, he determined to prove his case. "It seemed to me, in reading this beautiful composition," he wrote the poet diplomatically, "that it presents a noticeable analogy in style and feeling to your first acknowledged work, *Paracelsus*: so much so indeed as to induce a suspicion that it might actually be written by yourself." Gabriel signed it as "Your distant respectful admirer," and Browning, receiving it in Venice, acknowledged that Rossetti had penetrated his secret. Had Gabriel been preparing for a career in literary scholarship his discovery would have been useful; he was making no progress toward a profession in art, although no one reminded him of that when he would return home at dusk, often having been at the British Museum reading or drawing rather than at the place for which his tuition was being paid out of William's earnings.

At Charlotte Street Maria was gone, but her unhappiness at being a governess was the theme of every letter home, where—she wrote early in

1846—"it would be very pleasant to remain always." But she thanked God, in a letter certain to raise feelings of guilt in Charlotte Street, that she had been endowed with "talents which enable me to assist my dear father by removing the burden of my maintenance which he has borne for so many years with so much loving care. Might I only remove as easily the anxieties which weigh upon his heart, and all the vexations that oppress his mind." To "Willie," nevertheless, she commiserated that he could not enjoy the country air, the primroses and the nearly tame owls at Longleat, which privately she would have traded for the fogs and mists of London.

Maria's ambitions were still vaguely literary, but weighed down by the excessive piety which provided her only impetus to compose. In 1843 she had written a *Vision of Human Life* for one of the children's scrapbooks. In 1846, while she was still with the Thynnes, it was published at a shilling, as *The Rivulets, A dream not all a Dream.* It was a short religious allegory about four children, each of whom is to guard a rivulet from pollution. The rivulets, a convenient catechism at the end explains, represent the human heart; and the children have instructive German names—Liebe, Selbstsucht, Eigendünkel and Faule (Love, Selfishness, Conceit and Laziness). Liebe's devotion earns a place in heaven, and the only one irretrievably lost is Selbstsucht; but if there were a family allegory suggested, none of the Rossetti children ever openly related the four characters in *Rivulets* to themselves. Few copies were ever sold, and Maria at nineteen remained in literary obscurity at Longleat, Gabriel writing to his mother, then off to visit Maria in the country in the summer of 1847, "I hope you told Lady Charles that poor Maggy is not to be bullied and badgered out of her life by a lot of beastly brats; and that Lady C. fully understands the same, and has already provided the said Maggy with a bamboo." But Maria may have been less preoccupied by the behavior of the Thynne children than of their father, who had found that High Church Tractarianism was insufficient and was on the verge of going over completely to Rome. Eventually Maria extricated herself from papistic Longleat and became governess to the family of a Mr. Read, who lived in the Finsbury Pavement area not far from the Excise Office. There Christina sometimes visited and gave her some relief from child care. Maria felt less desolate.

Christina had been saved from governessing first by her youth and then by her frailty. In 1846, when her ailments were relatively new, her physician, Dr. Charles J. Hare, found only that she was "pale (anaemic)." It was a chronic nineteenth-century complaint among housebound older women, who remedied it by frequent dosages of "tonics" which were largely a substitute for the unavailability to them of the local public house. But Christina was fifteen. And it seems clear that the largely undefined illness—whether it was neurotic or had a physical basis—was timely. "As an invalid," William later wrote of her, "she had courage, patience, even cheerfulness. I have even heard her dwell upon the satisfaction—such as it is—of being ill, and interdicted from active exertion. . . ." Many years later she confessed to her publisher, Alexander Macmillan, "I am not very robust, nor do I expect to become so; but I am well content with the privileges and immunities which attach to semi-invalidism." One such immunity was identified in a letter to Swinburne, when she was long past any breadwinning necessities: "I myself feel like an escaped Governess. . . ."

There were liabilities as well as satisfactions in adolescent illness. Her own frequent betakings to bed were echoed in such verses as

> Sleep, let me sleep, for I am sick of care;
> Sleep, let me sleep, for my pain wearies me.
> Shut out the light; thicken the heavy air
> With drowsy incense. . . .

And that poem, copied as it was in Christina's notebook in her mother's hand, suggests that there were times when she was too feeble to produce a fair copy on her own.

Frances Rossetti had little time in which to feel sorry for herself. She hurried each weekday between caring for the *Professore* and the homes where she gave lessons. There was little time for indulging Christina, although she was left alone with her poetry. Or almost alone, since inevitably she became companion and substitute nurse for her father, who was morose and enfeebled, and sometimes longed loudly for death to end the decay of his faculties. The warm, cheerful family was only a memory. By day she was the only child at home, to muse over the mutability of life in the society of a sick old man who was its very symbol. Her youthful poetry darkly reflected the experience, as even "in the flowers she saw decay." Her interests in love and sex which were beginning to emerge as they might in any other girl of her age were darkly colored, too, by the realization that sooner or later they ended with "utter desolation," and that the only way to escape was to cultivate "indifference." Her own life would be too short for love, she suggested in December, 1847, in

> The roses bloom too late for me:
> The violets I shall not see. . . .

Yet after composing a poem she titled "Love Attacked" she thought better of such feelings and in "Love Defended" asked, "Who extols a wilderness?" and labeled her pessimism as "foolish" and "devoid of sense." The brave affirmations became persistent. Love was a way out of the stricken nest in Charlotte Street, and the thought exhilarated her almost as much as its likely realities repelled.

The solemnly titled *Verses by Christina G. Rossetti* was the chief satisfaction of 1847 for her. Old Polidori not only made good on his promise of publication, but included a frontispiece pencil portrait of her in profile by Gabriel as well as four of his illustrations for her poems. Privately printed in a small edition, and given away to friends and relatives rather than sold, the book made no impact whatever on the literary scene; but it gave Christina the feeling that she was not writing in a vacuum. Someday a wider world might discover them. That it might discover her too was no consideration. Any visions of worldly fame would have been thrust aside with a shudder as sacrilegious and sinful.

Vanity would always be, to both sisters, one of the most venial of sins, and their renunciation of it conformed to the pattern of renewal within the Church of England with which Maria and Christina identified. For years, English divines had subscribed genially to the Thirty-nine Articles, while their parishioners maintained a becoming and dignified loathing of Dissenters and of their misplaced zeal, and of Romanists and their papist adoration of ritual. Not until the winds from Oriel College, Oxford, began stirring new pieties in the Established Church, had fervor and ritual and doctrine become newly fashionable. Christina's faith, William later wrote, was "always of the most absolute and also of the most literal kind . . . , not doctrinal or didactic: doctrine is presupposed. . . ." So it was even in her earliest poems, where (as in "A Testimony") everything from laughter to health is "vanity beneath the sun," and men walked "in a vain shadow." Man flourished—and faded—"as a green leaf," and left "no track," for both hopes and bodies were doomed to decay, and death alone was "the lot of all." Maria and Christina embraced that certainty as if it were a valuable personal treasure, and found joy in the thrill of their devotions, Maria turning them into Sunday School lessons for younger children, Christina into beatific visions in verse. Although she could not have perceived it as such, she was leaving a palpable "track."

While Christina added to her poetry notebooks at home, Gabriel had encountered a curious notebook at his free university, the British Museum, at a time when he should have been copying plaster casts in the Royal Academy's Sculpture Room. In April, 1847, a Museum attendant named Palmer, noticing that the young man with the neglected hair and clothes was interested in poetry, offered to sell him a manuscript book he had apparently acquired legitimately, crammed with prose, verse and drawings by a little-regarded eccentric of a generation before, William Blake. The price asked was ten shillings, which Gabriel thought a bargain, considering that Blake, although no darling of the orthodox literati, had written *Songs of Innocence and Experience*. A glance through the notebook showed, William remembered, "outspoken epigrams and jeers against such painters as Correggio, Titian, Rubens, Rembrandt, Reynolds, and Gainsborough—all men whom Blake regarded as fulsomely florid, or lax, or swamping ideas in mere manipulation. These were balsam to [Gabriel's] soul, and grist to his mill."

Gabriel had no money, but applied to William, and the manuscript changed hands. Although Gabriel held it in reverence all his life, it was not for him a mere curiosity for display. Since the pages were a tangle of abandoned starts, alternative lines and cancellations, the brothers decided to copy out what they could, Gabriel taking the poetry and William the prose. From the verse, Gabriel learned in subtle ways which would influence his own writing. The prose reinforced all his misgivings about the stagnation of an Antique School education in art:

The Man who on Examining his own Mind finds nothing of Inspiration ought not to dare to be an Artist.

Reynolds thinks that Man Learns all that he knows. I say on the Contrary that Man Brings All that he has or can have Into the World with him. Man is Born Like a Garden ready Planted & Sown.

The Man who never in his Mind and Thoughts Travel'd to Heaven Is No Artist.

What has Reasoning to do with the Art of Painting?

Knowledge of Ideal Beauty is not to be Acquired. It is Born with us.

In 1847 William could better afford the Blake purchase, having been "put on the establishment"—the permanent staff—at the Excise Office, and given a £10 annual increase. By then he was employed as clerk in the English Correspondent's Office, his assignment to communicate with Excise officials in England and with English traders paying Excise duties. The work was dull, but the head of William's section was kindly; and the second-in-command enlivened the department by being unpunctual on the then-frequent days when a criminal was hanged. An undersized, elderly man who dressed in out-of-fashion knee breeches, he had a passion for public executions and a nearly infallible memory for the fatal statistics and for the final speeches and confessions of the condemned. At the beginning of 1848 William moved to the Secretary's office, where the primary hazard was the religious zeal of the chief clerk, a red-haired, red-faced Low Church loyalist who passed out Evangelical tracts each Saturday morning. "Mercifully," William remembered, Mr. Corbett "abstained from inquiring how I liked them."

The routine at Old Broad Street was so fixed that only one day in William's early years there remained memorable—April 10, 1848, on which was scheduled a great Chartist demonstration on Kennington Common. The year 1848 was one of revolutionary enthusiasm across the Channel, and William's radical Idealism was widely shared, but not by his brother. Gabriel had little interest in any politics but the politics of art, and to him the Chartists who had frightened the government were only a mob of low-class "cads." Since revolutionary ideals were impolitic for a young civil servant, William kept his opinions to himself. To counter the radicals the government nervously deputized whatever civil servants were available as special constables. Although William was not detailed for street duty he was invested with a constable's staff for garrisoning the office; he remained through the night despite the petering out of the demonstration. "If I had to break a Chartist's head with my staff," he thought later, "I suppose I should have tried to do so, but . . . I was considerably in sympathy with the Chartists, and had no inclination for breaking of heads, theirs or my own."

No friendships resulted from William's early Excise Office experience. His circle of acquaintances became Gabriel's own, as Gabriel had a way of attracting followers as well as friends; and, as he had already shown with Browning, he had no hesitation about seeking friends among already established artists. For William Bell Scott, a visit to Charlotte Street confirmed the impression he had received from a Rossetti letter. The saturnine, thirty-six-year-old Scott, then Master of the Government School of Design at Newcastle-on-Tyne, was also a poet—a combination of interests clearly appealing to Gabriel, who had written to him in November, 1847, praising Scott's ambitious blank-verse poem, *The Year of the World.* Puzzled and intrigued by the Italianate name, Scott returned a polite acknowledgment. Gabriel reacted by packaging copies of his completed verse manuscripts and sending them to Scott identified collectively as "Songs of the Art Catholic." All Scott knew about the young man was his confession that "the object of my ambition is to deserve one day the name of painter, to which end I am at present a student of the Academy." The poems suggested that he was much closer to another ambition, as they included drafts of "The Blessed Damozel" and "My Sister's Sleep," awesome accomplishments for a nineteen-year-old art student. Scott decided that he had to meet the young man.

It was close to Christmas when business brought Scott to London. Calling at Charlotte Street, he found the eye-shaded *Professore* in the small front parlor, dwarfed in a large chair by the fire, a table nearby on which rested a large manuscript book "and the largest snuff-box I ever saw beside it conveniently open." Neither Gabriel nor William were home, but by the window, writing at a high, narrow reading desk, stood "a slight girl with a serious regular profile, dark against the pallid wintry light." Christina curtseyed, then went on writing. At seventeen it was inappropriate that she do more, although Polidori had published her *Poems* that year, and she would have been of immense interest to the visitor had he known what she was doing, and what she had already done. Young Gabriel was away painting, the *Professore* explained. Scott promised to look him up.

Scott remembered finding Rossetti at the studio of Holman Hunt. This would have to have been half a year later, for Gabriel, frustrated at the Academy school, would decide that he would only learn how to apply paint to canvas by wielding a brush in close proximity to a working painter. Backed by a promise of modest financial help from his Aunt Charlotte for six months' instruction, Gabriel looked for an artist under whom he could learn. His first choice declined. In March, 1848, he wrote to his second choice, who wondered whether his leg was being pulled. At twenty-six, the burly Ford Madox Brown was a largely unsuccessful painter whose prospects as a Royal Academician were remote, and who was further embittered by his early widowerhood. The letter listed the "glorious works" by Brown which Rossetti admired, and emphasized his "constant study" of Brown's neglected painting, *The Execution of Mary Queen of Scots*, a continuing examination made possible (it went unsaid) because it hung for years in the Pantheon Bazaar, awaiting a buyer. To it Gabriel predicted indebtedness "if ever I do anything in the art." Then Gabriel came to his proposition—that in order to obtain "some knowledge of colour (which I have as yet scarcely attempted), the hope suggests itself that you may possibly admit pupils to profit by your invaluable assistance."

Brown suspected a hoax, and set off from his studio nearby, with a "stout stick" in his hand. At the address on the letter he had received he knocked, but would not enter or give his name, awaiting Gabriel, whom he asked, first, "Is your name Rossetti and is this your writing?" and then, "What do you mean by it?" Assured that Gabriel meant everything he had written, Brown was disarmed by the naïve sincerity as well as the charm of his supplicant, and agreed to teach him without fee. Gabriel dropped out of the Antique School and began spending his days at Brown's studio in Clipstone Street, Marylebone, and his nights at a life class in Maddox Street which Brown had recommended. Aunt Charlotte duly provided the half-guinea weekly for the four-evenings-a-week sessions, which lasted through the spring—about as long as Gabriel's first apprenticeship.

The friendship with "old Brown" was lifelong. But Brown, exacting as Gabriel's earlier teachers, insisted on painting medicine bottles and pickle jars. "He set me to fag at some still life—drawing and painting both,"

Gabriel later wrote to Scott, "but I could not stand that sort of thing; and after a time or two gave it up." His impatience at having to master his craft was part of a lifelong artistic schizophrenia, for he was already showing Brown his poems, and was exhilarated by the results of having sent copies of his poems to the critic and essayist Leigh Hunt. To Hunt he had confided that he was at a loss to know which of the arts was his most appropriate vehicle. The critic had observed that the samples he was shown suggested that Gabriel's poetry was "not so musical as pictorial." Judging from the original verse rather than the translations, he

recognized an unquestionable poet, thoughtful, imaginative, and with rare powers of expression. I hailed you as such at once, without any misgiving; and, besides your Dantesque heavens (without any hell to spoil them), admired the complete and genial round of your sympathies with humanity. I know not what sort of painter you are. If you paint as well as you write, you may be a rich man; or at all events, if you do not care to be rich, may get leisure enough to cultivate your writing. But I hardly need tell you that poetry, even the very best—nay, the best, in this respect, is apt to be the worst—is not a thing for a man to live upon while he is in the flesh, however immortal it may render his spirit.

Poet or painter? Whether he wanted to be one more than the other altered with the external circumstances.

Gabriel had barely begun work with Brown, but the drudgery of still-life painting already oppressed him. He had been less than diligent in his six years of schooling; yet he felt beyond mere prentice work. Somehow he drifted out of regular attendance at Clipstone Street without injury to his relationship with Brown, and began a search for a new instructor at whose side he might be an instant artist.

Rather than confess failure at Brown's by remaining at home, he worked alone at the little-used studio of a former schoolmate, a shriveled, squeaky-voiced sculptor of bas-reliefs, John Hancock. The hiatus was brief. His next painting master was a former Academy student only a year older, the one contemporary whom Gabriel had not dominated with what A. C. Benson later called his "natural kingliness." Comparing his work to that of Holman Hunt, Gabriel recognized his technical insufficiencies, especially when the Academy Hanging Committee accepted Hunt's canvas, *The Eve of St. Agnes*. In any case, Rossetti would have responded to Hunt's inspiration having come from Keats's poetry, but in the Architectural Room where the picture hung, he declared loudly to the painter that it was the best canvas in the exhibition. Hunt hardly knew Rossetti; his best painter friend then was John Millais, whom everyone outside the current Academy committee recognized as a young genius. Because of Gabriel's irregular attendance, Hunt had only been "on nodding terms" at the school, and knew of him only as a member of the Cyclographic Club, where each, according to the rules, had to produce a drawing a month as well as a criticism of the drawings of the other members.

Gabriel, determined that William learn something about art, took him to one Cyclographic meeting. Hunt recalled attending another, at Millais' parents' handsomely furnished house in Gower Street, where neither Rossetti was present. There the monthly portfolio was opened, and Gabriel's drawings "attracted our regard as an exception to the general level of the contributions, which could not be considered high in character; indeed the Club was already in danger of splitting up, owing to the glaring incompetence of about three-quarters of its members, and the too-unrestrained ridicule of the remainder."

At the Academy School, Hunt recognized the rare days when Gabriel was present by his "following of clamorous students, who . . . were rewarded with original sketches . . . of knights rescuing ladies, of lovers in medieval dress, illustrating stirring incidents of romantic poets." In the Architectural Room, standing under Hunt's canvas, they discussed favorite quattrocento paintings, and arranged to meet again in Hunt's studio to see his work in progress. Hunt's "studio"—the best the impoverished young man could afford—was a cubicle in his parents' home, which was a second-floor flat above an upholsterer's shop. To Gabriel it was suffused with poetry and art, for it was there that *The Eve of St. Agnes* was painted, and he confessed his frustrations with the tutelage of Madox Brown, the painting of bottles and the copying of a Brown picture of cherub angels. Other meetings above the upholsterer's shop followed, and at one of them Gabriel inquired how necessary it was, in Hunt's opinion, to follow the Brown regimen.

Diplomatically, Hunt—who was in the Academy's Life School—suggested that in the sequence of composition the still-life portions of a canvas were stages of proficiency until the artist was ready to paint the figures in the picture. The concept bridged the gap for Gabriel. Could he put the method into practice under Hunt's instruction? Young Hunt—only a student—was flattered. To further the persuasion Gabriel pressed upon him copies of "The Blessed Damozel," "My Sister's Sleep" and "Jenny," which illustrated the artistic dilemma he had already posed to another Hunt—the critic and poet of the immortal "Abou Ben Adhem."

Gabriel had every right to feel pleased with his own poetic production. His first published effort, in which

> The blessed damozel leaned out
> From the gold bar of Heaven. . . .

evoked the pictorial naïveté of a painting by Giotto or Cimabue; but later Rossetti claimed that its subject, if not its texture, had originated out of his love for Poe's "The Raven." Poe, he said, "had done the utmost it was possible to do with the grief of the lover on earth, and so I determined to reverse the conditions, and give utterance to the yearning of the loved one in heaven." * It was a charming conceit, completely effective, although it was unlikely that the poet had drawn any of it from life. What in his experience or observation resulted in "My Sister's Sleep" is more curious, for the poem concerned the Christmas Eve death of Margaret, the narrator's sister. According to Gabriel it had "no relation to actual fact," but to the Rossetti family, Maria was known as "Maggie." Was Gabriel fantasizing, even subconsciously, because of some half-forgotten sibling hostility?

"Jenny," the longest of the works he showed to Hunt, was a Browning-like dramatic monologue related by a client of

> Lazy laughing languid Jenny,
> Fond of a kiss and fond of a guinea,

who reflects that

> It was a careless life I led
> When rooms like this were scarce so strange
> Not long ago. . . .

Rossetti drew his sentimentalized prostitute from the London streets and from his increasingly bohemian associations. A pen-and-ink drawing initialed "G.C.D.R." and sketched no later than the "Jenny" period depicted two bonneted and cloaked women determinedly pinning a man against a wall which ironically carries placards about the Society for the Promotion of Christian Knowledge, venereal disease, and a production of Mrs. Cowley's comedy *The Belle's Stratagem.* On an upper corner of the wall the setting is identified as "Marlboro' Street." When Gabriel was drawn back to his poem nearly a decade later, and revised it extensively, he had already acquired a Jenny of his own, who was lazy and laughing and languid, and both fond of a kiss and fond of a guinea. The Rossetti of 1848 had few golden guineas to spare.

Gabriel realized that his plea to work under Hunt was unrealistic. In the cubicle above the upholsterer's shop there was no space for another easel. But when Hunt sold his *Eve of St. Agnes* for £70, and began negotiating for

---

* Poe stimulated the artist side of the teen-age Gabriel also. Among his early drawings are four versions of "The Raven" as well as illustrations of "The Sleeper" and "Ulalume."

a studio of his own at 7 Cleveland Street, Fitzroy Square, in which he also planned to live, Gabriel offered—probably assuming Aunt Charlotte's further bounty—to pay half the rent in return for work space and guidance. Hunt rented an extra room (as he had first contemplated sleeping in the studio) and his new friend prepared to move in his brushes and paints.

While William continued to walk each morning to the Excise Office and each evening back again, Gabriel slept at home less and less, charming his way into offers of hospitality or merely bedding down in a borrowed studio. He slept little, and that badly, and late, acquiring a hollow-eyed look that might have been thought romantic by the impressionable.

At Charlotte Street when William and Gabriel were away, a young man of much less romantic appearance was then the subject of discreet conversation, but in any case the pair would not have seen him, since Mrs. Rossetti and her sisters first noticed him in church. James Collinson, five years older than Christina's eighteen, was a stocky Nottingham painter who had come to London on an allowance from his widowed mother to study art. Early in 1848 he managed an introduction to Christina, and the elder women whom Maria and Christina accompanied to Christ Church, Albany Street, approved of his "heedful and devout bearing," and his pious glances in the direction of their pew. So far as any of the Rossetti women knew, his attendance had begun not in pursuit of Christina, but because of the Rev. Dodsworth's High Church leanings, which stopped just short of Rome. Collinson was an earnest follower of Newman and Pusey, but to the sheltered Christina he was the romantic answer to the melancholy appeals which suffused her poetry. "Who will love me?" she had asked in a poem written in November, 1847, and in "Repining," a ballad dated December, she wrote of a lonely girl who "sighed for love, and was not satisfied" until a demon lover spirited her away.

No one was less a demon lover than the timid Collinson, but by February, 1848, Christina was writing, "I do not look for love that is a dream," and "I thirst for love, love is mine only need." Collinson came regularly to church, and soon was a visitor at Charlotte Street. He talked of painting with Gabriel and William, and confided to the family that he also wrote poetry. By August, 1848, as Gabriel was about to move into Hunt's new studio, he had already introduced Collinson to Hunt and Millais. Soon he was writing to Mrs. Rossetti (then at Brighton with Christina and Polidori, who apparently paid the bill) that Collinson's poem, "The Child Jesus," was "a very first-rate affair." Collinson was beginning to sound like a good match indeed, with Gabriel assisting in the wooing for him.

Gabriel worked in Christina's behalf in still other ways. With both her brothers Christina often played the literary game of *bouts-rimés*, where each competitor received a series of rhymed endings to be used in writing a poem. They knew it was more than a game: they played their minds against each other, honing their literary powers; and by using the sonnet form they further refined their abilities in versification. Sometimes William would provide the challenging rhymes, Christina would write the sonnet, and Gabriel would pen suggested revisions. Only the more serious Maria, certain there was no future for her in literature, stayed aloof from the activity; but for William it was a mind-clearing challenge after the monotony of the tax office, and for Christina it was a medium for emotional release. One *bout-rimé* in the summer of 1848 suggested her morbid and manic side, as she reacted both to William's rhymed endings and to her feeling of being trapped in a hopeless life:

> I sit alone all day I sit & think—
> I watch the sun arise, I watch it sink
> And feel no soul-light tho the day is clear
> Surely it is a folly; it is mere
> Madness to stand forever on the brink
> Of dark despair & yet not break the link
> That makes me scorned who cannot be held dear.
> I will have done with it. . . .

At the bottom of her manuscript she noted that the entire sonnet had taken her eight minutes to compose. The time has a significance beyond pride in literary dexterity, for she was here recording a mood as it was felt, not artistically refashioning it in tranquillity. That she had the impulses she jotted down so darkly is obvious. Later, in an autobiographical novel, *Maude*, which she would not publish in her lifetime, she explained her gloom away in the third person—that "it was the amazement of everyone what could make her poetry so broken-hearted as was mostly the case. Some pronounced that she wrote very foolishly about things she could not possibly understand; some wondered if she really had any secret source of uneasiness; while some simply set her down as affected. Perhaps there was a degree of truth in all these opinions."

The novel as well as some of her poetry suggested also that she thought of herself as an attractive young woman whose womanliness was doomed to be wasted. "Her features were regular and pleasing," she wrote accurately of her autobiographical heroine; "as a child she had been very pretty; and might have continued so but for a fixed paleness, and an expression, not exactly of pain, but languid and pre-occupied to a painful degree. Yet even now, if at any time she became thoroughly aroused and interested, her sleepy eyes would light up with wonderful brilliancy, her cheeks glow with warm colour. . . ." Gabriel thought so too, and found her also to be a compliant model as well as one available without fee. He had already painted a small head of Christina that was so well realized that his godfather, Charles Lyell, now commissioned a portrait of Gabriele, probably as consolation for the old man, who, too blind and infirm to continue any pretense that he would ever teach again, had already resigned his professorship at King's College. Unwisely, Lyell gave his godson a £10 advance, which ended Gabriel's progress on the painting. Instead, he began thinking of a way to use Christina again, but postponed that project as well, the excuse being that Hunt's new quarters had to be cleaned up by the landlord before it could be used as a studio. Holiday funds in hand, he went off with Hunt on a Thames steamer to Greenwich and Blackheath. The *Professore* was bitter. "I say nothing to him," he reported to his wife, still away in Brighton, "for fear of some insulting reply. You know him well enough. The money has simply led him astray, not reconciled him to his work." It would happen again.

III

The Brotherhood
1848-1849

As Gabriel began his withdrawal from Charlotte Street, Maria made her return. Life as a governess was an exile. With some of her father's pupils available to be tutored, she, Christina and their mother would go out to teach Italian or the classics; but Frances Rossetti quickly realized that there was not enough work for all three. She began thinking of another way to insure an income: perhaps a school.

Gabriel was becoming proficient in living on other people's money. Lyell's advance had run out in ten days, and Gabriel returned to Charlotte Street, only to find that William, too, had gone off to what Gabriel referred to in a letter to him as "dreary, snobbish Brighton." Gabriel was beginning a picture and had made a nude study for the St. Anne figure—very likely from the Maddox Street life class—for when they returned from the seaside his mother and Christina—clothed—began sitting at home for St. Anne and Mary in his *The Girlhood of Mary Virgin*. At Hunt's he and his mentor, foreseeing in the discontent of the membership the imminent dissolution of the Cyclographic, were busy planning a new society of the elect. They had, he wrote William on August 30, "prepared a list of Immortals, forming our creed, and to be pasted up in our study for the affixing of all decent fellows' signatures. It has already caused considerable horror among our acquaintance. . . . The list contains four distinct classes of Immortality; in the first of which three stars are attached to each name, in the second two, in the third one, and in the fourth none. The first class consists only of Jesus Christ and Shakespear."

It was a curious document, one which, for example, gave the young Thackeray, who had just published his first novel, eminence superior to Milton, da Vinci, Newton, Columbus, and Joan of Arc. "We, the undersigned," the preamble began, "declare that the following list of Immortals constitutes the whole of our Creed." The creed became better defined as Hunt and Rossetti, in the backroom Cleveland Street studio by day, and together with John Millais in his comfortable studio at home in Gower Street at night, confided to each other their heretical opinions about the artistic establishment. Intense and rebellious, Hunt was a self-proclaimed disciple of John Ruskin, having read the first two volumes of *Modern Painters*, which called for "a just representation of natural objects in a scientific spirit." All three agreed that contemporary academic painting was dishonest and uninspired. Millais, at nineteen the youngest, displayed to the others an oversized book of engravings of fourteenth-century Pisan frescoes which the three concluded represented a simplicity, innocence, and careful observation of nature worth aspiring toward.

Inwardly skeptical and unwilling to be stampeded, Gabriel visited Brown and asked him doubtfully about Lasinio's engravings, and Brown told him to go look at them again, as they were "the finest things in the world." Hunt at the Academy School had been derided, Gabriel knew, for his denunciation of the great Raphael as pompous and false, and had been labeled with scorn as "Pre-Raphaelite." When next the three met Hunt suggested that perhaps the label fit their vague aesthetics. It certainly fit the simplicity and technical innocence of Gabriel's first studies for his new canvas. Agreeing, he suggested the addition of the word "Brotherhood." It had romantic, conspiratorial connotations reminiscent of his several unfinished melodramas, as well as the ring of the early Christian monastic tradition they saw in fourteenth-century art. But a Pre-Raphaelite Brotherhood required brethren—a secret society of three would hardly shake the system. Besides, Gabriel had a brother, and a future brother-in-law, and the familial tradition was strong among the Rossettis. He proposed William and Collinson. And he almost ended the Brotherhood before it had even begun by also nominating Christina.

Not only would his sister's entry into the exclusive society insure its domination by the Rossettis: she was, after all, a female interloper proposed for membership in a brotherhood. To Hunt, Gabriel further suggested reducing the exclusivity of art in the circle by gradually including "all the nice chaps we know who do anything in the literary line." Hunt restrained himself from an outburst which would under the circumstances have been reasonable, but indicated in a note that Gabriel's arrogance in redesigning the Brotherhood by adding a literary auxiliary had become insufferable.

Backing down, Gabriel explained, "When I proposed that my sister should join, I never meant that she should attend the meetings, to which I know it would be impossible to persuade her, as it would bring her to a pitch of nervousness infinitely beyond Collinson's. I merely intended that she should entrust her productions to my reading; but [I] must give up that idea, as I find she objects to this also, under the impression that it would seem like display." So ended the prospect of Christina's becoming an official Pre-Raphaelite, and with it went Gabriel's hopes for a coordinate fellowship of writers; yet he would remain attracted to painters who were also poets, and poets who could wield a brush as well as a pen.

The shy Collinson, among his talents, included poetry, but his chief claim to membership—pressed by Gabriel for him—was that he had exhibited a picture, *The Charity Boy's Debut*, at the May 1847 Academy show, the *Athenaeum* praising it as auguring "great future excellence." Another exhibited in the 1848 show received no attention, but Gabriel, in a confusion of motives, referred to him anyway as "a born stunner." Hunt found him, at worst, amiable, and likely to fall asleep* whenever the conversation was not about religion. And in the company of Millais and Rossetti talk seldom touched upon that subject. Still, he was acceptable and possibly even promising as a painter, which was hardly true of William Rossetti. William's only qualification to be a member of a society of artists was his attendance at the evening drawing school in Maddox Street, which was more conscientious than his brother's but nevertheless entirely a result of Gabriel's persuasion. He knew he would never resign a secure clerkship to hazard professional painting, and Gabriel knew that the family would not survive without William's salary; but Hunt and Millais saw nothing gained in refusing to be persuaded. After all, Gabriel had yet to exhibit anything himself, nor had the nineteen-year-old Antique School student Frederic George Stephens, whom Hunt then put forward and Millais seconded.

Why Millais never put forward his own brother is a puzzle. James Millais was a landscape painter of modest gifts, certainly much more of an artist than William Rossetti. It was almost as if John Millais understood the shaky nature of the P.R.B. and accepted Gabriel's enthusiasms only because Hunt did. He was interested in putting a sense of actuality into his work but was a friend of Hunt's, not an ideologue. Despite his own artistic gifts, and a Byronic profile—complete to tightly ringleted crown—he was still essentially shy and (living at home with his well-to-do parents) innocent of the world. But he may have sensed that the P.R.B. had gotten off to an unpromising beginning.

---

* Collinson could often be discovered asleep in his studio while a model sat patiently earning a shilling an hour.

Logically, Gabriel should have also nominated Ford Madox Brown, and indeed did mention the subject to him, but Hunt, worried that taking "into our boyish ranks one seven or eight years our senior . . . would have looked like an admission of weakness," made sure that no invitation followed. As a substitute Gabriel suggested another friend, Thomas Woolner, a robust twenty-three-year-old Academy student of sculpture. On the surface it was a curious choice, for Rossetti had no interest in sculpting, but Woolner was also an entertaining talker, an omnivorous reader and a self-taught poet. Rossetti steered Hunt to Woolner's studio in Stanhope Street, where Hunt was convinced—perhaps by Gabriel's rhetoric rather than by anything he saw—of the young sculptor's "energy and his burning ambition to do work of excelling truthfulness and strong poetic spirit." Millais was clearly unhappy but continued to make no public objection. But years later his private skepticism about being a member of a motley group of untried artists was still remembered by Hunt. "Where's your flock?" he jeered as Hunt arrived at the Gower Street studio. "I expected to see them behind you. Tell me all about it. I can't understand so far what you are after. Are you getting up a regiment to take the Academy by storm? I can quite see why Gabriel Rossetti, if he can paint, should join us, but I didn't know his brother was a painter. Tell me. And then there's Woolner. Collinson'll certainly make a stalwart leader of a forlorn hope, won't he? And Stephens, too! Does he paint? Is the notion really to be put in practice?"

On an evening in early September the four new members duly arrived at 83 Gower Street to be lectured by Hunt on the Pre-Raphaelite principles of simplicity, sincerity and fidelity to nature. Then Hunt asked them, in the interests of artistic solidarity, to add to their signatures on any works of art they produced, the initials "P.R.B." And they all swore a solemn oath not to reveal the meaning of the portentous initials, after which each endorsed Hunt's and Rossetti's idiosyncratic list of Immortals. Their next step would be to challenge the establishment with P.R.B.-identified art, and they set as their goal the May 7, 1849, opening of the next annual Royal Academy exhibition.

The means of all but Millais were limited, and the young men took at least one advantage of their Brotherhood by utilizing each other, whenever possible, as models. Millais began a *Lorenzo and Isabella*, inspired by Keats, and William—now balding rapidly—sat for the head of Lorenzo, with his brother and Stephens later posing for figures in the background; and Gabriel sat for the head in Hunt's *Rienzi Swearing Revenge over his Brother's Corpse*. They also began using "P.R.B." on their letters to each other, instead of "Esquire," and began holding monthly meetings at the homes of the members, which meant keeping some formal minutes; and in implicit acknowledgment that William could not be expected to do much more than sit for pictures, the others soon made him secretary of the Brotherhood.

During the months when the Brotherhood was fresh and active it was the most important thing in their lives, except for Collinson, who dozed at meetings, and looked forward to seeing Christina, to whom he was engaged at the price of his reluctant renunciation of Rome. When the Brothers were together, William recalled, "We had our thoughts, our unrestrained converse, our studies, aspirations, efforts, and actual doings; and for every P.R.B. to drink a cup or two of tea or coffee, or a glass or two of beer, in the company of other P.R.B.'s, with or without the accompaniment of tobacco (without it for Dante Rossetti, who never smoked at all), was a heart-relished luxury. . . . Those were the days of youth; and each man, even if he did not project great things of his own, revelled in poetry or sunned himself in art."

Soon after Hunt had made his studio available to Gabriel, and Gabriel had begun using members of his family as models for his new picture, Hunt was invited to dinner prior to a P.R.B. meeting at Charlotte Street. He came and was fascinated. The eye-shaded *Professore* arose from a group of Italian émigrés gathered about the fire and greeted him, in about the only words of English he used that evening, as "Mr. Madox Brown." Maria "rated him pleasantly." Then the elder Rossetti returned to his discussions in Italian and French so enthusiastically that, forgetting, he again confused Hunt with Gabriel's older friend. The political passions of the *Professore* and his friends, Hunt observed, "did not in the slightest degree involve either the mother, the daughters, or the sons, except when the latter explained that the objects of the severest denunciations were Bomba, Pio Nono, and Metternich." In reverent tones Hunt heard of Mazzini, Garibaldi and Louis Napoleon, who had once been a visitor at Charlotte Street. "The mother," Hunt wrote, "was the gentle and presiding matron we see Saint Anne to be in *The Girlhood of the Virgin.* The elder sister was overflowing with attention to all, . . . and Miss Christina was exactly the pure and docile-hearted damsel that her brother portrayed God's Virgin pre-elect to be."

Awaiting dinner Hunt watched the old ex-revolutionaries each in turn arise and speak excitedly, with broad gesticulations emphasizing his anger at the sad state of the Continent; and the others kept pace with a refrain of sighs and groans. "When it was impossible for me to ignore the distress of the alien company, Gabriel and William shrugged their shoulders, the latter with a languid sign of commiseration, saying it was generally so." Another aspect of the evening impressed Hunt. None of the refugee visitors was likely to be affluent, but all seemed to recognize a duty not to be a burden on the Rossettis. "As the dinner was being put on the table some of the strangers persisted, despite invitation, in going; some still stayed round the fire declaring solemnly that they had dined."

At dinner macaroni and other un-English dishes were served; and while everyone around the table conversed in English, the *Professore* continued his dialogue with those of his friends still at the fireplace, getting up to join them as he finished each course and remaining until called back for the next dish. Afterwards the women turned to dominoes and chess, old Gabriele to his remaining friends, and Hunt, Gabriel and William gathered upstairs in Gabriel's tiny fourth-floor workroom with the other P.R.B.'s, including the now familiar Collinson. The probationary members were to have brought samples—or at least evidences—of their future work, but of the four only William had a few of his "painstaking if very angular outlines from life." The others had "neither work nor apology, an omission which we tried to construe into evidence that extensive designs were being prepared as a surprise in store."

The Brotherhood not only brought James Collinson closer to the Rossettis but also required a beginning of the minuet of family contacts. Since it would have been indelicate for Christina, even as fiancée, to visit the Collinsons' home at Pleasley Hill, near Sherwood Forest in Nottingham-shire, William was deputed to meet her prospective mother-in-law and sister-in-law, and entrained north in late November with the future bridegroom. "Is either of these ladies *alarming?*" Christina wrote William. "Not to you of course, but would they be so to me?" And realizing that both William and Collinson were there to sing her charms, even to bringing with them a just-completed and barely adequate portrait in oils the sitting for which had given Collinson added opportunities to be with her, she chided, "You probably not only *profusely banqueted* but surfeited your victims with my *poetry;* but in this you may not have been the sole culprit." She was in love, or at least thought so, and rare traces of immodesty about the reaction to her glinted through chinks in her façade. She knew that the "celebrated portrait" was mediocre, and sensed that so might be Collinson; but he was an artist and a poet and a profoundly religious young man of good breeding who had weighed her against the insistent attractions of Roman Catholicism and she had won out. After some discreet months she might herself visit, preparatory to relieving the Rossettis of the burden of herself.

During the first months of the Brotherhood Gabriel progressed with his P.R.B. picture in Cleveland Street while making little headway with the portrait of his father commissioned by Charles Lyell. Finally, when the *Professore* in a letter to Lyell raised expectations of its completion, Gabriel felt forced to promise a likeness on a smaller scale, apologizing that his "first attempt in oils the size of life" had not been successful. Then he went on to describe the canvas he was "preparing for next year's Exhibition." Previous depictions of "the education of the Blessed Virgin," he explained, ". . . as I cannot but think, [presented the subject] in a very inadequate manner, since they have invariably represented her as reading from a book under the superintendence of her Mother, St. Anne, an occupation obviously incompatible with these times, and which could only pass muster if treated in a purely symbolical manner." Instead he was planning to represent the youthful Mary, while her mother watched, embroidering a tall lily, the symbol of purity, the flower she is copying held by two small angels. In the background would be seen her father, St. Joachim, outside pruning a vine. He had made several chalk studies, he told Lyell, and sketched the design on canvas, but had only painted in a part of the background "and a portion of the figure of the Blessed Virgin, for which Christina sits to me; her appearance being excellently adapted to my purpose."

Not only had Christina posed for the demure Virgin, and Mrs. Rossetti for St. Anne, but a Rossetti family occasional handyman, "Old Williams," who had a special affection for Gabriel, stood patiently in a difficult position, arms upraised, for St. Joachim. By November 21 Gabriel had progressed far enough to compose a descriptive sonnet, its last lines foreshadowing his next picture, which he may already have had in mind; but, having had difficulty with five successive child models for the only figure for which he could not depend upon No. 50 Charlotte Street, he had reduced his two small angels to one. His recurring problems were his own impatience with the task of painting, and his impulsiveness in dropping his brush to write—as with his sonnet on the incomplete panel, for while writing or sketching he would let his paint become too dry to work with further. Consulting Hunt, he was advised to rub out what he had done and begin again, "but he was reluctant to resort to such draconian measures, and essayed to treat the half-dried pigment like the tone on a mezzotint plate. Scraping through to the white canvas below with the point of a knife, he hatched and stippled the lights, and then the darks were expressed with touches from a brown brush, so that the effect at a distance was quite happy."

The whole process of Pre-Raphaelite painting defied contemporary practice. Hunt and Millais eschewed asphaltum (bitumen), the tarry brownish compound generally used as a ground, and the reason for the muted colors in the work of their Academy masters. Instead, they experimented with an adaptation of the techniques of the early Italian fresco painters, who spread only as much of the fresh, moist plaster as could be painted over at one sitting. Hunt showed Rossetti how to use a bright, whitish ground, over which first would go the outline of the painting, then a thin white coat through which the drawing was to emerge, and over which the color was to be applied while the segment of light ground was still fresh. The method made correction difficult, and required the artist's disciplining himself to record his intentions with his brushes precisely and unfalteringly. When the formula worked, the result was a brilliant canvas, for the ground reflected, rather than absorbed, light shining through the pigments.

Stage by stage, Gabriel's picture took shape under Hunt's tutelage. On a 33″ x 26″ panel he had drawn the architectural features of his design, and then transferred his nude studies of the four figures before clothing them and giving them features from his family models. Then, segment by segment, he painted the floor, the balcony and six oversized, symbolical books. By then the weather had become raw, and to paint an overhanging vine with appropriate Pre-Raphaelite verisimilitude Gabriel's mentor advised locating a conservatory where one was growing. For days the studio was quiet and Gabriel gone. When he returned, Hunt was startled by the "too crudely emerald green" vine, but prudently said nothing. Nor, after several attempts, did Hunt persevere further in teaching Gabriel the use of perspective, a technique which he dismissed as unnecessary and which he never mastered, William even remarking that his brother "was at all times almost indifferent to the question of whether his works were in perspective or out of it."

The piece-by-piece procedure was congenial to the systematic Hunt, who in any case seldom could snatch more than a few hours of painting time before or after his Academy life class, but Rossetti, with an excess of self-made leisure, found his patience strained, and at such times he heard the call of language even more clearly. There were days in Cleveland Street, Hunt remembered, when Gabriel's literary impulses obliterated all desire to paint. He had begun a translation of Dante's *Vita Nuova*, as well as some illustrations to it, and was also working on new poetry. "When he had once sat down, and was engaged in the effort to chase his errant thoughts into an orderly road, and the spectral fancies had all to be kept in his mind's eye, . . . he remained fixed and inattentive to all that went on about him, he rocked himself to and fro, and at times he moaned lowly, or hummed for a brief minute, as though telling off some idea. All this while he peered intently before him, looking hungry and eager, and passing by in this regard any who came before him, as if not seen at all. Then he would often get up and walk out of the room without saying a word."

Gabriel's compositional method suggested that he could exclude the outside world, but in reality the press of his creative fancies in both writing and painting often had the effect of canceling out each other, with his P.R.B. canvas suffering the most neglect. When another poem or drawing took possession of him he would refuse to leave the studio for home, meals or friends, dozing for an hour at a time where he sat, and eating whatever food was at hand. Eventually he would make a penitential return to his easel and dab at *The Girlhood of Mary Virgin* until his friends arrived, to Hunt's frustration, for "the precious daylight, . . . being of no account to them, they treated as without value to us." It became another unhappy aspect of the partnership, for some of the visitors Hunt was glad to see, yet he was suffering increasing anxiety about his *Rienzi*, which was a far more complicated production, only worked on in the hours before or after his attendance at the Life School. On returning home he would boil his coffee and sit down to his meal and a book before going to his canvas, but sometimes there would be Gabriel and William to join him in a supper that was meatless out of economy and the example of Shelley. Then "the hour of relaxation was all the pleasanter," but there were also times when Gabriel and "a small company" of his friends were gathered in the studio as Hunt returned, and if he delayed preparing his meal in hopes of feeding fewer guests Gabriel would scold, "Now, Hunt, don't keep us waiting any longer. I have promised them all supper."

Frustration with his technical inadequacies would suddenly turn Gabriel from carefree companion to temperamental Italian. Difficulties with the Virgin's drapery sent him for advice to Brown in what his "Bruno" described as "an almost maudlin condition of profanity, . . . lying howling on his belly in my studio." But the canvas was, somehow, completed. All three of the P.R.B. founders, as well as the somnolent Collinson, had a work ready on schedule. Millais had efficiently accomplished his *Lorenzo and Isabella* and Hunt, although close to desperation at times, had completed *Rienzi*; but the deadline was so close at hand that he carried the canvas personally to the Academy, arriving just short of midnight. By then they knew that Gabriel's painting would not be there, nor had he been in the Cleveland Street studio for weeks. Worried about possible reaction to its crudities, or to his having quit the Academy Schools, he had quietly diverted it to the Free Exhibition at Hyde Park Corner,* where one paid a fee for wall space, but had no fear of rejection. The Association for Promoting the Free Exhibition of Modern Art was only free in that artists were at liberty to exhibit, for the public also had to pay an admission fee; yet Gabriel felt it was a respectable as well as a prudent location to display his first work, for "Bruno" had sent a canvas as well. Hunt, however, first considered it treachery rather than prudence, an estimate reinforced by Gabriel's unannounced absence.

His canvas delivered, Millais went off to paint landscapes in Oxford-

---

* Which opened on March 24, 1849.

shire, and Hunt worked in unusual quietude until a carter came to haul Gabriel's properties back to Charlotte Street, in his hand Gabriel's announcement that effective with the previous Lady Day—the spring quarter day when quarterly rents and accounts were due—he had withdrawn from joint tenancy. Since it was April and he was already into the next quarter's lease, Hunt was responsible for the extra room he had rented at Rossetti's insistence, and—short in money—he worked out a compromise with his landlord to pay for it only until it could be acquired by another tenant. He had every reason to be furious with Gabriel, and to break up the infant Brotherhood, especially since *The Girlhood of Mary Virgin*, on view ahead of other P.R.B. work, was already spoken of as precursor of a new school. Yet Millais, Hunt and the other P.R.B.'s had a sincerity of purpose and sense of comradeship which soon enabled them to accompany Rossetti to the Free Exhibition one spring day, where they watched Gabriel proudly observe—so he wrote his Aunt Charlotte—"one of the critics of the *Art-Union* journal standing before my picture for a quarter of an hour at least."

In the *Athenaeum* his picture was plucked from "the mass of commonplace" to be described as "not from a long-practised hand, but from one young in experience, new to fame," who had painted "a work which, for its invention and for many parts of its design, would be creditable to any exhibition." While recognizing the immaturity in technique, the review perceived the unacknowledged P.R.B. ideal in the painting, seeing it as "full of allegory [and] . . . that sacred mysticism inseparable from the works of the early masters," and as having "the feeling with which the early Florentine monastic painters wrought." Its naïve sweetness had succeeded.

What saved the P.R.B. in the face of Gabriel's arbitrary behavior may have been the recognition by Millais and Hunt of an insecurity in their comrade which could reach panic proportions. On the face of it, however, the P.R.B. survived because its monthly meetings continued unabated, and its members sustained each other's enthusiasm in other informal ways. Led by Gabriel they would sometimes take long moonlit strolls, singing as they went, and rousing the sleepy Collinson to join them on walks along the Thames or hikes as far as Hampstead, from which they would return after dawn, Collinson propped up by his companions. There were times, too, when they would sit up, bantering and declaiming, often with non-P.R.B. cronies in the party, until dawn, when someone would propose a row up the Thames to Richmond, and fortified by bottles of wine or beer for breakfast and lunch they would bellow lines from Tennyson or Browning to passing bargemen.

At their formal P.R.B. sessions—the minutes of which William was deputed to record—they would also tell stories and recite poems, Gabriel intoning from memory, in a voice that could move his hearers to tears, pages from *Sordello* or *Paracelsus*. Gabriel even pushed his brother artists to versifying, Hunt protesting later that his "simple couplets" and Spenserian stanzas were only to record impressions of Nature, and not for print. Frederick Shields thought them "sombre, grand, like plumes of hearses," while William confessed that he was "not very clear as to their subject or mode of treatment." Still, Hunt, Woolner, Stephens and even William would read awkwardly from their own verse, and William would bring in so much of Christina's poetry that she became, in effect, the proxy P.R.B. Gabriel had pressed for months before. In one letter to William giving him permission to copy from her work, Christina, realizing her special status, even referred to her relation to him as a "double sisterhood." But she warned against exposing any of her verses which might be interpreted as "the outpourings of a wounded spirit" or as love poetry with a personal reference. With Collinson as an acknowledged suitor, she wanted no exposures of her emotional life which would be potentially embarrassing. Her brother duly selected innocuous verse, chopped out segments from other writings, and many years later even appropriately censored her published letters—as with this one, where Collinson's name is crossed out several times in William's hand. Even more innocuous was the first poem Christina had accepted for publication, in an annual called *Marshall's Ladies' Daily Remembrancer*, which was one of the many such publications which cluttered Victorian Christmases and household tea tables thereafter. According to the rules, entries for the 1850 volume had to be submitted before June, 1849. Payment to Christina was one copy of the book. Better-known contributors received two copies.

On the first Monday in May, 1894, the Academy's exhibition opened at noon, and Millais' painting quickly sold for £150 to a group of three Bond Street tailors who had bought it as a speculation. The *Athenaeum*, which had praised Gabriel's work for its antiquarian simplicity and sensitivity, saw only affectation in Hunt's and Millais' mixing up their considerable technique "with much that is obsolete and dead in practice." Through the months of the exhibition Hunt's picture went unsold, and he had to carry it home in August. Gabriel, however, had better fortune, although it seemed otherwise by his removal to the fourth-floor garret in Charlotte Street, where he painted beneath a picture of the *Spirit of Abstract Justice*, a Brown composition he had cut out of an illustrated magazine.

While his mentor's work languished unsold at the Academy, *The*

Girlhood of Mary Virgin was purchased for the list price in the catalogue—£80*—by the Dowager Marchioness of Bath. It happened that his Aunt Charlotte Polidori was governess, and later companion, in the family. Justice was indeed abstract.

Gabriel at first had been sent £60, but after some cautious correspondence—once he determined that the lady really wanted the picture—extracted the full amount. Then, on July 17, before delivery, he began repainting the angel which had caused him so much exasperation. Out went the head of Thomas Woolner's young half-sister and in its place, within the week, was the head of a new and more docile seraph supplied by Collinson.

A few days later Hunt heard repeated knockings at the street door below his studio. When neither his landlady nor her lethargic Irish servant answered, Hunt went down himself, and found the painter Augustus L. Egg, an R.A. He had come, he explained, to see *Rienzi* again, as it was a work he admired. Could Hunt arrange for an invalid friend who had not been able to go to the Academy to examine it at Egg's house in Bayswater? On an evening soon after, Hunt delivered it himself. The next morning his landlord, irate about the unpaid rent, seized all of his moveable property at Cleveland Street, and Hunt returned dejectedly to his father's house; but within the week Egg's friend had bought *Rienzi* for £100, generously writing the check for an additional five pounds for the frame. Taking the payment to the bank, Hunt opened an account, and delivered the first check to his landlord, recovering his sketches, furniture and books. He now deserved a holiday, he thought, and went off to sketch in the Lea Marshes of Essex. It was a time for reflection as well, and with his temporarily replenished purse his diminished anger with Gabriel diminished even more. He suggested that the two make their long-dreamed-of tour of French and Flemish art. In the waning days of September they would begin their education.

Exchanges of letters were so numerous that one would wrongly assume lengthy periods of separation of the Brethren, for under Gabriel's influence, all of them began writing as much, or more, than they painted or sculpted, usually raising the quantity rather than the quality of contemporary poetry. William had been the first P.R.B. to appear in public print, as early as September, 1848, when a mediocre poem of his appeared in the *Athenaeum*, and he versified at every opportunity, although constant practice never compensated for his thinness of poetic talent. On June 30, 1849, for example, when summer had parted the P.R.B.'s more than usual, he dashed

---

* Rossetti's biographer Doughty erroneously lists the amount in guineas, the gentleman's unit of price a later, more successful Gabriel adopted.

off some lines to Frederic Stephens which only proved that although he had nothing to say, and wrote business letters all day at work, the desire to communicate remained insatiable:

> It is now past the hour of 12;
>   Gabriel's dozing in his chair.
> And so this letter I will shelve,
>   As soon as can be, dear Brother.
> Not that I mean to go to bed
>   Quite yet. I have the P.R.B.
> Diary to write up instead.
>   Tho' there is nothing verily.

Although Woolner once sent a letter to William to congratulate him on having produced 103 lines of new verse, the P.R.B.'s claimed an interest in criticism which might have made the members more cautious in their own writing. One evening in August, meeting at Stephens's, they even dissected Keats's "Isabella"—a P.R.B. favorite—to locate infelicities in detail or in expression, and agreed upon twenty-four, with William overruled in his arguments for eleven more. Yet the Brethren continued to compose, for by then Gabriel had successfully made a case for a P.R.B. publication to feature their own work. The first entry on the subject in William's journal is dated July 13, 1849—that "In the evening Gabriel and I went to Woolner's . . . about a project for a monthly sixpenny magazine, for which four or five of us would write, and one make an etching—each subscribing a guinea, and thus becoming a proprietor." Soon after, William appeared in Newcastle on a visit to William Bell Scott, who confessed having been intrigued by the mysterious letters "P.R.B." which had begun appearing on the return address of his letters from Charlotte Street. Skirting the bond of secrecy William explained, "It's only a sort of club some of Gabriel's and Hunt's friends and other young fellows have planned out, and I, the youngest of the set, but no artist, am to be secretary. It's only friendly, [but] we are making a start on a new line." On leaving, William confided that the group was going to print something which Scott might soon hear of.

The project was one of passionate interest to Gabriel, although he intended to push the real work it would involve onto his brother; but when William went off to Ventnor, on the Isle of Wight, on his annual holiday from the Excise Office, Gabriel set about making his own inquiries to printers. Before he and Hunt had left for France he had tramped through publishers' offices in Paternoster Row and lined up promises of contributions from the P.R.B.'s.

While Collinson discreetly took his holiday with William, going as far as

Cowes and then returning to London, Christina was making her first and only visit to Pleasley Hill, which in late summer was no less dull than at other times. She longed for the mail, worked on a "dreary" poem, and listened to "perpetual" talk of *"beaus."* In "desperation" she "knit lace with a perseverance completely foreign to my nature," and sent William some rhymes for a *bouts-rimés* challenge. After a month, the tedious visit over, she returned home to find a curious letter from her prospective sister-in-law. "My correspondence with Mary Collinson," she wrote William in Ventnor, "has come to an end by her desire. Do not imagine we have been quarrelling: not at all: but she seems to think her brother's affairs so unpromising as to render our continuing to write to each other not pleasant. Does this not sound extraordinary? We are all much surprised."

Was Miss Collinson thinking of her lethargic brother's unpromising artistic future? Had her brother suddenly felt terror about a marriage he now wanted much less than a Mass? As early as April 18 Christina had begun a poem with

> My happy dream is finished with,
> My dream in which alone I lived so long.

Now she concluded one (October 10) with

> How should I share my pain, who kept
> My pleasure all my own?
> My Spring will never come again;
> My pretty flowers have blown
> For the last time; I can but sit
> And think and weep alone.

Christina kept her concerns to herself. Gabriel had deputed her to be unofficial sub-editor of the future P.R.B. magazine while he and William were away. No long-term solution to her private desperation, it was not even sufficiently therapeutic to keep her mind from morbid thoughts. She filled more pages of her notebooks.

IV

The Germ

1849-1850

For a time Collinson's relationship with Christina was more indirect than courtship implied. Letters were exchanged on P.R.B. business while Gabriel and Hunt remained away. And Gabriel, suspecting no impending rift, even had suggested to William before he left for France that Collinson's opinion on some new manuscript poetry be solicited. Nevertheless he added sarcastically about his prospective brother-in-law, "I suppose (ahem!) he works like a horse; of course I mean a Jerusalem pony." *

By October 4 Gabriel was in Paris, having written a blank verse travel journal en route, which for safekeeping he posted to William, accompanied by a similarly versified letter. He and Hunt were enthusiastic over Parisian bookstalls and printshops but with the condescension of immaturity he informed William about the old masters in the Louvre that aside from Leonardo, Mantegna and an Angelico fresco "there is a monosyllable current amongst us which enables a P.R.B. to dispense almost entirely with details on the subject." The word was "slosh." William had been working on what he called a "Pre-Raphaelite poem," the application to verse of the principles of "strict actuality and probability of detail," and rushed a copy to his brother for his criticism. Gabriel took hours out of his discovery of new pictures to elaborately praise, criticize, and recommend alterations to the seven hundred lines. Years later it would be published as "Mrs. Holmes

---

* An ass; very likely derived from the beast upon which Jesus made his entry into Jerusalem.

Grey"—a verse dialogue about a woman who dies in the home of a man for whom she had conceived an unrequited passion.

Passion, French style, was a shock to Gabriel. The great Rachel, in Scribe's *Adrienne Lecouvreur*, left them "inexpressibly astounded," and the cancan at Valentino's stirred Gabriel to a sonnet of moral indignation which he warned could not be shown to his family. The "frog-hop," he wrote, was

> A toothsome feast
> Of blackguardism and whore flesh and bald row,
> No doubt for such as love those same. For me,
> I confess, William, and avow to thee,
> (Soft in thine ear) that such sweet female whims
> As nasty backsides out and wriggled limbs
> Nor bitch-squeaks, nor the smell of heated q_____s
> Are not a passion of mine naturally.

The P.R.B.'s and their cronies were remarkably innocent bohemians. Although they were not immune to what Gabriel called "the fatal habit of intoxication," neither did they frequent the all-night gin shops, pubs and taverns, mainly because they enjoyed each other's company and their own self-entertainment enough not to need the fellowship of pub habitués or the salacious songs sung by patrons and performers alike. Few of the P.R.B.'s swore, or smoked, or ever thought of spending two shillings for a prostitute. Those receptacles of bohemian pleasure, easily available on almost any street in London, were aesthetically or ethically unappealing, or beyond the means of men just past being boys, who barely had sufficient shillings to purchase paint.

Although vulgarity and vice were just as prevalent in London as in Paris, Gabriel's insular superiority welled up in condemnations of most of what he saw. Frenchmen were "bland smiling dogs," and of their women, he wrote William, "We have not seen six pretty faces since we have been in Paris." That, and other aspects of Paris, moved him to verse—the bells of Notre Dame, which reminded him of France's most recent revolution, the previous year; the canvases of the Louvre, which made him and Hunt "yawn from school to school"; the intellectual darkness of a metropolis in which "no man asks of Browning"; the "fine churches" and "splendid inns" and "good dinners" which nevertheless could not erase the memory of police "Who spit their oaths at you and grind their r's / If at a fountain you would wash your hands. . . ."

After a fortnight they left for Belgium, Gabriel versifying en route, complete to a sonnet at Waterloo; and Antwerp and Bruges and the paintings of van Eyck and Memling inspired additional poetry; but Brussels, he wrote William, offered, in its "utter muffishness," insufficient materials for a sonnet. In early November they were back on familiar soil, Gabriel rejoicing at Dover in the sight of an English policeman, and returning with "an extraordinary self-concocting coffee-pot for state-occasions of the P.R.B., . . . a book containing a receipt for raising the Devil, and . . . a quantity of Gavarni's sketches." Work on the P.R.B. magazine had gone on in their absence, and they left it further to the others, more concerned about finding a new studio—even contemplating a large house on Cheyne Walk as a Pre-Raphaelite retreat, with "P.R.B." to be carved into the doorjamb so that only the elect would know that it did not mean "Please Ring Bell." But Gabriel, for a rent of £26 a year, settled on a small studio at 72 Newman Street, a haunt of artists across Oxford Street from Soho Square.

The new quarters were for beginning a canvas, again with Christina as model—an "Annunciation" which would be a logical follow-up to *The Girlhood*—and to do a picture based upon a Browning poem. Yet Gabriel could not entirely ignore the labor pains of the new P.R.B. publication for which he had pressed, and P.R.B. conviviality in general. The seven original members had doubled, although none, at Hunt's insistence, were formally given Brotherhood status, despite the need for their investment in shillings and in literary or visual art in what would finally be called *The Germ* (rather than *The Seed*), its fourth title after *Monthly Thoughts in Literature, Poetry and Art, Thoughts toward Nature* (Gabriel's suggestion) and *P.R.B. Journal*—which William opposed because it sounded like the transactions of a scientific society, and because it would imply that all contributors were legitimate Brothers.

At one meeting even before Gabriel and Hunt had left for France it had been decided that each P.R.B. would write a sonnet for the first issue which would describe the artistic aims which actuated the group, but as publication time drew near only William had produced a poem, having written the first eight lines, he had recorded in mid-August, "in a state of sleep." He knew it was beneath mediocrity, but it was sufficiently ambiguous—and opaque— not to go against the grain of any P.R.B. sensibilities. Early in November William was even mildly encouraged by a phrenologist he had consulted— he had a cautious curiosity—to believe that he had "an artistic development with symptoms of poetry"—but only "symptoms." Urged to leave a sample of his handwriting for analysis he succumbed to that as well, and when Cornelius Donovan furnished it he noted in his journal without elaboration that "Woolner and Gabriel, as well as myself, consider it very acutely judged and generally correct."

Despite his being the only member who had a job which kept him occupied all day, the others, having appointed William editor, left everything to him—the negotiations with the printer, the soliciting of subscribers (Gabriel sent him a list of potential patrons), the acquisition of publishable material. Coventry Patmore ("The Angel in the House"), whom the P.R.B.'s worshiped because he was the only recognized writer in London who was willing to associate his reputation with them,* offered a poem, but P.R.B. enthusiasm, as their projected December deadline approached, had not turned into finished copy. All agreed that the first number had to appear, but William, despondent over its prospects, convinced Stephens on the tenth that the first number—advertised for January, 1850—should also be the last.

Gabriel guiltily dropped his brushes on the seventeenth and resumed writing his trancelike prose tale "Hand and Soul." On the nineteenth, at an urgent meeting at Newman Street, a list of sixty-five possible titles was presented by Cave Thomas, and the final one decided upon by a vote of six to four, with Madox Brown, Walter Deverell, John Hancock and George and John Tupper also present, several of the non-P.R.B.'s casting ballots. John Tupper was an Academy sculpture student and his brother George a partner (with a third brother, Alexander) in the printing firm which was to publish *The Germ*. John Tupper was also the author of one of the few completed pieces for the issue, an earnest essay, "The Subject in Art." Woolner was supposed to have completed a poem by the following Monday, but when it did not arrive and William frantically searched for him, he discovered that it was not and would not be ready, nor did Cave Thomas have ready either his promised wrapper design or his article. Fortunately there was a batch of Christina's poems to be mined, and on the twenty-first Gabriel worked all day and into the night on his story, writing the epilogue the next day while William recopied for the printer the undecipherable sections.

Because of the haste in which most of it was written, "Hand and Soul" reveals more of Gabriel than he knew. The story is of Chiaro dell' Erma, an artist of such exquisite sensibility that his "extreme longing after a visible embodiment of his thoughts" causes him to "feel faint at sunsets and at the sight of stately persons." Guilty about his ambition for worldly fame through art he first explains his art as a means by which to worship God, but comes to realize "that much of that reverence which he had mistaken for faith had been no more than the worship of beauty." He had, in fact, regretted to himself that beauty in the form of a living woman to love had

---

* But not their literary deficiencies, Patmore finding in William's long unfinished realistic poem "a most objectionable absence of moral dignity, all the characters being puny and destitute of elevation." (*P.R.B. Journal*, 12 November 1849)

never happened to him, as he had left no room in life for it. To compensate for his unspiritual excesses he turns to the creation of works of moral instruction, but one day discovers his huge allegorical fresco of Peace, painted on an exterior church wall, spattered by the blood of townsmen fighting among themselves in the town square. Despair overtakes him, but a vision appears, "of the fair woman that was his soul," and he knew "her hair to be the golden veil through which he beheld his dreams." She directs him not to worry about whether he is fulfilling God's will. "What he hath set in thine heart to do, that do thou; and even though thou do it without thought of Him, it shall be well done. . . . Chiaro, servant of God, take now thine Art unto thee, and paint me thus, as I am, to know me. . . . Do this; so shall thy soul stand before thee always, and perplex thee no more." It is God's will, Gabriel suggests, that the artist work for art's sake, and not out of any ascetic or spiritual purpose. But it was Gabriel's will, the author implied between the lines, that was weakening under pressure of awakening and unsatisfied sexual passion. It was no longer enough merely to paint it or write about it.

On December 28 William corrected the second set of galley proofs (the first was full of errors) and filled the remaining empty space with an uninspired sonnet of his own, as other material in hand was too long. The other P.R.B.'s were of little help. Hunt even found time on his hands because a model failed to keep an appointment, and busied himself catching sparrows in a trap at his window, painting their heads green, and then letting them go. When he tired of that, he visited William at Charlotte Street and watched him spend the evening on the second proof of the last sheet, which Aleck Tupper had carried over himself. It was almost a ceremonial occasion: Stephens and Deverell stopped by as well. But Gabriel remained at his studio, with Collinson, both ostensibly painting.

On the last day of the old year the first fifty copies of *The Germ* came off the presses, and William went by to carry off twelve, selling three en route to Gabriel's studio, where Collinson and Woolner approved of the first number's appearance. But fortunately William had not ordered 4,000 copies, as he had thought of doing in the enthusiasm of October. Of the 700 copies printed, about a hundred were sold by the printers and another hundred by the P.R.B.'s and their friends. The porter at Somerset House was offered ten shillings to sell copies to students at the School of Design. More were given away: to Lord John Russell, Sir Robert Peel and other well-known persons, and to the clubs they frequented and the publications they read.

Some efforts worked. Douglas Jerrold, playwright and future editor of *Punch*, invited William, as editor, to tea. The editor of *Art Journal*, Samuel

Carter Hall, promised a review: and to try to lure one out of the *Athenaeum*, William inserted a modest advertisement. *John Bull,* the *Guardian*, the *Critic*, the *Morning Chronicle*, the *Spectator* and several smaller papers reviewed *The Germ*, but most notices were both patronizing and late. Still, William went on to prepare a second number, to include Collinson's "The Child Jesus" and additional poems by Christina, which he copied out of her notebooks, Gabriel a week later inventing the name "Ellen Alleyn" for her contributions. Deverell came by with a tale for the next issue, "which he read," William noted; "but becoming disgusted with it in the course of the evening, tore it up, and threw it away." With material short, William gratefully wrote out an acceptance for two poems William Bell Scott had sent Gabriel, had Patmore check proof of a poem of his as well as Collinson's, helped Stephens revise an article on Italian art, and wrote a review of Matthew Arnold's newest book; and Gabriel supplied his latest version of "The Blessed Damozel." More was needed, and in exasperation William appealed for material at a January 20 meeting in the Newman Street studio. With sales poor, contributions to the sequel were only lamely offered, and the atmosphere was uncharacteristically melancholy. In a mock-Keatsian sonnet, "St. Wagnes' Eve," Gabriel described the scene to Christina, a contributor denied by her gender any opportunity to sample the pervading gloom herself:

> By eight, the coffee was all drunk. At nine
> We gave the cat some milk. Our talk did shelve,
> Ere ten to gasps and stupor. Helpless grief
> Made, towards eleven, my inmost spirit pine. . . .

Two days later, when William prepared to send copy to the Tuppers for the next issue, he had still not received promised contributions from Patmore, Thomas and Madox Brown. He resorted to three less-than-mediocre sonnets by Deverell—who was better at painting—and padded the text with two uninspired poems of his own. But not his lengthy "Plain Story of Life" in blank verse ("Mrs. Holmes Grey"), which, already condemned by Patmore, had been labeled by Scott as "a curiosity" which was "wrong in its delineation of character." (Later another friend thought it was "more than half intentionally comic.") Still, William hoped that the magazine would survive long enough to publish his masterwork.

P.R.B. conclaves were not solely to agonize over *The Germ*. Winter evenings at Woolner's high-ceilinged sculpture studio in Stanhope Street made the chamber, Hunt recalled, seem vast and ghostly, because the only light came from the opening of the stove. The wreaths of tobacco smoke from a few pipes rose above their circle, and "seemed to elevate us above immediate cares. The world was then too agitated with discontent not to call forth all our political views; those of our host were strong, and decidedly complicated. 'I loathe from my very soul,' he said, 'all money grubbers, all who grovel in muck to scrape up filthy lucre.' Most severe was his disdain for our governing and wealthy classes. . . . His scornful sentiments might be traced to an unquestioning adoration of Shelley's wildest poetry [but] . . . he wisely took occasion to seek Gabriel's and William's opinions in turn on disputed judgments of standard poems. . . ." Yet their passionate arguments over poetry, and promises of productions of their own, left William with little matter for future issues, although the meetings would end convivially, and they would often sing their way home, the refrains continuing "until we came to our successive parting points, and ceased only when each felt responsible for his own share in the revelry."

Although Gabriel had contributed a major work to the second number and had convened two P.R.B. monthly meetings in succession at his studio, the reason was less dedication to *The Germ* than desire to remain close to his canvases. His sonnet on "The Girlhood of Mary Virgin" had prefigured a sequel, in lines that

> . . . one dawn, at home,
> She woke in her white bed, and had no fear
> At all,—yet wept till sunshine, and felt awed:
> Because the fulness of the time was come.

It was another family production. In William's journal for November 25, 1849, he had written, "Gabriel began making a sketch of the Annunciation. The Virgin is to be in bed, but without any bedclothes on, an arrangement which may be justified in consideration of the hot climate; and the angel Gabriel is to be presenting a lily to her." In a full nightdress Christina sat for the Virgin, and Gabriel completed a preliminary sketch which resembles, even in facial features, a nude sketch in the same position he apparently did from another model, in order to get the position of the legs accurately fixed, superimposing his sister's face. Had she seen the nude study her modesty would have been affronted, but it remained in the studio while Gabriel would carry his stretched 32″ x 17″ canvas to Charlotte Street to work from Christina.

At first he used a paid model for the angel, but the day after the first issue of *The Germ* went to the printer, Gabriel told his brother that the model was "useless." On December 30, between other occupations, William had begun sitting for the head of the archangel; and when he was not available Gabriel worked on studies for a large many-figured picture based on Browning's song in *Pippa Passes*, "Hist! said Kate the Queen." It concerned the love a page had for a queen, he wrote his Aunt Charlotte—"a subject which I have picked upon principally for its presumptive saleability. I find unluckily that the class of pictures which has my natural preference is not for the market." It was a persuasive line to the pious Charlotte Polidori but hardly even half-truth.

By the time the second *Germ* was published, Gabriel had completed to his satisfaction all of the Virgin but her hair. And William was too busy to sit for the angel's arms, compelling Gabriel to invest in two models. He had become enchanted by young women with red hair, and wanted a model with such accouterments. It was almost a premonition of his fate that when he found her in March she was a Miss Love. Since paid models could ill be afforded by the impecunious P.R.B.'s, Hunt foraged in Battersea Fields for gypsies appropriate for a canvas in which druids would figure, and located, William reported in his journal, "some of the most extraordinary people conceivable. He found a very beautiful woman for what he wants, fit for a Cleopatra; she consented to sit for £5 an hour, but finally came down to a shilling."

Only forty copies of the second *Germ* were sold: "The last knockdown blow," William groaned. He was ready to give it up and cut the P.R.B. losses, but George Tupper saw the journal as a prestige opportunity for his firm. Hoping that it might still win an audience, he offered to make good the losses on at least two further issues. On an evening in mid-February, in Gabriel's garret workroom in Charlotte Street, those of the faithful whom William could reach hastily by post gathered to hear Tupper's offer, made before he had received a farthing of their debt. They accepted.

The result was that William, after his hours at the Excise Office, was in effect the unpaid employee of the printers, who promptly renamed the forthcoming issue *Art and Poetry, being Thoughts towards Nature.* As he put it, "I naturally accommodated myself more than before to any wish evinced by the Tupper family." But the public remained unpersuaded. The March issue appeared a month late, and the April issue ended the experiment. The Brethren collectively owed £34 and seventeen shillings, which William computed in careful letters to the investors, at three pounds, fourteen shillings and sixpence each. Some of the P.R.B.'s squabbled over the bill, and William naturally paid Gabriel's share. More than two years later the indebtedness was still partly unpaid, Hancock (who had published nothing in it) having defaulted. William then dutifully advanced the amount out of his own pocket, and George Tupper tried to collect portions of it back for him from the remaining Brethren.

Perhaps William realized that despite the depressing, unremunerative work he had put into *The Germ*, only for him was the publication worth anything. With it he had served his apprenticeship as editor and critic, two occupations he would retain—along with the Excise Office—all his working life. The *Guardian* had observed that "some of the best papers [in *The Germ*] are by the two brothers named Rossetti." And several poets—notably Arthur Clough, Coventry Patmore and William Allingham—commented appreciatively on William's criticism. Further, his and Gabriel's friend Major Calder Campbell, who had contributed a sonnet to *The Germ* no worse than the *bouts rimés* efforts with which William padded the copy, had shown an issue to Edward William Cox, a barrister who edited the *Critic*, then a modest rival to the *Athenaeum*. The result was an offer to William to become the magazine's art critic. The post paid no better than *The Germ*, but it was a chance to champion P.R.B. causes and a respectable entrée into London critical journalism.

In the spring of 1850 P.R.B. painting needed all the help it could get. Again, prior to the opening of the Academy's annual, Gabriel, along with Deverell, defected to what had been the "Free Exhibition" the previous year, but was now called the "National Institution," this time located at the Portland Gallery in Regent Street. "Some spirits of wine and chloride of something," William noted on April 7, served to make the flame for the Archangel's feet, and the canvas, endowed with a Latin title, signed with the "P.R.B." code and listed modestly at £50, went off to what Gabriel hoped would be a kinder fate than he expected his brethren would encounter at the Academy. Alexander Munro, a sculptor acquaintance, inquired about the meaning of the mysterious initials, and Gabriel told him in confidence. Munro then told a writer-friend and fellow-Scot, Angus Reach, presumably also in confidence. Reach published his scoop in the *Illustrated London News*, to the outrage of the Brethren and the anguish of Gabriel, who was duly blamed for disloyalty. His cup was running over, for he had already had sufficient outrage directed at himself in the press for his offenses against art.

William and Christina, who had sat patiently for portions of the canvas, found the results described in the April 20 *Athenaeum* less than rewarding. "A certain expression in the eyes of the ill-drawn face of the Virgin affords a gleam of something high in intention, but . . . the face of the Angel is insipidity itself. One arm of the Virgin is well drawn. . . ." Otherwise, No. 225, *Ecce Ancilla Domini*, by D. G. Rossetti (he had decided to exploit the *Dante* in his name), was described as "a perversion of talent" and full of "infantine absurdities." Gabriel could not have been worse served had he exhibited at the Academy, and consoled himself with *The Times* review that slated his painterly weaknesses but recognized his picture as "the work of a poet."

Although Gabriel's friends had cause for unhappiness about his public decoding of the P.R.B. symbol, other revelations in the press suggested that other Brethren were not close-lipped either, for the very issue of the *Athenaeum* which condemned Gabriel had intimated the existence of a society of rebellious young artists; and the *Literary Gazette*, on the same day (May 4) as the *Illustrated London News* story, identified Deverell's painting as of "the *Pre-Raphael School*," and Gabriel's as "*Pre-Pre*, or ancient Byzantine." And on the same day the *Spectator* published a preliminary report of the Academy show, in which it described the canvases by Millais and Hunt as "leading types of the pre-Raphael school," and "monstrously perverse."

What was to be expected from the press about the P.R.B.'s was already clear on Varnishing Day at the Academy, when painters from seven until noon on the Monday morning of the opening could retouch or revarnish their work already hung. Millais had brought Hunt to see his "Carpenter Shop," which had cost him immense labor as he painstakingly sought a sense of raw actuality for the life of the young Jesus at home with his parents. He had painted for hours each day in a drafty, unheated carpenter's shop to get the setting and lighting just right, and paid the price in a series of severe colds; and he had even used models whose musculature had come from the kind of work he was portraying. (Only once thereafter, when he painted a drowning Ophelia from a model he had immersed fully clothed in a tub of water, did he attempt to secure such reality from which to work, as his aim was always a picture, not a P.R.B. manifesto.) But too shy to admit his pride at his accomplishment, Millais self-deprecatingly cautioned Hunt as they arrived before the canvas, "It's the most beastly thing I ever saw. Come away!"

As Hunt began protesting, two Academy School artists "rollicked into the room" and laughed loudly at the picture. It was too much for Millais, who alone among the P.R.B.'s—despite his words to Hunt—always had a sense of his own worth. Laying a hand on the shoulder of "the least imbecile" of the two (as Hunt described it), he cautioned them, his voice rising in fury, "Do you know what you are doing? *Don't you see that if you were to live to the age of Methuselah both of you, and you were to improve every day of your life more than you will in the whole course of it, you would never be able to achieve any work fit to compare with that picture?*" They slunk away, but not before Millais added that they were "egregious fools." Yet they were in tune with the critics, although the *Athenaeum* identified Gabriel—who was devoid of aesthetic theory—as "the chief of this little band," which could not have made Hunt and Millais happier. The two had worked earnestly, by P.R.B. principles, on canvases which they felt certain would win over the doubters.

Hunt, like Gabriel, had utilized his friends as models whenever he could. *A Converted British Family Sheltering a Christian Priest from the Persecution of the Druids*, was a crowded canvas nearly as large as its title, and inevitably William Michael Rossetti sat for the head and hands of the principal figure, an occupation which had kept him busy as late as April 7. He was loyal but increasingly uncomfortable as a model for at twenty he was nearly bald, and shy about it. "This, in youth" he wrote, "was anything but pleasant to me. In particular I used to dislike entering a theatre or other public place with my hat on, looking, as I was, quite juvenile, and then, on taking off my hat, presenting the appearance more like a used-up man of forty." People speculated in his hearing that the phenomenon was a symptom of dissipation, for which he could have had little time and less inclination.

On the basis of his brother's reception and then that of Hunt, whose work was called "uncouth" and "objectionable," William could have reasonably assumed that his appearance in a P.R.B. picture was bad luck for the painter. Millais, however, took the most brutal punishment of the three. His associating a scriptural subject with P.R.B. realism made *Christ in the House of His Parents* "a pictorial blasphemy," and the reviews ranged from "unpleasant" to "disgusting." It is difficult now to associate the hysterical outpouring in the press with the placid spirituality and mild realism of the painting; yet Charles Dickens in his magazine *Household Words* wrote savagely and over-imaginatively, "In the foreground of that carpenter's shop is a hideous, wry-necked, blubbering, red-haired boy in a night-gown who appears to have received a poke in the hand from the stick of another boy with whom he has been playing in an adjacent gutter, and to be holding it up for the contemplation of a kneeling woman, so horrible in her ugliness that (supposing it were possible for any human creature to exist for a moment with that dislocated throat) she would stand out from the rest of the company as a monster in the vilest cabaret in France, or the lowest gin shop in England."

Millais' parents blamed Gabriel Rossetti. He was "a sly Italian," and had been deceitful in diverting his picture to an exhibition where it had been viewed earlier. "What's the good of an ally who keeps out of the fight?" asked the elder Millais to his son and Hunt. But Gabriel had not kept out of the fight. Indignant at the *Athenaeum*'s mean-spirited criticisms, he had already written a bitter rebuttal. When the editor refused to publish it, Rossetti privately vowed never to send a work to public exhibition again.

The P.R.B., reeling from the debts brought on by the death of *The Germ* and the reviews of Gabriel's, Hunt's and Millais' work, and the failure of others to produce, suffered still another but more bearable blow after the Academy show. Ironically, while one of the criticisms of P.R.B. paintings concerned their alleged "popery," an accusation strengthened by the sacred themes of their work and even by the Latin title of Gabriel's picture,* James Collinson was making good his defection from the Brotherhood because there was not enough popery in the Protestantism he had resumed in order to court Christina. Possibly more afraid of marriage than damnation, late that spring he renounced Christina and the P.R.B.'s simultaneously, claiming that he could not "consciously as a Catholic, assist in spreading the artistic opinions of those who are not," as he would "dishonour God's faith" and the "Holy Saints." The withdrawal came in a letter to Gabriel, to whom Collinson appealed, "Please do not attempt to change my mind." No one did. William copied down the text of the letter in his diary. Christina accepted what she had expected from her long-absent lover. Going off to briefly recover in Brighton in the company of Maria and her mother, she managed to inquire from there to William about how Collinson's canvas *St. Elizabeth of Hungary* was proceeding. He had apparently not entirely disappeared from sight or mind. "Whilst I am here," she added, "if you can manage without too much trouble, I wish you would find out whether Mr. Collinson is as delicate [in health] as he used to be: you and Gabriel are my resources, and you are by far the more agreeable."

She could not forget Collinson easily. The P.R.B.'s had often made private fun of him but she had hung her hopes for happiness on him. Later in the year she wrote a poem on the subject of his painting, although she did not identify it that way, and her poetry of personal feeling registered her loss. One, afterwards retitled by William "Shut Out," in manuscript was called "What happened to me," and described iron bars as falling over her life. "So now I sit here quite alone," she wrote, "blinded with tears. . . ." She would not publish the poem for the feeling was too intimate. Nor another, written in the expectation of Collinson's break with her, which confessed,

> Now all the cherished secrets of my heart,
> Now all my hidden hopes, are turned to sin.
> Part of my life is dead, part sick, and part
> Is all on fire within.

"Being of a highly sensitive nature," William wrote, "and feeling keenly for him as well as for herself, she suffered much in forming and maintaining her resolve. A blight was on her heart and her spirits, and the delicacy of health which had already settled down upon her increased visibly. I remember that

---

* Recognizing the problem Gabriel soon afterward altered the title of his picture to *The Annunciation.*

one day—it may have been within four or five months after the breaking-off of the engagement—she happened to see Collinson in the neighbourhood of Regent's Park, and she fainted away in the street." * At almost exactly that time William was recording in his diary (Oct. 27, 1850) a visit to Coventry Patmore's house, where his host was reading to a small group "a translation, by Charles Bagot Cayley, with whom I have lately become acquainted, of some cantos of the *Inferno*, left by me . . . ." Patmore had promised William he would try to find a publisher for Cayley. And, after much diffidence, Cayley would become Christina's next serious suitor.

Despite financial problems and professional frustrations, the remaining P.R.B.'s and their cronies continued to see each other regularly, and Gabriel often worked his old magic in giving them cause to remain together. William Allingham, Coventry Patmore and William Bell Scott would join them when in town, as would the American poet-painter Buchanan Read; and William Rossetti, as a critic, now had access to review copies of new books, which gave him a new importance. One night at Gabriel's studio in Newman Street the group awaited William, who had gone to check on the possible arrival of an advance copy of Tennyson's mysterious new volume. "After long waiting," John Clayton, one of the number remembered, "when the clock indicated nearly midnight, there was a ring at the bell, and footsteps on the stair intensified expectation, until William burst into the room, waving the little brown cloth book over his head in triumph. It was *In Memoriam*. The volume was at once passed on to Gabriel, who then read the whole of it without faltering in his unapproachable tones and inspired interpretations, to the delight and amusement of all present, who had listened in rapt silence."

Publicly Gabriel was outgoing and optimistic, although he lived largely on "loans" from William and gifts from his aunts, and was even reduced, in mid-1850, to having no clothes not better hidden under his painting smock. From Newman Street one morning he sent an urgent appeal to William at the Excise Office. "I know not whether you have to go anywhere tonight, but . . . you have put on the only pair of breeches in which it is possible for me to go to the Opera tonight. Unless you *do* want them yourself, I wish if possible you would manage to be at home by five, in order that we may make a transfer. . . ." It was not easy to affect gaiety at the opera when so hard up, but Gabriel managed, and often stayed up so late thereafter visiting friends—he had no work to go to the next day—that once at Hunt's,

---

* Eventually Collinson married a sister of the wife of J. R. Hubert, R.A., thus remaining within a family of artists. He and his wife had one son.

Allingham remembered, his host lay himself determinedly across three chairs to sleep, as he still went to Academy classes each morning. Only when Gabriel rose did the party break up, with the early morning light already revealing from Hunt's window the shapes of barges on the broad Thames.

At least once in the frustrating summer of 1850 Gabriel was even embarrassed by poverty not his own. The tenant of his building, the proprietor of a dancing school from whom he subleased the rooms above what he called the "hop shop," defaulted on his rent and Gabriel's goods were seized. Buchanan Read lost the luggage he had stored in the studio, and Gabriel's books were only saved because William managed to smuggle them to Madox Brown's. Why Gabriel had to be in hiding, since he was not the guilty party, is not clear, unless his sublease made him doubly liable; but Christina wrote cautiously to William from Brighton, "If his whereabouts is to be kept secret, pray do not let me have his address." This time it was Aunt Margaret rather than Aunt Charlotte who bailed Gabriel out of what he described to her as "the late unlucky pickle." He paid his rent to someone, and sent Margaret Polidori a sketch of his *Kate the Queen* as evidence of his application to his work. He would soon be hiring models again, he told her. Yet he was already planning to put the work aside, explaining to William that it could not be completed in time for the next annual exhibition.

He was more frank about his brother's work, pressing him to write more lucidly. "I have just read your review in the *Critic*," Gabriel observed, ". . . many parts of which I do not understand. What do you mean by the 'enforcement of magnificence having a tendency to impair the more essential development of feeling'? This smacks villainously of Malvolio's vein." But although Gabriel could urge his less talented brother to work, William regularly put in a day's labor at a regular job before he began his after-hours' writing. Gabriel could write hortatory letters, but was doing less painting than before, or at least not carrying anything to completion, and returning more to the unremunerative solace of composition and translation.

A new try at a picture spurred Gabriel to travel to Sevenoaks, in Kent, where Hunt (with Stephens and soon Woolner, as company) was using Knole Park as setting for his *Two Gentlemen of Verona*. Translating the *Vita Nuova* had suggested to Gabriel a seven-foot-long *Meeting of Dante and Beatrice in the Garden of Eden*, but Knole was too rainy for sustained work, even, as Gabriel discovered, with an open umbrella lashed to his chest. Soaked, he wrote home for his "other breeches" and, in the continual autumn downpours, made further struggles to paint from nature. One stroller in the park, looking at a Rossetti sketch, told another that the artist was apparently drawing a map; while a boy insisted loudly that what was actually the beginning of a landscape was a deer. After three weeks Gabriel gave up, rolled up his canvases, and returned to London. There was a model he wanted to hire, whether or not he had a picture to paint.

V

Arlington Street
1850-1853

To William early in September, 1850, Gabriel had sent a short poem he later called "The Mirror," with a prefatory query, "Can you explain the following?" "She knew it not," the poem began, and decades later William explained that what the woman did not know was that a man was deeply in love with her and would not declare himself, but only bore his "most perfect pain" with "silent patience." Earlier in the letter Gabriel had joked that he had little news of the P.R.B.'s other than that Hunt and Stephens had "been playing off a disgraceful hoax on poor Jack Tupper, by passing Miss Siddal upon him as Hunt's wife." As soon as he heard of it, Gabriel added, he insisted that Hunt write an apology to Tupper. It was not that he had Tupper's well being in mind. Whether or not he even confessed it to himself, Gabriel could not bear the idea, even as a joke, that Miss Siddal could belong to someone else.

When he first saw Elizabeth Siddal, Gabriel once told Madox Brown, "he felt his destiny was defined." Yet he did not know what he could do about it, for he needed money, had no picture project going which could elicit it, had no published work which had earned a farthing, and remained a family burden at a time when family poverty made departure from Charlotte Street to less expensive quarters necessary. Early in 1851 the Rossettis moved to 38 Arlington Street, in the northern outreaches of London near Mornington Crescent and close to Madox Brown's new North London School of Design which Christina had begun attending intermittently. William Bell Scott, who directed one of the Schools of Design which the

Board of Trade had established in Newcastle, out of curiosity went to visit it, and found the shy young girl he had first seen standing at a writing desk at the Charlotte Street house now "among the pupils, who were all drawing not from casts or beautiful objects of any kind, either from sculpture or ornament, nor even from symmetrical forms, or solids to illustrate perspective—from nothing in short but wood-shavings picked up from a joiner's yard."

Christina was not a serious student, being in the vicinity only because her mother had moved in order to open a day school for daughters of tradespeople in the neighborhood: "the hairdresser, the pork butcher, etc.," as William put it. "Though she had no propensity to educational and other drudgery," he wrote of Christina, she assisted her mother, and Maria continued to go out to tutor the three or four pupils she had. Into her poetry and an autobiographical novel, *Maude*—a novel, she thought, might earn a few pounds—Christina poured her misery, keeping it back especially from her unhappy father, who paced in the patch of garden on clear days, and complained of his own frailties and of Gabriel's failure to be anything more than a financial embarrassment to the family. *Maude*—a thin, self-pityingly sentimental fiction—was, fortunately for Christina's reputation, unpublishable. Like the author, the poet-heroine had a sister, Mary, but Christina wrote in a sibling who resembled the heroine, something the plain, moon-faced Maria did not. Like the Rossetti girls, the teenage sisters are pious to the point of overscrupulousness, and for recreation play *bouts-rimés*. And Maude herself is "delicate" in health, confessing, "I begin to acquire the reputation of an invalid; and so my privacy is respected."

The novella ends with Maude's death, and with a striking anticipation of an episode in Gabriel's life still a decade away. The heroine, on her deathbed, leaves instructions to have her manuscript book buried with her, and her friend Agnes proceeds to carry out the task. "The locked book she never opened; but had it placed in Maude's coffin, with all its words of folly, sin, vanity; and she humbly trusted, of true penitence also." And as she places it by Maude's side she clips a lock of her friend's hair. Fiction would foreshadow life.

Gabriel was still managing to keep such melodrama remote from his own existence. He neither desired to live at a high emotional pitch, repressed or otherwise, nor did he wish to fulfill himself, in proper Victorian fashion, in work for its own sake. Carlyle had proclaimed that "All work, even cotton-spinning, is noble; work is alone noble." But even William, Gabriel knew, did not profess to be exhilarated by his hours at the Inland Revenue, and Maria tutored her pupils in Italian only because it was a means of income, acquired from her father, which saved her from the dread nineteenth-century living death of governessing. The cult of work no more appealed to Gabriel than the cult of moral earnestness, and to lower the implicit pressure on him to become a wage earner, he devised an appropriate gesture. After preliminary publicity at home, he betook himself to Nine Elms Station, on the South Bank of the Thames east of Battersea, to investigate a position, then open, as a railway telegraph operator. He examined the apparatus and explained courteously to the authorities, as he did afterwards to his family, that he could never understand telegraphic code or the complexities of the device. Then he left, having fulfilled, for the rest of his life, his obligations to salaried employment.

Father and son seldom spoke, although Gabriel usually slept at home. By day he slipped away early to the studio to which he had moved from Newman Street, one he shared with his friend Walter Deverell at 17 Red Lion Square, just above Holborn and east of Bloomsbury. It was from there that early in 1851 he explained his situation to his Aunt Charlotte, who had sent him one of the checks from relatives which constituted his major means of support. Having first cashed the check, he then wrote her a letter of thanks, pointing out brashly that he was sure that she would agree with him that living on what he called loans would enable him to get on with his real career, while "minor employment," which might provide "just the means of daily subsistence," would also cause him "to lose entirely what ground I have already gained with the public; which, I may add without vanity, is much more than most young men have gained upon the strength of two small pictures." He had not sold his "last year's picture," he explained, and had to exist on "several pounds which I have been forced to borrow of Mamma from time to time," but he could get on with a new big canvas.

What he failed to confess was that he had given up on his "Kate the Queen" picture and was exploring new ideas. Abandonment of the canvas he had begun meant that he would have nothing to exhibit in the spring shows, but outwardly he evidenced no distress. As Madox Brown recorded, Gabriel had "thrown up" his picture, but "his head and beard grow finer every day, and he had . . . some designs which are perfectly divine . . . but paint he *will not*. He is too idle." He "purports to keep himself," Madox Brown noted shrewdly. "I had thought for some time there had been some estrangement between Rossetti and his brother, and I asked Deverell. . . . He said no. That he believed they were as good friends as ever, but that he supposed his brother did not call on him oftener than he could help because he was ordered peremptorily to hand over all the cash he had about him." Somehow William's relationship to his brother survived such episodes, but they were seeing less of each other. William worked all day, and Gabriel often stayed evenings at the Red Lion Square studio, where his (and

Deverell's) landlord, concerned about the young women who entered alone and remained for hours, stipulated in his lease that models had to be "kept under some gentlemanly restraint, as some artists sacrifice the dignity of art to the baseness of passion."

At Red Lion Square there was that possibility, for Elizabeth Siddal was now a frequent visitor; and although she modeled for other painters in Gabriel's group, it was by then acknowledged that she was otherwise his. The P.R.B.'s were always looking for interesting faces and figures to paint, William Rossetti writing in his journal on December 7, 1850, that he had encountered Millais, Hunt and Charles Collins (painter brother of novelist Wilkie Collins) "parading Tottenham Court Road . . . on the search for models." And when they found "one or two adaptable for Millais—the best being in the company of two men"—their courage failed, as they worried that addressing her would bring "the likelihood of a cry of 'Police.'" Gabriel no longer had such problems. And when Hunt and William hired horses and "galloped full pelt" down Oxford Street and into the nearby fields, they may have been working off frustrations Gabriel no longer felt. His own prowling had ended.

When Deverell first told Hunt about the "stupendously beautiful creature" he had found plying her needle in a milliner's shop in Cranbourne Alley, where he had accompanied his mother, Hunt was too busy. It was then March, 1850, and Academy submissions were a month away. "By Jove!" he had gone on; "she's like a queen, magnificently tall, with a lovely figure, a stately neck, and a face of the most delicate and finished modelling. . . . Wait a minute! I haven't done; she has grey eyes, and her hair is like dazzling copper, and shimmers with lustre. . . ." And she would be at the Red Lion Square studio the next day to pose in page's garb for Viola in Deverell's *Twelfth Night*.

So was Gabriel, who sat for the head of the Jester in the picture. "To fall in love with Elizabeth Siddal," William Rossetti afterwards wrote, "was a very easy performance, and Dante Gabriel transacted it at an early date." "She's really a wonder," Deverell had said; "for while her friends, of course, are quite humble, she behaves like a real lady, by clear common-sense, and without affectation, knowing perfectly, too, how to keep people at a respectful distance." Gabriel was enchanted, and could not be kept at distance; nor did Miss Siddal act aloof. She agreed to sit for him, although he had no picture planned in which he could use her. He watched her sit for Deverell, and then Hunt, and did his own sketches, drawings, and watercolors of her. By the end of April Deverell had exhibited his painting, and had also done an etching of Elizabeth Siddal which appeared in the final number of the ill-fated *Germ*. Familiarly she was now "Lizzy," and in such demand among the P.R.B.'s that she made an arrangement to work a reduced schedule at the milliner's in order to have time for the more congenial and more rewarding employment of modeling. But whether Gabriel ever paid her anything more than compliments is unknown. She was not quite seventeen, and Gabriel had dark, brooding eyes, and spoke with the tongues of angels. Soon she was spending her off-duty hours with him, and by the end of the year it was understood in their circle that only for Gabriel was she anything more than a model.

Perhaps to keep her at more of a distance from his cronies—especially the attractive, mustached Walter Deverell—Gabriel had given up his joint tenancy of a studio with Deverell that May, and moved in again with Madox Brown at 17 Newman Street. "Bruno"—a widower with a small daughter— had remarried, this time an uneducated teenage farmer's daughter, Emma Hill. Since Brown spent much of his time with her in a cottage in Hampstead once their first child was born, his studio was a convenient place for Gabriel to paint—and to be alone with—Lizzy, who was already, privately, his "Guggums."

Somehow the disintegrating Brotherhood survived not only Gabriel's romantic defection but the critical onslaught from without when its newest works were shown. Gabriel, of course, had nothing. Lizzy that spring sat for his watercolor *Beatrice at a Marriage Feast Denies Dante her Salutation*, but it was not for exhibition, and hardly represented the likely relationship between model and painter. Other P.R.B.'s needed to sell their work but it cost Gabriel nothing to have Lizzy—who was earning a salary and modeling fees from his friends—pose, and Aunt Charlotte sent further checks and money orders.

How much the family—or both families—knew by 1851 is not certain. Lizzy's father—a former Sheffield cutler with a mentally defective son among his other children—did not have Lizzy as a burden to support, although she still came home evenings to sleep. None of the Rossettis but William as yet saw Lizzy, who as Madox Brown put it, could be "beautifully dressed for about three pounds, altogether looking like a queen," and spoke with a soft voice which belied her origins. Certainly the Rossettis hoped for a fine match for Gabriel, considering themselves of "good family," but at worst William assumed that she would be no added drain on his own finances.

As the family's had declined, William's had improved. He had confided to his diary about work as an after-hours critic that he would "certainly be glad to do for something, and with better prospects, what I am now doing for nothing," and he did get an offer to write art criticism for the *Spectator* from its proprietor, Robert S. Rintoul. It paid relatively well—£50 a year, which in addition to William's £110 from the Inland Revenue (its altered name), made him, as he put it, almost a capitalist among the P.R.B.'s. (Only Millais earned more, selling his paintings easily regardless of critical disapproval.) But William made the brotherly mistake of inducing Rintoul to offer assignments he could not handle himself to Gabriel, who should have needed the money, William and the others in Arlington Street having no idea of the extent of Gabriel's gifts and loans and near-extortions from relatives, including themselves. About an art exhibition he was to review while William was away visiting Bell Scott in Newcastle, Gabriel lazily wrote his brother, "I am not well enough to stir out tonight . . . but will write an article from recollection and catalogue—which Brown has got. This I suppose will be sufficient. The P.R.B. business will not lose. . . ." But it was, and had been, losing in the press.

Again the exhibition season was opened by the "Free Exhibition," which included a canvas by Deverell, *The Banishment of Hamlet*, and Collinson's finally-completed *An Incident in the Life of St. Elizabeth of Hungary.* One artist was not an official P.R.B., and the other had resigned from the group, but both were attacked as members of the faltering Brotherhood. To evade criticism the band had even disavowed the notorious P.R.B. symbol, and had demonstrated such lack of filial loyalty that William as Secretary desperately formulated rules which no one heeded, among them fines for absences from meetings, which no one paid. And he pleaded for a declaration of artistic principles, which Millais—out of William's hearing—called nonsense, and which only the press seemed to believe existed in practice.

At the Academy, Millais, Hunt, Collins and Brown were all attacked as Pre-Raphaelites, whose faith, *The Times* declared on May 7, "seems to consist in an absolute contempt for perspective and the known laws of light and shade, an aversion to beauty in every shape, and a singular devotion to the minute accidents of their subjects, including, or rather seeking out, every excess of sharpness and deformity." William's contrary opinion in the *Spectator* remained almost the only exception to the general humiliation, and Millais pressed Coventry Patmore to work on his influential friends to publish something in defense of P.R.B. art. One emerged in John Ruskin, then thirty-two and on the rise as a critic as a result of his *Modern Painters, The Seven Lamps of Architecture* and *The Stones of Venice.* Two letters of his appeared in *The Times* before the month was out, each mildly criticizing P.R.B. failings in technique and in "Romanist and Tractarian tendencies," while praising "the perfect truth, power and finish" of other aspects of their work, in which he saw a common aesthetic pattern William Rossetti had never been able to elicit from the artists themselves. And in a peroration

Ruskin warned that if the young men were not driven from the scene by "harsh or careless criticism" they might "lay in our England the foundations of a school of art nobler than the world has seen for three hundred years."

Hunt and Millais posted a joint letter of thanks, and Ruskin was so pleased with himself that he and his young wife, Effie, unheralded, drove off to 83 Gower Street—the return address on the letter—and carried Millais off to stay with them for a week at Camberwell. It was a valuable friendship for the P.R.B.'s, and they cultivated it with caution. (It was useful, too, for Ruskin, who eventually extricated himself from his unconsummated marriage when Millais began finding in Effie attractions which had seemed to repel her sexually underdeveloped husband.) The immediate impact of Ruskin's support was that Hunt's reviled Academy picture won a £50 prize at an exhibition in Liverpool, where he took it in August after it was taken down in Trafalgar Square. Mixing his metaphors, William wrote excitedly in the *Spectator* that "one of the most advanced signs of the times shoots meteorlike from the provinces across the London fog which encrusts Trafalgar Square." Soon after Hunt received an offer from Belfast shipping agent Francis MacCracken to buy *Valentine Rescuing Sylvia*, which he had not seen, for the catalogue price of £150.

Millais had sold his pictures before they left the Academy and had immediately employed Lizzy Siddal to pose for another he had already begun, *The Death of Ophelia*. With scrupulous fidelity to botanical detail, he had painted in the countryside, at Ewell, that autumn a leaf-filled stream (complete to water rat he then rubbed out). Lizzy was to lie in it to simulate the drowning of Hamlet's betrothed. But in December the stream, too, had to be simulated, and Millais rigged a large bathtub with heating lamps beneath, in which Lizzy lay, fully clothed, in water. During the final modeling session the lamps burned out, but Lizzy, knowing that the first duty of the model was to pose without disturbing the concentration of the painter, lay uncomplainingly and benumbed in the cold tub. She came down with a severe chill, and her father, angry when he discovered why, threatened to sue Millais. After Millais agreed to pay her medical bills, Siddall relented. Privately, Gabriel did not. It was an excuse to keep Lizzy more to himself. She never afterwards sat for another painter than Gabriel, and even left her millinery job at the end of the year, to spend more time with him. "How he managed to support himself, much less Miss Siddal," William wondered afterwards, "is a mystery."

With all her availability to Gabriel, Lizzy appeared on canvas during the next exhibition season only as Ophelia, for Gabriel again submitted nothing; yet the Brotherhood was well represented in Trafalgar Square. Lizzy, her red hair floating in Millais' painstakingly detailed stream, had posed for one of the supreme achievements of Pre-Raphaelitism, and his work and Hunt's—although not Brown's—were hung "on the line," a sign of respectability. Brown was furious, and swore never to exhibit at the Academy again. Hunt and Millais nevertheless applied for membership, explaining that it was proof that their work was not subversive to the artistic Establishment; but both were rejected. Hunt would not reapply, and Millais announced a similar intention; yet when he learned that his application had been disapproved only because he was a year too young, he prudently kept his papers in order.

Gabriel was seldom seen. He had again drifted out of Madox Brown's studio and taken advantage of a friend's offer to use his secluded, semi-rural London cottage—appropriately christened *The Hermitage*—while the occupants were visiting in Normandy. In the garden was a building separate from the house, and covered with ivy, and it was there that William Bell Scott was directed to look for Rossetti in the cool of a summer evening when he had come down from Newcastle. Climbing up the wooden steps, he entered in the dusk and encountered Gabriel "and a lady whom I did not recognise, and could scarcely see. He did not introduce her; she rose to go. I made a little bow, which she did not acknowledge; and she left. This was Miss Siddal. Why he did not introduce me I cannot say."

Despite Gabriel's withdrawal, he turned up with regularity at Arlington Street—alone—and felt comfortable referring to "the Sid" in the bosom of his family. On the surface the P.R.B. seemed still alive in the summer of 1852. Gabriel, in the interests of realism, had even queried John Tupper about the possibility of finding a dying and hospitalized boy to paint. He was interested, too, in the "consequent emotions" of onlookers, especially a mother. If such a boy were accessible, Gabriel urged coldly, "I wish you would let me know before the looks are entirely vacant." It suggested that he was looking beyond Lizzy for a pathetically saleable subject. William, too, seemed involved in P.R.B. activity, taking a week's vacation so that he could go to Clivevale Farm with Hunt, to visit Edward Lear, who was trying to complete his brooding paintings of Italian scenes under English skies. Millais turned up on a weekend, as well as Thackeray, with whom they had become friendly. But the activity was deceptive. As Gabriel wrote to Bell Scott in July, 1852, the important event "among us" then was "Woolner's exodus to the diggings." Sculpture had not made him a living, and he and two artist friends had decided to join the Australian gold rush, all three, as Gabriel described, "plentifully stocked with corduroys, sou-westers, jerseys, fire-arms, and belts full of little bags to hold the expected nuggets. Hunt, William and myself deposited them in their four months' home with a due mixture of solemnity and joviality." When the ship sailed from Gravesend, with it, in effect, went the disintegrating Brotherhood.

The actual end dragged out for some months, for some of the Brethren still saw each other, and on occasion helped each other. Hunt, working on a painting of a lantern-carrying Jesus, *The Light of the World*, which he was sure would make his fortune if not his reputation, still painted by strict P.R.B. principles. It meant painting by moonlight if the setting were moonlit, keeping owl-like hours for weeks, and using a head he had modeled from his friends rather than try to get them to sit up with him in the small hours on his balcony in Chelsea. William disappeared into the composite head, but for the face itself Hunt went to his surrogate P.R.B., Christina, trying to capture what he called her "gravity and sweetness of expression." Mrs. Rossetti accompanied her to Hunt's studio one morning, where he painted directly onto the canvas; thus beneath the bearded Jesus is the flesh of Christina, her large, heavy-lidded eyes, eyebrows and eyelashes. Hunt knew what he was doing. On seeing it Thomas Carlyle called it a "mere papistical phantasy," but on completion it sold for 400 guineas, and created such a demand for copies that Hunt further sold the copyright for an additional £200. He began planning a trip to Egypt and the Holy Land, to paint appropriate subjects on site.

Millais prospered even sooner than Hunt, but the others not at all. Gabriel remained immersed in drawings of "Guggums," and wrote Christina, then away on a visit to friends in Staffordshire, that with him while Lizzy was also away he had "a lock of hair shorn from the beloved head of that dear, and radiant as the tresses of Aurora, a sight of which may perhaps dazzle you on your return." By August, 1852, Gabriel was planning complete removal from the family; in order to be with Lizzy he wanted a domicile of his own, which he explained to his mother (the prospective "lender" of the money) as a place for William and himself. William in fact had to sign as co-tenant, at £40 annual rent, since Gabriel was jobless and could not guarantee the £40. But he could wheedle the furnishings, enlisting Christina to itemize the kitchen implements and furniture he would borrow, including the two best family mirrors, which he claimed would be essential to his painting. On November 22, 1852, the move was accomplished, aided by gifts from his aunts (Margaret Polidori provided a lamp) and the strong back of "Old Williams," the family servant who had posed for St. Joachim in *The Girlhood of Mary Virgin*. At twenty-four, with almost no income, and the prospect of supporting a mate as well as the rent, he was on his own.

Three days after his move to the three-room upstairs flat at 14 Chatham Place Gabriel wrote William, "I have Lizzy coming, and of course do not wish for anyone else." He was referring, he added, having framed the warning too accurately, to a possible visit from Hunt, and indeed offered William dinner if he came over after his Friday at the office, but the implication remained. Although Chatham Place was for more than painting and writing, P.R.B. conviviality—next to having Lizzy over—had a low priority. But Lizzy was not going to be living there, ostensibly, and Gabriel relented and began inviting his cronies as soon as he acquired enough ancient secondhand chairs to seat them.

One such occasion that winter included seven artist friends, but although Gabriel took his guests through the rooms to see his pictures and curios—including a copy of a death mask of Dante—he showed them no work of his own, other than a slight sketch accidentally left visible. Still, the conversation was boisterous over roasted chestnuts and coffee, and hot spirits and honey, and the view of the Thames at evening, with lights flickering on the bridge and quays and boats, charmed painter George Boyce. He noted it in his diary—and also his return the following Thursday when Hunt and Millais joined the company. But such conviviality at Chatham Place grew more rare as Gabriel became more absorbed in his passion for "the Sid"—the term he usually used in referring to her when he wanted to deflect suggestions of intense intimacy.

He was drawing from Lizzy or taking inspiration in his writing from his involvement with her; and he was optimistic about increased earnings. Working in watercolors was less demanding, and the low prices one could then ask seemed to him good business. Why struggle for a year to finish, at most, one or two meticulously detailed canvases for an obtuse Academy?

He permitted two Dantesque pictures, one of them modeled from Guggums, to be shown at an exhibition in Pall Mall, greatly concerned all the while that they might be rejected, but busy, nevertheless, with more watercolors. Writing came more easily, too, in the ebullience of his relationship with Lizzy, and he even dashed off a poem on the occasion of the death of the "Dook," the hero of Waterloo. His poetry about Guggums, except for bantering doggerel of a kind written by lovers, celebrated such joys and frustrations as suggested that if Lizzy was withholding anything of herself, Gabriel expected all obstacles would soon be removed. In the meantime he identified his situation with Dante and his Beatrice, and described his love poetically as being that of the lover who watches his young beloved mature into nubile womanhood.

On New Year's Eve, as 1852 became 1853, he saw the year in with William and Maria at Arlington Street, where Stephens and Hunt ("jollier than ever, with a laugh which answers one's own like a grotto full of echoes") had joined them for dinner. Then, with guests departed, Maria gone to bed, and William slumbering in a chair, one candle guttered out. Gabriel awakened William to ask for help in finding another ("He says 'no' . . . and falls asleep again. But he is wrong, for I have found one.") and began a long letter to the absent Woolner in Australia. Interweaving his gossip with caricatures of their friends, Gabriel described his own professional progress realistically ("art—the last thing with me as usual") before deciding that he had reason for optimism about his prospects. He had "got rid" of his "white picture"—the *Ecce Ancilla Domini*—"to an Irish maniac," the Belfast shipper MacCracken who had encountered the P.R.B.'s through Hunt. "I find I am pretty certain of selling any water colour drawings I make, and advantageously," he crowed; "the two exhibited have drawn a good deal of attention. . . ."

His sale to MacCracken had actually not yet been consummated. The canvas needed restoration, as Gabriel had not known how to handle his pigments, but he attributed his problems with the Archangel's head to "William's malevolent expression," and induced his brother to sit again on his Sunday off from work. By the end of the month "the blessed white daub"—retitled *The Annunciation*—was en route to Belfast for £50, Gabriel having prevailed in a tiff with the purchaser as to whether Ruskin could first view the canvas to assure MacCracken that it was all right. Woolner had made only £20 digging in Australia.

Although Gabriel had rejected Ruskin's intervention, it was Ruskin who induced MacCracken, once he had seen his purchase, to commission a companion, *Mary in the House of St. John*, for which £150 was to be paid; and a Liverpool shipowner, John Miller, who had seen *The Annunciation*, also wanted a picture. By the time Rossetti began the picture for MacCracken, it was too late for a sale, and Miller waited years for his picture to be begun, let alone completed. Gabriel did not need much money and could wheedle much of that, content with his "professional prospects."

Prospects for his mother, father and sisters were increasingly poorer, but that did not seem to disturb Gabriel greatly. The school in Arlington Street had been a failure, and Mrs. Rossetti, insistent that a day school somewhere was a solution to their problems—especially to what to do with daughters who had no livelihood—gave up the house in London in April, 1853, and moved with Christina to Frome, in Somersetshire. Gabriel wrote Woolner that he hoped his father's health would benefit from the change, and that "I shall thus have a *pied-à-terre* whenever I am able to get into the country, which shall be very jolly, but I shall miss them here. . . ."

Collinson had gone into a Jesuit college in the country, information about his whereabouts passed on to Christina by her brothers. (The new Academy show had gone without a new work of his, nor one of Gabriel's, but Hunt and Millais again exhibited, more successfully than before.) Of the family, only Maria and William remained. Since their lease of the Arlington Street house ran until the end of the year, they postponed any move, Maria keeping house and going out to her Italian-language pupils, and William making the long walk to Somerset House each morning.

The opportunity in Frome had come about because a High Church clergyman ousted from his London living because of his Puseyite leanings had been presented with a living there by the Dowager Marchioness of Bath, who lived nearby at Longleat. Through Aunt Charlotte, the invitation to open a school at Frome then materialized, and Christina and Mrs. Rossetti settled in Brunswick Place, Fromefield, a Somersetshire market town with hilly streets which led out to nearby farms, and to few potential students. By the time the ailing *Professore* arrived, it was already clear that the school would be even less of a success than the London attempt. Maria, on the other hand, acquired a new, young pupil of her own in London, ten-year-old Lucy Brown, daughter of Madox Brown by his first marriage. His young second wife, Emma, was being patiently educated by Brown himself, and had the beginnings of a new family to also occupy her. Lucy was to be taken off her hands to be an informal day pupil, who would be brought by her father to Arlington Street, as Christina put it from Frome, "for the advantage of her acquaintance." Maria would lunch with her, give her lessons in what was more a social than a tutorial atmosphere, take her to nearby Regent's Park to "Zoological Gardenize," and have her father over to tea at times to demonstrate what, among the civilized graces, Lucy had begun acquiring. Sometimes, after his day at the Inland Revenue, William was also home while Lucy went through her paces, but he showed little more than polite interest. There were exhibitions to cover, after hours, for the *Spectator*; new books to read and reviews to write; besides, the family of the journal's proprietor was beginning to take a proprietary interest in William himself, perhaps because there was a daughter of more than marriageable age at home—home being Henrietta Rintoul's apartment on the upper floors of the publishing office of the *Spectator* in Wellington Street, just above the Strand at Aldwych, and conveniently across the street from Somerset House.

Christina had few preoccupations other than the torpor of her own life. She sent William *bouts-rimés*, sonnet endings and a poem on the P.R.B. which included a couplet on William as critic, who "calm and solemn / Cuts up his brethren by the column," and she tried to fill her solitude by experimenting with drawing and watercoloring, and with poetry that had become more stoical than self-pitying:

> Our heaven must be within ourselves,
> Our only heaven the work of faith,

> Thro' all the race of life that shelves
> Downwards to death.

Life did not race in Fromefield, but it was clear that although Christina's perspectives had shifted somewhat, it had not affected her preoccupations. There was even a playful note to her morbidity, as in "Charon" she wrote of "my cottage near the Styx," a conceit accurately representing her view of Frome but which William said "tickled . . . Maria uncommonly" when sent in a letter to London, and which Gabriel described as having "brought to light a neatly-paved thoroughfare between Maggie's ears."

They were snatching at a cause for laughter. With the *Professore* clearly in his last enfeebled months, and isolated at dreary Frome, far from his dwindling band of émigré cronies, it was a dismal period for the splintered family, except for Gabriel, who was too preoccupied with "the Sid" and with his own professional activity to be of much solace. He was also intermittently ill himself, possibly from the foul atmosphere of Chatham Place, the pilings of which were awash in sewerage when the Thames was at high tide; but the picturesque location near Blackfriars Bridge, looking out over the river, kept him there. When summer came and the air was especially bad—he attributed some of Lizzy's chronic bronchial illness to it as well—he borrowed a carpetbag and "ten or twelve pounds" from Aunt Charlotte through the good offices of Maria and went off to visit Bell Scott in Newcastle, telling his aunt that he needed the sea air at Tyneside. And from there he pressured William—who slept at Blackfriars sometimes—to pay the rent at Chatham Place. Meanwhile, although he continued his travels about England through the summer, all he could do was profess anxiety to his mother "to find my way to Frome, and see your dear face again before long—also as much as is visible of the governor's,* and Christina's almost stereotyped smile." In the early autumn "Maggie" went up from London to Frome, but Gabriel complained of a boil, and of the need to work on a watercolor for MacCracken.

Old Gabriele's *Arpa Evangelica*, the reaction of a dying man to a religious life that had been more Florentine than Roman, had been printed privately for him, copies arriving at Frome in September. To William he sent instructions for distributing books among designated friends, and suggested that he would value the criticisms of both his sons. "I started this letter," he concluded sadly, "with the idea of filling the four little pages, but having got half way down the second I cannot see to write any more."

Gabriel was given his copy by William, as well as the admonition to

---

* A reference to his perpetual wearing of a cap with eye-shade.

reply, and sent an appreciative and understanding letter, receiving in return a long, admonitory letter in Italian:*

My Dearest Gabriel,

For some while past I have been feeling a strong impulse to write to you, my dearly beloved son; and to-day I will obey this imperious inner voice.

I am glad that you have undertaken to read the *Arpa Evangelica*. . . . You should, however, always bear in mind that this book is the outcome of only three months' work, and was written with the intention of its being amenable to every grade of intelligence.

I am extremely pleased at the progress which you are making in your beautiful art, and at some profits which you are earning from it to maintain yourself with decorum in society. Remember, my dearly loved son, that you have only your abilities to rely upon for your welfare. Remember that you were born with a marked propensity and that, from your earliest years, you made us conceive the brightest hopes that you would become a great painter. And such you will be, I am certain.

* * * *

Good-bye, my most lovable Gabriel, and believe in the constant affection of
Your affectionate father
GABRIELE ROSSETTI.

P.S.—I perceive that I have not spoken to you at all about the state of my health. And what can I say of it? It is the same as it was in London; betwixt life and death, but more tending to the latter than the former.

Gabriel understood the criticism implied, and in an unusually sensitive defense, in Italian, responded:

In your letter, my dear Father, you speak of my profession. I can assure you that now I am not negligent in that respect. With me progress is, and always will be, gradual in everything. Of late also health has not been favourable to me; but now I am well and at work, and also I find purchasers, and I can see before me, much more clearly than hitherto, the path to success. How much do I owe you, and how much trouble have I given you dearest Father, in this and in all matters! Needless were it to ask your loving heart to pardon me; but I must always beg you to believe in the real and deep affection with which I remain,
Your loving son,
DANTE GABRIEL ROSSETTI.

The exchange left him wondering whether a trip to Frome was a good idea after all, but indirectly Gabriel kept that possibility alive by finding that he had an excuse to travel there if Christina could locate for him there an

---

* Quoted from here in William Rossetti's translation, as also is the following letter.

appropriate brick wall to paint. He had a piece of Pre-Raphaelite realism in mind, which required also a calf in a cart. But whatever his distance from Frome, he had not forgotten Christina's problems in trying to break into print, which her separation from London had made worse. Not only was he trying to find a publisher for a short story she had written, but pressing her to write verses other than the morbid ones Maria had recently shown him which "smack rather of the old shop." What he wanted to see her try was some P.R.B. realism— "any rendering either of narrative or sentiment from real abundant Nature, which presents much more variety." He would also teach her something about painting, he volunteered, "but I am afraid you find art [to] interfere with the legitimate exercise of anguish." He had an immense amount of news for a short letter, even noting off-handedly that he had escorted Maria to Christ Church, Albany Street the previous Sunday (November 6), certainly one of his rare appearances in a pew. Much had happened to the splintering P.R.B.'s, he told Christina. Woolner was still in Australia, using his sculptor's talents to fashion gold into medallions rather than vainly digging for it. Deverell, the handsome young artist who had first found Guggums, was bedridden, dying of kidney disease. Hunt would be leaving in a week for Egypt. And "Millais, I just hear, was last night elected Associate [of the Royal Academy]." Clearly it was a turning point, and he portentously added, " 'So now the whole Round Table is dissolved.' "

Two days later—from what she had called "the Frome forlorn hope"—Christina responded, with a wit that did not smack of the "old shop." Yet it was an elegy:

> The P.R.B. is in its decadence:
> For Woolner in Australia cooks his chops,
> And Hunt is yearning for the land of Cheops;
> D. G. Rossetti shuns the vulgar optic;*
> While William M. Rossetti merely lops
> His B's in English disesteemed as Coptic;
> Calm Stephens in the twilight smokes his pipe,
> But long the dawning of his public day;
> And he at last the champion great Millais,
> Attaining Academic opulence,
> Winds up his signature with A.R.A.
> So rivers merge in the perpetual sea;
> So luscious fruit must fall when over-ripe;
> And so the consummated P.R.B.**

---

* A reference to Gabriel's reluctance to exhibit his art publicly.

** It updated the doggerel she had tried out on William the previous September, in which she toyed with the names of the six who "Embodied the great P.R.B."

VI

Chatham Place
1854-1856

He showed me a drawer full of 'Guggums,' " Madox Brown wrote after a visit to Gabriel. "God knows how many . . . it is like a monomania with him." "Catty," Madox Brown's daughter Catherine,* remembered how, when she was a small child in her father's house in 1854, she observed Rossetti, suspended momentarily in daydreaming, the beloved one absent, murmuring "Guggum, Guggum." Most of his days, and many of his nights, were spent with her, although at first she was rarely mentioned in his letters and was referred to in the presence of his friends mainly to warn them away from Chatham Place when she was there. She became "so much of a settled institution," William remembered, "that other people understood that they were not wanted there . . . —and I may include myself in this category. . . . This continual association of an engaged couple, while it may have gone beyond the conventional fence line, had nothing in it suspicious or ambiguous. . . ." It was unquestionably unambiguous, although there was an unearthliness about her frailty and passivity that seemed at the farthest remove from sensuality.

When Christina had visited at Gabriel's flat and begun to know the quiet young woman whom her brother symbolized pictorially as a dove, the poem "Listening" apparently resulted:

> She listened like a cushat dove
> That listens to its mate alone:

---

* Later Mrs. Franz Hueffer, mother of Ford Madox Hueffer (Ford).

She listened like a cushat dove
  That loves but only one.

Not fair as men would reckon fair,
Nor noble as they count the line:
Only as graceful as a bough,
  And tendrils of the vine:
Only as noble as sweet Eve
  Your ancestress and mine.

And downcast were her dovelike eyes,
And downcast was her tender cheek;
Her pulses fluttered like a dove
  To hear him speak.

To Gabriel, Elizabeth Siddal's beauty, ethereal in its contrast of consumptive pallor and coppery-gold hair, was enhanced by what he considered native, untutored literary and artistic genius. Although she had been an unschooled apprentice in a bonnet shop, she was nonetheless intelligent, full of folk learning, and more than merely literate, encountering Tennyson by discovering his poems printed on a piece of paper used to wrap butter which she brought home to her mother. Gabriel encouraged her to write verses herself, and after he had her read Wordsworth's poetry she began a drawing based on "We Are Seven." Reading and drawing filled her long, empty hours when Gabriel was away, and he encouraged her to do designs from her books—from Browning, Keats, the old English ballad of Sir Patrick Spens, and Gabriel's friend William Allingham's "Clerk Saunders." And she did a remarkable self-portrait, her progress inspiring him to write Madox Brown (January 3, 1854), "Lizzy* sits by me at work on her design, which is now coming really admirable. She has also finished the *Lady of Shalott* sketch, and made quite another thing of it. She has followed your suggestions about her [self-] portrait, and done several things which improve it greatly."

Gabriel had written to Woolner of his delight with his rooms from which he could look close on the left at the bustle of traffic over Blackfriars Bridge, and directly south at the ceaseless activity on the Thames. There was, he wrote, "a large balcony over the water, large enough to sit there with a model and paint—a feat which I actually accomplished the other day for several hours in the teeth of the elements." Seldom that hardy, his chief

---

* Gabriel made her drop the final *l* in her name, believing that *Siddal* seemed more aristocratic. He also called her by the unaristocratic name of *Lizzy*, sometimes also spelling it *Lizzie*. Except in quotations, she will be referred to by Gabriel's earlier version.

and almost only model was becoming more wan and wasted. Lizzy ate little and slept badly, and was seldom at the tiny flat which Gabriel insisted that she take nearby to preserve the convention of separate living quarters. They took their meals together, worked together and spent most of their days and nights together. "Why doesn't he marry her?" Madox Brown wondered, as did their other friends; and Lizzy was at times unreasonable and even hysterical in her demands on Gabriel, although it is likely that the reluctance to marry was at first shared—because one worried over committing an active man to the care of a chronically ill wife and the other had doubts about giving up the freedoms still possible to the technically unmarried, one of those freedoms the privilege of drawing upon his unending credits with his slightly more moneyed relatives. Long, desultory engagements were common in Victorian England, but seldom if ever did the "engaged" couple live together as openly as did Gabriel and his "Sid." It showed in everything he drew. "One face looks out from all his canvases," Christina wrote,

> One selfsame figure sits or walks or leans:
> We found her hidden just behind those screens,
> That mirror gave back all her loveliness.
> A queen in opal or in ruby dress,
> A nameless girl in freshest summer-greens,
> A saint, an angel—every canvas means
> The same one meaning, neither more nor less.
>
> He feeds upon her face by day and night,
> And she with true, kind eyes looks back on him,
> Fair as the moon and joyful as the light:
> Not wan with waiting, nor with sorrow dim;
> Not as she is, but was when hope shone bright;
> Not as she is, but as she fills his dream.

There were times when Gabriel felt that Christina did not like his Lizzy, and she may have hoped for a better marriage for him than her own dimming prospects seemed to indicate for herself; but it is clear from the way in which she wrote about the pair that she understood both of them.

Times had changed for the young men of the P.R.B. They were older and wiser and a little more moneyed, and sex was no longer a vicarious pleasure indulged in life classes. Holman Hunt had left for the lands of the Bible to paint, and even managed an amorous encounter en route, writing about it to Millais, who prudently inked out the racy paragraph before passing the letter on to Charles and Wilkie Collins, and then to Gabriel and William Rossetti. The proper fictions had to be preserved, even among intimates, Millais writing Hunt that it was "not desirable" that their cronies should learn of "the little impropriety in the French railway carriage which would alarm them mightily particularly as it is understood you are principally induced to go to the East from religious notions and such an effort could be certainly misunderstood—would appear a contradiction."

For one crony there would be no need for concern about Victorian social conventions. On the second of February, 1854, the handsome and promising young artist who had first brought Elizabeth Siddal into the P.R.B. orbit died. Less than a fortnight before, Gabriel had gone to see him. Deverell had not been told that he was in his last illness, and—worried more about supporting his fatherless younger brothers and sisters—continued painting almost to the end. His unfinished last canvas was to be titled *The Doctor's Last Visit*, and pictured a concerned family learning that there was no hope for the patient. Walter Deverell had begun it when Gabriel was still sharing his studio, before art had anticipated life. At the end—still conscious—he was told that he could not live through the day, which Gabriel reported to Bell Scott, Deverell "heard quite calmly, only saying he wished they had told him before, but that he supposed he was man enough to die." He had "no older or more intimate friend," Gabriel added, but it was the new Academician, Millais, who had remained with Deverell to the end.

Other deaths affected Gabriel's life more directly. In December 1853 his grandfather Polidori died at a tenacious eighty-nine, just before William and Maria, who had given up their Arlington Street lease, prepared to move at Christmas to lodgings over the shop of a pharmacist (and amateur watercolorist) in Albany Street, near the Euston Road. A small inheritance, partially dissipated by loans from her sisters, who would also share it, was due Mrs. Rossetti, and she began thinking about the possibility of using it to extricate Christina, herself and her rapidly failing husband from the frustrations of Frome. William had been pressing her vainly to return to London for some months, for he had been promoted at the Inland Revenue, as well as given the then-comfortable salary for a twenty-four-year-old of £250 a year, with assurance of annual increments; and he had his additional income from the *Spectator*. Maria, too, had her tutorial income, which made her feel self-sufficient although William paid the household expenses.

Christina was in no position to stand on pride. Only her unremunerative writing, and the continuing *bouts-rimés* exchanges with the compliant William, were sustaining her at Frome, her sonnet rhyme-endings being mailed to him almost until she and her parents were reinstalled in London early in the spring of 1854. Her lonely father had been overjoyed at the possibility. On December 23, 1853, he had written to his wife, who had been away on business connected with the deaths of her parents, "When are you going to return, when? . . . Christina and I await you with open arms; but as yet in vain. Have you then decided to abandon Frome and to return to London? Hurrah! Our good William is earning enough to persuade you to do that?"

To consolidate the family William leased a house at 45 Upper Albany Street,* near the dwellings of the devout aunts Eliza and Margaret, and eccentric Uncle Henry, who had become English—he thought—by changing the spelling of his name from Polidori to Polydore. For William it would continue to be a long walk to Somerset House, but his mother would remain close to her family.

Two exceptions marred the reintegration of the Rossettis. Gabriel would only be a visitor, as the requirements of his relationship with Lizzy Siddal as well as his desire for a bohemian independence, made any return on his part impossible. And old Gabriele was so failing by the time he was returned from Frome that for him the move became only a convenience enabling him to die in the bosom of his adopted city. On Easter Sunday, April 16, he took a turn for the worse, his condition having been complicated by diabetes and general debility. Having been apart from her father for months because of the Frome venture, Maria became especially attentive, even to noting down the last exchanges with him. His last sightless glance was in William's direction, Maria asking him, *"Lo conoscete? È Guglielmo."* ("Do you know him? It is William.") *"Lo veggo,"* he answered, *"lo sento, mi stà scritto nel cuore"* ("I see him, I hear him, he is written in my heart.") William remembered only his father's ironic *"Che consolazione aver tutti i figli intorno a me! E non poter vederli!"* ("What a consolation to have all my children around me! And not to be able to see them!") On the evening of the twenty-fifth the old atheist and revolutionary, having been without speech through the day, suddenly cried out loudly, *"Ah Dio, ajutami Tu!"* ("Ah, God, help me Thou!") The next day conscious almost to the end, although speechless as well as sightless, he died as his wife read to him from an Italian translation of the Anglican liturgy.

The children stood by, as well as Gabriele's aged cousin Teodorico, and Christina noted in her mother's diary of Gabriele's last days, "Mr Cayley called twice at the very last, and waited, but did not see my father, much endearing himself to us." The quiet, studious Charles Bagot Cayley had been a pupil of the *Professore*'s and a translator of Dante, and had lingered on the periphery of the P.R.B. To three of the four Rossettis he had become a respected, if not close, friend. To the fourth, Christina's note made obvious, he was now something more. But this was not something she could tell him.

---

* Afterwards renumbered 166 Albany Street.

Several years later, Gabriel produced a memorial sonnet, "Dantis Tenebrae," suggesting that his father had, at baptism, dedicated him to art and poetry

> . . . when at the font
> Together with thy name thou gav'st me his,
> That also on thy son must Beatrice
> Decline her eyes according to her wont. . . .

As soon as the return from Frome had been accomplished, Gabriel had set about trying to get his mother and sisters more favorably disposed toward his Beatrice. Since they considered themselves to be of a gentility superior to that of a cockney shopgirl-daughter of a former Sheffield cutler, he understood that what was to him an ideal romance was to them a misalliance. (William's far more discreet relationship with the aloof Henrietta Rintoul was more appropriate, as her father was editor of the *Spectator.*) Christina had only been back in London a few days when Gabriel had used William as his intermediary to induce his sister to visit Chatham Place not only to see Lizzy but also "Gug's" artistic "emanations." Clearly Lizzy would be more respectable as an artist than as a model or ex-shopgirl, and Gabriel was impressed by her progress. But in April, as his father failed, Lizzy became seriously ill, and Gabriel had to appeal for help and advice. There was no evidence of a specific disease, although her frailty suggested what was then classified as consumption or "decline." Whatever the organic complaints it is clear that there were also neurotic symptoms, which would increase as Gabriel forced artistic growth on an unprepared, lower-class girl and added to such pressure the problems of economic survival and bohemian quasi-marriage. (She toyed with food, ate little, and vomited much of that; and doctors of later generations than her own might have classified her, with what little evidence there was to go on, as a classic case of anorexia nervosa, not having the laboratory opportunity to check for tuberculosis or even leukemia.) If nothing else, a rest-cure was indicated, to get Lizzy away from the emotional pressures of bohemian London as well as the health hazards of Chatham Place, for Gabriel lived in an area known as "London's Maremma." The built-over Fleet River which emptied into the Thames nearby was even then described as "a sewer roofed over," and at least one letter from Gabriel to a friend explains his absence from Blackfriars as "because of the state of the river."

A new artist friend, Barbara Leigh Smith,* who came from a well-to-do family which had an estate and farmlands in Sussex, near Hastings,

---

* Barbara Bodichon after she married an eccentric French army physician.

recommended a place in Hastings as "cheap and nice." The area was popular for convalescence because of the proximity to sea air and the likelihood of more sunshine than elsewhere in the south of England. But planning the retreat to Hastings was difficult, as it coincided with the old *Professore*'s last days and came when Gabriel had no new picture-sales income.

For the first eventuality he could make no preparations; for the second problem he had begun shrewdly assessing the value of his increasingly close—but until that month only epistolary—association with John Ruskin. As a critic Ruskin had supported the Pre-Raphaelites (making an exception for Madox Brown, whom he passionately disliked). As a person, Ruskin was having difficulties with the one Pre-Raphaelite he had befriended, as the handsome and attentive John Millais had made Effie Ruskin realize the futility of remaining any longer in her unconsummated marriage, which survived only because of the expected social repercussions to both parties of annulment proceedings. Gabriel, who did not know that the Ruskin marriage was about to break up, nevertheless shrewdly intuited that Ruskin preferred not only artistic women, but artistic women who made no implicit sexual demands upon him. To Madox Brown, Gabriel wrote in mid-April that he intended to show Lizzy's pictures to Ruskin, "who, I know, will worship her." And to Ruskin, who visited one morning at Chatham Place, just after Gabriel had returned from taking Lizzy to Hastings, he explained that she was his "pupil." Ruskin was interested—in fact, as Gabriel wrote William Allingham, "he yearneth."

While lunching at Ruskin's London home at Denmark Hill—on the very day that Ruskin was served with notice of annulment proceedings—Gabriel had to be summoned away to the bedside of his father, who died the next day. After that the two, each drawn to the other for his own reasons, had to be temporarily apart, Gabriel going to Hastings after the funeral, and Ruskin discreetly going abroad after writing Gabriel vaguely on the very day of the funeral—May 3—about "some grievous family misfortune" (as Gabriel identified it) that would soon become public knowledge.

In Hastings, Lizzy had been without Gabriel, but had not been alone. The energetic Barbara Leigh Smith had summoned her artist-friend Anna Mary Howitt and her poet-friend Bessie Rayner Parkes (afterwards Belloc) to help, explaining to Bessie Parkes that Lizzy was Gabriel's "love and pupil," as well as an artistic genius, "her gift discovered by a strange accident such as rarely befalls woman." If she lived, she would be "a great artist," but her life had been hard and her fate in doubt. "Rossetti," she confided, "has been an honourable friend to her and I do not doubt if circumstances were favourable would marry her. She is of course under a ban, having been a model."

Later she reported to Bessie Parkes (whose assignment had been to give Lizzy tea and find her a room) that she and Miss Howitt had seen Lizzy and Gabriel sitting atop the East Cliff apparently happy and cheerful, but she still believed that Lizzy was "going fast," and that Gabriel was "like a child. He cannot believe she is in danger." To his mother Gabriel wrote that "no one thinks it at all odd my going into the Gug's room to sit there; and Barbara Smith said to the landlady how unadvisable it would be for her [Lizzy] to sit with me in a room without [a] fire." Presumably the landlady was to have been frightened by visions of Miss Siddal cuddling into his arms for warmth if no other source of heat were available. In any case, fire or no, Gabriel had a room in the same house on the High Street. A sonnet he dated much later seems either first begun in those days, or recalled from them, when love was "our light at night and shade at noon":

> Sometimes she is a child within mine arms,
>   Cowering beneath dark wings that love must chase,—
>   With still tears showering and averted face. . . .

Lizzy seemed to improve at Hastings, perhaps even more when the alternative to Mrs. Elphick's lodging house was the Sussex Infirmary, where—Gabriel explained to Bessie Parkes—Lizzy "would be surrounded by persons of habits repulsive to her, and by scenes likely to have a bad effect upon her spirits." To remain at Hastings was expensive, for Gabriel still had the upkeep of domiciles in London to consider. He may have hoped that the kind and amply proportioned Barbara Smith (Anna Howitt even painted her as Boadicea) would take them both as guests at her estate at Scalands, but visits there remained only visits. Meanwhile the Academy spring exhibition had opened, and Gabriel was away from it. "I wish you would tell people I am not dead," he wrote William. But artistically he might as well have been dead. William had sent art supplies, and Gabriel sketched Lizzy but little else. Even she, although ill, did more drawing than he managed. He was not only bored with the slow pace of Sussex life, but also paralyzed with concern, as he confessed to Allingham: "I am melancholy enough here sometimes. . . . Lizzy is a sweet companion, but the fear which the constant sight of her varying state suggests is much less pleasant to live with."

Allingham understood. While Gabriel might idealize his surrogate Beatrice, his blood quickened at the sight of a "stunner," and although brother William could continue a celibate existence while engaged to a woman who insisted upon waiting until the wedding night, Gabriel required more than an invalid love. Once, at Hastings, seeing a dark gypsy girl, he was impressed by her "image of savage, active health," but to Allingham, who inquired about his extracurricular amorous life, he confessed that he missed dining at the Belle Sauvage Inn on Ludgate Hill near his Blackfriars flat, where a "cordial stunner" took their orders. "I shall have no chance against you any more."

To remain at Hastings into June, Gabriel had to solicit funds from William, still assuming that if Lizzy returned to London she would need hospitalization. Barbara Smith had suggested a new "Sanatorium" in Harley Street, managed by a relation, a Miss Florence Nightingale, where "governesses and ladies of small means are taken in and cured," and Gabriel asked his sister Maggie to investigate the possibility. She did, and although it was an alternative to managing as before, late in June they gave up the rooms and the sunshine at Hastings and returned to London, where Gabriel, exhilarated by the familiar sights and sounds—and smells—produced several sonnets he would not publish for fifteen years. Dr. Garth Wilkinson, a homeopath and Swedenborgian whom at Barbara Smith's urging they had been consulting by mail when away from London, pronounced Lizzy "better," although his initial diagnosis had been curvature of the spine. Gabriel saw nothing to which to look forward except her continued decline, writing Allingham, "It seems hard to me when I look at her sometimes, working or too ill to work, and think how many without one tithe of her genius or greatness of spirit have granted them abundant health and opportunity to labour through the little they can do or will do, while perhaps her soul is never to bloom nor her bright hair to fade, but after hardly escaping from degradation and corruption, all she might have been must sink out again unprofitably in that dark house where she was born. How truly she may say, 'No man cared for my soul.' " Clearly he did not feel that he was an exception, so long as he shrank from marrying her. And she did not ask. In fact, as he wrote Allingham, "I went to the Belle the other day, and was smiled on by the cordial stunner, who came in on purpose in a lilac walking costume. *I am quite certain she does not regret* YOU *at all.*"

By August Gabriel was desperate enough about money to write the usual letter to Aunt Charlotte, beginning painfully with "I am afraid you will guess, before reading this letter, what it is likely to relate to." A money order followed, and the Chatham Place landlord satisfied. Relieved, Gabriel began utilizing the good weather, while it remained, to paint a brick wall near Chiswick that would be background for his sole venture into Pre-Raphaelite realism, the never-to-be-finished *Found*.

Lizzy had been unable to accompany Gabriel on his painting excursion. Madox Brown found her at Chatham Place early in October "looking thinner and more deathlike and more beautiful and more ragged than ever. A real artist, a woman without parallel for many a long year. Gabriel as usual diffuse and inconsequent in his work. . . . However, he is at the wall, and I am to get him a white calf and a cart to paint. . . ." At Finchley, near Brown's home, where he slept on a mattress on the floor, Gabriel soon began painting the calf which, trussed in the cart, was to be set before the brick wall, the implied marketing of the calf to be symbolic of the prostitute also to appear eventually on the canvas. The cooperative farmer kept his uncooperative calf tied for hours each day as model. "The view of life induced at his early age by experience in art," Gabriel wrote Allingham about the calf, "appears to be so melancholy that he punctually attempts suicide by hanging himself at 3-½ daily P.M."

There was excitement in the Albany Street household while Gabriel tediously and Hunt-like painted his calf, seemingly hair-by-hair. War against Russia in the Crimea had begun the previous March, but enkindled no patriotic enthusiasm among the Rossettis, although some of the ladies of Christ Church, Albany Street, volunteered for local nursing duty. In June a British contingent landed at Varna, on the Bulgarian coast of the Black Sea, to assist the besieged Turks. Cholera broke out, added to which were high casualties from the first engagements near Sevastopol. By mid-October *The Times* correspondent on the scene had shocked England by revealing the total inadequacy of arrangements to cope with the thousands of sick and wounded, and the indefatigable Florence Nightingale, at thirty-three now a veteran hospital administrator, set out on October 21 with thirty-eight hastily assembled women volunteers, some of them nurses but others ranging from Roman Catholic nuns to drunken drabs. One of the thirty-eight was Christina's aunt Eliza Polidori. Christina, too, had applied to go, but was refused because of her youth. Disappointed, she withdrew into desultory social activities—once, even, a masquerade party—and her writing, and then retreated into a familiar escape of her youth, being ill again from March to July, 1855. Into her poetry she poured her frustrations, dreaming of such lovers as one who "took me in his strong white arms" and bore her away on a horse, never asking her consent:

> He made me fast with book and bell,
> With links of love he makes me stay;
> Till now I've neither heart nor power
> Nor will nor wish to say him nay.

Away from London to recuperate, Christina had missed seeing more of Charles Cayley, but Gabriel, loyally trying to promote Cayley's translation of the *Divine Comedy*, had even sent a copy to Ruskin, who replied in his usual manner by disliking it. The book was obviously sent to solicit praise, Ruskin began, but since "no poem *can* be translated in rhyme," he had only faint sympathy for the work, which he downgraded by elaborate comparisons demonstrating that the translator had substituted "insipidity for simplicity." Cayley never knew, and continued in his unreal world of hand-to-mouth literary scholarship, Madox Brown observing him at Chatham Place on an especially hot evening that summer with Gabriel and William, Bell Scott and half a dozen other writers and artists. No poetic hero on horseback, Cayley, Brown noted, "looks mad, and is always in a rumpled shirt, without collar, and old tail-coat." He would remain tenuously attached to the Rossettis, through William's good offices sometimes securing a meal and a warm fire at Albany Street, where men were less and less in evidence.

Despite deficiencies in talent or in its application, Gabriel from the start reigned among his friends like Arthur among his knights. In Elizabeth Siddal he had his Guinevere and at Chatham Place his Camelot. The charisma he carried would persist all his life, one of his last young followers, Philip Bourke Marston, writing to a friend, "What a supreme man is Rossetti! Why is he not some great exiled king that we might give him our lives to try to restore him to his kingdom!" Even the unsentimental William Bell Scott wrote afterwards that he began then "to feel some sort of fascination about the personality of D.G.R." that made one "accept certain peculiarities in him. I found all his intimate associates did so, placing him in a position different from themselves, a dangerous position to a man whose temperament takes advantage of it." It gave Gabriel, Bell Scott felt, "a sort of supremacy." His deep-set dark eyes, his rich voice, his combination of Latin grace and Anglo-Saxon wit, deflected skepticism and induced the impecunious to lend him money, the cautious to trust him with their wives and mistresses, the wary to offer him friendship, the discreet to confide in him, and the cynical, despite themselves, to admire his poetry or his painting. And like any king worth his scepter, Gabriel supported his royal style by taxing his willing subjects, living off subsidies from his mother and his aunts, his brother and his friends, eventually, too, his admirers and his patrons. Whatever the manner of service, somehow those Gabriel used found in it a kind of fulfilment, and in a subliminal way the cult of medievalism to which his circle responded may have acquired new force.

With bad weather in November and December, Gabriel had abandoned his outdoor painting ("the calf would be like a hearth-rug after half an hour's rain"). He had accomplished nothing he could sell, had gone through the money he had "borrowed" from his aunt, and in his last days at Finchley again importuned William for "tin." He had "an awful lot of claimants,

Mrs. Burrell foremost. . . ." She was the housekeeper at Chatham Place. To John Millais in a New Year's letter (in which Effie Ruskin remained unmentioned) Gabriel put the best face on his artistic activities. His picture in progress was "lamentable," because of "wretched weather" and his "deficient practice in painting that sort of thing." He had done "a good many things" but they made "as usual precious little when put together." He had done some drawing and writing, and was devoting his evenings—he ignored the days—"to translating the pre-Dantesque poets, and have done upwards of fifty poems from them. . . . I calculate on the triumph of being the first man in England who was ever beforehand with the Germans in translating any important work." Life at Chatham Place clearly included Lizzy, although he never mentioned her name, the plural personal pronoun being enough. "We have no companions here except a serene cat, a mezzotint from Murillo, an ideal head of Charles 1st as a martyr, and the injured ghost of Sir Hoshua Kennels. . . ."

Somehow Lizzy bore the January cold, and worked at watercolors while Gabriel worked at new sonnets, one ending with a simile based upon a fact of country life told to him by Hunt before he had left for the Holy Land, in which sleep soothes

> Even as the thistledown from pathsides dead
> Gleaned by a girl in autumns of her youth,
> Which, one new year, makes soft her marriage bed.

Marriage for Lizzy seemed no closer in the new year, but solvency seemed ahead after Ruskin returned from Switzerland, for in March, 1855, he invited Gabriel and Lizzy to his parents' home in London, where Ruskin pronounced her a "noble, glorious creature," and his father allowed that by her manner and appearance she might have been born a countess. Then Lizzy's drawings were examined, and Ruskin offered to buy them all. First he paid £30 for sketches and watercolors for which Gabriel asked £25, and, telling Gabriel that they were better than anything he had done, offered to settle £150 a year on Lizzy for all the art she produced, and that if he sold any she would also have all the profits above that amount. Then Ruskin supplied her with a quantity of ivory dust to be made into jelly, supposedly for its medicinal properties. It had been worth Gabriel's offering to teach art, from half-past seven until ten on Monday evenings at the new Working Men's College, which had grown out of Frederick Denison Maurice's Christian Socialist fervor, and held classes in a building at Red Lion Square,* where Ruskin himself, a believer in using art for social

---

* Now, generations later, at Crowndale Road, Mornington Crescent.

improvement, taught drawing on Thursday evenings. Yet Ruskin's interest in the welfare of the cool, quiet Elizabeth Siddal—whom he insisted on calling "Ida" after Tennyson's "Princess"—had more behind it than Rossetti's careful scheming. Ruskin thought he saw genius in Gabriel's "pupil's" work. But whatever her fragile gifts, Lizzy was freeing Ruskin from memories of the alienated Effie.

To Gabriel, the gaunt, "hideous" Ruskin was someone to be used, and Ruskin's own generosity, chivalric on the surface, filled his own needs to replace not only Effie but his artist-protégé who had flown with her. To Lizzy herself Ruskin appealed that she should not be too proud to accept his help, if not for Gabriel's sake, at least for her own. "The plain *hard fact* is that I think you have genius; that I don't think there is much genius in the world; and I want to keep what there is, in it. . . . Utterly irrespective of Rossetti's feelings or my own, . . . I should try to save a beautiful tree from being cut down, or a bit of a Gothic cathedral whose strength was failing."

The impact of Ruskin was even felt at Albany Street, Rossetti writing to Madox Brown, "Lizzy will take tea, perhaps dinner, at my mother's tomorrow. . . ." Brown was invited as well, and remained overnight, talking late into the evening with Mrs. Rossetti after Gabriel—according to Brown's diary—"saw her home." There could have been only one subject, the same one aired by Ruskin immediately thereafter. "I should be very grateful," he wrote, "if you thought it right to take me entirely into your confidence, and tell me whether you have any plans or wishes, respecting Miss Siddal, which you are prevented from carrying out by want of a certain income, and if so what certain income would enable you to carry them out." Gabriel had no honest answer that would have pleased Ruskin. His mother had finally met Lizzy for the first time—and under her own roof—but he would not be bribed into marriage. With no response forthcoming from Gabriel, Ruskin wrote again, somewhat embarrassed by his earlier bluntness, that he didn't want his new friend's "greatest genius" stifled by unhappiness and dissipated by extraneous problems, and that he would buy what Gabriel produced, up to a particular annual value, to enable him "to paint properly and keep your room in order."

Now Gabriel was forced to answer, and agreed to paint for Ruskin, mentioning—it seems implied from Ruskin's response—that Lizzy was unlikely, given her chronic illness, to want to burden a husband. With Lizzy presented in such a romantically self-sacrificing role, Ruskin would not be satisfied until he had effected her cure as well as her marriage. Yet he was not all sentiment. He realized that by far the greater talent was Gabriel's, and that it was paralyzed by indecision. Ruskin would play God.

The relationship with Ruskin became almost a family affair. In the first enthusiasm of his arrangement he invited Maria to join Gabriel and "Ida" at dinner. It was the beginning of what could only be called, given the innocence of men on Maria's part, a "crush" on Ruskin, who apparently was attentive partly out of reaction to the disappearance of Effie from his life, and partly out of a desire to keep close to the Rossettis. Rich, and still only in his mid-thirties, the lean, ascetic Ruskin was theoretically a great catch, although Gabriel by then knew otherwise. Maria never knew, or understood, and accepted him as an admirer. What never was, would never be, and Christina later wrote, in her amalgam of meditation and memoir, *Time Flies*, that "one of the most genuine Christians I ever knew, once took lightly the dying out of a brief acquaintance which had engaged her warm heart, on the ground that such mere tastes and glimpses of congenial intercourse on earth waited for their development in heaven." In the margin of the copy she presented to her Aunt Eliza she penned, "Maria with Ruskin." Later, painter Charles Allston Collins showed some interest in Maria, and again Maria read into it more than was there. She had no one outside her family and her Italian language pupils. Her father's daughter, she turned to a study of Dante. Collins married a daughter of Charles Dickens.

In the summer of 1855, Mrs. Rossetti and the ailing Christina had gone to Hastings to sample the invigorating sunshine and sea air, and Gabriel—still showing evidences of romantic feeling for his Sid, instructed his mother where she and Christina, on their walks, could locate places—a large rock, and the wooden door of an old hut—where he and Lizzy had scratched their initials the previous year. He even wrote Allingham that his *"rapports"* with the Belle Sauvage stunner had "stopped some months ago after a long stay away from Chatham Place," partly from his "wish to narrow the circle of flirtations, in which she had begun to figure a little." Still, he confided, "I often find myself sighing after her, now that 'roast beef, roast mutton, gooseberry tart,' have faded into the light of common day."

Lizzy, little better—frailty would be her constant condition—had tried the country air in Somersetshire, and at Ruskin's behest—and with his funds—had gone to Oxford to consult the distinguished and hospitable Dr. Henry Wentworth Acland, Professor of Clinical Medicine at the University. His diagnosis was curious but shrewd. "Acland examined her most minutely," Gabriel wrote his mother, "and [he] was constantly paying professional visits—all gratuitously, being an intimate friend of Ruskin. I . . . was glad to find that he thinks her lungs, if at all affected, are only slightly so, and that the leading cause of illness lies in mental power long pent up and lately overtaxed." Acland advised her to abstain from work for a while, and to find a warm climate for the winter.

The "wizard" making her recommended trip south possible, Rossetti was not embarrassed to inform his friends, was Ruskin. But if he hoped for easy acceptance of his own painting by Ruskin, he was quickly disappointed. A watercolor *Nativity* on which he spent a week and for which he asked fifteen guineas, Ruskin complained about, withholding payment for months until it was improved to his specifications. Drawing examples to make his point that much in it was *"Wrong,"* he explained, "A human arm—on the one hand, is not this—as the academicians draw it—but neither is it this—as *you* draw it. Flesh is not Buff colour—as Mr Neabert draws it—but neither is it pea-green." A list of additional anatomical failings followed, evidence of Gabriel's many absences when at Sass's, concluding with an objection to Pre-Raphaelite realism: "If there is anything—in an idiosyncratic way—which I *particularly dislike,* it is dirty naked old men with the soles of their feet turned up. I have seen much [of] both of them in Italy—and perceived with other senses as well as eyes." Ruskin was a prematurely old fairy godfather to Gabriel and Lizzy, and in the circumstances absolutely essential to them; but the friendship while it lasted would be a difficult one.

To Dr. Acland, Lizzy presented her watercolor landscape, *We Are Seven.* He was impressed. "That a girl brought up in London, within a street or two of the Elephant and Castle, should have selected such a subject and executed it from pure imagination, is most remarkable." Gabriel's own painting failed even to satisfy himself, but his hopes rested on his translations of medieval Italian poetry, in which the publisher Macmillan had expressed an interest, and which he hoped Ruskin might subsidize, and in eventually bringing Ruskin around to appreciating his painting for what it was. But he erred in thinking that Ruskin would pay for his work in advance. He had already asked MacCracken for an advance, and saw no reason to expect difficulty from Ruskin. In fact he would ask every patron thereafter for advance payment, assuming that the rebuffs were worth absorbing if some "tin" resulted.

Ruskin was offended. He was already paying Lizzy's pension, which was implicitly Gabriel's as well, and had stood their holiday in the country as well as the Oxford stay. Depending on his regular although substantial allowance from his parents, Ruskin had depleted his resources in their behalf without informing the elder Ruskins. Brusquely he informed Gabriel that there would be no money for him without finished pictures, unless it were "a question of sheriff's officers." Lizzy's guaranteed income had other repercussions for Gabriel. Although she holidayed in the country with him, and spent most of her nights in London at Chatham Place, the informal liaison which had lasted for five years now seemed to her insufficient. The money was ostensibly her own. There were quarrels and reconciliations, and for a time Gabriel was angry with Christina, according to Brown, "because she and Guggum do not agree." William thought the reason was that Gabriel's "ardour for Miss Siddal made him think that Christina was not adequately impressed by her." Yet it may have been that Gabriel was attempting to display an ardor for Lizzy which had become increasingly fragile. Lizzy, on the other hand, demonstrated her unhappiness with Gabriel by demanding repayment of £20 of Ruskin's pension money he had spent, forcing Gabriel to appeal to Brown for a loan. Her only close female friend and visitor was Emma Brown, and often Madox Brown had to defend his wife against Gabriel's accusations that they were encouraging Lizzy to demand a wedding ring. Even if they were not, Emma was a conspicuous example of a young uneducated girl who had nevertheless been made a wife by a sophisticated artist. Once when Ruskin called at Chatham Place he found utter idleness and disorder. The Browns were there, and Lizzy and Emma half-dressed. Emma's baby, Oliver, was crying; Brown was in shirt sleeves, smoking his pipe while Gabriel held forth on art and poetry. With their dislike of each other unconcealed, Ruskin and Brown were rude to each other; Brown huffily left the room; and Ruskin wondered why his attempt to play Pygmalion had gone wrong.

The solution Ruskin proposed was to send Lizzy, with a distant Rossetti relative, a Mrs. Kincaid, as companion, to the Continent for her health. With Ruskin's money as well as money Gabriel borrowed from Madox Brown on the strength of Brown's sale of his *The Last of England* (for £150), Lizzy left for France in late September. Once she was gone, Gabriel became restless. He visited the Brownings on two successive evenings, on one of them, when Tennyson was also present, bringing William to hear the poet laureate—until long after midnight—read his *Maud* "through from end to end," unaware that Gabriel was sketching him. But Gabriel did little other drawing until, six weeks after Lizzy had left, he received a letter from her confessing that she had spent all her money in Paris—apparently in the fashionable shops—and had no funds to continue to Nice, her original destination. Suddenly there was pressure to paint.

Gabriel put aside half-finished canvases, worked for a week, often long into the night, on a gloomy *Paolo and Francesca*, extracted thirty-five guineas for it from Ruskin (for a lady in Leeds), and, refusing Ruskin's request that he give some lectures in Italian art in Manchester, set out for Paris with the money. There, where Lizzy was again ill, unable to leave her room, the pair were again affectionate as before. After he put her and Mrs. Kincaid on the train to Nice he returned to London, where he had been bickering with Ruskin about unfinished and unsatisfactory canvases. Of one, Ruskin asked that Rossetti "try to get it a little less like worsted-work," and of another, *Dante's Vision of Rachel*, Ruskin had written to Ellen Heaton in Leeds, "The Rachel is a curious instance of the danger of interfering with R. I wanted some illustrations from Dante for myself and chose seven subjects, of which this was one—& gave them to R. He didn't do any of them for a long time, until I provoked & said I thought it was very bad of him and then he did this. . . . It is a portrait of the young girl whom I told you of—who draws so well."

While Chatham Place remained quiet, the Albany Street household was also reduced by a member, Christina having gone off, apparently to a household in the Hampstead Heath region, when a temporary live-in tutoring opportunity came up. She had earned no income on her own, and although she disliked the idea of being a second-class resident in someone else's home, she did not know how to refuse. Quickly, however, she found her health not strong enough for the work, and on November 13, 1855, announced her discovery to William: "I am very comfortable in my exile; but at any rate I know I am rejoiced to feel that my health does really unfit me for miscellaneous governessing *en permanence*." William had his numerous jobs and after-hours activities to keep him busy, and what one of those activities still was, Christina alluded to in her letter: "I dare say you know I have written to Henrietta; to whom my cordial love *should you chance* to see her." William's informal engagement had been of nearly as long a duration as Gabriel's, and seemed as little likely to end in marriage, even after William formally proposed in January, 1856, and was accepted. "In refinement of mind, character, and demeanour," he thought, Henrietta "stood on a level which I have seldom known equalled, never surpassed. That she had some degree of liking for my society and myself was plain enough. I did not for a while attempt to test how far this liking might extend. . . ." Neither of her parents thought the match was good enough for her, although she was approaching an age when any match might have been the last opportunity. Her father, for whom William wrote in the *Spectator*, even preferred spinsterhood for Henrietta to William. But, cool and correct, the engagement was permitted to stand, having not altered matters at all. If it were not what William had in mind, it was definitely the kind of relationship Henrietta Rintoul found appropriate.

Absence was having the effect of repairing Gabriel's relations with Elizabeth Siddal. His drawings and unfinished paintings of her in Chatham Place were so numerous that he hardly missed her as model; but on February 15, 1856, he sent her a day-late verse Valentine concluding fondly,

Come back, Dear Liz, and looking wise
In that arm-chair which suits your size,
Through some fresh drawing scrape a hole.
Your Valentine and Orson's soul
Is sad for those two friendly eyes.

Not until spring had thawed the English climate did Lizzy return, having remained at Nice despite Ruskin's entreaties that for her artistic education it was essential that she visit Swiss mountains and Italian museums. She was no better in health, but seemed sturdy enough when she discovered that during her absence Gabriel had been seen more often than necessary with Annie Miller, the pretty model Hunt was planning to marry after he returned from Egypt and Palestine. Hunt had given her permission to sit only to Rossetti in his absence, assuming that Gabriel was sufficiently preoccupied with his Guggum, but he had not known when he left that so would Lizzy be leaving London, and that Annie would do more than sit. Hunt, who felt that Gabriel had "beguiled the girl away from him," eventually broke his engagement, and even William, long afterwards, conceded that his brother was "properly, though I will not say deeply censurable." William hedged not merely to protect his brother's reputation, but because he knew that although Annie Miller spent many days—and nights—at Chatham Place while Lizzy sulked in Weymouth Street, she was flirted with as well by Boyce and Stephens and even William himself, who took her out on the river as an antidote to the unpromising courtship of Miss Rintoul. That Annie shared her charms among others than Gabriel could hardly placate Lizzy. Valentine sentiments long forgotten, she would wax hysterical, flee—usually to the Browns—and permit a reconciliation. Gabriel was getting even less done than before, although his frustrations resulted in some morbid poetry. Even Lizzy found her poetic voice,

Gazing through the gloom like one
Whose life and hopes are also done,
Frozen like a thing of stone.

Both yearned for the simpler days, when she could respond to the passionate needs for which Gabriel was certainly searching elsewhere for solutions, Lizzy asking,

Can God bring back the day when we two stood
Beneath the clinging trees in that dark wood?

It may be that her brother's dilemma was in Christina's mind when, in July, 1856, she wrote a long poem, "Look on this Picture and on this":

> I wish we once were wedded—then I must be true:
> You should hold my will in yours to do or undo:
> But I hate myself now, Eva, when I look at you.
>
> You have seen her hazel eyes, her warm dark skin,
> Dark hair—but oh those hazel eyes a devil is dancing in;
> You, my saint, lead up to heaven, she lures down to sin.

There were forty-six triplets altogether, about a man—the narrator—torn between love and passion. If it were not for the name *Eva*, William wrote, annotating the poem when he published about half of it posthumously, "I should be embarrassed to guess what could have directed my sister's pen to so singular a subject." But *Eva* was a character in a novel by Maturin whose situation was much like that of the first love in her poem—a novel, William wrote of Christina, by "a favourite romancist of her girlhood." The name was convenient. William as well as Christina implied Gabriel's problems. The saintly love appears to be Elizabeth Siddal; the dark lady was neither Annie Miller, nor the "cordial stunner" who did more than wait on tables at the Belle Sauvage. She suggests, rather, all the fleshly temptation into which the passionate but trapped young man of twenty-six could be lured.

In September, 1856, Mrs. Coventry Patmore wrote a friend that both Gabriel and William had become formally engaged, but named no names. Even earlier Stephens had written Holman Hunt that Millais—who had finally married the former Effie Ruskin—was "gloriously happy and there is a rumour about that both the Rossettis are to marry. . . ." Madox Brown, in a badly spelled letter to Hunt, corroborated the news:

> Millais is married, you not being well aware of this fact strikes one with a painful sense of your isolation from polite society burried as you seem to be amid a heap of monomaniacs and people out of senses and out of elbows. He has *taken a wife* to himself in good earnest—construe the meaning of the sentence as you will—since which I am told that he writes from Perth his present residence, most feelingly on the forlorn condition of all unhappy young men not married, so you know what to expect. Collins had I believe received peremptory orders to marry himself forthwith and is I suppose going to do so. Gabriel Rossetti still prudently holds aloof from any measure of the kind likely to break in upon his artistic and poetic reveries, but there are rumours of William, that hitherto young man, having seriously taken some step or steps towards the estate, pronounced by Millais, now, to be of such "indescribable bliss". So you see that in coming home you are only hastening to a sort of maelstroom of matrimony round which you may describe a few convolutions more or less, but in you will plunge over ears for consummation with most invitable summersault. The English are a marrying people and just at present it seems to be what they are most fit for. . . .

William, eschewing publicity, had considered himself engaged for years. As far as Gabriel's loyalties were concerned, any public confirmation was a technical victory over Lizzy. He would, he announced, marry her and take her to Algeria, where the climate had attracted consumptives, including Isabella Leigh Smith, the sister of the hearty Barbara. At half-past three one morning that autumn he even kept Madox Brown from his bed with his explanations about his decision. But Lizzy refused to hear of Algeria, and Gabriel then decided to postpone the wedding until he received payment for a picture. When the money arrived, however, and he found another excuse for delay, Lizzy took Ruskin's quarterly allowance and fled in a fury to Bath, vowing never to return. At Brown's, life quieted down, and Madox Brown placidly took time off evenings from a commissioned canvas to continue a portrait of his friend William Rossetti, who could sit only from eight until midnight, in order to be up early enough to walk to work in the morning.

Not knowing anything about Gabriel's renewed problems, the helpful Bessie Parkes forwarded in November additional information about Algeria, and Gabriel replied, vaguely, that Algiers was "not very promising" in his case. "Miss S. is at Bath just now, and a little better than she has been lately." Early the next month Gabriel betook himself to Lizzy's redoubt at Mrs. Green's lodging house in Bath and indirectly reported success. "I think it is likely Lizzy may be in London again at the end of a week," he wrote Madox Brown. "She sends love." Yet it may have been when alone at Mrs. Green's that Lizzy had composed her verses suggesting other sentiments, almost certainly referring to Gabriel:

> Ope not thy lips, thou foolish one,
>   Nor turn to me thy face;
> The blasts of heaven shall strike me down
>   Ere I will give thee grace.
>
> And turn away thy false dark eyes,
>   Nor gaze into my face:
> Great love I bore thee; now great hate
>   Sits grimly in its place.

It took longer than a week to convince Lizzy to return to Chatham Place, but by the end of the month—and the year—she was applying oils to a canvas, and both had returned to an unsatisfactory London. Even Christmas, Gabriel wrote Allingham, was "neither a bright day nor a dark day, but a white smutty day—piebald—wherein accordingly life seems neither worth keeping nor getting rid of." Clearly he had more in mind than the weather. The year was well over.

VII

Oxford and Aftermath
1856-1859

Although by the end of 1856 the Rossetti spell was losing its grip upon Elizabeth Siddal as well as upon such P.R.B. worthies as Hunt, Gabriel was working his magic anew among fresh disciples. An Oxford student supposedly destined for the ministry, Edward Burne Jones, had seen Gabriel's illustration to "The Maids of Elfinmere" in a book of Allingham's poems, and thought it was the most beautiful drawing he had ever encountered. When he heard that Rossetti gave lessons at the Working Men's College he hurried to London to see the artist himself, and soon after found an excuse to meet him. Before long, he had left Oxford without a degree and was learning painting under his hero; and William Morris, his best friend at college, a burly, well-to-do aspiring poet, nicknamed Topsy by his cronies, was also learning to draw. To the young men, Rossetti's mostly unfinished canvases were a revelation of unearthly beauty, and his poems seemed an unique complement to his genius. Morris had begun financing a shilling monthly, the *Oxford and Cambridge Magazine*, as a place to publish his own writings, and to it, nostalgically recalling *The Germ*, Gabriel offered some of his own poetry, including a revised "Blessed Damozel."

The friendship had grown amidst the dust and disorder of Chatham Place because Lizzy was so often in self-exile, and through dominating them Gabriel was reliving as well as refashioning the glorious early days of the P.R.B. As a result it was fitting that he should charm the pair into renting the rooms at 17 Red Lion Square which he had once shared with Deverell. The area was drab, and the flat dark, despite the window facing the square having been extended to the ceiling; but the Master had suggested the location, and the rooms were thus suffused with the spirit of Art. For Morris and Jones everything Gabriel touched was gilded by the romance of the artist's existence. "There was a place in Cheapside," Jones remembered, "with a board up to say, 'Dinners for 4d.,' and you could have sausage, and a lump of stale bread, and a glass of beer for fourpence. Gabriel used to lean against the counter, and pull out of his pocket a *Morte d'Arthur* and read bits aloud whilst we ate." There were, he would tell them, for the moment forgetting Dante, only two books in the world, the *Morte* and the Bible, and Jones "accepted it and stored it up as a precept in life." Some evenings they would go to the theatre, Lizzy being left in her discreet Weymouth Street rooms, or at Chatham Place. Jones had never been in a theatre before and would sit in rapture whatever the bill, until Gabriel would say, "This play is a curse, Ned; let us come away." And meekly Jones would agree, "Yes, Gabriel, let us go away," all the while longing to stay; but Gabriel would be in full stride toward the Judge and Jury, to observe, for the price of the cheapest mug of beer, the patrons of the public house in more informal performance.

By November, 1856, Morris and Jones had moved to Red Lion Square, Morris putting an end to his magazine in order to concentrate on his new career in London, which included making his own medieval-inspired furniture to complement his literary and artistic interests—"tables and chairs like incubi and succubi," Gabriel wrote Allingham. The new friendships spurred Gabriel's own work, which had not lacked for beginnings of pictures, but which suffered from his inability to complete them. He was doing more watercolors, which he knew Ruskin could dispose of, and he had agreed to join the group of well-known artists whom the publisher Moxon had invited to illustrate a new edition of Tennyson's poems—on condition that he could choose those poems to illustrate "where one can allegorize on one's own hook." Because of new complications in his life his blocks were ready for engraving later than all the rest, although he had extracted £30 each for his five, while the others—including Millais and Hunt—had accepted a standard £25. Even at that Tennyson was unhappy with Gabriel's gratuitous medievalism, but the publication, later in 1857, was the first to bring his name and art to a wide public, and Thomas Plint, a Leeds stockbroker who had become interested in Gabriel's work, offered forty guineas for a drawing of the illustration to "St. Cecilia."

The *Moxon Tennyson* suggested a new respectability for the P.R.B.'s, spurring Brown, who had been one in all but name, to produce a free Pre-Raphaelite exhibition at a large private house in Fitzroy Square. Even Lizzy was included, but when Hunt was escorted by Gabriel to see the "stunning drawings" by his Sid, he was offended by what Hunt intended as praise—that they could have been "happy designs by Walter Deverell." To Gabriel, old loyalties forgotten, they were "a thousand times better." * Hunt might have been less kind had he known of the tantrums of the Sid over the idea of a "college"—actually a joint establishment of living quarters and studios for artists. Morris, Jones and Brown were interested, and Gabriel—assuming that he and Lizzy would be married by the time the scheme became operative—suggested that if two or three married couples should initiate it, he would be willing. Lizzy heard that Hunt would be involved, and objected—apparently hysterically—to "living where Hunt was," Gabriel attributing the outburst to her illness, and the editors of Rossetti's letters to the practical joke of seven years earlier, when John Tupper was told that Lizzy was Hunt's wife. But Lizzy, sufficiently embittered to leave Gabriel again, this time to stay with her sister, must have had something more immediate in mind—very likely the realization that a communal "college" that included Hunt would very likely also include Annie Miller. The "college" idea faded.

Lizzy, Gabriel had written Brown before she left at the end of February, "does not better in health, never eating anything to speak of, and I am most wretched about her. What to do I know not." Of course he knew what to do, but put marriage out of mind, telling Brown instead, "I cannot . . . feel any anger at her, only constant pain at her sufferings. Kind and patient has she been with me many and many times, more than I have deserved." But he suggested no concrete amends, settling only for the ritual breast-beating.

One of the results of the rifts between Gabriel and Lizzy was the refusal of Lizzy, by mid-1857, to continue her arrangement with Ruskin. He had seen less and less of them, and heard little from Gabriel unless Gabriel needed "tin" or had a scheme to promote. Lizzy, realizing that Gabriel was acquiring commissions, wanted to be dependent upon him rather than Ruskin's charity, particularly since she was doing little drawing, and Ruskin extracted payment through his interference in her life. Ruskin apparently understood. "The only feeling I have about the matter," he confessed to Gabriel, "is of some shame at having allowed the arrangement between us to end as it did, and the chief pleasure I could have about it now would be her simply accepting it as she would have accepted a glass of water when she was thirsty, and never thinking of it any more." He would not be seeing the reluctant "Ida," but he pressed Gabriel and his "sister" for further visits to

---

* Although Gabriel's work received the most attention from the critics, probably because he had refused to exhibit elsewhere publicly, Lizzy's—identified in the *Saturday Review* as displaying "all the most startling peculiarities of Mr. Rossetti's style"—was highly praised.

lunch and dinner. "If Ida can't come, it's no reason why Miss Rossetti shouldn't."

As far as Ruskin was concerned, Gabriel had only one sister. One 1857 letter to Gabriel concluded with Ruskin's "sincere regard for you, your brother, and Miss Rossetti—just as much as ever." The talented and attractive Christina seemed not to exist, and Maria's faint hopes fluttered at such signs of interest; yet Ruskin encouraged only sexually undemanding female relationships. Eventually Gabriel sent him manuscript copies of some of Christina's poems, but although Ruskin acknowledged their "beauty and power" he was convinced that they were so full of "quaintnesses and offences" as to render them unpublishable. "Irregular measure," he pontificated, ". . . is the calamity of modern poetry." Since Homer, Vergil, Dante, Spenser, Milton and Keats wrote without violating the metrical rules, "your sister should exercise herself in the severest common-place of metre until she can write as the public like." Finally—as representative of "the public"—he recognized the existence of the second sister.

William's life was subtly altering while the melodramatics remained part of the everyday life of his brother. Although William gave his daily hours unstintedly to the Inland Revenue, his life was really elsewhere. Literary and artistic journalism took up those of his evenings and weekends not devoted to Henrietta Rintoul. Tight-lipped and high cheekboned, she looked even more imperious than she was, and William counted himself fortunate to be on the verge of moving up in the English caste structure by marrying into her family. But *she* would set the date. In the meantime he courted her decorously and wrote for her father's journal.

Besides the *Spectator* he was London correspondent for the American art journal the *Crayon*, and assisted a nonprofessional, a retired army captain, Augustus A. Ruxton, in organizing an exhibition of British paintings to be shown in New York, Philadelphia, Boston and Washington.* He was to be further involved with America through William Bell Scott, who sent him a copy of Walt Whitman's *Leaves of Grass* early in 1857. "Obliterate utterly with the blackest ink half-a-dozen lines and half-a-dozen words, ignore the author altogether, and read as one does the books that express human life like the Bible—books that have aggregated rather than been written—and one finds these *Leaves of Grass* grow up in a wonderful manner. The book is very like opening into a quite new poetic

---

* A new American depression hurt art sales; a *Venus* by Leighton offended the modesty of New Yorkers and had to be removed; and a rainstorm damaged a Madox Brown watercolor.

condition." Bell Scott had given a better gift than even he knew. In 1868 William Rossetti would become, implicitly following his astute friend's instructions for discreet expurgation, Whitman's first editor abroad.

In the spring of 1857 Lizzy was sheltering in Sheffield, at the home of her cousin William Ibbitt. Away from Gabriel her health was good, and she joined a ladies' art class and visited about the area, where there were additional cousins and acquaintances. Unaware, Barbara Leigh Smith—Mrs. Bodichon as a result of her voyage with her ailing sister to Algeria—invited Gabriel and Lizzy to spend a summer week away from London at Scalands, for the sake of Lizzy's lungs. The letter was forwarded to him at Oxford, from whence he replied that much as he liked the idea, it was impossible. "What do you think I and two friends of mine are doing here? Painting pictures nine feet high with life-sized figures, on the walls of the Union Society's new room here. . . . The work goes very fast, and is the finest fun possible. Our pictures are from the *Morte d'Arthur*."

The new University Museum and Union Society Debating Hall had been designed by Ruskin's friend Benjamin Woodward, and on a trip to Oxford Gabriel had been attracted to the ten bare—but windowed—bays set into the walls of the Hall. Impulsively he suggested decorating them during the University's long summer vacation if he and his painter-friends could have their materials and living expenses paid. To have Ruskin's chief disciple do a series of pseudo-medieval murals was an exciting prospect to the architect, who persuaded the interim Union executive committee to accept the offer. Soon Gabriel had Morris and Jones move to Oxford from Red Lion Square, and by mid-August several even younger painters as well as older friends joined them. The work, they thought, would take six jovial weeks, but none of them knew anything about fresco or any other kind of mural painting, and Ruskin wrote skeptically to William Rossetti, "The roof *is* and is *not* satisfactory—clever, but not right. You know the fact is they're all the least bit crazy, and it's difficult to manage them."

On the raw plaster Gabriel and his crew painted in tempera, and the pictures either fell off in flakes or sank into the unprepared wall like ink into blotting paper. They began improvising, while Morris, who painted boldly and rapidly, outdistanced the others. It was Gabriel's happiest and most irresponsible summer. At twenty-nine he was suddenly an informal collegian, free from financial cares and almost forgetful of the claustrophobic life with Lizzy in the sickroom which Chatham Place had become. Between brush strokes they emptied paint pots upon each other, squirted soda water at each other, short-sheeted each other's beds, and otherwise regressed to undergraduate behavior. By October the work was far from complete, and the crew had to evacuate their rooms for incoming students and move to other quarters. Still, the jovial breakfasts with Morris, Jones and the others who still remained continued, as did the jolly evenings spent playing whist, or listening to "Topsy" Morris read from his own verse narratives. "Grinds," Gabriel called them. "Well, if this is poetry," "Top" had declared when first told so as a student, "it is very easy to write." By mid-1857, with Gabriel's encouragement, he was planning to put his best verses into book form; and another Oxford poet, the red-haired young Algernon Swinburne—who looked like a boy of twelve—had attached himself to the group and burned, too, with medieval ardor.

At Oxford Gabriel painted in a plum-colored frock coat he was still using as a smock years later, and his crew used each other as models, wearing visors, mail or whatever seemed to the purpose for everything from St. George to Lancelot. Forty years later Arthur Hughes remembered "how Rossetti once went in beautiful evening dress to some . . . stately feast [at Oxford], and only late in the evening feeling for his handkerchief discovered no pocket, and looking down, [saw] many smears of paint, having his trousers and waistcoat correct enough, but in the dark had slipped again his old painting coat on, and how magnificently and like a prince, he passed it off!"

When it came to Iseult, or Guinevere and other ladies of Arthur's court they needed local models. At the theatre Gabriel and Ned Jones found one, a tall dark young girl of seventeen with a long neck and a mass of black, crinkly hair. Immediately Gabriel's ideal of feminine beauty altered. Jane Burden was the daughter of a stableman, and from her swarthy complexion it has been guessed that there was gypsy blood in her family; but no one among the young painters at the Debating Hall asked for her pedigree, only that her father permit her to model. William Morris, shy and awkward with women, was smitten. On the back of a study of her as Guinevere he confessed, "I cannot paint you, but I love you." Gabriel's first pencil study of her was inscribed, more laconically, "J.B. Aetat xvii, D.G.R. Oxoniae primo delt. Oct. 1857." There was still a pale, red-haired young woman—no longer a girl—to whom the claims of duty attached him. He had not seen her in months.

The other Rossettis led less romantic existences, although Christina's inner life, if one judged from her verses, still seethed with frustration. Her life seemed restricted to the axis of Albany Street between her home and her church, and the interesting men and women she met were largely through the pages of her correspondence. In her poetry she raged silently, for she had no expectation of publication. In one poem she wished "the terrible pain" were over. At twenty-six she brooded on "the short past and the long to-come," and insisted, grimly,

> Dumb I was when the ruin fell,
> Dumb I remain and will never tell. . . .

She daydreamed, in another mid-1857 poem, with a "longing" and a "languour," but her nights, in a fragment published posthumously, could be punctuated by a "friend in ghostland" who was "early found" and "ah me how early lost." Was it the very-much-alive but inaccessible Collinson, spectrally disguised? Or a perverse and dreamlike embodiment of her deeper longings:

> If I wake he hunts me like a nightmare:
> I feel my hair stand up, my body creep:
> Without a light I see a blasting sight there,
> See a secret I must keep.

Yet in manic-depressive fashion she could also write lyrics of passionate joy, as if she were leading a fantasy life of such amorous intensity that it intermittently filled the void. "My heart is like a singing bird," she wrote ecstatically in November, in a poem that is deservedly one of the great love lyrics in the language. But after the first metaphoric stanza ("My heart is like an apple tree . . .") the second and last turns, with decorative abandon, to "Raise me a dais of silk and down" because "my love has come to me." The decorative details of the dais—carved with "doves and pomegranates" and "peacocks with a hundred eyes"—seem less significant than that the dais (one must recall that the writer is a proper Victorian maiden) is very likely a bed.

An undated note from Lizzy Siddal to "My dearest Gug" asks him to return to her and help her with a figure she is painting as "I am too blind and sick to see what I am about." Whatever the occasion on which it was sent, something of like urgency arrived at Oxford on November 14, 1857, and Gabriel rushed to Matlock, in Derbyshire, where Lizzy was taking a "hydropathic cure." His panel, Val Prinsep, remembered, had on it "a vision of angels, and Lancelot lying asleep. . . . But there was a large gap of bare wall which Rossetti never took the slightest trouble to fill." With Gabriel's going, the group of young painters began scattering. None of them were being paid, and they were largely doing the work in order to sit at the young master's feet. Some never finished their panels, not that it would make any difference, as all of it was doomed to disappear. Gabriel never returned.

From Matlock he reported to Allingham that Lizzy had been "terribly ill" but had improved somewhat. From William he begged for "the loan of as many pounds as you can manage." Beset by bills he had been ignoring, many of them accompanied by lawyer's letters, he was forced to use most of an £84 advance he had wheedled from Thomas Plint to pay old debts. At the beginning of the new year Gabriel was still marooned at Matlock with his Sid, and his appeals to Ruskin for funds were answered by Ruskin's offering to cancel a £70 debt if Gabriel would paint a second panel at the Oxford Union. Gabriel realized he could not, but responded that he would.

Spring came, and he was still mired at Matlock, with only "Top" remaining at Oxford. By then Morris had become engaged to Jane Burden, but whether he had been pushed by Gabriel into his declaration is unclear. Morris had worshiped her in the languid medieval manner, ending a poem about her in which he was humble supplicant that his lady seemed to be "Waiting for something, not for me." Young Algernon Swinburne, whose interest in women was then vicarious at best, felt that the burly Morris's relationship to "that wonderful and perfect stunner of his" somehow violated the rules of aesthetics. "The idea of his marrying her is insane," Swinburne wrote a friend, Edwin Hatch. "To kiss her feet is the utmost men should dream of doing." Whether Morris, shy with women, had been persuaded from Matlock, or had been pressed to declare his intentions as Gabriel prepared to rush off to the desperately ill Lizzy, it seems that Gabriel's goal was to retain Jane Burden within his circle as model since he could not retain her himself on any terms. Fourteen years later, while staying at the Morris's house, he wrote a story that one of his biographers suggests transposes the 1857 situation at Oxford safely into the Middle Ages. In "The Cup of Cold Water" a young king is hunting with a knight, his best friend. They stop at a forester's cottage for refreshment, and the forester's daughter offers a cup of water. Both men are immediately taken with her beauty, but the king has long been affianced to a princess whom—until he has been confronted with a new vision of beauty—he has thought he has loved with a pure love. The knight, understanding this, realizes that he may be in trouble for doing so, but declares his love to the girl, who confesses that she loves his friend, whose identity she does not know, and who has not given any indication of his true feelings. The knight tells all to the king, asking his help, and the king pleads his friend's cause with the girl, not hiding his own passion, but declaring that since he has no choice but to sacrifice his feelings in order to do the honorable thing by his betrothed, so should she accept a noble man whom the king loves better than all men and whom she will surely love as well. And she does.

Was Gabriel the king? And were Morris and Jane the knight and the forester's (rather than stableman's) daughter? Was the story a view of how Gabriel felt in 1857–58? Or had he revised his memories? Whichever the real situation, in 1858 Gabriel was still with Elizabeth Siddal nine years after he had first become infatuated with her. He was no longer faithful to her, as he knew she knew; but unless she threw him over he felt both pity and obligation, and both impulses grew in the forced intimacy of Matlock, along with a renewed tenderness and solicitude which, with Gabriel remote from the temptations of London, seemed much like the old love.

On April 12, 1858, he wrote Brown from Matlock that he was nearly penniless—with just enough funds to return them to London, along with a few drawings he had done. "I must trust, like Mr Micawber, for something to turn up in the matter of selling them, as none of them have immediate prospects." Through the spring and summer, with borrowed money and funds representing partial new advances for pictures he had not begun, he and Lizzy lived quietly at Chatham Place, Gabriel pressing to complete his translations of sufficient poems for his *Early Italian Poets* and to paint a triptych for the Llandaff Cathedral in Wales. His architect friend John Seddon was restoring the cathedral, and had persuaded the bishop to commission Gabriel years before to do a painting for the altar. Seddon's brother Thomas "asks if I think *Rossetti would undertake it,*" Madox Brown had written bitterly in his diary on Good Friday, 1855, "when he [Seddon] had bought my *King Lear* at auction for £15, and knows I am on the point of being driven out of England through general neglect. I do not grudge Rossetti the work, but in truth Seddon need not ask my opinion about it." It was the way Gabriel acquired such of his funds as he did not borrow, for he never exhibited his work and few connoisseurs had ever seen a real Rossetti canvas or watercolor. Yet his very aloofness from exhibition and even from public sale gave his work an exoticism and rarity which only increased the desire of prospective purchasers, while his friends continued loyally as missionaries for unpainted Rossettis. One could not become well-to-do, however, on advances upon uncompleted commissions, and Lizzy no longer talked of marriage. It might raise their cost of living, and they had little enough.

All the Rossettis visited William Bell Scott in grimy Newcastle at one time or another, and for Maria or Christina it was one of the signal events of any year. In June, 1858, it was Christina's turn, and she met whatever artistic people in the area Scott could gather together, then entrained with the Scotts to Sunderland, where they picnicked—as she recorded in a doggerel poem—on tarts, sandwiches, potted jam and "rough-coated sunburst oranges." William and Maria came later in the year, meeting Thomas Dixon, the artistic cork-cutter and friend of Ruskin who had recommended Whitman's poems to Scott, and indirectly to William; and remembering the visits Dixon wrote William, "The pieces by your sister are just of that kind as I should expect; full of that quiet peaceful piety and faith, such as I always remember in thinking over the few hours' conversation I have had the pleasure of having in her presence. I see now as I write this, in my mind's eye, the quiet face, and hear the calm quiet voice—so full of the spirit that one finds in the simple though expressive old Fathers' a reflection to me of a deep lover of Thomas à Kempis, and of one who had achieved that rare and arduous task in this life, the realization in actual life of the teachings of that beautiful book. . . ." Maria was writing a devotional work—the only kind of book she felt equipped, in her family of writers, to produce.

During the August doldrums when there were no exhibitions to review or interesting new books to criticize, William took his annual holiday from the Excise Office and went to his favorite watering place, the Isle of Wight. Christina and Maria went no farther than the nearby Regent's Park Zoo, which had become for them a familiar yet always exotic place. His letters from Freshwater Bay, Christina wrote, "cheer us like sunbeams and produce in us a moon-like content." That the expression of vicarious pleasure included their sister was indicated by the use of *moon,* for moon-faced Maria was often slyly alluded to that way in the family code. "We have revisited the Zoological Gardens," she added. "Lizards are in strong force, tortoises active, alligators looking up. The weasel-headed armadillo, as usual, evaded us. . . . The blind wombat and neighbouring porcupine broke forth into short-lived hostilities. . . ." On the Isle of Wight, Tennyson—who lived there—looked William up and invited him home, and from Freshwater William also kept up with Tennyson's peer Robert Browning, who was interested in Gabriel's poetry but from Italy realized that if he wanted his English interests to be looked after competently, William was the more prudent and businesslike brother. Thus William was detailed to have an engraving made from a photograph of Mrs. Browning for a frontispiece to an edition of her *Aurora Leigh.* And to his publisher Browning wrote, "We have many artistic friends in London generous enough to care about our concerns and help us in such a matter: but I think William Rossetti is our man just now."

At Freshwater William had visited with Miss and Mrs. Rintoul, but that long-standing engagement was no closer to ending in marriage than was Gabriel's with Lizzy. Although Robert Rintoul's health was sufficiently frail, and his years advanced, to induce him to relinquish the *Spectator*—to which William then ceased contributing in December, 1858—he was still not eager to relinquish his only daughter. Reviewing for other journals, William did not at first miss his regular appearances in the *Spectator*, but the end of the relationship gave him fewer opportunities to press his suit with Henrietta, as the publication's offices were still below the flat in which the Rintouls lived when in London.

Since Gabriel knew that his mother and sisters could get along without William's income he badgered his brother regularly for money, on the last day of the year confessing shame at plaguing William for another ten pounds until "the Llandaff people" sent him some money. He was doing his best to keep at work at Chatham Place, he insisted, but was being driven mad by bill collectors. He had tried vainly to sell something to Charles Eliot Norton (a Ruskin acquaintance) across the Atlantic at Harvard, and tried through his aunt Charlotte to sell drawings to Lady Bath and a Miss Baring, and averted further recourse to William or to the pawnbroker (his "uncle" in their parlance) by a sale to Miss Baring and another—two drawings for seventy guineas—to "Old Plint." Temporarily he was solvent. To Madox Brown he wrote that "Plint bites already," and after Brown sold an old canvas to a Newcastle lead merchant, James Leathart, converted to art patronage by Bell Scott, Gabriel predicted hopefully to Brown that Leathart might become "a victim of Art in the future. Who knows that he may not even pair with Plint some day as twin lambs at the altar of sacrifice." It was not an Art for Art's sake attitude. The purpose of Art was to feed artists.

On April 26, 1859, Gabriel was not present at St. Michael's, Oxford, when Jane Burden was married to William Morris. The rest of the Oxford brotherhood apparently attended the quiet wedding. Was Gabriel unable to face the loss-and-gain for him inherent in the ceremony? He said and wrote nothing about the event, and returned to his painting while Top and Janey honeymooned on the Continent before returning to London and then to "The Red House," a red-brick and red-tile country house Morris was refurbishing according to his pseudo-medieval fancy. Whatever the cause— it may have been the marriage—Gabriel alternated visits to the Morrises, where he was helping to decorate the Red House, with nocturnal wanderings about London, sometimes with a P.R.B. or Oxford Brotherhood companion. With little work accomplished, his problem remained "hard-upishness," and in June, after being "literally penniless for two days," he managed to borrow two pounds from William. The same month saw Ruskin criticize Gabriel's drawings as well as his Italian translations. "I am beginning to have a very strong notion," he wrote, "that you burn all your best things and keep the worst ones." There was no mention of money.

In addition to balancing all of his own activities and trying to tread the thin line between financing Gabriel and encouraging him, William was exploring publishing opportunities for his sister's writings, for he would not accept her protestations of content with the creativity itself. To John Millais he proposed that for the magazine *Once a Week*, with which Millais had an association, the artist illustrate a poem by Christina, thus guaranteeing that poem as well as picture would be published. For the purpose Christina cut down a forty-three stanza ballad, "Maude Clare," to twelve, and it duly appeared with a Millais drawing. The year 1859 saw a flood of long poems from Christina, one in March suggesting the disparity between her inner (or upstairs) life with her outer (or downstairs) appearance:

> Downstairs I laugh, I sport and jest with all;
> But in my solitary room above
> I turn my face in silence to the wall;
> My heart is breaking for a little love. . . .

Chief outlet for her affections was Maria, who could not have guessed at the intensity of repressed and unrecognized erotic feeling which was subconsciously transferred to her, even when Christina produced a strange and powerful poem which ended with a tribute that "there is no friend like a sister. . . ." "Goblin Market," completed on April 27, 1859, became on publication several years later a Victorian nursery classic, like many works somehow considered appropriate for children—*Alice in Wonderland* was the prime contemporary example—actually full of sinister, subterranean echoes fortunately too sophisticated for their understanding. It is quite possible that Christina herself, in her lurid tale about two maiden sisters who become involved with a tribe of scary goblins, had no idea how deeply she was probing her own psyche. Even her relationship with her brothers is implicitly questioned, for the goblins themselves, although not brothers to heroine-sisters of the poem, are described as

> Leering at each other,
> Brother with queer brother;
> Signalling each other,
> Brother with sly brother.

But "Goblin Market" is more about an emotional relationship between sisters that can only be contemplated through the veil—and the subconscious self-censorship—of art.

The long poem—nearly seven hundred lines—tells the story of Laura and Lizzie, two sisters who are tempted by tiny goblin merchants who haunt the woods and glens at evening, hawking—for a penny—ripe, delicious fruit. Laura succumbs, but the goblins' victim is never granted a second taste although the result of the first taste is a wild craving for more. To save her sister's life, Lizzie makes the perilous journey into the dark wood and exposes herself to the temptation of the goblins' fruit in order to secure the "fiery antidote" which will quell Laura's desperate craving. She is bullied and coaxed, but refuses to open her lips. The evil little men even pour the luscious juices over her face to no avail. Defeated, they fling back her penny and let her go, whereupon she runs home to her sister, crying,

> Come and kiss me,
> Never mind my bruises,
> Hug me, kiss me, suck my juices
> Squeezed from goblin fruits for you,
> Goblin pulp and goblin dew.
> Eat me, drink me, love me. . . .

Laura clings to her sister, and kisses away the juices of the forbidden fruit, which are now like "swift fire." She falls insensible, "Pleasure past and anguish past." But she awakes as from an innocent dream, the poisons in the blood purged.

To Ellen Moers in *Literary Women* (1976), *suck* "is the central verb of 'Goblin Market'; sucking with mixed lust and pain is, among the poem's Pre-Raphaelite profusion of colors and tastes, the particular sensation carried to an extreme that must be called perverse. I am not suggesting that 'Goblin Market' belongs to the history of pornography as Victorian celebration of oral sex, but that Christina Rossetti wrote a poem . . . about the erotic life of children." What Ellen Moers does suggest is that in close-knit families where children were also close in age, erotic fantasies could emerge (and linger) "from the night-side of the Victorian nursery—a world where childish cruelty and childish sexuality come to the fore. . . . Several Victorian women writers—the Brontë sisters and Christina Rossetti among them—derived a valuable professional leavening from starting out as infant poets, dramatists, or tellers of tales with an audience of enthusiastic and collaborating siblings. That not only much of the technical expertise but also some of the material of their adult work derived from the nursery circle should not surprise us. . . . The rough-and-tumble sexuality of the nursery loomed large for sisters: it was the only heterosexual world that Victorian literary spinsters were ever freely and physically to explore." Could the poverty of Christina's physical experience, and the disproportion of her sexual hunger, subconsciously directed here, it seems, toward Maria, have led to "Goblin Market"? Certainly the poem is more than an entertainment, and probably more, far more, than Christina knew.

A pen-and-brown-ink drawing by Gabriel survives which looks as if it could be an illustration to "Goblin Market." In it a slim young woman brushes with her lips the face of a darker, more stocky young woman while embracing her. The two almost could be Christina and Maria—or even the two sisters of Christina's poem. Yet the drawing anticipates the poem by half a dozen years, and was intended as an illustration to an abortive *Book of Old English Ballads* in which Lizzy Siddal was to have collaborated, and for which she actually did several studies. Had Christina seen it? Did it suggest to her, even subconsciously, her own tale of two sisters? There seems now no way to know, yet the drawing at the very least seems to be a striking anticipation of, perhaps even a biographical gloss upon, "Goblin Market."

There is little need to examine Christina's oft-documented literary sources, from the elves and fairies in the *Sagen und Märchen* she read under Dr. Heimann's tutelage as a child, to various Christian tales of temptation and sin, from the forbidden fruit in Eden to the ripe pears of St. Augustine's *Confessions*. Clearly Christina intended a Victorian moral tale. One sister is nearly destroyed by her own inability to resist temptation. The other—was the name *Lizzie* an unconscious recognition of Elizabeth Siddal's stubborn holding out for marriage?—cannot even be corrupted by the taste of the forbidden fruit forced upon her lips. Was the "Eat me, drink me, love me"—as a Christina Rossetti biographer contends—a "bold application of the Eucharistic principle to a human relationship"? William Rossetti had been asked by Christina's first biographer why the published poem had not only concluded with the famous lines identified with Maria but had even been dedicated to "M.F.R." It did "indicate *something*," William thought: "Apparently C. considered herself to be chargeable with some sort of spiritual backsliding, against which Maria's influence had been exerted beneficially." From what had Maria saved her? Had the straitlaced Maria sensed the subtle eroticism in her sister's poetry? Violet Hunt, daughter of Oxford don Alfred Hunt, although not born at the time, suggested that she had learned from private sources that "Maria did not, like Lizzie to save Laura, hold converse with goblin men on the hillside, and eat their delicious deadly fruits. But for a week of nights, the kind, sonsy* creature crouched on the mat by the house door and saved her sister from the horrors of an elopement with a man who belonged to another." She identified the tempter as James Collinson, who had spurned Christina nine years before, but allegedly returned, a married man, to ask her to run off with him. The melodramatic story has nothing to substantiate it. "Goblin Market" suggests other sources. Christina's decade of repression had engendered within her lurid sexual fantasies she would have rejected with horror had they been explained to her.

Gabriel was indulging his own fantasies. For a time, partly because Ruskin admired the actress Ruth Herbert (Mrs. Crabbe), Gabriel painted

---

* sonsy: buxom; handsome; pleasing; comfortable; good-natured

the tall, golden-haired model, assuming Ruskin would buy. "I want you to get her beautiful face into your picture as soon as possible," he once commanded. And Rossetti once wrote around the sides of a small watercolor "Beatrice Helen Guinevere Herbert." With the alienated Elizabeth Siddal in the Midlands, or Bath, or Hastings, or elsewhere for her health much of the time, Miss Herbert was a radiant substitute for the frail Sid; but Gabriel's real indulgence involved another woman who had captured him in part by her "harvest-yellow" hair. Since the days when he first decided upon her as his fallen woman in the still-unfinished *Found*, and she had compliantly fulfilled other needs of his than those of a model, he had often gone off without brush or pen to visit Fanny Cornforth at 24 Dean Street, Soho, or her later, less sleazy address in Tennyson Street, Battersea.

Four years older than Gabriel, and lushly beautiful, Fanny was really Sarah Cox, but in London she had adopted her grandmother's name. The stories about her first meeting with Gabriel—including Fanny's own—are contradictory, but her most reasonable recollection was that it was while promenading in the Old Surrey Gardens with a cousin on a visit from the Sussex countryside to see a fireworks exhibition celebrating the return of Florence Nightingale from the Crimea in the spring of 1856. Rossetti, with several painter-friends, had succeeded in colliding with her soft curves, and tumbling down her mass of yellow hair, as a means of making the acquaintance of a potential model. Gabriel glibly turned his apology into an invitation to pose, and the next day, said Fanny, "he put my head against the wall and drew it for the head in the calf picture." What spell the coarse, barely literate Fanny cast over Gabriel was inexplicable to his sophisticated friends. Swinburne called her a "bitch" and classified her as "at the other pole of the sex" from Elizabeth Siddal. But this was exactly what Gabriel wanted. Her vulgarity and vitality were his antidote to the etherealized "Sid," and her simple, unromantic submissiveness—at a price—to Gabriel's wants was the antithesis of Lizzy's proud independence.

By February, 1859, Gabriel had moved her from Soho to Tennyson Street in Battersea, and had cadged £40 commission from his watercolorist friend George Boyce (who was Fanny's closest friend among Rossetti's cronies) for an oil portrait of Fanny. By October he had actually completed it, writing Bell Scott that he had succeeded in "a half-figure in oil," an experiment in "rapid flesh painting." Boyce was delighted. It was "splendid." And it was finished. Young Swinburne, in a letter describing the "head in oils of a stunner with flowers in her hair, and marigolds behind," judged it as "more stunning than can decently be expressed." The very title of the canvas, from a sonnet by Boccaccio, suggested Gabriel's feelings. The portrait of Fanny was the *Bocca Baciata*—the "kissed mouth" which "loses not its fascination but renews itself as doth the moon."

That he was able to do the canvas suggested not only the creative energy Fanny's sexuality tapped but a profitable new direction for Gabriel. Sensuous portraits of sensuous women would dominate his work, and appeal to wealthy patrons whose puritanical lives permitted what at the time, even without nudity, was near-pornography—if it were packaged as Art and labeled with literary titles. As Rossetti's biographer Doughty put it, "Guinevere replaced Beatrice, 'Body's Beauty' (or 'Lilith') ousted 'The Blessed Damozel.' Yet the earlier, ascetic ideal was neither destroyed nor banished." What happened, however, is that the concepts clashed thereafter, both in life and in art. "Rossetti," said a friend of his Oxford Brotherhood days, many years later, "was addicted to loves of the most material kind both before and after his marriage, with women, generally models, without other soul than their beauty. It was remorse at the contrast between his ideal and his real loves that preyed on him and destroyed his mind."

Lizzy apart from Gabriel was often physically more vigorous than with him, although in an era when tuberculosis was the equivalent of the common cold she was unlikely ever to get better. Dr. Acland may well have been right when he suggested that her lungs were not nearly as disabled as her ability to cope with her exterior problems, but his prescription, as well as that of later physicians, would reinforce the ailment. To suggest, for example, that Lizzy should scrupulously refrain from drawing would truly have eliminated the strain of her attempting to rise to Rossetti's, and then Ruskin's, romantic expectations. To suggest—as was often done—convalescence somewhere remote from Gabriel's center of activities might have removed her from the strain of rising to the level of cultural sophistication of Gabriel's friends and relatives—a strain she often compensated for by passivity and long silences when in such company, and in the comfort of friendship with the unlettered Emma Brown. But when the physician treats the totality of symptoms as having an organic basis and advises prolonged rest, especially rest in bed, and the avoidance of what seems really important in life, the patient's own natural tendency to regard the illness as real and disabling is reinforced by outside authority. If, further, the medical recommendation includes pain-killing drugs or alcoholic "tonics"—upon either of which the patient is likely to become dependent—the prescription as well as the ensuing dependency reinforce and even aggravate the sense of serious illness. Lizzy was a victim not only of her unresolved conflict between what she wanted to do and the circumstances—including her own anxieties—which prevented her from doing so, but also of Victorian medical practice.

While her frailty kept Gabriel supportive, it also prevented Gabriel from satisfying, with her, his increasingly urgent sexual needs; and her illness kept him from marrying her although marriage would have made her more sexually accessible. Gabriel's barely-hidden straying only reinforced her insistence on marriage at a time when her emotional and physical decline was making her less and less marriageable, while reinforcing Gabriel's own sense of guilt both in straying and in not marrying. With Lizzy he had retreated to an association that was more sentimental than sexual, but no less powerful.

By the close of 1859 he was again involved with Annie Miller, who according to Boyce "looked more beautiful than ever," Gabriel was also filling his sketchbook with voluptuous visions of Fanny Cornforth. It had been years since his "Sid" had regularly sat for him, or since he had wanted her to do so. "Oh never weep for love that's dead," she wrote in another melancholy verse, "Since love is seldom true." The concluding lines seemed almost a message to the errant Gabriel:

> Sweet, never weep for what cannot be,
>   For this God has not given:
> If the merest dream of love were true,
>   Then, sweet, we should be in heaven;
> And this is only earth, my dear,
>   Where true love is not given.

VIII
An End in Blackfriars
1860-1862

In 1860 the long engagements into which the two Rossetti brothers had entered both ended, only one of them with a marriage. The unexpected element was not only that it was Gabriel who was marrying, but that the bride was the long-suffering Lizzy Siddal. At Hastings she appeared again to be dying, and Gabriel, at what seemed his final bedside watch, felt his guilt acutely. He renewed his abandoned offer. "Like all the important things I ever meant to do," he wrote his mother on April 13, "—to fulfil duty or secure happiness—this one has been deferred almost beyond possibility. I have hardly deserved that Lizzy should still consent to it, but she has done so, and I trust I may still have time to prove my thankfulness to her. The constantly failing state of her health is a terrible anxiety indeed; but I must still hope for the best. . . ." Then he explained lamely that improved "money prospects" made marriage possible when it had been impracticable before.

William immediately dispatched a congratulatory message, to which Gabriel responded with a brotherly letter rare in that it did not ask for money. "I am not short at present," he noted, "though I only have it as an advance on work to do." Even that money he did not have with him when he rushed to Hastings, and had to return to London to fetch it when a long stay in Hastings seemed at least as likely as a funeral and more likely than a wedding trip. He had already made what seemed to be the essential purchase for Lizzy's rallying, a marriage license, but validation required a church ceremony, which seemed impossible, and to William he conceded that a costly special license was too great an extravagance.

Ten days after Gabriel had arrived in Hastings it appeared that Lizzy was over the worst. To Madox Brown he reported that she had seemed about "to die daily and more than once a day. It has needed all my own strength to nurse her through this dreadful attack. Since yesterday there has been a reaction for the better. She has been able to get up and come downstairs, and eats just now—though not much—without bringing up her food—which she has done till now, generally a few minutes after swallowing it." He felt "as if I had been dug out of a vault," and hesitated "to put full trust" in her recovery. His thirty-second birthday, May 12, was set for the wedding, but Lizzy was too weak to withstand the ceremony. Finally on the morning of May 23 they were married at St. Clement's Church, Hastings, with only the required two witnesses present, and went on to Folkestone en route to Paris.

The Hôtel Meurice was fashionable but too expensive. After a week they moved to lodgings in the Rue de Rivoli, from which Gabriel sent William a wedding notice to post in *The Times*. In Paris he drew two pen-and-ink sketches which have survived, the gloomy *How They Met Themselves* (a Doppelgänger drawing) and *Dr Johnson at the Mitre*, and began studies for an oil portrait of Lizzy, which became *Regina Cordium*.* With Lizzy at first too weak for wandering Parisian streets or shops, he read to her from *Pepys's Diary*, stole away briefly to the Louvre to marvel at Veronese's huge and populous *Marriage Feast at Cana* ("the greatest picture in the world without a doubt," he wrote William), and began to chafe at his inactivity. In London Boyce found Fanny chafing over her neglect. "Called on Fanny Cornforth who, I heard . . . was ill," he noted in his diary on June 5. "Found her so in bed. It appears she frets constantly about R, who is with his wife in Paris. . . . F was seeing a doctor and was in very nervous, critical state."

Four weeks after the wedding Gabriel was not only bored, but short in funds. Any thoughts of a trip to the presumably healthful south of France were abandoned, and they took the boat train back toward London. But in the first newspaper Gabriel picked up in England he read of the death of Robert Brough, an acquaintance whose comic writings,† he knew, could not have left much wherewithal for a widow and two small children. As he and Lizzy had already called for a cab, they directed it first to a familiar

---

* *Queen of Hearts*. Ironically it later passed into the hands of Fanny Cornforth, who may have merely appropriated it.
† His satiric verses, "Songs of the Governing Classes," had been dedicated to Gabriel.

pawnshop, where Lizzy pledged the new Parisian jewelery she was wearing. Then they went on to Mrs. Brough's lodgings, left her the money and proceeded, nearly penniless, home.

Home remained Chatham Place, although Gabriel had promised his bride more salubrious surroundings. For a while they would rent a house at Downshire Hill, Hampstead, to be intermittently near the Madox Browns; but the familiar damp pile at Blackfriars remained Gabriel's place in which to paint if not to sleep. With Lizzy now his wife, Gabriel determined to acquire for her acquaintances more appropriate than Emma Brown, and arranged for her to have dinner with his mother, brother and sisters, and to meet the wives of his friends Morris and Jones. For a time after their securing Spring Cottage at Hampstead Lizzy was again ill, and Dr. Crellin—who had seen Lizzy at Chatham Place—was sent for although it was far out of his normal range of calls. Gabriel offered the physician "2 guineas at least," recognizing the extraordinary service; that he had the price, and more, was a result of his newly learned dexterity in balancing advances from his patrons and attracting interest from dealers. A Colonel Gillum, who had been steered to Gabriel by Browning, was providing quarterly payments, and other moneyed collectors like Plint* and Leathart were jostling each other for priority now that dealers like Gambart were willing to take Gabriel's canvases and sell them at higher prices than Gabriel would ask himself. In part it reflected the success of the lush portrait of Fanny, the *Bocca Baciata*, which he could have sold several times over and which Boyce boasted, with useful publicity for Gabriel, was his favorite picture. But Fanny herself had been discreetly shunted into the background.

In July, 1860, once Lizzy was well, Gabriel suggested that the Browns and the Joneses meet them at "the Wombat's Lair" at the Zoo, wombats being his favorite among furry creatures. "Georgie" Jones—Ned Jones had married petite Georgiana Macdonald—remembered Lizzy then as slender, graceful and elegant, and Gabriel as feuding with an owl in a cage, and rattling his walking stick on the bars. The Joneses returned with the Rossettis to Hampstead, and the brides adjourned to Lizzy's "little upstairs bedroom with the lattice window," where she took off her bonnet, revealing to Georgie "the mass of her beautiful, deep-red hair . . . very loosely fastened up, so that it fell in soft, heavy wings," and her delicate complexion, "as if a rose tint lay beneath the white skin." There Lizzy showed her new friend a drawing she had been working on, illustrating

---

* Plint died soon after, having advanced Gabriel £714 for three undelivered pictures. The executors found Gabriel difficult as he had neither the money nor the paintings, and settlement was drawn out for years.

Gabriel's unfinished "Bride's Prelude." Lizzy had titled it *The Woeful Victory.* She had depicted the *finale* to a joust where a lady with proud, averted head gives the required prize to the knight who had slain her lover. The title had no symbolic relationship to Lizzy's marriage but reflected, rather, her affinity for melancholy themes; yet Georgie was uneasy. "I know," she wrote many years later, "that I then received an impression which never wore away, of romance and tragedy between her and her husband."

Gabriel had work to do, which meant Chatham Place, where Lizzy hesitated entrusting her frail health; and Hampstead was lonely although Gabriel returned evenings to sleep. Brighton beckoned, for its sea air and because her sister Lydia—Mrs. Wheeler—suggested the spot. Gabriel was not sorry to see her go. Weak lungs, wan appetite, and laudanum—the latter the drug which doctors had recommended to appease her gastric spasms and assuage their pain—had left her listless. Opiates were often used to quiet the pangs of intestinal tuberculosis (which was never diagnosed in her case), and laudanum itself—a tincture of opium—enjoyed an immense vogue during the nineteenth century and was for a time prescribed almost as a specific for consumption.

For three pounds a week Gabriel kept both sisters at bay. "Dear Gug," she apologized in one letter from Brighton, "I am most sorry to have worried you about coming back when you have so many things to upset you. I shall therefore say no more about it. . . . Perhaps after all I am better here with Lyddy than quite alone at Hampstead. . . . I should like to have my water-colours sent down if possible, as I am quite destitute of all means of keeping myself alive." She remained and George Boyce found Gabriel at Chatham Place at the end of July, working on the Llandaff triptych with an Italian male model; and before Boyce left, he noted, "Morris and his wife (who he familiarly addresses as Janey), came in. . . ."

Boredom had set in too for the females at Albany Street, and Christina had broken away in the only respectable way she knew, which meant finding a religious outlet for her yearnings. She became an Associate (an "outer sister") of St. Mary Magdalene's Home at Highgate, a refuge for what William called "the reclamation and protection of women leading a vicious life." Letitia (Mrs. William Bell) Scott found her there, wearing her habit, a "simple, elegant" black dress "with hanging sleeves, a muslin cap with lace edging, quite becoming to her with the veil." After "Goblin Market" Christina had written almost nothing for half a year, and her verse during the months when she spent intermittent periods at Highgate was far less than her usual outpourings, only four poems appearing in her 1860 notebook. Something about being among "fallen women" seemed emotion-ally satisfying.

None of the four Rossettis, despite their heritage and interests, had ever ventured to Italy, and when William finally did so, taking his annual holiday in September, it was for un-Italianate reasons. The Brownings were there, and had invited him to Florence. When William arrived, with the young barrister Vernon Lushington as traveling companion, the Brownings were instead at Siena, and William followed. The result was a series of useful introductions to the Anglo-American artistic colony which radiated from Florence, and an introduction, too, to spiritualism, about which William—a skeptic—became fascinated. Contrary to her husband, Mrs. Browning was a believer, and one of their Florentine friends, the English painter Seymour Kirkup, had a housekeeper-mistress, Regina, who was noted as a medium. Browning regaled William with stories about Regina, and William managed to meet the painter—who had once corresponded with old Gabriele about Dante—and his clairvoyant. Later William and his brother would investi-gate the phenomenon in London.

In October he was back, and found Gabriel and Lizzy planning to move into Chatham Place to stay. They had given up on Hampstead. Every house they sought, Gabriel wrote Allingham, seemed "to slip through just as we think we have got it. For one in Church Row . . . which has just escaped us, my heart is in doleful dumps: it having a glorious old-world garden worth £200 a year to me for backgrounds." Instead, Gabriel prevailed upon his landlord in Blackfriars—who owned both number 13 and number 14—to cut a door into the second floor of the next house and thus double the rooms available without necessitating a move. Having camped rather than dwelt in Chatham Place before, the couple, inspired perhaps by the fact of legal domesticity, set out to clean up the clutter and decorate. Unlike the moneyed Morrises in their Red House at Upton, the Rossettis could neither build what they wanted nor buy the expensive new or the expensive antique; they made do instead with secondhand furniture and china (Lizzy liked willow-pattern dishes), and Gabriel covered the shabby fireplace with blue Dutch tiles, designed his own colorful wallpaper and painted all the doors bright green. The sitting room was "completely hung round with Lizzy's drawings," he wrote Allingham. The kitchen made little difference. They made breakfast in it, and tea, and when the light failed at dusk, Gabriel would put away his paints and they would look for dinner at a nearby restaurant, generally unfashionable but inexpensive.

"No place out of my studio," he wrote Bell Scott, "must know me this autumn, in spite of various invitations, tempting to wife and myself." He was determined to prove up to his new legal responsibilities, and worked with a tenacity he had not known before, seeing little of his brother, sisters or friends but for a trip to the Red House with Lizzy to paint a panel for Top. Even a visit to Albany Street, at his mother's invitation, was put off, Gabriel blaming Lizzy's "unsettled" condition, caused "by constant moving about." The problem, he did not say, was that she was pregnant.

Some days were better than others. One fine fall day they took a steamer up the Thames with Ned and Georgie Jones to Hampton Court, to inspect the maze, and at other times Top and Janey came in from the country, or—at Christmas—they went to the Morrises, Lizzy traveling ahead and Gabriel following when he had painted himself into need for a rest. All was going unpredictably well, and even the visits of Fanny to sit for one of the Llandaff pictures (*The Seed of David*) or for *Fair Rosamund* provoked no outbursts from Lizzy; the lush Fanny—who seldom now saw Gabriel—was now Mrs. Hughes, having married a mechanic whom Gabriel then enlisted, when Timothy Hughes was sober, to sit for David in the triptych. And Lizzy herself still drew, as Gabriel boasted to Allingham. "Her last designs would I am sure surprise and delight you, and I hope she is going to do better than ever now. I feel surer every time she works that she has real genius—none of your make-believe—in conception and colour, and if she can only add a little more of the precision in carrying out which it so much needs health and strength to attain, she will I am sure paint such pictures as no woman has painted yet. But it is no use hoping for too much."

Ironically it was the prudent William who had hoped too much. After years of waiting for Robert Rintoul to assent to his daughter's marriage, William saw his hopes rise when Rintoul had died in 1859. But Henrietta then pleaded the needs of her ill and aged mother. Then, in October 1860, when William was in Italy with the Brownings, Mrs. Rintoul died. Returning home, William proposed, and the next month—William wrote discreetly in his memoirs—"the lady announced to me that, consequent upon her grief for her mother's death, she viewed with dismay the idea of forming any new ties, and she preferred that the engagement should be regarded as at an end. Against myself no sort of complaint was made or suggested. I was unable to consider this second rupture of the engagement entirely reasonable. I submitted to it, and determined to remain a bachelor." He was diplomatic. Henrietta had agreed to marriage—but on her terms. Four years older than the thirty-one-year-old William, she may have feared a pregnancy at her age, or, after half her life spent in cautious suppression of the primal urges, she may have feared them altogether. She proposed a sexless union, and William refused.

While he was indignant, she was prostrated. Recovering sufficiently to pick up her pen, Henrietta sent a doleful note to Christina, explaining that they would not be sisters-in-law after all, and Christina (who had already heard from William) rushed over to comfort her. What separate explanations the estranged pair gave Christina is unknown, but the two repressed virgins held each other fast, Henrietta's thin body trembling in Christina's arms as, crying, she kissed her, and poured out her new misery. What she confessed to Christina about the past filled William's sister with pity, and she wrote to William that she wished that he and Henrietta were "compatible," but that if not, the brother who was the man she loved most in the world had to have her support in the matter. She remained vaguely friendly with Henrietta thereafter, but William never saw Henrietta again.

While William was recovering stoically from the shattering of his long-nursed hopes, Gabriel and Lizzy were enjoying the brief summer of their marriage. Her health seemed improved by pregnancy, and the stability of the marriage seemed enhanced by their mutual eagerness to make Chatham Place more habitable. The London winter was suddenly tolerable; Gabriel's friends, old and new, were greeted in Blackfriars with jollity—the Joneses, the Morrises, the Browns, Ruskin (who came on a January evening), a witty young novelist named George Meredith, the even younger poet Swinburne, who quickly developed an adolescent passion for Lizzy; and among intimates, Georgie Jones remembered, Lizzy would become "excited and melancholy, though with much humour and tenderness as well." While Gabriel ebulliently reigned over his guests, often inventing absurd limericks describing them (". . . a poor creature named Georgie / Whose life is one profligate orgy. . . ."), Swinburne—so ribald with his cronies—often sat, literally, at Lizzy's feet, charming her with his reading of the Elizabethan dramatists, carefully expurgating the unseemly passages as he took all the roles. (He thought of her as he would a sister, although in decorous Victorian fashion they did not call each other by their Christian names.) "I shall never forget her delight . . . ," he wrote thirty-five years later; "I can hear the music of her laughter to this day." In his novel, *A Year's Letters*, begun that January but not published for more than forty years, he wrote poetically of her face, "pale when I saw it last, as if drawn down by its hair, heavily weighted about the eyes with a presage of tears, sealed with sorrow, and piteous with an infinite, unaccomplished desire." *

The new Rossetti energies radiated from Chatham Place into Albany Street. Gabriel, with his *Early Italian Poets* nearly ready for publication, pressed William into collating the translations against the originals, and

---

* The relationship of Swinburne's Mademoiselle Philomene to Lizzy is set forth with additional quotation in Doughty's biography of DGR.

pushed Ruskin to say a good word about Christina's poetry to W. M. Thackeray, then the editor of the *Cornhill*, while Gabriel himself tried personally to extend Christina's success with Alexander Macmillan, co-founder with his brother of the publishing house and magazine of the same name. Few journals had seen, or printed, Christina's poems until *Macmillan's Magazine* read her "Up-hill," which Gabriel described as her "lively little Song of the Tomb." It was published in the February 1861 issue, after which Gabriel suggested "Goblin Market" to Macmillan, writing William that Ruskin's strictures about the poem were "most senseless, I think." Gabriel also told Macmillan about Christina's supernatural tale "Folio Q," about a man whose tragedy it was not to be reflected in a looking glass. It was, William thought, "perhaps the best tale she ever wrote in prose," but when Gabriel tried to have it published he discovered that his overcautious sister had destroyed her only copy—according to William because, although the author was unaware of it in the writing, "it turned out to raise—or *seem* as if it were meant to raise—some dangerous moral question." Still, Gabriel reported to Macmillan—so he told Christina—that there was "a good deal of poetry," enough for a book. "I wish you would make a collected copy in printing-form of all the most available, and allow me to give an opinion beforehand as to which should be included. I believe they would have a chance with Macmillan." William, and even Maria, were writing also, one a translation of Dante, with critical preface, the other a long interpretation of Dante, almost as if the ghost of old Gabriele still stalked the Rossetti household.

"Lizzie is pretty well for her," Gabriel wrote somewhat anxiously to Allingham, "and we are in expectation (but this is quite in confidence as such things are better waited for quietly) of a little accident which has just befallen Topsy and Mrs T. who have become parents. Ours, however will not be (if at all) for two or three months yet." Despite the obvious concern, Gabriel pressed on with his siege of Macmillan in Christina's behalf, testing her poems on a friend "conversant with publishers . . . who thought them so uniformly excellent that there could be little doubt ever of their finding a publisher, not to speak of a public. Really they must come out somehow." He suggested a change of title for one poem, which Christina accepted, and sent the collection "at once" to Macmillan.

On April 20, Gabriel wrote to Blake biographer Alexander Gilchrist of new concern about Lizzy and her baby, "She has a doctor in whom I have confidence, and an excellent nurse, and we have also seen Dr. Babington, head of the Lying-in Hospital, so I feel sure all is being done for the best. She has too much courage to be in the least downcast herself. . . . So we can but wait and trust for a happy termination." What his fears were had their confirmation in a brief note to his mother on May 2: "Lizzie has just been delivered of a dead child." It had been expected for several weeks. Denied his daughter, Gabriel's chief anxiety was for Lizzy, about whom he wrote friends that he could feel "nothing but thankfulness" that she had come through the ordeal.

But she had not come through unchanged. In the new gloom at Chatham Place, Georgie and Ned Jones found Lizzy "sitting in a low chair with the childless cradle on the floor beside her, and . . . and she cried with a kind of soft wildness as we came in, 'Hush, Ned, you'll waken it!' " Years later, in a cryptic verse autobiography he called "Chimes," Gabriel wrote of:

> Lost love-labour and lullaby,
> And lowly let love lie. . . .

It suggested what had upset the delicate balance and returned Lizzy to what would be a pervasive melancholy, now aggravated by intermittent hysteria. For Gabriel, who brooded over the disaster without such outward show, the stillborn daughter would be suggested in his poetry, in his describing Death as a small child, two poems even being titled "Stillborn Love" and "Newborn Death." A few months later, when the Joneses were expecting their first child, Lizzy tried to press "a certain small wardrobe" upon them, and Gabriel appealed, "But don't let her, please. It looks like such a bad omen for us."

In the months following the stillbirth, with Lizzy too frail to think of bearing another child, she and Gabriel tried to adopt a little girl who later became the actress Nellie Farren. But her father, Nellie recalled, "thought it an odd way to start married life—especially as they seemed to have no money. Of course he wouldn't give me up, but I often used to go with her [Lizzy] and sit in the painting room." Brooding over her loss, Lizzy turned again to her gentle, ballad-like poetry, where it was not the child (here transformed from daughter to son) who would die, but the mother. Almost certainly she wished it so.

> O mother, open the window wide
>   And let the daylight in;
> The hills grow darker to my sight,
>   And thoughts begin to swim.
>
> And, mother dear, take my young son
>   (Since I was born of thee),
> And care for all his little ways,
>   And nurse him on thy knee.

And, mother, wash my pale, pale hands,
　　And then bind up my feet;
My body may no longer rest
　　Out of its winding-sheet.

And, mother dear, take a sapling twig
　　And green grass newly mown,
And lay them on my empty bed,
　　That my sorrow be not known.

And, mother, find three berries red
　　And pluck them from the stalk,
And burn them at the first cockcrow,
　　That my spirit may not walk.

And, mother dear, break a willow wand,
　　And if the sap be even,
Then save it for my lover's sake,
　　And he'll know my soul's in heaven.

And, mother, when the big tears fall
　　(And fall, God knows, they may),
Tell him I died of my great love,
　　And my dying heart was gay.

And, mother dear, when the sun has set,
　　And the pale church grass waves,
Then carry me through the dim twilight
　　And hide me among the graves.

Gabriel only saw the verses when it was too late. He was busy with his own, which he was fair-copying into a new calfskin manuscript volume to show to a publisher, and with Christina's, and with his painting—which lagged so far behind the advances he had collected that there was no likelihood of his ever making good on all of them. Yet still he solicited more. Leathart sent him half of a £50 note—their usual way of doing business—and Gabriel requested not only the other half as well, but an additional £50,* while fending off Ernest Gambart, the dealer representing the Plint estate, by telling him "that if I take my own time they shall be good pictures, but if I am hurried they will be bad ones." There was no income he could count on from his *Early Italian Poets*, which had appeared through Ruskin's publishers Smith and Elder just as Lizzy had been hospitalized. The book was not a failure, although only six hundred copies

---

* Gabriel had again commissioned the unfinished *Found*.

were sold over the next eight years, the first £100 in profits going to Ruskin, who had covered the publisher's risk to that amount. In the end Gabriel earned a reputation among the literary critics for his work, but only nine pounds.

Encouraged by his appearance in print, he pressed on with his own poetry, but soon discovered that his priorities had to lie where income would result, and dropped pen for brush. With only her verses Christina had no such choice, but was buoyed by publication of another poem in *Macmillan's Magazine* in April, with yet another scheduled for August. It looked as if a book were in the offing when in June William took his mother and Christina to France for a holiday, their first trip to the Continent, for which Christina was willing to forego a residency at the Charity Home. But new sights and sounds meant little to her, and although she remembered the church of Notre Dame de Bonsecours near Rouen and "the splendid effect of sunshine after storm . . . near Avranches," the apex of the excursion was the large Persian cat at their hotel in Normandy, remembered by Christina as "the cat of St. Lo," which—so Maria told Swinburne about her mother and sister eleven years later—was petted and fed and "lived on as a family tradition since."

Staying on in London, Gabriel worked hard at painting and at evading the emissaries of Plint's executors, who very rightly did not believe the charwoman's story that he was in the country. That June there was, in fact, what Gabriel's friend Mary Howitt described as "a great Pre-Raphaelite crush," a private preview in which the most public of Pre-Raphaelites was again not represented by a picture, although his influence was pervasive in the work of his friends and the clothes of their women, who came attired as if to model for a Rossetti painting. "Their pictures covered the walls and their sketch books the tables. The uncrinolined women with their wild hair which was very beautiful, their picturesque dresses and rich colourings, looked like figures out of some Pre-Raphaelite picture . . . . I think of it now like some hot struggling dream in which the gorgeous and fantastic forms moved slowly about. They seemed all so young and kindred to each other that I felt out of place, though I admired them . . . ."

Gabriel's public invisibility as a painter, as well as his failure to deliver commissioned work, seemed only to drive his prices up. A Rossetti was a rarity. Even Lizzy laughed over Gabriel's evasion of his creditors, and collaborated with him on what Swinburne called an "unwritten dirge" on Plint. "Hers was the best line," Swinburne thought. But Ruskin was outraged by Gabriel's exploitation of his friends and patrons, and wrote— not entirely in jest—that August, "I hope somebody will soon throw you into prison. We will have the cell made nice, airy, cheery and tidy, and you'll get on with your work gloriously." The problem was that Gabriel had accepted too much work in order to collect the cash advances, and managed to finish few he had begun. And since he still needed more money—for completing a painting already paid for in full brought in no new income—he was doing drawings for stained-glass windows ordered from what he referred to as "the Topsaic Laboratory at Red Lion Square." With Brown, Jones, Rossetti and several Oxford friends, Morris had established early in the year the firm of Morris, Marshall, Faulkner and Company, "for the production," as Gabriel explained to Allingham, "of furniture and decoration of all kinds . . . . Each of us is producing at his own charges, . . . not intending to compete with Grace's costly rubbish . . . but to give real good taste. . . ."

Trying to keep ahead of his debts, he had little time for Lizzy when she was not sitting to him. She worked at her watercolors, penciled scattered lines of melancholy poetry, and went docilely, at Gabriel's urging, to visit Janey Morris, or Georgie Jones, or Emma Brown. Yet twice she suddenly disappeared and was discovered later at home, once when Gabriel himself was away in Yorkshire doing a patron's portrait he would give the same title as his head of Lizzy—*Regina Cordium*. (*Queen of Hearts* may have improved the price of the product, for later he did a third *Regina Cordium*.) In a panic, with William away, Gabriel wrote to his mother to furnish funds to Lizzy, as "I know there was not a half-penny of money at Chatham Place." Thanking her afterwards he added, "No doubt you've heard of Christina's luck with Macmillan." It was not luck, but the conclusion of a brotherly campaign to convert the publisher to her unconventional poetry, and the three samples which had appeared in the *Magazine* had caused contributors to tell Macmillan—as Gabriel put it in a note to Christina—that he had "got a poet at last in your person." Besides, Gabriel had offered to design the binding and furnish woodcut illustrations, spurring Alexander Macmillan to write Gabriel in October, "I was hoping to . . . talk to you about your sister's poems. I quite think a selection of them would have a chance—or to put it more truly that with some omissions they might do. At least I would run the risk of a small edition, with the two designs which you kindly offer. My idea is to . . . bring it out as a small Christmas book. . . ."

Christina, now thirty-one and somberly celibate, went off to her fallen women at Highgate "on condition," she told William, "that I shall have leisure to attend to proofs." Her life was becoming complicated in yet another way, the same letter revealed: "The 2 Misses Cayley called the other day. Sophie (in a bonnet and not very good light) handsome and striking, ready and amusing in conversation; Henrietta [Cayley] you know. . . ." It was likely, one of Christina's biographers writes, "that this formal call was the opening salvo in [Charles] Cayley's campaign of the

1860's to win the younger Miss Rossetti as his wife." Cayley, meanwhile, was shyly paying calls on the Rossetti ladies ostensibly, as a Dante scholar, to help Maria—the elder Miss Rossetti—with her own Dante book and to elicit Maria's advice, as a Greek scholar, on his translation of Homer, her letters afterwards suggesting improved readings, and questioning "a mysterious compound epithet." Both books were slow going, and Cayley's visits prolonged, not to his dissatisfaction.

At Chatham Place, while Lizzy nursed her pain and desolation with laudanum, taken—to dispel the taste—in brandy, Gabriel seemed unaware that her old discontent had given way to a profound resignation. He saw the familiar lassitude, not reading into it her hopes for reunion with her stillborn child and with that the end of pain. In a "very shaky and straggling" hand, which William surmised meant that it had been written under the influence of laudanum, she composed what was for her a long poem with such dark refrains as "Lord, have I long to go?" and "Lord, may I come to thee?" She wrote of "Loved eyes, long closed in death," which watched over her while her "outward life" was "sad," "still," and "frozen."

> I am gazing upwards to the sun,
> Lord, Lord, remembering my lost one.
>   O Lord, remember me!
> How is it in the unknown land?
> Do the dead wander hand in hand?
> Do we clasp dead hands, and quiver
> With an endless joy for ever?

The lines went on to speculate beyond the grave, but, to Charles Eliot Norton, Gabriel—unaware of Lizzy's lines about the "Hollow hearts" and "Soulless eyes" near her which "have ceased to cheer me"—described all he understood, that his wife was now "unhappily too confirmed an invalid to leave a hope . . . that she will ever be able to make the most of her genius. Indeed the strength to work at all is only rarely accorded her." Her genius, such as it was, had been forced. As Sacheverell Sitwell put it, "Her destiny was to be brought out into the light and to die of it. . . . As a person she was abnormally sensitive, and had been given a soul, which, because it had arrived so mysteriously, could find nothing else to live upon but that other heart out of which it had been born. He was her only affection." For the sake of Lizzy's health Gabriel would "at once" have given up Blackfriars, and the cozy old rooms—"if I found a nice place elsewhere, and hope to do so before long." But while there he regularly invited "a few blokes and coves" among his writing and painting friends—William almost always included—"to participate in oysters and obloquy."

Not invited to such gatherings, Christina nevertheless knew of Lizzy's deepening depression each time William returned to Albany Street, and as William believed, intuited its outcome in a poem she wrote then, "Wife to Husband":

> Pardon the faults in me,
>   For the love of years ago:
>   Good-bye.
> I must drift across the sea,
>   I must sink into the snow,
>   I must die.
> You can bask in this sun,
>   You can drink wine, and eat:
>   Good-bye.
> I must gird myself and run,
>   Though with unready feet:
>   I must die. . . .

Lizzy's spirits waxed and waned through the winter months. The day before Christmas, 1861, Gabriel had written to Ellen Heaton (whose portrait he had painted in Yorkshire) that he was finally doing a watercolor for her, *St. George and the Princess Sabra*, "having been delayed in carrying it on by other work, and also by my wife's delicate health making it difficult for her just now to sit to me for the lady's head which however she had done now." He made several studies for it, and Lizzy continued to sit for him until early in February, Gabriel unaware of the gloom she was confining to the verses he was not shown. One fragment attributed to her was particularly foreboding, in its seeming pun on the drug she relied upon to blot out her misery:

> Laden autumn, here I stand
>   With my sheaves in either hand.
> Speak the word that sets me free,
>   Naught but rest seems good to me.

Early in the evening of February 10, 1862, Gabriel called for a cab to take them to dinner at a Leicester Square hotel where they would meet Swinburne. The two men found the atmosphere of the Sablonière exciting because it was frequented by Continental revolutionaries who popped in and out of exile. For Lizzy it was a sort of celebration. She had just bought a new mantle as a going-away gift to herself, and was planning on a short holiday to escape the lagging winter days, having earned her jaunt after some six weeks of intermittent sitting for Gabriel. Much of what happened thereafter was reported in a London newspaper:

DEATH OF A LADY FROM AN OVERDOSE OF LAUDANUM

On Thursday Dr. Payne held an inquest at the Bridewell Hospital on the body of Eliza[beth] Eleanor Rossetti, aged 29, wife of Dante Gabriel Rossetti, Artist of No. 14 Chatham Place, Blackfriars, who came to her death under melancholy circumstances. Mr. Rossetti stated that on Monday afternoon (February 10, 1862), between six and seven o'clock, he and his wife went out in the carriage for the purpose of dining with a friend at the Sablonière Hotel, Leicester Square; when they got about halfway there his wife appeared to be very drowsy and he wished her to return. She objected to their doing so, and they proceeded to the Hotel and dined there. They returned home at eight o'clock when she appeared somewhat excited. He left home again at nine o'clock, his wife being about to go to bed. On his return at half-past eleven o'clock he found his wife in bed utterly unconscious. She was in the habit of taking laudanum, and he had known her to take as much as a hundred drops at a time and he thought she had been taking it before they went out. He found a phial on a table at the bedside, which had contained laudanum, but it was empty. A doctor was sent for and promptly attended. . . . He saw her on Monday night at half-past eleven o'clock and found her in a comatose state. He tried to rouse her and could not. . . . He and three other medical gentlemen stayed with her all night, but she died at twenty minutes past seven o'clock on Tuesday morning.

The coroner's jury brought in a verdict of "accidental death." It was almost certainly a merciful evasion. The family escaped the embarrassment that one of its members might have deliberately sought death, and the unfortunate young woman escaped the indignity of burial outside the churchyard walls. Before Lizzy had even died, Gabriel in despair had left the doctors and rushed off to Brown—arriving at five in the morning, Brown afterwards told William—with a note withheld from the inquest which Gabriel had found pinned to his wife's nightgown—"Take care of Harry." The faithful Brown put it in the fireplace.

Henry was the somewhat retarded Siddall brother. There was another, James. At the moment when the temptation to have done with life was too powerful to resist, Lizzy thought of something other than an affectionate farewell to her husband, the natural impulse toward the helpless brother suggesting hostility-by-omission toward Gabriel. He understood. Remorse and self-accusation would be a fact of his life thereafter. He had left after nine to go to the Working Men's College, but although it was his regular evening there Lizzy must have assumed that since the hour was late for a regular class, he must have intended going elsewhere—perhaps to the detestable Fanny in Battersea. Yet he was home again little more than two hours later, to find Lizzy already unconscious. Anything more than the most hasty assignation in Battersea would have been more than a two hours' round trip from Blackfriars, even if he had encountered no difficulty in locating a conveyance. Besides, with Lizzy about to leave London, Gabriel would have to wait only a few more days for—if he wished it—uninterrupted dalliance. He had probably been telling the truth, but his duplicity in the past left him haunted nevertheless. If he needed someone else, then he did not love her. She could not, in her unsophistication about the world's ways, see any other answer, nor did she realize how much Gabriel had suppressed his passionate spirit in adapting, in his fashion, to her frailties.

Gabriel took care of Harry Siddall,* and for years after Gabriel's death William continued his brother's ghostly penance. "At intervals," William's daughter Helen remembered, "a bent and rather dilapidated man would call at our house and my father always welcomed him into his little library and there for a while remained with him in talk, reaccompanying him to the front door with his wonted courtesy. On one occasion, happening to be entering the house myself at the moment, my father said to me, as he closed the door behind his visitor, 'That aged man is a brother of Gabriel's wife, Lizzie.' And then he told me that for many years he had helped him with a small allowance." After Harry's death, William also supported James. Fifty years to the month after Lizzy's death, James Siddall too finally passed beyond earthly assistance.

Chatham Place was repellent to Gabriel once Lizzy was gone. He fled to Albany Street, where to his mother and sisters (as Swinburne described it) "with sobs and broken speech he protested that he had never really loved or cared for any woman but the wife he had lost; with bitter self-reproach he referred to former professions [he had made] not ostensibly consistent with this assertion: he appealed to my friendship, in the name of her regard for me—such regard, he assured me, as she had felt for no other of his friends—cleave to him in this time of sorrow, to come keep house with him as soon as a residence could be found." He wept, William recalled, by Lizzy's bier, pleading for her to come back to him, and on the second or third day after she had expired he refused to believe that she was dead, so lifelike was her appearance, perhaps because of some quality in the drug. Dr. Marshall was recalled to verify for Gabriel the fact of death.

On the third day, too, Ruskin called at Chatham Place to view the body of his lost Ida, who had once given him "a bride's kiss," and Mrs. Siddall and her daughter Lydia came, William receiving them because Gabriel was unable to do so. Self-reproaches consumed him. He knew when he married his Sid that she was doomed to a short life, but her body even in death

---

* A letter from Gabriel exists noting a £10 payment to Harry Siddall in August 1867, and "evidence of like kind goes on as late as 1878" (WMR in his memoir of DGR).

showed no signs of the wasting away that would have been her lot had she lived many melancholy years longer with her apparent tuberculosis. She had spared herself (and Gabriel) further agonies, but the fact of her suicide, with the implicit condemnation of Gabriel in her final message, he told a friend when in his own last illness, "had left such a scar on his heart as would never be healed."

Burial was at Highgate on February 17. For nearly a week Lizzy's body had reposed, in an open coffin, in Chatham Place, and just before the lid was closed, Gabriel, unseen, deposited his manuscript book of his own poems, which had already been advertised as forthcoming in his *Early Italian Poets*, next to Lizzy's pale face, concealing it with her golden hair. George Meredith afterwards thought his friend was influenced by real sentiment when he impulsively sacrificed publication, while Holman Hunt, estranged now from his P.R.B. associate, insisted all his life that the gesture was theatrical. "Gabriel," he said, "had a copy or knew his poems by heart." But to Brown, Gabriel confided what he had done. "I have often been writing at those poems when Lizzie was ill and suffering, and I might have been attending to her, and now they shall go." Realizing that not all of the poems in the calfbound manuscript book existed in publishable copies otherwise, Brown appealed to William to help change Gabriel's mind, but the renunciation of possible poetic fame had its impact upon the usually cool and unsentimental brother. "Well," said William, "the feeling does him honour, and let him do as he likes." With the Siddall and Rossetti families present, and a few other mourners, the coffin was lowered. Returning to Chatham Place, Gabriel's mother fetched Lizzy's beloved bullfinch in its cage and took it to Albany Street.

IX

Christians and Heretics
1862-1867

oblin Market was published only a fortnight after Elizabeth Siddal's funeral. Despite the devotional quality of much of the book beyond the title poem, it was revolutionary in its metrics and in its diction. Its impact was far in excess of Macmillan's modest sales, and Christina discovered herself among the first poets of the day while the household at Albany Street, augmented by the distraught Gabriel, was still recovering from the shock of Lizzy's death. Had he been well known, the notoriety of his wife's method of departure might have spread far beyond the Rossetti circle of friends and relatives; but he had refused to exhibit his paintings publicly, and had literally buried his poetic fame in the grave. As a result, when he made his next visit to Newcastle later in the year, the inquisitive literary cork-cutter of Sunderland, Thomas Dixon, turned up at Bell Scott's to query Gabriel not about him but about his sister. "He is exceeding anxious," Gabriel wrote him delicately, ". . . as to the allegorical meaning of *Goblin Market*, so Christina knows what to expect next she sees him."

Christina had sent a presentation copy to their old friends the Heimanns, especially calling their attention to one poem, "Christian and Jew," as an example of her "longing and praying" for their conversion, adding naively that she hoped they would take no offense at her feelings. Adolf Heimann responded kindly, apparently more concerned—because of the morbidity of her verse—for her emotional well-being. "If *sad and melancholy,*" she responded defensively, "I suggest that few people reach the age of 31 without sad and melancholy experiences: if *despondent,* I take shame and blame to myself, as they show I have been unmindful of the daily love and mercy lavished upon me." But her poems were, she confessed, "not mainly the fruit of effort, but the record of sensation, fancy, and what not, much as these came and went." There were no further efforts to convert the Heimanns.

Gabriel was busy with his own efforts at conversion. He had never slept a night at Chatham Place after Lizzy's death, but while at 166 Albany Street, and temporary rooms at 50 Lincoln's Inn Fields, he worked at convincing his brothers and sisters that they could all settle together with him in a new house, along with such friends of his as he felt might provide him with useful companionship—in particular, the eager Swinburne. The idea was hardly practical, although William was agreeable and Mrs. Rossetti easily convinced; and Gabriel went ahead to lease the large property at 16 Cheyne Walk, Chelsea, with its pre-Embankment grounds sloping down to the Thames, and its vistas of riverboats and barges, and Battersea beyond.* He relinquished Chatham Place to George Boyce, and a trunk of Lizzy's "things" to his mother, to be held for the Siddalls, but the objections to his moving the family wholesale, to assuage his own increasing fear of solitude, grew. Not only was a family of women involved, including Mrs. Rossetti and the near-invalid aunt Margaret Polidori, but Maria, who continued to go out to give lessons in Italian, would have been remote from her pupils in still-suburban Chelsea. To have the pious, reclusive women in the same house with the blasphemous, noisy, often-inebriated Swinburne would have created more problems than it solved.

William agreed to pay part of the £100 annual rent, advance Swinburne's out of his own pocket, and stay overnight at least three days a week at "Tudor House," so named because it was reputed to have been part of the red-brick pile to which Queen Catherine Parr had retired after the death of Henry VIII. The women gratefully agreed to abide where they were. Old fashioned and many-roomed, Tudor House had a large back garden dominated by an ancient mulberry tree. Since P.R.B. days Gabriel had coveted a Cheyne Walk house.

Although restless while awaiting the move, he refused to join William and Bell Scott on an excursion to Italy. Gabriel preferred London. A non-smoker, he nevertheless frequented, during his period of limbo, the "cigar divans" which had grown up as informal public clubs for men, where for a shilling one could acquire a cigar, a cup of coffee, and access to the latest newspapers and magazines (from which he copied out reviews of *Goblin Market* for Christina), or find a partner for backgammon or chess.

---

* And just over Old Battersea Bridge, Fanny.

And he escaped from his memories during wanderings about the city, often with Boyce or Swinburne or his other future tenant, Meredith, and in one moment when he could not avoid contemplation wrote the only sonnet he dated from that period, "Lost Days," about times like "golden coins squandered and still to pay," and like grain grown for food "but trodden into clay." After death, he suggested, the faces he would see would be his murdered selves, each saying, "I am thyself,—what hast thou done to me?" But Gabriel was not so despondent as to encourage the companionship of the dour, domineering Ruskin, who from Milan in July (he had been living disconsolately on the Continent) had written that he was "thinking of asking if I could rent a room in your Chelsea house."

On October 23, 1862, Gabriel took possession of Tudor House, his three subtenants moving their belongings in desultorily afterwards, William beginning by setting his pewter tobacco box on the mantelpiece, Swinburne and Meredith arriving with their belongings days later. Early in November Gabriel could write to Madox Brown, "I have reclaimed my studio from the general wilderness, and got to work." Filling the other rooms took longer. He acquired old furniture from his mother and aunts, bought secondhand tables and chairs and beds, and gradually accumulated pictures and hangings and curios. In the long drawing room with its seven windows overlooking the Thames, he hung Lizzy's pen-and-ink drawings and watercolors. There, Georgie Jones thought, "if ever a ghost returned to earth, hers must have come to seek him."

Soon after, Boyce called at 16 Cheyne Walk and found Fanny there, and early in December he again found Fanny there, but was invited nevertheless to stay and have dinner, leaving afterward with a pencil sketch by Gabriel of Fanny "as she lay on a couch, hair outspread." Soon Fanny was a fixture at Cheyne Walk, sometimes identified as housekeeper, Gabriel having complained of his inability to retain servants who could work efficiently without supervision. Yet she behaved as if she were mistress of the house, which indeed she was, except when Gabriel's mother and sisters were visiting, at which times she discreetly disappeared to her own house, nearby in tiny Royal Avenue, off the King's Road. Soon, too, Gabriel acquired an assistant and quasi-pupil, the young artist W. J. Knewstub, who also lived in (without salary), to help set up and prepare Gabriel's canvases, and even to make copies of some works, the production of Rossetti "replicas" soon becoming a lucrative industry.

The very need for an assistant suggested prosperity, and for Gabriel it was a curious affluence. Most of his income came from commissions he secured, or copies he made. The commission income was always spent long before a picture was produced, if one were produced at all, and there was constant haggling with patrons over the delays in delivery. Tudor House was run on a generous and indulgent scale, often with money borrowed from William, some of which went to finance formal dinner parties in honor of moneyed patrons who were flattered by their proximity to Gabriel's literary and artistic friends. That the guests often included Gabriel's lawyer (Anderson Rose) and physician (John Marshall) showed his additional prudence, yet that prudence seemed not to result in his saving or investing anything. "Gabriel," Madox Brown once told him, "you really ought to pay William; it isn't the thing, my dear fellow, to be so much in his debt." And Gabriel said, "Pay my brother William? Good God, Brown, you must be mad."

Gabriel's purchases were lavish. Since childhood the four Rossettis had loved small animals, and one wrench Maria and Christina were spared when they did not have to give up 166 Albany Street was their proximity to the Regent's Park Zoo, where they would go to contemplate the wombats or armadillos. Tudor House and its garden gradually became Gabriel's own zoo, as he withdrew more and more into a self-enclosed world of his own making. The walled garden beyond the avenue of lime trees near the house became cluttered with cages and enclosures for animals and birds, many with their doors left open so that the creatures wandered freely into the house; and the untended grass (". . . a wilderness in most people's opinions. I prefer to compare it to an Eden," he wrote his Aunt Charlotte in 1866) would remain long, dry, weedy and withered, part of it covered in summer by a luxuriously outfitted tent, complete to Persian rugs and oriental cabinets, in which Gabriel entertained on warm evenings. It was a curious polarity of affectionate interest in his friends and family, and need for relief from humanity via his domestic zoo. There was a raccoon which liked raw eggs, and a pet wombat which died of eating too many of the cigars Gabriel kept available for his guests. There were also peacocks, which roamed the house except when fastidious guests were expected, at which times the birds were let out into the garden; and there was a gazelle, who fought with one of the peacocks, "until," Jimmy Whistler—a neighbor—remembered, "the peacock was left standing desolate with its tail apart strewed on the ground." Because of the raucous cries of the peacocks the ground-landlord, Lord Cadogan, appealed to by residents nearby, wrote into future Cheyne Walk leases a clause forbidding tenants to keep peacocks. He might also have included Gabriel's armadillos in the prohibition, as they had a tendency to burrow, and would reappear in the manicured lawns nearby, to the consternation of the residents.

Even more destructive than the peacocks were the kangaroos, mother and son, which apparently killed each other. The mortality rate in Gabriel's menageries was high. Ellen Terry remembered the party Gabriel gave to celebrate the awakening of his white dormice from winter hibernation. "They're awake now," he announced, "but how quiet they are! How full of innocent repose." Then prodding them encouragingly he said, "Wake up!" But they were dead. Ellen Terry also recalled the zebu, which Whistler christened a "Bull of Bashan," bought because Gabriel thought it had "eyes like Janey Morris." With money borrowed from William, it was bought in April 1864 for £20 at the Cremorne amusement gardens upstream from Chelsea, "brought home by two men, led through the hall, out into the garden at the back, and its rope fastened to a stake." Gabriel was assured that it was quite tame and would only cost "about 2s 6d. a week for keep." At least the former was accurate, and Gabriel, Whistler recalled, "used to come and talk to it. One day the bull got so excited it pulled up the stake and made for Rossetti, who went running round the garden, tearing round round and round a tree, a little fat person with coat tails flying, until, at last he managed to rush up the garden stairs and slam the door. . . . Then he called his man and ordered him to go and tie up the bull, and the man, who had looked out for the rest of the menagerie, who had gone about the house with peacocks and other creatures under his arm, rescued arma- dillos, captured monkeys from the tops of chimneys, struck when it came to tying up a Bull of Bashan on the rampage, and gave a month's warning."

Grotesquely spendthrift about animals, Gabriel thought of buying a lion which was being offered at a bargain rate, but his friends convinced him that he would then have to heat his jungle of a garden with hot water pipes during the winter. Georgie Jones recalled Gabriel's desire to have a young elephant, and Browning's puzzled, "What on earth do you mean to do with him when you have him?" "I mean him to clean the windows," said Gabriel, "and then, when someone passes the house, they will see the elephant cleaning the windows, and will say, 'Who lives in that house?' And people will tell them, 'Oh, that's a painter called Rossetti.' And they will say, 'I think I should like to buy one of that man's pictures'—and so they will ring, and come in and buy my pictures."

One of the many paradoxes about Rossetti was his willingness to collect creatures which had the freedom of the house, including the dinner table, while he simultaneously acquired rare Orientalia, especially fragile seven- teenth- and eighteenth-century blue-and-white porcelain. In the latter love he had a formidable rival in Whistler. To Whistler's chagrin he sometimes found his friend bidding against him and raising the prices for both of them, at the firm of Farmer and Rogers in Regent Street, whose manager, Lazenby Liberty, foreseeing the spread of the cult, soon opened his own shop on the opposite side of the street. When it came to Nankin blue-and-white, Gabriel, whose resources—and zeal—were greater than Whistler's, would not be outdone. According to one story which appears in various versions, a friend of the poet, who collected old china, once invited a number of people to supper in order to exhibit a valuable plate he had just purchased. Among the guests was Rossetti, who made an excuse to stay the night and left early the next day. Soon after his departure it was discovered that the priceless plate was missing; but its owner* said nothing, instead contriving soon afterwards to get invited to dine and sleep at Tudor House. In the middle of the night he got up and prowled the cupboards for his treasure, finding it eventually under a pile of clothes at the bottom of a wardrobe, wrapped in drapery. Substituting an ordinary dinner plate from the kitchen, he took his property home in the morning. Fascinated by, but still dubious about, the occult, Gabriel was briefly convinced by the metamorphosis. "God in Hell!" he shouted. "See what the blasted spirits have done!" But soon afterward, when his suspicions had become more earthly, he called on his friend. "I never saw anything like it!" he exclaimed. "I'm simply surrounded by a set of confounded thieves. What do you think? You know that plate of yours? Gone, my dear fellow! Stolen, and a common piece of crockery left in its place!"

The obsession could cause peculiar difficulties for Rossetti's or Whistler's hosts. The first time Rossetti dined at the home of Whistler's friend Albert Moore he was served soup. "I say, what a stunning plate!" he cried, and forgetting its contents turned it over to look for its mark. The flood that followed came as a complete surprise. Yet for Whistler and Rossetti, collecting blue-and-white satisfied more than an aesthetic or acquisitive craze. Both he and Rossetti used their purchases as props in their pictures, and were in the vanguard of the boom which Du Maurier would satirize in *Punch* in 1880, where the cartoon's Aesthetic Bridegroom, admiring a blue-and-white wedding gift, breathes, "It is quite consummate, is it not?" And the Intense Bride, cradling the object in her hands cries passionately, "It is, indeed! Oh, Algernon, let us live up to it!" By 1880 both men were out of the competition. Gabriel's collection was sold in 1872. Whistler's creditors seized his in 1879.

The collecting mania that had helped Gabriel furnish, with Lizzy, his Chatham Place rooms, became more important to him as he began looking for exotic paraphernalia for backgrounds in his canvases of beautiful women, and for exotic costumes in which to portray his models, even when he sometimes painted from the nude in order to get the limbs right and then

---

* C. A. Howell.

painted the models clothed. Mirrors, chests, furniture, robes, brocades and tiles made a museum of Tudor House and gave him a sensual pleasure the earthy Fanny, with her billingsgate invective* and repertoire of snatches of popular melodies, never understood. But attired in garments which Gabriel chose, and with backgrounds from his collection of exotica, the lushness often intensified by masses of flowers, he would paint her as symbol of sensual beauty. In a poem describing a sultry portrait of her, *Lady Lilith*, he wrote,

> The rose and poppy are her flowers; for where
> Is he not found, O Lilith, whom shed scent
> And soft-shed kisses and soft sleep shall snare?

But explaining to William Allingham what he was doing, he once used the presence of his resident model to indicate her finer points for the artist, and as he followed her curves with demonstrative finger, Fanny, her "ample charms [spread] upon a couch," would giggle, "Oh, go along, Rissetty!" Lilith existed only on canvas.

Early in the summer of 1864, Allingham, visiting unannounced, discovered Gabriel "painting a very large young woman, almost a giantess, as *Venus Verticordia*"—Venus, the turner of hearts. "I stay for dinner and we talk about the old P.R.B.s. Enter Fanny, who says something of W. B. Scott which amuses us. Scott was a dark, hairy man, but after an illness has reappeared quite bald. Fanny explained, 'O my, Mr. Scott *is* changed! He ain't got a hye-brow or a hye-lash—not a 'air on his 'ead!' Rossetti laughed immoderately at this, so that poor Fanny, good-humoured as she is, pouted at last—'Well, I know I don't say it right,' and I hushed him up." Gabriel had been looking for a new and striking model for his *Venus*, which had been commissioned by a patron in Bradford, and "noticed in the street," his brother recalled, "a handsome and striking woman, not much less perhaps than six feet high." She turned out to be "a cook serving some family in Portland Place." Gabriel painted her clothed only in a background of honeysuckle and pink roses. She exuded a lush sexuality, but he was dissatisfied with it until he later painted another model's head over that of the busty cook. Seeing the result, a rare Rossetti nude, Ruskin complained about the "coarseness" of the flowers, perhaps evading the real cause of his uneasiness. Gabriel was sarcastic: "I suppose he is reflecting upon their morals, but I never heard a word breathed against the perfect respectability of a honeysuckle. Of course roses have got themselves talked

---

* But when Gabriel would use a "bloody" in company, Fanny would warn, "Rissetty, I shall leave the room!" or "Rissetty, I'll put you in the scullery!"

about from time to time, but really if one were to listen to the scandal about flowers, gardening would become impossible."

At Albany Street the most frequent visitor was the shy, unworldly Charles Cayley. Christina had sent a book of his to Gabriel just as her brother had moved to Cheyne Walk. It may have been his unsuccessful volume of original verse, *Psyche's Interlude* (1857), or his translation of an Italian novel, *Filippo Malicontri* (1861), both published at his own expense and both stillborn. "Will you thank Christina for the *Cayley*, who seems lower in the scale of creation than ever," Gabriel wrote his mother. Very likely she relayed the thanks but no more, as the cruel but concise judgment would have been too much for Christina to bear, although she may have been amused years before when her brother drew an affectionate but unflattering pen-and-ink sketch of Cayley, dressed in disheveled morning clothes and hurrying somewhere with a serious look on his face, as if he were worried about being late. He always looked serious, even when his abstracted look only meant that he was woolgathering.

Cayley had become an earnest, if undemonstrative suitor, and to Christina, still a slender, dark, attractive young woman but now in her early thirties, he may have seemed like her last opportunity to escape spinsterhood. In 1863 Cayley, the son of an English merchant who had settled in St. Petersburg, was forty. Once he had possessed a comfortable inheritance, more than enough to finance his scholarly interests, but a friend had induced him to invest in a company which had been formed to place advertising posters in public places, especially railroad stations. The venture—a generation ahead of its time—failed. After that he survived in genteel poverty, passionately studying languages and publishing his translations and his antiquarian scholarship, when he could, at his own expense. He produced versions of the *Divine Comedy*, the *Iliad*, *Prometheus Bound*, the Psalms (from the Hebrew), and even translated the Gospels into the Iroquois language.

William, who also knew Cayley's elder brother Arthur, a Cambridge mathematician, sympathized with his friend's suit, but realized that "he made hardly anything by literary work, and was, [in] spite of his genuine talent and many acquirements, . . . entirely alien from putting himself forward in any practical sphere of life." His self-effacing courtesy and tremulous sadness left little room for wit or humor, and he smiled, as William remembered, "much in a furtive sort of way, as if there were some joke which he alone appreciated. . . . To laugh was not his style. Cayley's costume was always shabby and out of date, yet with a kind of prim decorum in it too. His manner was absentminded in the extreme. If anything were said to him, he would often pause so long before replying that one was inclined to 'give it up,' but at last the answer came in a tone between hurry and confusion." Madox Brown painted him in a Manchester fresco as an abstracted astronomer dropping his tape measure while recording the Transit of Venus, and Brown's precocious son Oliver in a juvenile novel drew him as an absentminded professor immersed in his huge and never-to-be-completed *Studies Toward a Topographical and Archeological and Historical Account of North Devonshire.* His absentmindedness, his unobservant blindness, perhaps even his reluctance to recognize the nature of Christina's reciprocal affection, seem playfully described in bantering verses she dated August 15, 1864:

> The blindest buzzard that I know
> Does not wear wings to spread and stir,
> Nor does my special mole wear fur
> And grub among the roots below;
> He sports a tail indeed, but then
> It's to a coat; he's man with men;
> His quill becomes a pen.
>
> In other points our friend's a mole,
> A buzzard, beyond scope of speech:
> He sees not what's within his reach,
> Misreads the part, ignores the whole;
> Misreads the part, so reads in vain,
> Ignores the whole though patent plain,
> Misreads both parts again.
>
> My blindest buzzard that I know,
> My special mole, when will you see?
> Oh no, you must not look at me,
> There's nothing hid for me to show.
> I might show facts as plain as day;
> But, since your eyes are blind, you'd say,
> 'Where? What?' and turn away.

Cayley's very eccentricities endeared him to Christina. When, in decrepit tailcoat, he paid his morning or afternoon calls, his fund of small talk with both sisters and their mother was full of erudite quips and subtle puns and the nuances of Italian translation, the latter possibly one of the reasons that, when Christina began a series of love poems in December, 1862, which she kept locked all her life in her writing desk, they were written in Italian. Cayley, after all, had been her father's favorite pupil.

Il Rosseggiar Dell' Oriente (*The Reddening Dawn*) has little if anything to do with Cayley, but a lot to do with Christina. The very first poem confesses that love for her "sweet friend" did not become her, since her heart had been "killed" by an earlier beloved. But she permitted Cayley's gentle and decorous courtship, privately derided by Gabriel yet actively encouraged by William. In a way she even felt guilty about encouraging Cayley, for she knew she would not have him so long as he was remote from her religious views. Collinson and she had parted because of a matter of Anglican or Roman ritual. Cayley—like her brothers—was not even a believer. "I lock my door upon myself," she wrote in a poem in 1864. "God harden me against myself. . . ."

Christina had sufficient scruples with which to supply all four Rossettis with a complete set. Gabriel had nearly none. He could not afford them, whether they concerned love or money. Painting almost without let-up, to keep pace with his debts, he seemed to owe everyone his life touched, even "Red Lion Mary," Morris's factotum. In an apologetic note to her about "tin" in the spring of 1863 Gabriel had added, intimating his domestic situation, "Fanny says she would like to know what I am saying to you as I am writing such a lot, so I had better leave off before I am scratched about the nose and eyes." Husband-and-wife servant teams replaced each other with regularity at Tudor House—Baker and wife, Weir and wife. . . . But Fanny seemed always present when Gabriel's friends called, although there was still a Timothy Hughes somewhere.

By August, 1863, Meredith had "evaporated for good" from Tudor House, as Gabriel wrote Allingham. The jovial quarter of occupants was beginning to disintegrate. Only Swinburne still seemed at home among the curiosities Gabriel collected at Cheyne Walk. A wispy carrot-colored mustache and thin beard attested to the frailty of his masculinity more than did his lusty ballads about cruel and beautiful women, and his closest relationship to a real woman remained his brief brother-sister idyll with the unforgotten Lizzy. Bachelor parties at Cheyne Walk, with bottles to empty and bawdy songs to screech left him ready to slip away, in top hat and frock coat, to a discreet house in St. John's Wood where he paid two "golden-haired and rouge-cheeked" women to whip him. Gabriel and William knew of Swinburne's foibles and fetishes, since the poet made little secret of his love for the literature of flagellation, or for the liquor which left him surrounded, morning, noon and night, by a haze of whiskey and often resulted in his being returned to Tudor House at all hours by sympathetic policemen or small boys.

Swinburne had begun his habitation in Chelsea, Gabriel had complained, "madder than ever," drink fortifying his urge to race about naked, and turning his conversation inevitably to sex, "not exactly of the sexes—but of each sex with itself." Still he hung on, Gabriel and William loyal, and certain of Swinburne's genius. William urged him, usually in vain, to make his writings more palatable to publishers and public, for Swinburne, quoting William's words against him, would explain, "I think it advisable to eschew allusions to the identity of sex between lovers—which 'no English mother could explain to her younger daughters'. . . ." William even accompanied him to Monckton Milnes's home when Swinburne was interested in examining, among Milnes's hoard of erotica, his de Sade manuscripts, William discreetly looking instead at rare samples of Blake. And at Tudor House Swinburne and William argued often about the Civil War in America, the poet insisting that even the slaveholding South had the right to rebel.

George Meredith's stay at 16 Cheyne Walk was more brief, as Gabriel concealed an imperious presence beneath his brooding eyes and baggy clothes. He had given a dinner on April 30, 1863, for several of his patrons, including Leathart, during which Meredith, turning his wit almost entirely upon ridicule of Rossetti's pictures, had been in unusually brilliant form. Mortified by such a scene in the presence of people who bought his work, the painter decided to ask Meredith to reside elsewhere. Two months later he was still paying his share of the rent and had no idea he was so out of favor, but he had indiscreetly mentioned some difference of his with Gabriel to a cabman—perhaps the dinner—and the cabman afterwards conveyed both Gabriel and the tale. Gabriel had often presided at dinners with elan, but sometimes the dishes seemed to misbehave, as when he began carving one of a pair of ducks served in the same vessel, and in his ferocity the other flew into the lap of journalist George Augustus Sala. "I say, Sala," Gabriel had drawled unabashed, "just hand me back that duck." The last supper with Meredith had begun in typical Tudor House fashion, with Swinburne declaiming between dishes from *Leaves of Grass* while the pet wombat nibbled from Gabriel's plate. But Gabriel could not be distracted from his subtenant's indiscretion. Although Meredith had been living with him practically as a guest, if he could gossip to cabmen he was no gentleman— and for emphasis Gabriel slapped a serving spoon into the dish of meat in front of him, the hot gravy splashing into Whistler's face. Meredith took his bags and his leave.

Gabriel worked intensively on his canvases through the summer of 1863, painting as long as daylight permitted, then often entertaining in his garden (and tent) or his drawing room during the evening. His mother and sisters visited, and such luminaries as Ruskin ("he talked such awful rubbish") and Browning ("very jolly indeed") added importance to his invitations. But when William, about to leave on his annual holiday, suggested that Gabriel accompany him on a gallery-hopping trip to Belgium,

Gabriel agreed, running away, he confessed to Allingham, from "some copies, only doing [them] for filthy lucre's sake from some things of my own." Returning to his potboiling, he felt "quite as bad again" as before he left. But Ruskin's secretary, Charles Howell, a charming and unscrupulous half-Portuguese rogue, who more and more was permitted the run of Tudor House, rummaged among old and unfinished pictures, and came back with one—sometimes they did not come back—which he had cleaned and relined. It was a life-sized head of Lizzy, intended (as Gabriel wrote Ellen Heaton) "to represent Beatrice falling asleep by a wall bearing a sundial; and I have pencil sketches for it. . . . I remember you once asked me whether it would be possible to do anything of the kind from recollection. . . ." Then he had said *no*. But with the head already laid in, he returned to the canvas to paint the episode from the *Vita Nuova* in which Beatrice dies. Trancelike, her eyelids shut, Elizabeth Siddal emerged posthumously in one of Gabriel's most compelling works. But returning to Lizzy was not easy. Begun just before Christmas in 1863, it was not completed until just after Christmas in 1870.

Even to his Aunt Charlotte he felt prepared to confess that he was never so prosperous before, with "quantities of commissions." Yet he was still repaying advances for work he had never done, fending off entreaties for delivery of unfinished work for which he had accepted payment, and painting pot-boiling copies of successful earlier works. Later even the magnificent *Beata Beatrix* would be replicated (and not very well) for 900 guineas. But with prosperity—and confidence—came eagerness to promote the talents of Christina. Maria had her work, and was uncomplaining; William was a respected civil servant and carried on his double life as a critic and editor; only Christina, perhaps the most gifted of them all, seemed without occupation, although her *Goblin Market* gave rise to even greater expectations. Gabriel pressed her to produce another collection for Macmillan, but she responded, "Why rush before the public with an immature volume? I really . . . think of waiting the requisite number of months (or years as the case may be) until I have a sufficiency of quality as well as quantity." In the meantime she had her small inheritance to live on—in her brother's house—and her Charity Home.

The first printing of *Goblin Market* sold out, and Macmillan proposed a volume augmented with new poems, rather than a new printing. Christina refused, politely. But Gabriel persisted, inducing her to turn a brief verse into a long narrative poem, "The Prince's Progress," as the future title-work of the next collection. And he went through each poem she let him see, including two she singled out as having "won a word of praise from Mr. Cayley," Gabriel carefully offering praise, suggesting changes or vetoing a work altogether as a contender for the new book. Gratefully she sought—and accepted—the editorial assistance, although she was far the better-known poet. In one case a poem to which Gabriel objected was "meekly" returned, "pruned and re-written to order." Two weeks later, after still more objections from Gabriel as well as "six well-defined . . . paroxysms of stamping, foaming, [and] hair-uprooting" of her own—presumably all private and figurative, she again went along with her brother's emendations. Yet not always, for Gabriel insisted upon putting a tournament into the poem and Christina refused to tinker so drastically with it. "How shall I express my sentiments about the terrible tournament? Not a phrase to be relied on, not a correct knowledge on the subject, not the faintest impulse of inspiration, incites me to the tilt: and looming before me in horrible bugbeardom stand TWO tournaments in Tennyson's *Idylls*. . . . You see, you were next to propose my writing a classic epic in quantitative hexameters or in the hendecasyllables which might almost trip-up Tennyson, what could I do? Only what I feel inclined to do in the present instance—plead good-will but inability."

The emotional effort drained her, and she was physically exhausted as well. During the winter of 1864–65 Christina—like Lizzy years before—retreated to Hastings in search of health. She had, she knew, a "delicate chest," and racked by persistent coughing, she was certain she was coming down with consumption. But at Hastings she worked over the proofs of the new edition of *Goblin Market*, and a project of Maria's. "Have you heard of Maria's astute plan for an Italian exercise-book?" she wrote Gabriel. "I am doing some of the subordinate work for her down here in my hermitage. Truth to tell, I have a great fancy for her name endorsing a book, as we three have all got into that stage, so I work with a certain enthusiasm."

To fatten Christina's completed work into a book Gabriel hinted that some of Lizzy's poems might supplement it by sending a packet of copies to Hastings. Looking forward to it Christina wrote him, "I wonder if possibly you might ever see fit to let some of dear Lizzie's verses come out in a volume of mine; distinguished, I need not say, as hers: such a volume would be very dear to me." Once she read them she changed her mind. "How full of beauty they are, but how painful—how they bring poor Lizzie herself before one, with her voice, face and manner!" Their pathos remained overwhelming. Posting them back to Tudor House she diplomatically suggested that the "honour" of publication should be in a volume by Gabriel, but that they were "almost too hopelessly sad for publication *en masse*. . . . Perhaps this is merely my overstrained fancy, but their tone is to me even painfully despondent. . . ." She was unable to see how melancholy were her own writings.

Scheduled for 1865 publication, *The Prince's Progress* did not appear until a year later because the two drawings for it Gabriel promised Macmillan "as soon as possible" in April 1865—already a year late—were undelivered until many months afterward. Still, she wrote him, "Your protecting woodcuts help me to face my small public. . . ." But his dilatoriness did not extend to his close supervision of the final texts as well as the printer's proofs, and he even tried to alter her business relations with her publisher, which until then had been based on half-profits—the sharing of profits with no preliminary financial risk for the author. For a Charles Cayley this would have been indeed an advantageous contract, but Gabriel, used to advances on his paintings and convinced of his sister's genius, wrote Alexander Macmillan, "Now couldn't you be a good fairy & give her something down for this edition,—say £100? You know she *is* a good poet, & some day people will know it. That's so true it comes in rhyme of itself! She's going to Italy and would find a little moneybag useful." In great distress about his own financial affairs, for patrons were demanding long-paid-for portraits, and canceling commissions, Gabriel was borrowing money again where he could, and although he had no designs on his sister he was more money-conscious than ever.

Christina was embarrassed. Advances, to her pious soul, were unearned pounds, and she rebuked Gabriel gently for his "brotherliness in helping me as to business matters." Then she wrote to Macmillan assuring him that her trip to Italy was assured by "unfailing family bounty," not her new book. "So please wash your hands of the vexatious business," she wrote Gabriel; "I will settle it now myself. . . ."

With *Prince's Progress* done, the title work about a prince's hazardous—and heavily symbolic—pilgrimage to win his bride, she had written a brief poem beginning,

> Thou who didst hang upon a barren tree,
> My God, for me,
> Though I till now be barren, now at length
> Lord, give me strength
> To bring forth fruit to Thee.

At thirty-five she may have meant it literally still. But the "peccant chest," as she described it, "entered a protest against being considered well," and the trip South became more important, pressed upon her by William while Gabriel suggested "some well-bodied wine," preferably Madeira, and shipped her half a dozen bottles. (She had already become a patient of Sir William Jenner, who prescribed sherry.)

While Gabriel dallied over the woodcuts for Christina's book, working at his oils in order to "come up to the Scratch," as he put it to Rose, his harassed lawyer, William escorted his mother and Christina to Italy, the trip taking from May 22 to June 26, and including a stop in Paris—where a year before Gabriel had brazenly taken Fanny—and another in Lucerne. (In Paris William went to the Théâtre Français alone; out of some "moral scrupulosity," he wrote, Christina had ceased theatregoing at eighteen.) They crossed into Italy over the Gothard Pass, with Christina sufficiently awed by the Alpine grandeur to break into verse, her poems collectively titled *En Route* becoming her reminiscences of their Italian stay as well as the journey there. The last poem was a passionate farewell to Italy, and the "half familiar speech," which she called, in a companion piece written from "that bleak North" of London in July, a "country half my own."

Back home William reported to Macmillan that, although the weeks away had been "a great delight," Italy "did not produce the sensible improvement [in Christina] I had hoped for." Awaiting publication of her book, frustrated by Gabriel's failure to produce two illustrations for it, and still feeling unwell, Christina lapsed into a new depression. Nine days before Christmas, 1865, she was writing the obvious to Macmillan—that "as for the old sore: you know the woodcuts cannot be ready for Xmas?—I hardly know how to ask you now to keep back *P.P.* after your 'few days' advertisement; yet if you agree with me in thinking Gabriel's designs too desirable to forego, I will try to follow your example of patience under disappointment."

With nothing around him going right, William found it difficult to keep up his air of busy serenity, and surprised the guests at the splendid wedding of Holman Hunt to the well-to-do Fanny Waugh, where he was a witness (while Gabriel was absent altogether), by being genial. According to Frederic Stephens, William had "for some reason been against everyone and everything lately," but had recovered his good humor. Very likely he had merely put it on for the wedding. Holman Hunt was thirty-eight, and his bride thirty-two. Thirty-five himself, and with his bald head and greying beard adding even more years to his appearance, William could have been pardoned for thinking that he had wasted his chances on the wrong woman; but if Hunt were an example, William still had his life to live.

Gabriel wasted no time on further self-pity. To his uncle, Henry Polydore, from whom he had borrowed money, he had written in November, "Referring to my diary, I find there have been only twelve days during the five months ending with the close of October which have not been spent by me in work at my easel. I have completely missed all exercise and change of air this year." And to Allingham the day after Christmas he insisted, "I have not had a single day out of London this year except once to

Greenwich with Boyce, and once walking to Tottenham. For all that I've not done half I meant to do."

Early in February, 1866 he had finally finished sketches for two wood blocks for Christina's book, and promised a third "when that is cut." None was done, and Macmillan waited no longer once he had the two blocks in April, one of them the frontispiece illustration representing the prince who, having tarried so long on the way, finds his bride dead when he arrives. The episode may have had special meaning for Gabriel, complicating his already fragile balance. It was a low period for him. He was getting paunchy; his hair and beard, trimmed infrequently, were beginning to grey; his eyes were invariably hollow with fatigue. His energies had declined after a winter of sleeplessness and overwork, and he was also suffering the discomforts of a hydrocele,* for which he would need intermittent surgical relief and which at intervals complicated—perhaps even seemed to him a judgment upon—his sexual life. At times it appeared that he was losing his grip on himself. Boyce, for example, described an excursion they took on Whit Monday—May 21—to Rye House to Hertfordshire, having jointly hired a hansom for twenty-five shillings for the round trip. "It being a brilliant day and the meadows thick with grass and buttercups and the trees gay with young green leaves, we enjoyed the trip very much. . . . Got some grub with difficulty. . . . Gabriel somehow or other, perhaps by taking whisky, etc. on an empty stomach, got rather drunk and quarrelsome and fell down in the dark passage leading to the dungeons and lost his overcoat. Fortunately I noticed his disappearance and pulled him up or he would have been trodden on by the streams of people. After some fuss the overcoat was regained, though torn." Some of Gabriel's confidence was going.

Early in June *The Prince's Progress* was finally out. Christina received her first copies while at Alice Boyd's Penkill Castle, inland from the Firth of Clyde, having traveled to Scotland with the complaisant Letitia Scott, whose husband had acquired the wealthy Miss Boyd as mistress seven years before. The *ménage à trois* had prospered, although the innocent Christina may not have known it existed. Alice Boyd would winter in London with the Scotts (who had moved there from Newcastle), and Bell Scott, with or without his wife, would spend the summer and fall at Penkill. To her brother William, again in Italy, she wrote happily, "You are not badly off if you are only in country as fine as this." Her health had improved. She was being congratulated, she wrote, on her "looks and *fat*."

Part of her happier frame of mind may have been due to her deliberate escape from London and the ordeal of confronting reviews of her book,

---

* A painful accumulation of fluid in the testes, relieved by tapping.

although she discovered little to fear, William furnishing discreet support by inserting into a long review of Swinburne's *Poems and Ballads* he had published as a small book praise of his sister's "internal sense of fitness, a mental touch as delicate as the finger-tips of the blind." Defusing adverse criticism in the press proved unnecessary, the *Athenaeum* only regretting her "religiously submissive" tone while the *Saturday Review* praised her poetry in Shelley's definition as "a record of the best and happiest moments of the best and happiest minds." She was satisfied, and let her "poor brain" continue to "lie fallow" while she savored her comparative solitude, which was apparently so complete, despite the presence of Miss Boyd and Mrs. Scott, that among her satisfactions of such a stay—perhaps this one, since there were only two—was an incident (recalled in her *Time Flies*) remarkable for its picture of her reverence for life:

Once in Scotland, while staying at a hospitable friend's castle, I observed, crossing the floor of my bedroom, a rural insect. I will call it, though I daresay it was not one in strictness, a pill millepede.

Towards my co-tenant I felt a sort of good will not inconsistent with an impulse to eject it through the window.

I stooped and took it up, when in a moment a swarm of baby millepedes occupied my hand in their parent's company.

Surprised, but resolute, I hurried on, and carried out my scheme successfully; observing the juniors retire into cracks outside the window as adroitly as if they had been centenarians.

While Christina remained at Penkill, Gabriel was working on the first of what would be many portraits of a woman he had tried to dismiss from his life when his duties lay elsewhere. He had always remained friendly with Jane Morris, but there was nothing in his courtly relationship with her and his bantering relationship with "Top," to outwardly suggest his story, "The Cup of Cold Water." He had drawn her the year before, but had even refrained from painting her, alternating instead between Fanny and hired models, his favorite of them beginning in the mid-1860s and continuing long thereafter the attractive and loyal Alexa Wilding, whom he had met, like so many earlier models, casually in the street.* Reporting his beginning of a canvas of "Janey," to Madox Brown, Gabriel curiously added a sketch

---

* A letter from her, dated April 8, 1865, from 23 Warwick Lane, Newgate Market, declares that "she has obtained her Mamma's permission to sit for any picture. . . ." Rossetti kept her on a weekly retainer of thirty shillings thereafter to secure her exclusive services. Another, a pretty laundress named Ellen Smith, became his model under similar circumstances, but had worse luck. When she was disfigured by a brutal soldier who had dallied with her, her career as Gabriel's model was over.

of himself he titled "Physical condition and mental attitude." Beneath he wrote, "The burden of conscious fat and hypocrisy, the stings of remorse, the haunting dread of exposure as every motion wafted the outer garment to this side or that, the senses quickened to catch the sound of fatal rents,—all this and more over the scene that veil which Fate respected." He drew himself tearing his hair, and with a tear in the back of his waistcoat; and cartooned in the background were Morris, Madox Brown and his daughter Lucy, and others. It was apparently intended entirely as jest, but was more than that. He was covering some real concerns with a caricature.

On Christina's return from Penkill, prompted, perhaps, by the long separation from her, the undemonstrative Cayley brought himself to propose marriage. While she withheld an answer, clearly concerned about his lack of wherewithal to support a wife as well as his lack of religion, William interposed. A promotion at the Excise Office was impending, he knew, and with it some added income.* He also had no expectations for himself except continued bachelorhood. "While the question was still somewhat in suspense, and when I had become aware of my sister's feelings," William remembered, "I urged her in express terms not to hesitate to marry, as she and her husband would be most welcome to live in my house as members of the family." Christina needed time and distance from Albany Street to think it over. Finally, on September 11, 1866, William received a penciled note from her:

I am writing as I walk along the road with a party. I can't tell you what I feel at your most more than brotherly letter. Of course I am not *merely* the happier for what has occurred, but I gain much in knowing how much I am loved beyond my deserts. As to money, I might be selfish enough to wish that were the only bar, but you see from my point of view it is not. Now I am at least unselfish enough altogether to deprecate seeing C.B.C. continually (with nothing but mere feeling to offer) to his hamper and discomfort: but, if he likes to see me, God knows I like to see him, and any kindness you will show him will only be additional kindness loaded on me.

I prefer writing before we meet, though you're not very formidable.

In rejecting William's proposed financial sacrifice, Christina made no effort to win Cayley to a religious accommodation with her. She was prepared to reject, at thirty-six, a last chance at matrimony rather than to reject a single tenet of her faith, or coerce Cayley into obvious religious hypocrisies. As William explained it, Christina understood that Cayley was

---

* In July 1866 the Keepership of the Print Room of the British Museum had fallen vacant and William proposed that either he or Bell Scott bid for the job. Scott declined, and told William that for him, too, it would not be "worth your while."

"either absolutely not a Christian, or else so removed from fully defined religious orthodoxy that she could not regard him as sharing the essence of her own beliefs. She consequently, with a sore heart, declined to be his wife." But she did not stop seeing him on the old terms. The cautious minuet of small courtesies and small talk was apparently preferable, at thirty-six, to more intense intimacies. On the surface it may have been to Christina a profound matter of conscience, but in her way she had succeeded where Henrietta Rintoul had failed.*

In 1870, with nothing changed, Christina wrote a poem, "By Way of Remembrance," in which she asked "my brother and my friend" to have patience with her "till the hidden end":

> I love you and you know it—this at least,
>   This comfort is mine own in all my pain:
>   You know it, and can never doubt again,
> And love's mere self is a continual feast:
> Not oath of mine nor blessing-word of priest
>   Could make my love more certain or more plain. . . .

It was addressed to Cayley. But rather than let him see it, she put it in a drawer.

At Cheyne Walk, Gabriel made no pretense that William's aid offered Christina could not be put to other use. He would not have let William pay the rent, he confided to his mother just before Christmas, "but for unusual pressure." The white mice had disappeared, he added, but he hoped they would "pick up a living," and the hedgehogs had been "let loose in the garden, being rather troublesome indoors." Despite the hazards of the menagerie, all the Rossettis but Maria dined at Tudor House on New Year's Day, 1867, the repast resulting from William's money. Snow fell through the evening, turning his garden, Gabriel exulted, into a North Pole. But it meant that Mrs. Rossetti and Christina had to spend a rare night in a Tudor House bed, and Fanny a rare night out of one.

Maria had not joined the others. Although she made rare, dutiful visits to Tudor House to accompany her mother, the unseen presence of Fanny loomed large in her mind. Coincidence or not, Gabriel insisted on not accepting social invitations for Sundays, which he kept free for Fanny, who felt "dismal" about being left alone. And on a Sunday none of the Rossetti women would travel farther from home than the Albany Street church. Still, Gabriel respected Maria's pious snubs, and even offered his help when, early

---

* As part of Henrietta's campaign to forget William, she made a trip to Russia in 1864–65, but nevertheless kept in intermittent touch with Christina.

in 1867, her *Exercises in Idiomatic Italian*, together with its companion "key," *Anedotti Italiani*, were ready for the printer. Adolph Heimann had recommended the publisher, Williams and Norgate, and William and Gabriel scrutinized the contract as if the work would become a bestseller. The idea was to teach idiomatic Italian by putting together words which in English sequence seemed grotesque yet when translated literally made good Italian. But it only worked in one direction: Italian students who might have experimented with English by using the method in reverse would have evoked laughter.

The method had worked well for Maria's pupils, but sold to others very slowly. At the end of the first year only eighty copies had been disposed of, while only fifty of the key. The publishers were patient. Twenty years later it was turning out a profit. But Maria, copies in hand for her own students, returned immediately on publication to her long-planned study of Dante.

By January 11, Gabriel was hard up once more, plagued by a butterman's long accumulated bill of "£50 odd." He sent his manservant, Loader, to Somerset House to have William cosign a note so that the money could be borrowed, and went back to toiling over pictures long due, interrupting work on them for potboiling over "replicas" and watercolors which would bring in quick income. The large canvases, especially those paid for, were losing their interest for him, and he even made efforts to abrogate his pledge to complete *Found* for James Leathart. He would paint other pictures and refund the rest of the money—when he could—in order, he wrote the Newcastle lead merchant, to leave the impression that he had not "behaved badly in the long run." Nothing was going right. Leathart wanted all of his money rather than substitute pictures. A "maniac" solicitor, L. P. Valpy, who was so terrified of nudes that even bare arms disquieted his Victorian soul, wanted to buy a Rossetti canvas—but only one already sold to Frederick Craven, and thus to Gabriel "a dead 'oss." And when Gabriel finally thought he had convinced him to purchase other pictures, he dropped out of the market altogether. "Valpy has proved a bad lot," Gabriel complained to Madox Brown in the summer of 1867. "Just as he was beginning to buy, he has engaged to get married and is done for." Even worse, Ind Coope brewer C. P. Matthews, who suddenly appeared as a *deus ex machina* offering fifteen hundred urgently needed guineas for an unpainted *Perseus and Medusa*, afterwards took fright at the thought of Medusa's severed head and serpentine locks, and canceled the commission. Then the shade of Lizzy even appeared at Cheyne Walk in the form of a begging letter from Harry Siddall, and Gabriel sent ten pounds he could not spare.

Although in 1867 Gabriel would generate an income of over £3,000, in the process reducing his debts to £1,000, the reason lay in Treffry Dunn, his replacement for Knewstub as art assistant. But for the central figures themselves, Rossetti's lucrative "replicas" saw little of the Rossetti brush, except when it was in Dunn's hand. An artist of integrity, he would not pass off someone else's work as his own, but background and what he called "accessories" were something else. "I would like you to get the reduced outline exactly correct first," he wrote to Dunn about one copy, "after which you might proceed to lay in the background in oil, but the whole of the figures would have I think to be done by myself. . . ."

Despite his beginning of a profitable trade in replicas, in midsummer of 1867 Gabriel was more harassed by claims upon his canvases and his cash than ever before. The small army of tradesmen who had furnished him with everything from paints and frames to animals and port wine, continually pressed for payment. The burden of meeting his debts and his artistic obligations affected both Gabriel and his work, both often becoming coarsely commercial. As his biographer Doughty put it, "Consequent over-work, inevitably often inferior painting, mental and physical fatigue, financial worry itself, and lack of exercise, all gradually wore down his morale, encouraged his tendency toward neurotic anxiety previously induced by his natural disposition and unhappy past." The resulting insomnia wrecked his nights and defeated his days.

William slept well. In 1867 he was promoted to Committee Clerk at the Excise Office, putting him in direct working contact with one of the Inland Revenue Commissioners. A "larger and better-looking house" was in order, especially since he now expected to house indefinitely his mother and sisters and surviving aunts Eliza and Charlotte. For £125 annual rent,* he settled on 56 Euston Square (afterwards renamed 5 Endsleigh Gardens), with a front vista of treelined square. Late in June, 1867, the family shifted addresses, and William was able to spend his evenings again at literary work, which did little more than pay the rent, but was one way in which he maintained his contacts with the less dull world in which he would have rather moved. The other way was always expensive and never without interest. For William it could have been a full-time occupation to be his brother's keeper, and some days, and weeks, it was.

---

* Part of it paid by his mother and aunts Eliza and Charlotte. Margaret Polidori had died.

1. *The Girlhood of Mary Virgin,* by Dante
Gabriel Rossetti. Oil on canvas. Dated
"PRB 1849." Gabriel's mother and sister
sat for St. Anne and the Virgin. Tate
Gallery No. 4872. *Courtesy the
Tate Gallery.*

4. Ford Madox Brown, by Dante Gabriel Rossetti. Pencil. Dated "Nov/52." National Portrait Gallery, London, No. 1021. *Reproduced courtesy the National Portrait Gallery.*

6. William Holman Hunt, by Dante Gabriel Rossetti. Oval. Pencil. Dated "12th April 1853." Once attributed erroneously to F. G. Stephens. Birmingham City Museum and Art Gallery No. 392 '04. *Courtesy the Birmingham City Museum and Art Gallery.*

2. *Ecce Ancilla Domini (The Annunciation)*, by Dante Gabriel Rossetti. Oil on canvas mounted on panel. Dated "March 1850." The Virgin is painted from Christina, the head of the Angel from William. Tate Gallery No. 1210. *Courtesy the Tate Gallery.*

3. Dante Gabriel Rossetti, by William Holman Hunt. Oval. Dated "1853." Birmingham City Museum and Art Gallery No. 33–61. *Courtesy the Birmingham City Museum and Art Gallery.*

5. D. G. Rossetti sitting to Elizabeth Siddal, by Dante Gabriel Rossetti. Dated "Sept 1853." Birmingham City Museum and Art Gallery No. 480 '04. *Courtesy the Birmingham City Museum and Art Gallery.*

7. William Rossetti in 1855, by Ford Madox Brown.
Wightwick Manor. *Courtesy of Lady Mander.*

8. Gabriele Rossetti, in his familiar
cap with eye-shade, by Dante
Gabriel Rossetti. Pencil. Dated
"April 28/53." *Courtesy of Mrs.
Roderic O'Conor, Henley-on-Thames.*

9. Charles Cayley, by Dante
Gabriel Rossetti. Pen and ink. Ca.
1853. Once owned by W. B. Scott
and/or Alice Boyd. *Courtesy of
T. R. R. O'Conor,
Goring-on-Thames, Reading.*

10. *Ophelia*, by John Millais.
Oil on canvas. Elizabeth Siddal
posed for the drowning Ophelia.
Tate Gallery No. 1506.
Courtesy the Tate Gallery.

11. Elizabeth Siddal, by Dante Gabriel Rossetti. Pencil. 1854. Birmingham City Museum and Art Gallery No. 260 '04. *Courtesy the Birmingham City Museum and Art Gallery.*

12. Elizabeth Siddal, by Dante Gabriel Rossetti. Pencil, pen and ink. Dated "Hastings June 1854." Fitzwilliam Museum No. 2147. *Reproduced by permission of the Syndics of the Fitzwilliam Museum, Cambridge.*

13. Elizabeth Siddal, by Dante Gabriel Rossetti. Pen and brown and black ink. Dated "Feb 6th 1855." Ashmolean Museum No. E 1152. *Courtesy the Ashmolean Museum, Oxford.*

14. *Study of Two Girls,*
by Dante Gabriel Rossetti.
Pen and brown ink and
wash. Originally intended
for "The Ballad of Fair
Annie" as part of an
abortive mid-1850s project
for an illustrated *Old
English Ballads.* Possibly
an influence upon
Christina Rossetti's
"Goblin Market" (see
chapter VII). Birming-
ham City Museum and
Art Gallery No. 360 '04.
*Courtesy the Birmingham
City Museum and Art
Gallery.*

15. *Head of a Girl* [Fanny
Cornforth], by Dante
Gabriel Rossetti. Pencil.
Dated in the hand of the
purchaser, G. P. Boyce,
"July 23, 1859." The
young woman is Fanny
at a time when her friend-
ship with Gabriel was still
relatively new. Tate
Gallery No. 4286a.
Courtesy the Tate Gallery.

17. William Michael Rossetti as a young man. *From a photograph reproduced courtesy of Professor W. E. Fredeman, and first printed in his edition of WMR's* Pre-Raphaelite Diary *(1975).*

16. Dante Gabriel Rossetti. Self-portrait. Pencil. Dated "Oct. 1861." Birmingham City Museum and Art Gallery No. 479 '04. *Courtesy the Birmingham City Museum and Art Gallery.*

18. Charles Cayley. From a photograph, probably taken in the 1860s, reproduced in William Rossetti's *Some Reminiscences.*

19. *Beata Beatrix,* by Dante Gabriel Rossetti.
Oil on canvas. 1863-64. Painted by DGR
from studies of his late wife. Tate Gallery
No. 1279. *Courtesy the Tate Gallery.*

21. Maria Francesca Rossetti. A
photograph taken around 1874,
when she became an Anglican nun.
From William Rossetti's *Some
Reminiscences.*

20. Study for the Prince, by Dante
Gabriel Rossetti, for an illustration
for Christina Rossetti's *The
Prince's Progress.* Pen and India
ink over pencil. Ca. 1865-66.
Birmingham City Museum and
Art Gallery No. 424 '04. *Courtesy
the Birmingham City Museum and
Art Gallery.*

22. *Perlascura*, by Dante Gabriel Rossetti. Pastel on pale
green paper. Dated 1871. Painted from Jane Morris and
emphasizing the long sweep of her neck. Ashmolean Museum
No. E 1136. *Courtesy the Ashmolean Museum, Oxford.*

23. Lucy Madox Brown Rossetti (Mrs. William Rossetti),
by Dante Gabriel Rossetti. Chalks on pale green paper.
1874. *Courtesy of Mrs. Roderic O'Conor, Henley-on-Thames.*

24. Christina Rossetti and her
mother, by Dante Gabriel Rossetti.
Colored chalks. 1877. National
Portrait Gallery, London, No. 990.
*Reproduced courtesy the National
Portrait Gallery.*

25. Henrietta Rintoul at about
thirty. William Rossetti kept her
picture all his life, and near the end
of her own life his daughter Helen
gave the photograph to
W. E. Fredeman.

26. *The Day Dream*, by Dante Gabriel Rossetti. Oil on canvas. Dated
1880. Commissioned by Constantine Ionides from a drawing of Jane
Morris dating back to at least 1872, but painted as well from life.
Ashmolean Museum No. E 1140. *Courtesy the Ashmolean Museum, Oxford.*

X
Omens
1867-1868

Increasingly haunted by remorse and anxiety, Gabriel was prey to any phenomenon which would reinforce his brooding. In 1865 and 1866, while Whistler's straight-laced mother was away, his red-haired mistress Jo would move in and entertain Gabriel and the otherwise unwelcome Fanny at Lindsey Row, where Jo would sometimes officiate at séances. In 1852 the first American medium to get extensive press coverage had arrived in London. Almost immediately, manifestations of rapping were recorded all over England, ladies even sending out invitations to "Tea and Table-Turning." Queen Victoria herself was alleged to have attempted communication with Prince Albert's shade, having, even earlier, awarded to one Georgina Eagle a medal for "Meritorious and Extraordinary Clairvoyance"; and from the Court down, interest in occult phenomena burgeoned.

"We often had table-turning at Jimmy's," Luke Ionides remembered, "but no very important results. He had an idea that Jo was a bit of a medium; certainly, the raps were more frequent when she was at the table, but I cannot recall any message worth repeating. Jimmy believed in it more or less." One day when Rossetti joined them, he broke up the séance after a time by warning, "You'd better stop that, otherwise you will all go mad." He knew why from experience.

Once, when Whistler was about to leave his studio with Jo (so he later told Mortimer Menpes, a disciple) he suddenly asked her to place her hands upon a table and use her willpower. She did, and soon there was a knocking and rapping seemingly emanating from the table. "Gentle spirit," Whistler inquired tentatively, "is it good?" There were more noises, identified as indicating that the spirit was saying, "No, it is bad." "Gentle spirit," said Whistler then, "don't come again!" And to make sure he removed the table.

Rossetti—for reasons of his own—encouraged Jo's experiments in spirit-rapping at his own house; however Whistler's memories were of Lindsey Row. "One day, I and the White Girl went into her room and just the two of us alone tried the same experiment, and a cousin from the South talked to me and told me the most wonderful things. Again by holding a lacquer box, a beautiful Japanese box, one of the many wonderful things in the Chelsea house, between us, we had the same sort of manifestations. But it is a study, really, that would engross a man's whole lifetime, and I have my painting to engross me. [Do] I believe? Yes." Browning dramatized the dilemma in "Mr. Sludge, 'the Medium' ":

> One does see somewhat when one shuts one's eyes
> If only spots and streaks; tables do tip
> In the oddest way of themselves; and pens, good Lord,
> Who knows if you drive them, or they drive you?

Yet Browning remained a skeptic, although his late wife to the end had thought that there might be something in it. So did Whistler. "The silliness, as a rule, of the spirit's performance? They may seem silly now, but wasn't the beginning of some of the wonderful electrical contrivances we have the mere dancing of little paper dolls on a table? The darkness that is always necessary? Why not? Everyone knows, there are certain chemicals that act only in the darkness. Why should it not be the same with the spirits? How can we understand the conditions that rule them? For myself, I have no doubt—the very fact that man, beginning with the savage, has always believed in them is proof enough."

To Gabriel, who had discussed the matter with her, Christina talked of the occult as threat to her religious beliefs. The Davenport Brothers, an American spiritualist group which specialized in pre-Houdini escapes from rope bindings, had been attributing their hairbreadth releases to the agency of spirits. "To me," Christina wrote Gabriel, "the whole subject is awful and mysterious; though, in spite of my hopeless inability to conceive a clue to the source of sundry manifestations, I still hope simple imposture may be the missing key." Further, she appealed, "Please God, I will have nothing to do with spiritualism, whether it be imposture or a black art; or with hypnotism, lest wilful self-surrender become my road to evil choice. . . ."

Haunted by what William called "poignant memories and painful associations" related to the death of Lizzy, Gabriel "was prone to think that some secret might yet be wrested from the grave." Seeking that secret in hope of allaying his own sense of guilt, Gabriel became an easy mark for the occultists, for although he was without religion, he was superstitious even to worrying over thirteen at the dinner table. Early in October, 1865, Bell Scott noted in a letter a piece of gossip he had picked up from William—that Gabriel claimed that his wife was "constantly appearing (that is, rapping out things) at the séances in Cheyne Walk—! William affirms that the things so communicated are such as only she could know. No reasoning seems to have the least effect with these absurd people. I am going to be present on Friday evening, but expect nothing but rubbish." William, Scott had realized, although the most thorough skeptic of the four Rossettis, and the natural person—as brotherly confidant—to supply the antidote, had found himself unable to furnish it. He wanted to experience the phenomenon himself, and in another setting than at his brother's house, to confirm his unbelief, but when he encountered the allegedly occult his curiosity was only whetted, and his growing inability to remain an unbeliever helped undermine Gabriel's tenuous hold on himself.

After William's first table-turning he wrote Anne Gilchrist, "I must avow, at the risk of seeming very absurd, that I am a believer—i.e., things do actually take place which I cannot account for by any physical hypothesis, or any deception of the senses, & which would be adequately accounted for by the spirit hypothesis, which therefore, till something better offers . . . , I feel no hostility to."

He had been invited by his entrepreneur friend Captain Ruxton, in November 1865, to a séance conducted by a washerwoman medium, Mrs. Marshall, at her home. Several correct answers rapped out at her table left him wondering. He and Ruxton had come unannounced, and he could not, he wrote Mrs. Gilchrist, "quite bolt the idea that Mrs. Marshall knew who I was, or that I was a friend of a painter deceased these three or four years & little known to the public named John Cross. . . ."

On January 4, 1866, at the home of the historian Thomas Keightley, William had managed, he thought, to communicate with Lizzy. A. C. Lyster, Keightley's nephew and a colleague of William's at the Inland Revenue Office, could get nowhere with the "spirit," which asked, rather, for William, who proceeded to elicit answers by first writing down an alphabet and then waiting for appropriate knocks as he touched the relevant letters. "Spell your surname." "EROSS." "Is E the initial of your Christian name?" "Yes." "Is *R* the initial of your surname?" "Yes." "Are you Lizzie, my brother's wife?" "Yes." Some reasonably right responses followed, but more that were ambiguous or wrong; yet it had been an improvement over one the Rossetti brothers had conducted, with Fanny, at a small, shaky japanned table in Tudor House six weeks before, where "ERSS" had been identified, and Gabriel had received an affirmative to "Are you Lizzie?" The rest had been muddled, but it had not prevented William from trying again at Scott's home in Elgin Road on November 25, where "Lizzie professed to come." From Penkill, Alice Boyd had cautioned Scott about involving himself with the occult, but he had answered, "You need not be uncomfortable about the bogies. I need only tell you it was simply childish, and lowers my two very dear friends William and D.G. immensely in my judgment. It is all [because of] that three-waisted creature, who makes society there intolerable." The increasingly plump Fanny was not one of Bell Scott's favorite females.

At Scott's home, the shade of Elizabeth Siddal recalled Scott but could not name the district of London in which she first saw him, considered that William was "an affectionate brother" to her, and claimed to have seen him with Gabriel at breakfast that morning in Chelsea. But she could not say who else had been present. (Mrs. Rossetti and Christina had also been there.) "What is my elder sister's name?" "MARI–." "My younger sister's?" There were no more raps, but Scott's skepticism was somewhat shaken. To William he wrote, "As Miss Boyd has expressed an extreme dislike to have anything to do with spiritualism, please don't mention to anyone our experience of Saturday, which was certainly remarkable enough to be worthy of mentioning. I do not wish she should know of all things in the world."

When William tried again at the Marshalls, returning with the puzzled but curious Scott, he asked to be put in touch again with "the same spirit who had communicated with me on the previous occasion." All the medium's efforts failed to raise Cross. "Surely if Mrs. Marshall could supply that name on the first occasion," he wrote Mrs. Gilchrist, "she could all the more do so on the second." It reinforced his intimations of the medium's integrity.

Scott, personally unknown to the Marshalls, asked, "I have a particular deceased friend in my mind: will he communicate with me?" "Yes." "What was your surname?" "Boyd." "Christian name?" "Spencer." "What was the name of my street in which you died?" "Elden Road." "How long ago?" "Eight months." Boyd had died in a house in *Elgin* Road ten months before. Scott was impressed, because the old washerwoman and her daughter-in-law were "uncultivated and mentally unfurnished." But a second visit "had the opposite effect. I saw in the approximation to truth the clever guessing of the practised thought-reader by the expression of the [visitor's] counte-nance. Every card-sharper has this faculty, showing him how far he may go. . . . It was at best guessing nearly right while the first clue guided. . . . Reading the expression is the art. . . ."

The next year, Scott still saw Gabriel as "gay and hospitable, carefully hiding the wound which . . . continued to bite." But Gabriel was experimenting further at table-turning in order to try to call up from Highgate the source of that wound. On February 16, in the studio at Cheyne Walk, while he worked by gaslight at a long-unfinished design of Hamlet and Ophelia, the woman having been modeled from Lizzy in 1858, William and Fanny sat at the familiar japanned table and successfully invoked the "bogey" of Lizzy, this time understanding "EERS" to be Elizabeth Eleanor Rossetti. Gabriel then took William's place at the table, William standing aside and recording what appeared to be tapped out as the alphabet was pointed to. Was Lizzy happy now? "Yes." Happier than when she began spirit communication? "Yes." Did she like Gabriel's last picture, *The Beloved,* just sent off to James Rae? "Yes." Soon there came a mental question from Gabriel: he had thought of a name, and wanted its initials. An *H* and an *S* were tapped out. He had been thinking of her brother Harry, the subject of the awful note that was still giving him sleepless nights. Other answers came, correctly, after which Gabriel asked, "So it was you who made raps in the bedroom the other night?" (Fanny had heard the tapping, presumably to her terror,* but not Gabriel.) The answer was "Yes."

Gabriel then left the table, changing places with William, and resumed his drawing. The rapping continued, responding to questions about Gabriel's patron James Rae, where Rae's new picture was hung, how many Rossettis he owned, until there was a long pause—about fifteen minutes—after which William felt prepared to ask whether during the long silence "Lizzy" had been looking into Rae's house. "Yes." "Can you give me any idea of the process by which you pass from one place to another?" "No." "Are you always about this house?" "Yes." Few answers were wrong, and even one thought to be off the mark, on investigation, proved to be right after all—that Lizzy's married sister Clara lived in Australia. After that, "the tendency of the table to move," William noted in his diary, ceased.

On May 12, 1866, in the back sitting room of Charles Howell's house in Brixton, the Howell family (some of them nervous), Gabriel and William tried table-turning by firelight, after pledging, each to the others, to "abstain from any tricks," a necessity with the charmingly untrustworthy Howell. First the table "ticked," then tilted, the hands of all parties presumably on the table, the feet of all parties presumably on the floor. Finally Gabriel asked, "Is any spirit present?" and the expected three tilts (for "yes") occurred. This time, not to Gabriel's surprise, the name spelled out began as

---

* At one table-turning session Fanny's mother professed to come but Fanny declined any communication.

"ELI"—after which he called a halt, and then "ROS"—after which he stopped to ask the last letter of the surname. It was an *I*. Understanding it to be "Elizabeth Rossetti," he asked, "Will you give [me] a message?" "Yes." "Give it." "Love your Liz." William's diary suggests that there was considerable surprise, after which the entry reads, "We did not pursue this line of questioning, nor did anything else of a marked kind occur."

Gabriel and William tried other séances over the months, with no reappearance of "Lizzy," but the need of the brothers to conjure her up remained powerful. Finally, near midnight on August 14, with the gaslight lowered at Cheyne Walk, William, Dunn and Fanny seated themselves at a sturdy round table in the studio, while Gabriel stood by in another room. Quickly, strong rapping and tilting began, and "ER" identified herself. Gabriel joined. "Are you my wife?" "Yes." "Happier than on earth?" "Yes." "If I were to join you, should I be happy?" "Yes." "Should I see you at once?" "No." "Quite soon?" "No." "Tilt the table to the person you like best." The table tilted toward Gabriel, who then asked whether she liked Fanny. "Yes." "But some while ago you used not to like her?" "No." * "Did you pull her hair on a particular occasion?" (William recalled being present when Fanny felt her hair being mysteriously tugged.) "Yes." Although "Lizzy" then offered to do it "now," nothing of the sort occurred, and after some desultory questions and answers Gabriel asked whether Lizzy knew his father "in the world of spirits." "Yes." The "bogey" of old Gabriele was summoned, and asked whether his theories about Dante were proved correct in the hereafter. "Yes." "Will you speak to me in Italian?" "No." Soon the old *Professore* faded out, having been in error on the question, "Do you know where Christina is?" (She was away from London, in Leeds.) The purported shade of Lizzy returned, to be asked such questions as what would be the outcome of Christina's illness (she did not know), and her opinion of Howell ("disgraceful character"). It was two in the morning when the "manifestations" ceased. Whether Gabriel slept any the better is unknown. It was not the last time he sensed the presence of his dead wife, but it was the last of twenty séances William recorded. By that time Gabriel was in the throes of chronic and deepening insomnia, and was having serious problems with his vision. Finding daylight painful, he further curtained his rooms, and seldom left Cheyne Walk until after dark. Lizzy had never lived at Tudor House, but her presence there, whatever the truths of table-turning, seemed undeniable.

Had the "bogey" been correct about Christina, it would have known that she was out of London as much as at home, convalescing from what Dr.

---

* Presumably meaning "No, I did not."

Jenner described as congestion of the lungs, and indulging in her "invalid habits." In the summer of 1866 she spent six weeks at Penkill Castle, traveling back and forth with Letitia Scott, and modeling for Lady Jane Grey in the murals Scott was painting as his ostensible reason for living at the castle with Alice Boyd. Later he would ignore the proprieties.

"Christina and Letitia are here," Scott wrote William from Penkill in July, "and living with 3 ladies, religion and ailments forming a large portion of daily life and talk, is not exhilarating. As for Christina and I, we fight like cats, as is our nature. . . ." The report may have been ironic, given Christina's convalescent ways, but they could have argued about religion.* On her return to Euston Square Christina continued her routine of writing and churchgoing, which was sometimes interrupted by quiet dinner parties, usually William's doing, Browning turning up twice. At another Rossetti dinner Anne Gilchrist, whom both William and Gabriel had helped complete her husband's book on Blake, recorded that Madox Brown's artist daughter Lucy (now twenty-four) was present, as well as "a gifted man of the name of Cayley," who had joined with the Rossettis in coining an Italian name for their favorite furry animal, Christina afterwards writing verses on "L'Uumibatto." She sent them to Gabriel (who had purchased what William called a "lumpish" one for £8) with the explanatory couplet,

> When wombats do inspire
> I strike my disused lyre.

Cayley offered other additions to the menagerie, a friend needing someone to care for two peacocks for the summer. As fee Gabriel was to have any offspring. But at Tudor House only the nocturnal creatures saw much of Gabriel. The lights remained on, many nights, until dawn, as Gabriel wrestled with insomnia in his heavily curtained bedroom; and at his easel his eyes blurred, and he experienced giddiness, at exposure to the dull glare of the usual London day. He seldom went to the theatre, for gaslight tormented his eyes as much as daylight, and seldom was seen in public at all, evading attendance even at the wedding of his crony and picture-dealer Charles Augustus Howell, although William, and even Christina, signed the register at St. Matthew's Church, Brixton, and Madox Brown's two daughters were bridesmaids. Much of Gabriel's agony, William realized, resulted from the clash of Gabriel's two guilty loves, one dead, the other someone else's wife. Gabriel's friends assumed only the continuing remorse

---

* Lona Packer's *Christina Rossetti* (1965) manufactures a thesis that Christina had a decades-long frustrated emotional attachment to Scott, but the circumstantial and suppositional structure of her argument has been largely exploded.

over Lizzy. He had summoned her in séances, sent her verses to Christina, photographed her drawings and sent them to Allingham. "Short, sad and strange her life," Allingham mused in his diary; "it must have seemed to her like a troubled dream." But it was Gabriel's sleep that was troubled. In an 1868 sonnet, "Sleepless Dreams," he wondered,

> O lonely night! art thou not known to me,
> A thicket hung with masks of mockery
> And watered with the wasteful warmth of tears?

Nocturnal wanderings along the Thames, and into the narrow gaslit Chelsea streets, only postponed the inevitable retreat to his bed, where one "fearful" night succeeded another. When he closed his eyes he experienced a "whirling" and a "flickering," and symptoms he associated with approaching apoplexy; and he resorted at Scott's suggestion to "whisky-toddy," for which he had "no taste" but only need. Three eye specialists saw him. Gull found no organic disease. Critchett thought he detected a minor malformation of the eye for which his muscles could not compensate, and prescribed strong glasses. (Sometimes Gabriel wore one pair atop another.) Bowman sagely suggested that Gabriel leave Cheyne Walk for a while, and reduce his emotional strain.

His first such experiment took him to Lymington, where Allingham's Customs' duties had transferred him. The train from London arrived on the evening of September 11, 1867, after which Rossetti and Allingham talked into the morning, Gabriel not being eager to go to bed. Two days later he announced that he was ready to explore the area, and they walked about looking for roses suitable for a background to a picture he had brought with him. But for the most part he preferred to do nothing. Although Gabriel wrote his mother that he was walking ten miles a day for his health, Allingham's diary recorded that most days Gabriel had not been out at all, had not even opened his picture-case, and was instead reading *The Mill on the Floss*, and collecting money mailed him for copies being painted by Treffry Dunn at Cheyne Walk. One Sunday they walked to the seacliffs to admire the view toward the Isle of Wight, and talked of Home and other spiritualists, "about whom D.G.R. has at least a curiosity." With Gabriel trailing his umbrella behind, they visited dealers in old furniture, Gabriel's passion, and Tudor House acquired an old mirror and other objects to be shipped to London. But he was bored, and slept no better. Early in the evening of September 20 he entrained home, "without having put a single touch" upon his picture, "and while down here indeed never once handled brush or pencil, partly to save his eyes."

At home nothing was changed, except that Gabriel entertained his cronies until even later hours than usual. Reciprocating his hospitality, he invited Allingham to dinner with Fanny, Howell, Madox Brown and Treffry Dunn, Howell telling his tall stories as if authentic autobiography. "All sit late," Allingham recorded, "and supper being suggested, Howell and Dunn go down to the kitchen and bring up meat; H. says he 'saw a mouse eating a haddock' downstairs. 3 o'clock, R. goes to bed, Howell and Dunn go out in the rain to look for a cab, Madox Brown and I wait, sleepy, in hall—cab at last."

William assumed that "painful thoughts, partly but not wholly connected with [Gabriel's] wife and her death," were at the root of both the eye affliction and the insomnia. Certainly the two were at least related in that Gabriel's eyes were raw with sleeplessness and their muscles flickering painfully from strain.* Guilt was apparently absorbing his nights. Lizzy could not be exorcised. Fanny remained an awkward but necessary fixture. And even more necessary was Jane Morris, then beginning her sittings for *La Pia de' Tolomei*, Gabriel's representation of the Dantesque story of a woman imprisoned, Gabriel seemed to have concluded, more by himself, when he guiltily married Lizzy and left Jane to the adoring Top. He had not forgotten her, but discretion as well as the distance to Upton had kept them apart except upon social occasions. When Morris's £900 a year from family shares in a Cornwall tin mine shrank as the mine became less profitable, and he had moved his family from the expensive Red House to London, Jane became more accessible. She began sitting to Gabriel, and he made no secret of his new happiness, even hosting a dinner party in celebration of the beginning of *La Pia*.

Proud of his beginnings of new portraits of Jane, Gabriel lost no opportunity to display them, whatever the implications to visitors. One, early in July, was Whitehall civil servant Arthur Munby, a poet and compulsive diarist, who recalled finding Gabriel and William in the studio "full of great easels," and being shown "large idealized portraits of Mrs. Morris . . ., a glorious, heroic face. . . ." Gabriel, looking "like a younger Faust, in that weird chamber, . . . nursing a Canadian marmot in his arms," bade his guests, including Cayley, upstairs to "that large and lordly upper chamber . . . looking out on the river, . . . lit by red waxlights in silver candelabra. . . ." There Munby, whose secret mistress (and later wife) was a servant woman, and who was sexually aroused by coarse, worn servant

---

* In an essay on *La Pia*, W. D. Paden suggests that arterial hypertension "perturbed the delicate tissues of the brain" and caused Gabriel's sleeplessness, and "damaged the net of minute arteries in the retinas of his eyes," affecting his vision as well as "a number of apparently unconnected [later] disabilities." Medical evidence does not support this.

hands ruddy and worn with toil, paid special attention to the buxom woman who hovered about the dinner table—probably Fanny. The antique glass and china, he wrote, were "handed round by a single female servant; a robust and comely young woman, whose large strong hands, used to serving, contrast with the hands of her master, used to pictures and poems. She offers the dishes with a quaint simplicity, pointing out to you the best part of each. And we, we talked as of old. . . ."

Cayley and several others left at eleven, after coffee, but some returned to the studio, where Gabriel read aloud new poems by the blind young Philip Marston, after which "the talk turned on early memories; and the two Rossettis reminded each other of childish things; how Dante made drawings of his rocking horse, at the age of 4; how Christina, in those days, had such a dreadful temper; how they all talked Italian and English both. . . . At last, about 1 A.M., [Gabriel and William] opened the hall door and showed the moonlight shining on the river, through the lofty iron gates, between the ancient elms: and . . . I said Goodnight. . . ."

Gabriel, it was clear, was in one of his happiest moods, and all was right with the world. For the second time in his life he had found himself deeply in love, in a relationship which had nothing to do with his continued need for the vulgar, amiable Fanny, yet everything to do with his marriage to a young woman, since dead, his duty to whom—he now thought—had prevented a lifelong idyll with Jane. Nearly thirty and the mother of two girls, Jane could have discouraged Gabriel, but her marriage with William Morris, despite his great artistic and literary gifts and his affection for her, had been unsatisfactory. A many-sided genius to others, to her he was a loud bore whose enthusiasms she tolerated by retreating into silence and her embroidery. But Morris, insensitive to people in many ways, understood that with Gabriel his wife was happy. Reluctantly, he condoned the sittings, and hoped they were nothing more, for Gabriel offered him every opportunity to join Janey at Tudor House, where he passed the time by teaching himself Icelandic and completing the first volume of *The Earthly Paradise*. Still, the sittings were Gabriel's way of making love, and his letters to Jane arranging them were full of passionate declarations not meant to be hidden from her husband.

"Top" understood. Janey's large, sad eyes were

> . . . most times looking out afar
> Waiting for something, not for me.

In May, 1868, Gabriel had turned forty. The past could not be undone and relived; yet his rapture with Jane Morris restored both his painting and his poetic enthusiasms, and what he wrote suggests that Janey—for a time, at least—reciprocated his passion. Fanny, on such occasions, could be bribed with money—which she cherished above all else—and banished briefly to Royal Avenue; but Lizzy could not be so eliminated. His entombed sonnets to her, resting under her golden hair in the grave, Gabriel knew mostly by heart. They rang hollowly next to his impassioned new verses to Janey. One in 1868 even evoked her physically as he celebrated a portrait of her he had painted, where

> Above the enthroning throat
> The mouth's mould testifies of voice and kiss
> The shadowed eyes remember and foresee.
> Her face is made her shrine. Let all men note
> That in all years (O Love, thy gift is this!)
> They that would look on her must come to me.

No wonder his nights were sleepless, and that Janey—too late—began a cautious retreat into the assumed safety of protestations of ill health. The meetings continued, and Rossetti's sensuous, if not sexual, worship of Janey during his days were recompense for his literally dreadful nights. Scott's observation evokes Gabriel's similar worship of Lizzy years before. Coming from the Cheyne Walk studio he wrote their patron James Leathart, "10 life size heads of Jane Morris either painted or drawn in chalk in progress, and nothing else visible, or likely to be, as far as one can see."

William understood the anxieties which pressed upon his brother, yet accepted Gabriel's eye trouble as organic and his sleeplessness as related, although he had sat through the séances at which Gabriel probed his disquietude in the way one returns to a throbbing tooth.

There was still the appearance of normality at Cheyne Walk. Gabriel was producing pictures and replicas at a record rate, although *La Pia* seemed never to be near completion. Neither recurrent eye difficulties nor insomnia kept him from "a monster party to 120 friends and foes" given by Madox Brown, at which the close-packed guests managed "to amuse each other," he wrote Alice Boyd, "exactly according as they happened to be packed, making the most of the person next to them, like pick-pockets at a hanging." And for once he found himself able to aid William, who was in financial difficulties, having had his money stolen from his luggage while vacationing in Verona. To Venice Gabriel sent his penniless brother £30.

By September impaired vision and sleeplessness had reduced Gabriel to a morbid mental state, and to only brief sittings with Mrs. Morris for a canvas commissioned by William Graham, M.P. for Glasgow. Visiting at

Euston Square Gabriel, complaining that objects flickered before him, suggested that William accompany him to Germany, where an oculist at Coblenz had improved the vision of Whistler's mother, but William had no more vacation time. The idea was dropped. Several days later Gabriel spoke of being blind by Christmas, and hinted to William of an end to his troubles that suggested the example of Lizzy. "He talks of making a deed of gift of all his property to me; so that, whatever may befall himself, I may be empowered to do the best for all parties concerned." By "all parties" he almost certainly meant Fanny and Janey, and William understood. Gabriel also talked of forbidding the "posthumous exhibiting of his collected works," and William tried to divert his brother from "these gloomy anticipations," as did two physicians, one of whom bought a copy of the *Bocca Baciata* for 150 guineas. Gabriel promptly renamed it *La Bionda del Balcone*.

Rest, and distance from Chelsea, was the general prescription. Allingham again offered refuge along the Solent, but Gabriel wanted no "impending female photographers or even poets laureate," references to Allingham's vain attempts to have him photographed by Julia Cameron and to visit with Tennyson; and he unkindly considered the walks about Lymington "rather used up." In his wretched state Gabriel wanted even greater seclusion, and found it at Alice Boyd's Penkill, although traveling to Ayrshire with Bell Scott, he wrote William, required "toils worthy of Aeneas."

For "Scotus" the holiday with his old crony was unlike the convivial, whist-playing and gossiping sessions of the past. Unable to paint, Gabriel pushed the sedentary Scott into footpaths in the glen which no longer interested him, and regaled him with worries about impending blindness. And after dinner there were "the fearful skeletons in his closet that were [rattled] every night, when the ladies had gone, brought out for his relief and my recreation. These skeletons were also made to dance along the mountain highroad during our long walks." Morbidly Gabriel wondered of what use he was as a painter if his eyes failed him, and spoke often of "the short ending to his ills." Skeptical of the "monomania" about Gabriel's blindness Scott rejoined, "Live for your poetry," and seconded by his wife, by Alice Boyd and by Miss Boyd's wealthy old aunt Miss Losh, who secretly pressed a loan upon Gabriel, Scott urged him to try to recall more of his buried verses than Gabriel thought he had committed to memory. By the time they left for London in the chill early days of November, Gabriel—although still depressed, sleepless and impaired in vision—was writing some additional lines down, to compare to the poems he had in imperfect manuscript copies at Cheyne Walk.

While Gabriel had been en route home, William had finally extracted from Moxon, the publisher of the famed illustrated *Tennyson*, a contract to do an edition of Shelley's poetry with a prefatory life. It had long been his ambition to rehabilitate his literary hero, and the work on it helped create an atmosphere in which Gabriel not only offered his editorial assistance but furnished conjectural emendations which William diplomatically put aside out of a concern which he kept to himself that they might cause the edition to "fall into disrepute." But his brother was, at least, now thinking in poetic channels, and in his journal for November 27, 1868, William noted that Gabriel, "being still, from the state of his eyes, unable to resume painting, has been looking up his poems of old days ["raveled rags of verse," he deprecated them to Allingham], with some floating idea of offering some of them to *The Fortnightly Review*, and at any rate with a degree of zest which looks promising for *some* result with them." Dunn continued executing replicas to pay Gabriel's bills, and in mid-December William noted that his brother had "just written a series of four sonnets—*Willow-wood*—about the finest thing he has done. I see the poetical impulse is upon him again."

The Morrises were about to revisit Cheyne Walk, so that Gabriel could resume his carefully choreographed courtship by straining his still-weak eyes at the recumbent figure of Janey. The "Willow-wood" poems and their successors recorded his mood. He hinted of long-divided love now freed, "alive from the abyss," and "the shades of those our days that had no tongue" were exorcised in a flood of ecstatic new poetry unleashed by the brooding, half-mystical sexuality of his best friend's wife. Only months later Christina wrote "An Echo from Willow-wood," using a line from her brother's poem as epigraph, and describing "hungering hearts" which knew the "bitterness" of "craving each for each," which although "one moment joined," would have to "vanish out of reach." William, much later, first suggested that the reference was to Gabriel and Lizzy, then cryptically ventured that a "wholly different train of events" was in Christina's mind. Were they both alluding to Janey?

Bell Scott that November reported to Alice Boyd that Gabriel's "being so fond of Mrs. Top" was common gossip, and that Gabriel "understands they are being watched." Yet with that understanding came little conceal-ment of his ardor. At dinner for a dozen at Scott's on the 26th, the Morrises, and Janey's placid sister Bessy (whom Morris detested, but who often lived with them), joined Gabriel at the table, and Scott reported that Morris was in "great spirits" although his wife sat with Gabriel, "and I must say [he] acts like a perfect fool if he wants to conceal his attachment, doing nothing but attend to her, sitting side-ways toward her, [and] that sort of thing. . . . However, I have concluded they (G. & J.) will not go further than they have gone. She is certainly the most remarkable looking woman in the world, and *in expression* lovely. Of course a woman under such circumstances, before people, is a sealed book, still I think she is cool. As to Gabriel he forgets everyone else, . . . [even with] Morris looking at him all the time." How far Gabriel and Mrs. Morris had gone, or would go, Bell Scott could only speculate. Perhaps because of his confidence in Janey's ultimate caution, Gabriel would not let up the pressure on her, and her coolness—or appearance of it—would remain a vital part of her armor. Some months later, visiting Cheyne Walk, Scott found Gabriel "in the dumps, not painting . . . , but lounging about the room shouldering everything with his hands in his pockets, because Janey was ill and unable to come." Nothing had changed.

Sixteen sonnets, some of them new and the product of his passion for Janey, would appear in the March (1869) *Fortnightly*, a public resurrection for Gabriel as poet. And while he had written of, and painted, his beloved, her husband sat in another room in Gabriel's house working on more stanzas for his *Earthly Paradise*. Morris knew he had somehow failed Jane, but still worshiped at her shrine. His bluff, manic ways could not compete with a mystic rapport of souls, and he wrote bitterly of his frustration, giving the lines to a woman rejecting the poet, despite his kindness and "hungry eyes," her heart "grown silent of its grief,"

> "Yea gone, yet not my fault. I knew of love,
> But my love and not his; nor could I tell
> That such blind passion in him I should move.
> Behold, I have loved faithfully and well!"

Morris was not about to cast off Janey except in his poetry. When he left suddenly for Rome with Ned Jones, trying to save him from pursuit by Marie Zambaco, a Greek beauty from whom Jones was belatedly and unsuccessfully trying to extricate himself, Gabriel wrote Howell, "Janey has stopped her sittings by order during foreign service—just as I supposed." But the separation was brief. Morris was soon back at Queen Square, and Janey at Cheyne Walk.

When Henry James visited Queen Square in March he saw, as he wrote his sister, "a large, nearly full-length portrait" of Janey, "so strange and unreal that you'd pronounce it a distempered vision, but in fact an extremely good likeness." The portrait, he declared, "haunts me still. A figure cut out of a missal. . . . 'So did the woman herself.' Imagine a tall lean woman in a long dress of some dead purple stuff, guiltless of hoops (or of anything else, I should say), with a mass of crisp, black hair heaped into great wavy projections on each side of her temples, a thin pale face, a pair of strange, sad, deep, dark, Swinburnian eyes, with great thick black oblique brows, joined in the middle and tucking themselves away under her hair, a mouth like the 'Oriana' in our illustrated Tennyson, a long neck, without any collar, and in lieu thereof some dozen strings of outlandish beads."

To Gabriel, however, Janey was the incarnation of beauty, and as his devotion to her person resulted in more poetry as well as a strained intensification of his painting, he turned more—first subconsciously—to thoughts of recapturing the poems he had put into the grave. He did not have sufficient verse on hand for a book without some of those he described evasively as "lost." If Lizzy would return them to him, her spell over him, and his guilty conscience, would simultaneously disappear. (He felt no pangs of conscience over Fanny, his plump and fortyish "dear elephant" whose services were to him no more—or less—spiritual than he would have regarded a hearty dinner.) But what was taking shape in his mind, even as he refused still to admit it to himself, could be read between the lines of an incautious letter to his mother, which he intended to be jocular. "I send you my sonnets," he wrote on March 1, 1869, "which are such a lively band of bogies that they may join with the skeletons of Christina's various closets, and entertain you by a ballet. . . . As their own vacated graves serve them to dance on, there is no danger of their disturbing the lodgers beneath; and if anyone overhead objects, you may say that it amuses them perhaps and will soon be over, and that, as their hats were not buried with them, these will not be sent round at the close of the performance."

The thoughts he could not think kept his nights sleepless as he painted his Janey, perhaps more symbolically than he dared know, as Pandora. On Gabriel's canvas she clutches the fateful box described in a sonnet with an antique word which, after the fact, has an added dimension:

> The ill-born things, the good things turned to ill,—
> Powers of the impassioned hours prohibited.
> Aye, clench the casket now! Whither they go
> Thou mayst not dare to think; nor canst thou know
> If Hope still pent there be alive or dead.

He could not finish the painting. His eyes swam and his head ached. Janey, too, complained of exhaustion, and in July had to be taken by Morris—who grumbled about his need to remain with The Firm—to the spa at Bad Ems in Hesse-Nassau for the traditional healing waters. Gabriel had also been painting her as Beatrice, identifying her thus with his dead wife, who remained much in his mind—so much that he wrote Charles Eliot Norton, then visiting from America, that he would gladly purchase from him the "Clerk Saunders" drawing "by my late Wife" which Norton owned, and would either pay for it or furnish one of his own—worth two or three times as much. Every year, he wrote, he valued her work even more, "apart from other personal interest to me."

As the Morrises departed for Germany, Gabriel began to send to Messrs Strangeways, a London printing firm, manuscripts of his poems to be set in type in order—in that pre-typewriter era—to visualize them better for a future book. Unthinkingly, perhaps, he described the result as "dead stock." And on July 30 he wrote passionately to Jane, after brooding about their parting,

All that concerns you is the all-absorbing question with me, as dear Top will not mind my telling you at this anxious time. The more he loves you, the more he knows that you are too lovely and noble not to be loved: and, dear Janey, there are too few things that seem worth expressing as life goes on, for one friend to deny another the poor expression of what is most at his heart. . . . I can never tell you how much I am with you at all times. Absence from your sight is what I have long been used to: and no absence can ever make me so far from you again as your presence did for years. For this long inconceivable change, you know now what my thanks must be. But I have no right to talk to you in a way that may make you sad on my account when in reality the balance of joy and sorrow is now so much more in my favour than it has been, or could have been hoped to become, for years past.

Rossetti's language was not only a fervid wooing of Jane but an intimation that his passion had not been without response. Yet it also seemed clear to him that her recurrent illnesses were not merely a safety valve to secure her against scandal, but a result of the strain under which she played out her dual role as William Morris's dutiful wife and Dante Gabriel Rossetti's inamorata and inspiration. Gabriel's constant and extravagant concern for Jane's frail health ("a capricious malady") in his correspondence thus became itself a way of wooing, as to her "dear health" he vowed to sacrifice "all else." In one of his notebooks he wrote, obviously of her,

> My world, my work, my woman, all my own—
> What face but thine has taught me all that art
> Can be and still be nature's counterpart?

She *was* his world as well as his work; but in the shadows lurked Lizzy, and at Queen Square there was Janey's lawful husband. In Gabriel's agitated state of mind he may have expected a more persuasive protest from the grave than from the unhappy, but resigned, Morris. Thus before he fled again to Penkill in August he wrote cautiously to Howell, "I feel disposed, if practicable, to go in for recovery of my poems if possible, as you proposed some time ago." It was to be someone else's idea, although it is unlikely that the shrewd "Portugee" would have made the offer without a strong hint from Gabriel. The suggestion otherwise would have been potentially offensive. (He had earlier described it to Howell as a "ghastly business.") It was a matter, Gabriel confided, that was causing him "some real anxiety" since he began going through his surviving manuscripts.

After first thinking that it would be more prudent to leave the matter for his return, Gabriel found that circumstances at Penkill were altering his outlook. His memory refused to release the lost lines, yet he could think of little else but the grave. He talked daily of suicide, and on visiting one glen with Alice Boyd and Bell Scott, he peered over a sheer precipice with an expression Scott interpreted as "One step forward and I am free!" Then Gabriel turned round "and put his hand in mine, an action which showed he was losing self-command and that fear was mastering him."

There was no such danger again, but an incident occurred the next day which left Scott wondering how it could have happened to "a man writing his best poetry, painting his best pictures, and exercising a daily shrewdness of business habits." Ascending a hill they saw a small bird, a chaffinch, in the road. As they advanced it remained motionless, until Gabriel was near enough to scoop it up in his hand. Still it refused to fly. "What is the meaning of this?" Scott heard Gabriel say to himself, his hand trembling with emotion. Realizing the peculiar mental strain his companion appeared to be under, Scott suggested, although it was an unlikely circumstance in the sparsely populated area, that the bird was probably a tame one, escaped from a cage.

"Nonsense!" said Gabriel. "You are always against me, Scott. I can tell you what it is; it is my wife, the spirit of my wife. The soul of her has taken this shape; something is going to happen to me." * Scott said nothing, and they returned to Penkill in silence, where Miss Boyd rushed out to tell them that the gate bell, which took a strong pull to ring, had been ringing although no one was in sight to have done it. Gabriel asked when the incident had occurred, and—Scott recalled—"finding it must have been just about the time when we met the bird, he turned his curiously ferocious look upon me, asking me what I thought now. . . ."

From London, Gabriel had brought with him a pile of proofs for his "trial book," and anticipating additional poems, decided to warn his family. "I am calling in William's valuable aid for revision," he explained to his

---

* Years later Gabriel described—or imagined—such an episode:

This little day—a bird that flew to me—
Has swiftly flown out of my hand again.
Ah have I listened to its fugitive strain
For what its tidings of the sky may be?
   (*Works*, dated 1880)

In the fragment, however, the bird does not refuse to fly away, perhaps the triumph of art over reality.

mother. "My object is to keep them by me as stock to be added to for a possible future volume; but in any case I thought it necessary to print them, as I found blundered transcripts of some of my old things were flying about, and would some time have got into print perhaps—a thing afflictive to one's bogie." His choice of words continued to suggest what was on his mind, and there was confirmation in his exhortations to Howell to explore the matter of Highgate Cemetery. To William there was no hint of any plan to extract the book from Lizzy's grave, but only a stream of exchanges dealing with editing the newly printed proofs, and even a letter to Maria about one of the Italian poems which William felt was too weak to include. The family was not to know. Yet on September 1 Gabriel's solicitor friend Henry Virtue Tebbs called on William (since Gabriel was away, and his brother had long been assumed his other self), "and began talking about the volume of MS. poems by Gabriel which he suppressed at the time of Lizzie's death, and buried in her coffin." Tebbs, William noted in his journal, offered the information that legal authorization would be needed to open the coffin, "but that he could without any difficulty obtain this for G[abriel], should the latter wish at any time to recover the poems. I said that I would bear the point in mind, and let G know of this in case the question should ever be in the way of arising." But William kept his own counsel, and—knowing of his brother's dangerous state of mind—did not inform Gabriel of the meeting, not realizing that Gabriel was actively planning the exhumation with Howell, who had already enlisted Tebbs.

Instead, William wrote to Gabriel, exhorting him to alter a line in a poem where the sea appeared in the wrong place. "Nazareth is *quite inland,* about equidistant from the Mediterranean and the Lake of Tiberias: the sea could no more be heard there than in London or Birmingham." Exasperated, Gabriel forgot his anxieties momentarily, answering William, "I fear the sea must remain at Nazareth; you know an old painter would have made no bones if he wanted it for his background."

The melodramatics of Gabriel's life penetrated Euston Square only dimly. What William knew he did not tell Maggie or Christina, and what Mrs. Rossetti knew she was informed of by Gabriel's usually cautious letters. There was sufficient worry about Christina's health, although during a July holiday at Penkill (none of the Rossettis, curiously, ever traveled there with another) she had been, according to William's diary, "uncommonly well." Maria remained immersed in her devotions and in Dante, and William rejoiced at a promotion that month to Assistant Excise Secretary at Somerset House, which meant £800 a year, and attending meetings of the Board of the Excise Office every second day of the week, after having prepared papers with recommendations for their disposal. It was a good professional income for the time, and even much later. Senior professors at major English universities got no more until after the First World War. Still, William longed for the life of the scholar and litterateur. He preferred to edit Shelley, and in fact was also at work (for £21 a volume) on a series of prefaces to "Moxon's Popular Poets"; and his most ambitious creative effort—"Mrs Holmes Grey," a long—and unsuccessful—poem he had begun in P.R.B. days—had finally been published in New York, in *The Broadway* for January, 1868. Spending his off-hours looking up old, abusive articles on Shelley in the British Museum; having the tough, seventy-seven-year-old seafaring friend of Shelley's, E. J. Trelawny (who burned the poet's drowned body on an Italian beach), visit at Euston Square; playing host Browning, who gossiped unashamedly about his rivalry with Tennyson; visiting Byron's aged ex-mistress Claire Clairmont in Florence; or drafting with Swinburne a letter—in Italian—expressing freethinking sympathy to the Anti-Catholic Council in Naples in December, 1869—these were William's joys. But he spent his Mondays-to-Fridays "reading and considering a number of letters addressed to the [Excise] office on a variety of subjects; making orders upon some of them; presenting others to a commissioner or to the Board, to obtain signatures to orders, or to have the orders made; revising the drafts of the letters written to carry out all those orders; and signing the letters themselves." And William was of sufficient importance that visitors on personal business were free to stop by without embarrassment to him, an improvement in his situation which made the slow-moving bureaucratic hours easier to bear.

Gabriel, who had never known soul-deadening work, lived constantly at the opposite extreme of emotional tension. Recuperating during the early autumn in Ayrshire, he found that despite—or perhaps because of—the continuation of the mental strain that had brought him to Penkill, it was a fertile period for his poetry, some of his verses then too evidently connected with Janey, for he later lightened the dark hair of the beloved in a number of sonnets. One of his poems, "The Stream's Secret," a title he appropriated from one of Scott's sonnets, expressed not the secret of the rushing Penwhapple but of his own floods of passion and remorse; and other poems reached an erotic—or a morbid—intensity just short of hysteria.

He had to do something about the buried manuscript book. He may have felt, now, that the shade of Lizzy had been giving him all sorts of signs that she was willing, even eager, to give the poems back to him. He may even have felt that, if he retrieved his poems in usable condition, the shade of Lizzy would have thus signified her making peace with him. Bell Scott afterwards assumed that Gabriel's determination to exhume his poems was an outgrowth of the Penkill experience, for he had pointed out there that Gabriel's desire to include his prose tale "Hand and Soul" in a future book of verse "was an exhibition of [poetic] poverty not to be thought of," and that Gabriel had then determined to reclaim "Jenny" from the grave. But Gabriel had already been in obsessive communication with Tebbs and Howell, and before he left Scotland had sent his factotum a letter of introduction to the Home Secretary, Henry Austin Bruce (Lord Aberdare), in whose power it was to authorize the opening of the grave.

A complication followed. The cemetery plot was actually owned by Gabriel's mother, but Lord Aberdare wrote to Rossetti in Scotland "that the circumstances you mention justify a departure from the strict rule." With only the earth above the coffin now separating Gabriel from the end to his anxiety he packed his bags and with some excuses took the first train he could get to London.

At Penkill the first reaction to Gabriel's departure had to be one of grateful release. Still, the castle seemed not without him for long. Gabriel's habit at Penkill had been to take his proof sheets after dinner to the room above the drawing room, to check his lines by reading to himself, his voice "so loud," Scott recalled, "that we in the dining room beneath could almost hear the words." As they were sitting after dinner, "when he must have been approaching London in the train," they heard what seemed to be the usual voice over their heads. Scott looked at Alice Boyd, who was "listening intently till she could bear it no longer, and left the room." Several other dinner guests heard the voice, "sure evidence we were not deceiving ourselves. Next night it was the same, and so it went on till I left. When we tried to approach it was not audible, or when the doors of the drawing-room and its small ante-room communicating with the staircase were left open, we could make nothing of it. It gradually tapered off when Miss Boyd was left by herself; by and by the whole establishment was bolted and barred for the winter. Next season it had entirely ceased." Had the autumn wind been playing tricks upon their susceptibilities? Perhaps there was no more suggestible group than a society of skeptics.

On September 20, 1868, Gabriel arrived in London, William seeing him the next evening. "He has done a good deal of poetry," William noted in his journal. "He seems more anxious just now to achieve something permanent in poetry than in painting. . . ." But William also noted that Gabriel complained of being "very weak, perspiring excessively, losing sleep and [says] that his health is breaking up." Of the negotiations with the Home Secretary, William—who had done all of his brother's difficult errands for two decades—learned nothing. The exception had to be made because if their mother learned of the enterprise it was within her power to stop it.

On an evening in early October Gabriel sat with Kate Howell in Brixton while, by the light of torches and a fire built by the graveside at Highgate, workmen spaded the soil from a grave. Howell stood by with Tebbs and Dr. Llewellyn Williams, whose task it would be to disinfect and dry the book if it were salvageable. The coffin was soon exposed, and Howell lifted the lid. Lizzy's long hair was still golden. Howell lifted it to look for the book bound in rough grey calf—there was also a Bible buried with her—and drew it out, handing it to Williams. The coffin was resealed and lowered again, and the three left the aftermath to the workmen with their torches and spades.* With the deed done, Gabriel could write to William, explaining painfully on October 13—he could not bring himself to do it in person†—that "no mistrust or unbrotherly feeling" was involved, but that

the thing is done. All in the coffin was found quite perfect; but the book, though not in any way destroyed, is soaked through and through, and had to be still further saturated with disinfectants. It is now in the hands of the medical man who was associated with Howell in the disinterment, and who is carefully drying it leaf by leaf. . . . It was a service I could not ask you to perform for me, nor do I know anyone except Howell who could well have been entrusted with such a trying task. It was necessary, as we found, that a lawyer should be employed in the matter, to speak to the real nature of the MSS., as difficulties were raised to the last by the Cemetery Authorities as to there possibly being papers the removal of which involved a fraud. This service Tebbs rendered me. . . . I have begged Howell to hold his tongue for the future, but if he does not I cannot help it. . . . I suppose the truth must ooze out in time. It is very desirable, as you will think with me, that our family should not know of it.

The devoted William replied as expected. "Under pressure of a great sorrow you performed an act of self-sacrifice: it did you honour, but . . . you have not retracted the sacrifice, for it has taken actual effect in your being bereaved of due poetic fame these seven and a half years past: but you now think—and I quite agree with you—that there is no reason why the self-sacrifice should have no term." To Swinburne, who adored Lizzy, Gabriel furnished a sentimental rationalization—that "Had it been possible to her, I should have found the book on my pillow the night she was buried; and could she have opened the grave, no other hand would have been needed." Swinburne agreed, and Gabriel sent him grateful thanks, acknowledging, "I have undergone so much mental disturbance about this matter." It told in many ways, from his persistent sleeplessness to a "constant shaking of the hand . . . with corresponding internal sensations." He had to convince himself further that he had done the right thing, and the renewed presence of Janey as he painted, and prepared new poems for the

---

* Gabriel did not pay the two guinea charges until late in December.

† "He could do it, he could repent of it," Eleonora Duse told Arthur Symons in the 1890's; "but he should have gone and taken it back himself: [instead] he sent his friends!"

printer, was consolation. His letters to her took on a constant lover's plea, for she would sometimes withdraw herself on excuse of illness, and Gabriel no longer worried about caution. "To be with you . . . ," he wrote, "is absolutely the only happiness I can find or conceive in this world, dearest Janey; and when this cannot be, I can hardly now exert myself to move hand or foot for anything." Another letter between "sittings" emphasized that "places that are empty of you are empty of all life," and that "You are the noblest and dearest thing that the world has had to show me: and if no lesser loss than the loss of you* could have brought me so much bitterness, I would still rather have had this to endure than have missed the fullness of wonder and worship which nothing else could have made known to me." His intensity of passion was on the edge of hysteria.

The double boon of the book's retrieval and Janey's reappearance turned Gabriel to a sonnet in which he equated his two loves, one which now vivified his life after years of "waste remembrance," the other lying unforgotten with "all that golden hair undimmed in death." His poetry restored to him, although—he told Madox Brown—there was "a great hole through all the leaves of *Jenny*," he pressed on with preparation of a substantial volume to be published by Frederick S. Ellis, picking his brother's brains for emendations. One evening he hurried to Euston Square to read a new poem to his family, expecting the usual polite overlooking of the more passionate lines, although the really erotic verses—by Victorian standards—he usually expurgated for his sisters in advance. But the serpent-sex symbolism in "Eden Bower" was less cryptic than Gabriel thought, and both Christina and Maria retreated from the room. He was delighted, but did not tell William, who had not been present. Instead he confided his glee to Bell Scott, who then told William himself.

By January, 1869, Gabriel had designed the binding for his book, but a month later was still making meticulous changes within. Finally, with new anxieties cropping up as he began to worry about press reaction—for publication after all was akin to the public exhibition he had foresworn for his painting—he agreed to take a rest in "country air" as Christina's physician William Jenner had urged. He was, he confessed to Allingham, "hardly my own ghost."

With William's recently widowed friend W. J. Stillman—an American journalist once U.S. consul in Crete—as companion, he went off to Scalands, Barbara Bodichon's farm. It was a curious choice. He had not been there since the first days of his marriage. Few places were more suffused with memories of Lizzy.

---

* Presumably when he lost her to Morris and married Lizzy.

XI

Anxieties
1869-1872

In 1870 Christina was forty. A long illness had convinced her that she would never be wholly well again. A long courtship had culminated in a proposal of marriage—certainly her last—which she had rejected. Years of deliberate austerity had left her few ordinary joys in life to sustain her. Years of poetry writing had left her with a modest reputation yet only a small audience. Stubbornly, nevertheless, she affirmed her way of life:

> I would not if I could undo my past,
> Tho' for its sake my future is a blank;
> My past for which I have myself to thank,
> For all its faults and follies first and last.
> I would not cast anew the lot once cast,
> Or launch a second ship for one that sank,
> Or drug with sweets the bitterness I drank,
> Or break by feasting my perpetual fast. . . . .

In August, 1869 an anonymous series of three monthly articles on three of the Rossettis began appearing in the "Criticism of Contemporaries" feature of *Tinsley's Magazine*. First there was Christina, then Gabriel, then William, the unnamed author (H. Buxton Forman) finding Gabriel potentially the best writer, although conceding Christina "a genuine poetic gift" with a "sense of execution" exceeding that of Mrs. Browning. It was Gabriel who was exhorted to bring out a book of verse, "the sooner the better." By the time the article appeared he was hard at work on exactly that, and well before the end of the year he was able to utilize the exhumed manuscript book, although—Bell Scott, then back in London, wrote Alice Boyd—"It was so decayed through the *middle* part of the pages that he has had to *copy it himself.* A queer sensation it must give him." Undoubtedly it did, for as Gabriel confided to William* it also had "a dreadful smell—partly no doubt the disinfectants," and was in the handling an "unpleasant job." By the new year, when all that could have been copied had been extracted from the grisly book, it had long since been burned;† but for Gabriel it had not altogether disappeared. The book in preparation was a constant reminder of his theft from Lizzy's grave as well as his theft from Morris's bosom, and it is difficult to separate the two in his intimation to William that the dedication of the *Poems* to him would be "failing only one possibility which I suppose must be considered out of the question." If that possibility were his dead wife it would have revealed his robbery from her coffin. If, as is more likely, the "possibility" were Jane Morris it was no possibility at all. He would be either acknowledging the desecration of a grave or the desecration of a marriage. Thus, although there were jolly parties at Tudor House, and a display of Rossettian heartiness, the ebullience was often supported by brandy, and Gabriel had even begun limiting his breakfasts to sherry. William later denied Gabriel's dependence on alcohol, except as his brother used whiskey—neat—to wash down the sleep-inducing chloral; but he had no idea of the extent of Gabriel's craving for palliatives to his burden of anxieties. Not all of Gabriel's concerns were communicated to William. Only two years later, for example, did Gabriel confide his terror at a "supernatural visitation" he had experienced then. As his nights had become more sleepless, he had taken to drawing far into the night, illuminating his studio by a huge gaselier on a standard near his easel. (Then he would sleep late into the next day, compounding his inability to sleep the next night.) Sitting in the studio after midnight, after everyone else, as usual, had retired, he heard—or thought he heard—in the passage outside the room leading to the garden door, the whimpering of a child. The crying came near, then retreated, then came near again, as if the child were going up and down the passage, but there was no sound of footsteps. After what Gabriel thought was about five minutes, the sounds ceased. He went to the studio door and looked up and down the hallway, but there was nothing.

Perhaps, William suggested (when he finally heard of it), it was the raccoon, which had once been accidentally shut up in a drawer of a cupboard

---

* In a letter William drastically expurgated for the *Family Letters.*

† Three fragments purported to come from the exhumed manuscript survive. Two are in the British Museum; the other is at the Houghton Library, Harvard.

in that hallway. No, said Gabriel, it was no animal sound—only that of a child. Lizzy's—and his—stillborn child? He kept his interpretation of the occurrence to himself.* But soon after it had happened, he fled Cheyne Walk for Sussex.

Before he left for Scalands with Stillman, Gabriel's worries about the press reaction to his poems were directed toward William. "Top wants to do a notice of my book—he proposed the *Fortnightly* but there I believe Swinburne proposes to do so, and had long ago started the idea. Do you think the *Academy* would be available? And if so, would you propose the thing to the editor?" And he wanted William to dine with him the next evening to discuss other stratagems for insuring appropriate coverage. "Who could do it for the *British Quarterly*? I suppose you are shut out though that would please me better than anything, but then the book is dedicated to you. Do you think Scotus could get the job?" To Ellis, his publisher, Gabriel advised, "I want to appear when I know a few reviews are ready, to keep spite at bay. . . ." In particular he wanted to outmaneuver Robert Buchanan, a prolific (and mediocre) poet and reviewer whose tastes were conservative at best, and who seemed to be eager to settle old scores against what he called the Rossetti coterie, for years earlier, William—in reviewing Buchanan's *Idylls and Legends of Inverburne*—had dismissed him as "a poor but pretentious poetaster" while defending Swinburne's racy *Poems and Ballads*. Buchanan had evened the score by denouncing William's *Shelley* in the *Athenaeum* that January, provoking Gabriel to refer to the journal in a letter to Swinburne as the "Arse-inaeum." He fancied, he told Ellis, elaborating on the metaphor, that Buchanan has "his natural organ of speech hitched up for an utterance," and hoped that it would be "a silent emanation" which would leave him "nothing but the smell to enjoy." But the bawdy wit belied Gabriel's concern, and was another factor in the depression which he took with him to Barbara Bodichon's farm.

At Scalands there was no gaslight. He and Stillman took long walks and wrote letters during daylight hours, and retired at times when, if Gabriel had been in London, Swinburne would not yet have become noisy, let alone (in Bell Scott's description) "rampant, then unmanageable, and lastly inarticulate and helpless." At Cheyne Walk, with Gabriel and his manservant gone, Dunn managed affairs, with William stopping by regularly; and Fanny kept mostly to her rented house on Royal Avenue, where she was gradually

---

* Treffry Dunn believed in the raccoon explanation, although the sounds he described were different. The animal, living in the bottom drawer of a huge cupboard, "had been . . . prowling about the house at night in search of food. This accounted for certain mysterious noises which had occurred in the dark hours of the night—sounds, as it were, of a faint, flat footfall up and down the stairs. . . ."

hoarding possessions of Gabriel's which had some money value but which might not be missed—a dusty curio, a discarded drawing, a blue pot bereft of its lid. At the farm Gabriel drew a head of Stillman, and another of the gamekeeper's daughter, which he sold to Graham for fifty guineas. He craved additional companionship, and discreetly invited the Madox Browns as well as the Morrises, although Stillman was paying half of the rising house expenses. Janey even remained on—"in another house, lent by Barbara's brother," Gabriel explained to Bell Scott. (The proprieties, however, were mainly to permit Top to return to The Firm in London.)

Gabriel's eyes—and his health in general—improved in the simple seclusion of Scalands, but the penetration of his London problems into the country only aggravated his continuing insomnia, for the longer nights meant more hours of sleeplessness. Stillman helpfully recommended a new soporific, chloral hydrate, which produced in Gabriel a splendid stupefaction, but at the dosage Stillman recommended—"twenty grains dissolved in 3 ozs. of water, a tablespoonful to be taken three nights in succession, and then no more until three days had elapsed"—the relief was only for short periods of time. Gabriel stopped using it. Crankier, especially as publication day loomed, he behaved as if master of the house which had been lent to them jointly, and the financially hard-pressed Stillman, his expenses rising because of Rossetti's guests, decided to leave his companion to them, having agreed before departing to review the *Poems* for an American paper.

Late in April, with Janey nearby, Gabriel awaited publication, taking the train to London one morning in order to inscribe copies for Ellis. Bell Scott looked with distaste on Rossetti's "working the miracle"—using those of his literary friends in strategic places to puff his book. Yet Gabriel's efforts to promote his own book would become a commonplace of publishers' public relations, and was not, even then, a Rossettian invention. Swinburne, in fact, had to be implored not to praise the *Poems* "beyond my deserts," to which he replied that he would not—"to speak Topsaically—say a bloody word which is not a blasted fact." Only Top himself seemed to be producing his paean (for the *Academy*) with reluctance, his comment to his confidante, Aglaia Coronio, on the review ending with "ugh." But when Gabriel returned to London on May 9, 1870, he was more than merely famous. He was unique in his time as having proven his genius in both art and letters, and his twelve-shilling volume, with binding designed by himself, went into several printings in the first month of publication, bringing Gabriel £300 before the first few days of May had run their course. The first printing of a thousand copies had exhausted itself in a week, a remarkable record for a book of poems.

Christina was having far less success with the same publisher. Gabriel had hoped to "concentrate our forces" by having his sister and others of his circle publish under Ellis's banner, but Christina's first effort for Ellis, a collection of prose tales, was unfortunately, but accurately, titled *Commonplace* after the longest story, which Gabriel thought Jane Austenish but, from Scalands confessed to Christina was "not dangerously exciting to the nervous system." The other tales dated back as early as 1853, Christina's facility with prose not paralleling her production in verse. Only with "Commonplace"—published in a magazine in March—had she arrived at sufficient bulk for a book, and after some changes in it requested by Ellis agreed to generous terms Gabriel had proposed to the publisher—twenty-five percent royalty on the retail price of the first edition of five hundred copies. A week before the May 7 publication date she invited Ellis to a "kettledrum" at Euston Square, the tea intended to improve their acquaintance "beyond knowing each other's handwriting by sight."

To Ellis the arrangement with the Rossettis appeared at the time to be a profitable long-term investment. Gabriel seemed bound to follow up his first success, and Christina had already told Ellis of her work in progress, a collection of nursery rhymes and children's songs which Gabriel had already praised as "divinely lovely." Besides, there were two other Rossettis, both writers and critics. Ellis had high expectations as family publisher, while Gabriel worried more immediately about Christina's range as a writer. Her "proper business," he reminded her, was "to write poetry, and not *Commonplaces*." Impatiently she responded that it was "impossible to go on singing out-loud to one's one-stringed lyre." And if he thought she could extend her poetic opportunities by ranging outside herself, she had an answer for that too. "It is not in me, and therefore it will never come out of me, to turn to politics or philanthropy with Mrs. Browning: such many-sidedness I leave to a greater than I, and, having had my say, may well sit silent."

For once the brothers were working at cross-purposes, for as Gabriel was promising Christina's literary future to Ellis, William was still bargaining for her with Macmillan, using the Ellis invitation to attempt to get Macmillan to improve an offer Gabriel described to Swinburne as "mean" and "laughable." Christina finally settled the matter by closing with Ellis herself and arranging for *Commonplace* as well as for *Sing-Song*, prudently setting a terminal date for publication of the poems, after which—if *Sing-Song* were not in print—the agreement would lapse. It was a shrewd precaution, for massive indifference greeted *Commonplace* on May 7, although Christina left for a holiday at Folkestone a few days later to escape the assumed ordeal of the reviews. There were few.

While again reprinting Gabriel's *Poems*, Ellis cooled to the idea of still another book by Christina, especially after he saw Alice Boyd's weak illustrations for it, which were to be part of the package. A month after publication Christina sent Ellis a postal order for what she assumed would be the balance of the unearned advance she had received, and told him candidly that although she still hoped that favorable notices might rescue *Commonplace* from imminent oblivion, she saw no such prospect. Perhaps if Miss Boyd made no further large figure designs, she suggested—Alice Boyd seemed able only to draw animals—the illustrations for *Sing-Song* might yet be saved. But then she added unflinchingly, "I can readily imagine that if *Commonplace* proves a total failure, *Sing-Song* may dwindle to a very serious risk: and therefore I beg you at once, if you deem the step prudent, to put a stop to all further outlay on the rhymes, until you can judge whether my name is marketable." He did. Before she left Folkestone her relationship with Ellis was over, and she acknowledged to him that her next book "may well hide its diminished head" for a while. Suddenly she was without a publisher.

Outside events in the summer of 1870 ended Ellis's heady sales of Gabriel's book. With the outbreak of the Franco-Prussian War, reader interest, except in current events, slumped. Even Christina, despite her testy rejoinder to Gabriel about poetic themes, wrote two pro-French poems about "Sister France" and "Vine-clad France." Gabriel worried only that "all poetry will be as dead as ditch-water now with this blessed war." But there were ironic consolations. Thanks to Napoleon III, where Gabriel had not been able to rig enthusiastic reviews for his *Poems*, the chance of the opposite, in *Blackwood's* and the *Nation*, came "too late to smash me, as no doubt the war has been beforehand with them as regards poetry in general." He had heard a rumor that a turncoat friend had written one of the adverse reviews, and although he was relieved that the French and the Prussians had combined to undermine the conspiracy against his reputation, he seldom failed to see a conspiracy where criticism was intended.

Once the war began, William traveled to Germany, visiting the Rhineland and Bavaria, deliberately choosing sides because he considered the French criminal in starting the war. Although he sympathized with the French people, he felt that "to fight for the simple purpose of preventing Germany from being powerful and united was totally contrary to my conceptions of public right." The capture of Napoleon and the siege of Paris took hold of English imaginations, but William was more impressed by how little the war had touched Germany. "No warlike effervescences," he wrote Mrs. Gilchrist, "& passport never once asked for."

Not knowing William was away, Holman Hunt—estranged from Gabriel but still in tenuous communication with his brother—appealed to him on October 9, "Go and have a look at my little boy and tell me how he seems. I am wondering whether I shall ever get hold of him. I want him so much *here*. I must have someone to love near me." The widowered Hunt, painting in Syria, had been forced to leave his son, Cyril, with his late wife's mother. Old Mrs. Waugh had provided little news of him, and refused to send the boy to the dirty and disreputable East. William was at least a reliable informant, and early in November he was back; but before checking on Cyril Hunt he made his first stop at Cheyne Walk, where he found Gabriel in excellent spirits, working on a "glorious" big canvas, *Dante's Dream*, and aware of no difficulties with his eyes. Not only had success been a healer, but also silence. He had largely smothered attacks on his poems, was even talking about a show of his pictures toward the end of the year, and had taken time from new writing to advise, at length, a literary physician, Thomas Gordon Hake, about his poems and tales. Gabriel had even become interested in a loquacious young Irishman named John Butler Yeats who had abandoned Dublin, and the Law, to paint and write in London. William went as emissary to invite Yeats to Cheyne Walk, and although the offer was repeated, Yeats never came. Later he regretted his diffidence. "Better to have talked to a man like Rossetti than to travel a thousand leagues to see a thousand cities. Meeting a man like Rossetti must have been like sitting down to a great banquet in a King's hall." It was remarkable how often—and how consistently through the years—the stocky, unprepossessing Rossetti was referred to in royal metaphors. There was something charismatic about the man, from his magnetic, brooding eyes to the natural authority in his rich voice, and the range of his erudition, which—even in Gabriel's adversity—drew men to him.

With his self-confidence restored, he moved more about London. Bell Scott had taken a house nearby, near Battersea Bridge, which made for convenient Tuesday evening whist sessions; and Gabriel was also seen, in various stages of adoration, in the company of Mrs. Morris at artistic soirees ranging as far from Cheyne Walk as Madox Brown's commodious house in Fitzroy Square. Edmund Gosse remembered, as a young man, seeing Janey "in her ripest beauty" sitting on the painting throne at the Browns in a long, out-of-fashion gown of ivory velvet while Gabriel "squatted on a stool at her feet," and someone else recorded seeing him at a party at his solicitor's, Virtue Tebbs, feeding Mrs. Morris strawberries. "He was carefully scraping off the cream, which was bad for her, and then solemnly presenting her with the strawberries in a spoon." She continued to sit for Gabriel, often doing embroidery as he painted. When a curtain she had designed for her bedroom was finished, Whistler once gossiped, Howell was commissioned to hang it between the beds. It was short of the floor by a foot, Howell teased.

"Some night Topsy might crawl under." "He wouldn't dare," said Gabriel. "He wouldn't dare."

Apologizing to his old friend Frederick Shields early in 1871 for not being seen at new exhibitions in London, Gabriel noted that he had "got into such an absolute and undeviating habit of working all daylight somehow" that he was going nowhere. He had five large canvases in progress, but was no longer thinking about showing his pictures. For weeks he even postponed his usual visits to Euston Square, and not until spring did he invite his family again to Tudor House, after having canceled his New Year's Day dinner for them there. Work on pictures was going too well to stop. By the time his urge to complete his canvases had diminished, much had happened at Euston Square. The firm of Rivington and Co. had accepted Maria's *A Shadow of Dante*, to be published "at their own risk & expense, and after deducting from the proceeds of the sale the cost of production and advertising . . . the profits remaining to be divided annually into two equal shares, one moiety to be paid to the author. . . ." Delighted, Maria enlisted Gabriel and William to help design the book. William produced the initial design, Gabriel re-drew it, and Treffry Dunn made the finished sketch for the binders. A thousand copies were to be printed, although on April 8 the publishers cautioned Maria, "We do not think that there is sufficient interest in the subject in this country to make the book very saleable." With difficulty Christina had extricated her book from Ellis, offering *Sing-Song* to George Routledge, who also accepted it in April. Agreeing to terms, Christina wrote that she expected to leave town on the fourth of May, and that if she had not seen specimen pages by then, "my brother William Rossetti kindly undertakes to be the consulting party in my stead." The information did not sound ominous—apparently a spring holiday was in the offing—but her shaky handwriting appeared to be that of an old woman.

In February, in a letter to Gabriel, Christina had referred vaguely to being troubled by an "abscess." Later Dr. Jenner diagnosed severe aches as neuralgia. By April 28, two days after her letter about *Sing-Song*, she was writing Gabriel, "Sir W. Jenner saw me last Saturday and pronounced me seriously ill: to avoid stairs I am confined to the drawing room floor. . . . Please attribute intolerable hideousness [of handwriting] in part to weakness." She was too weak to do anything but remain on her sofa; her eyes bulged, her skin yellowed, she was subject to tremors, and flashes of fever and pain. Jenner still did not recognize exophthalmos, or Graves' disease, but as her symptoms waxed and waned she struggled to prepare her book for the printer and for Arthur Hughes, who had been engaged as illustrator. All that Jenner could suggest, her earlier attempt to leave London having failed because of her exhaustion, was a change of air, and on June 6 she moved with her mother to lodgings in Hampstead Heath, where she could be wheeled outdoors in a bath chair. Six weeks later she came home just long enough to look over the second proofs of *Sing-Song* and its illustrations, to help Maria choose a frontispiece for her Dante book, to be published in August, and despite her appearance permit Cayley to come to dinner and visit with her, lending him as he left her presentation copy of Joaquin Miller's *Songs of the Sierras.* (The exotic American poet had become a friend of William's.) She was, she told William, "less ornamental than society may justly demand," but Cayley was as near to family as it was possible to be, and in her isolation Christina could not afford vanity. Soon she was even further removed from her own limited circle, convalescing at Folkestone, again with her proofs, watching carefully for what William had identified as evidence of "speedy execution" in some of the illustrations. Hughes blamed the engravers, the Dalziel brothers, who had demanded twenty designs the first week. He reworked them, with Christina so pleased at the result that she felt his art "deserve[d] to sell the volume." She even insisted that his name be put in larger print on the title page.

Only William was having publishing problems. While Maria was correcting her proofs, and Christina was doing the same; while Gabriel was watching his *Poems* continue to prosper, despite his concern about adverse criticism, William was watching his favorite project, the Moxon "Popular Poets," become a dry well. Prompt payment for each volume had become no payment, and halfway through 1871, with six volumes issued and four planned, William had still received nothing. All his inquiries had accomplished was to secure the firing of Payne, the original editor, for the firm was discovering the extent of his mismanagement. While beginning legal proceedings against him, Moxon further discovered that William had never had a written contract with Payne, and instructed Beeton, his replacement, to curtail the series and settle with William. Calling on Beeton on June 26, William reluctantly accepted £50 instead of the £126 due him, and agreed to let the series continue in modified form. Something was better than nothing.

Although Gabriel had spent all but one weekend in London, he had seen little of his family. He professed to have been delighted with what appeared from messages he received to be Christina's improvement, but during her worst weeks in London had been to see his sister only twice. She excused him, observing that "his nocturnal habits are not adapted to a sickroom," but the real reasons were that sickbeds repelled him only less so than deathbeds, and he was trying to make up for months of painting he had lost because of his eye trouble. The one weekend away had been to travel with the Morrises to see an old farmhouse in Oxfordshire, near Lechlade, which had been advertised for rent at £60 a year. Morris's willingness to be in Gabriel's company for the journey was as inexplicable as his willingness to share the lease. If he schemed that he and Gabriel would reside there separately, thus removing Janey from him, it was not to be. A low-lying old manor house, ten-gabled and with tapestried interiors, Kelmscott had room for a studio for Gabriel, and he immediately set about having his Cheyne Walk studio renovated, to improve the light, moving to Kelmscott while the work was being done. Morris, having been interested for years in the Scandinavian epic, and having taught himself Icelandic, determined not to reside jointly with Gabriel but instead to take the fortnightly Danish mail boat for Iceland. A week after Morris left, Gabriel moved in, beginning the first of several long periods during which he lived under the same roof with Jane Morris, although his friendship with her husband became increasingly strained and their own joint residence would be restricted to a few weekends.

Morris had been working on a novel of contemporary life which dealt with the love of two brothers for the same woman. He abandoned it after a third of it was written, but the theme remained pervasive in his writing, especially—since the influence of the Arthur-Lancelot motif in Tennyson's *Idylls* was infectious—the unresisting behavior of a husband betrayed by his best friend. A year later Morris wrote without elaboration to Aglaia Coronio about "what horrors" the Iceland voyage "saved me from," for while he explored the land of the sagas Gabriel lived a secluded summer of connubial bliss with Janey. They walked for miles in the lowlands, painted and posed, decorated and furnished the house, played with the two Morris girls and acquired three dogs.* And they treasured what Gabriel described as

> This close companioned inarticulate hour
> When two-fold silence was the song of love.

The "drained flood-lands" became the setting for new sonnets to be added to "The House of Life," some of them more erotic than topographical, and it is difficult to accept such lines as

> Her arms lie open, throbbing with their throng
> Of confluent pulses, bare and fair and strong:
>   And her deep-freighted lips expect me now
>   Amid the clustering hair that shrines her brow
> Five kisses broad, her neck ten kisses long,

---

* Morris disliked dogs as well as other domestic animals.

as entirely the product of amorous speculation. But ironically Gabriel painted not only from life but had also agreed to do a replica of *Beata Beatrix* for Graham, who had written, "I know there must be a certain special reluctance, from the memories and associations of the *Beatrice*, to re-tread very sacred ground. . . . You know . . . that the *Beatrice*, from the first day I saw it, has appealed to my feeling altogether above and beyond any picture I ever saw, the *love* for it has only deepened with its growth and my knowledge of its history. Therefore I can come to you with clean hands and a pure heart, and say, 'Do it for me if you can without *hurt to yourself.*' " In the serenity of Kelmscott, even the shade of Lizzy could be exorcised, and Gabriel could write to Dr. Hake that copying the *Beatrice* was "not inspiring work but profitable." He set his price to Graham at 900 guineas. "I make lots of money (for a poor painter)," he wrote his uncle Henry Polydore, "and never have a penny to fly with."

To Hake in September Gabriel sent a poem, "Commandments," in which the Italy he had never seen provided a needed rhyme. The closing was lyrical and heartfelt:

> Let no priest tell you of any home.
> Unseen above the sky's blue dome.
> To have played in childhood by the sea,
> Or to have been young in Italy,
> Or anywhere in the sun and rain
> To have loved and been beloved again,
> Is nearer heaven than he can come.

The last two lines—the reason for the entire poem—needed no elucidation to those who knew what had been happening to Gabriel, but the heaven that was Kelmscott was about to close its doors. Morris returned with the autumn, visited twice, then took his family back to Queen Square. With the autumn rains the floodplain surrounding Kelmscott was largely under water, and the meadows over which Gabriel and Janey had walked daily could be traversed only in a small boat. Lonely in the isolated village and having tramped alone along the "stubble-fields and queer byways" which were the only dry paths, he returned to London in mid-October.

Emboldened by his months with Janey Morris, within days of his return Gabriel was seeing her again, and under circumstances which suggested—if one is to believe Bell Scott—that the lovers, still under the spell of their Kelmscott summer, had abandoned caution. Morris had invited a group of artist and writer friends to Queen Square for dinner, Scott among them, and the evening before Scott had asked Gabriel whether he would also be present. No, he said; he had another engagement—which turned out to be

Janey, who would be spending the night at Cheyne Walk. Until Scott arrived at Queen Square for dinner he remained unbelieving. But Janey was not there. "Is it not too daring?" he queried Alice Boyd, as if she had been a paragon of chastity rather than his mistress in a *ménage à trois* that had been carried on for years with careful Victorian decorum.

Although Janey apparently continued to visit Rossetti, the evidence of such contacts exists mainly on his canvases, as he entertained little while he caught up on his painting, and made no public show of the relationship to Janey he was enabled to maintain through Morris's pretended indifference. The year would pass, he wrote Alice Boyd's aunt, Miss Losh, without his hosting guests under the tent in the Tudor House garden. For the first time since he had moved to Cheyne Walk the tent had not been up. (There were other changes, too, as the studio windows overlooking the garden had been enlarged while he had been away, providing him with more light at a time when improved vision relaxed his earlier limits on hours of work.) Bringing Miss Losh up to date on his family he wrote that Christina was improving after her worst spell of illness, but was "completely altered and looking suddenly ten years older," and that his elder sister had just published "a compendious and most thoroughly executed" book on Dante which he had not yet read himself. Christina's condition had been alarming, and remained so, Gabriel crediting her with both "courage" and "endurance." In November her erratic thyroid was worse. The swelling in her throat made swallowing difficult, and she also suffered from what William described as "a fluttering of the heart" that was sometimes followed by breathing difficulties and loss of consciousness. Her head ached constantly, and her hands still shook. Unable to hold a pencil in her fingers without an intense effort, she could write almost nothing. The previous month William had gone over the final proof of *Sing-Song* for Christina, and her publisher rushed a bound copy to her on November 18, although it was to have an 1872 publication date, for it seemed important to get a book into her palsied hands in case 1872 would prove too late.

Having the book was a hollow triumph in the midst of her pain. William acknowledged that "as regards appearance, she is a total wreck for the present, and I greatly fear this change may prove permanent." Her scalp was coarse, and her hair falling out. (She had to wear a cap.) Her skin had become a dry rusty brown. Her eyes bulged even more prominently than before. Her face was drawn, with nose sharpened and cheeks sunken. Her voice rasped from her swollen throat. "But with all these disasters—and she is fully alive to every one of them," William noted, "her spirits are not so bad as might be expected; she shows a really admirable constancy, and the worst shafts of Fate find her their equal." Her symptoms were classic, but only after Sir William Jenner returned from Balmoral in Scotland, where he had been attending the Queen, and consulted with Dr. Wilson Fox who had treated Christina in his absence, did the two confirm what her ailment really was. For Christina it was no consolation to have her horrors given a name, and she turned, as always, to her steady source of comfort:

> Thou, O Lord, in pain hadst no pillow soft,
> In Thy weary pain, in Thine agony:
> But a cross of shame held Thee up aloft
> Where thy very mother could do nought for Thee.

Christina's lowest moment was Maria's highest. Early in November *A Shadow of Dante* was favorably reviewed in the *Athenaeum* and *Saturday Review*, the first of a number of good notices which propelled the book in sales beyond its publisher's expectations. It was almost a family affair. William and Gabriel had helped with its design. The title was taken from a passage in her father's *Veggente*, and the family link was emphasized by her use of quotations from William's flat translation of the *Inferno* as well as some of his notes on the poem. Yet her quotations from the *Vita Nuova* were her own translations, spurning Gabriel's eloquent version from the *Italian Poets*, while for the *Purgatorio* and the *Paradiso* she used Longfellow's blank verse rendering, which she called "faithful and beautiful." * Whether or not it was the debt to his countryman which inspired him, James Russell Lowell reviewed it with high praise as "the best comment [on Dante] that has appeared in English," the product of a "lithe mind" that has mastered "the metaphysical and other intricacies of her subject." She had gone right to the point—that Dante for centuries had been more praised than perused:

Dante is a name unlimited in place and period. Not Italy, but the Universe, is his birthplace; not the fourteenth century, but all Time, is his epoch. He rises before us and above us like the Pyramids—awful, massive, solitary; the embodiment of the character, the realization of the science, of his clime and day; yet the outcome of a far wider past, the standard of a far wider future. Like the Pyramids, again, he is known to all by name and by pictorial representation; must we not add, like them unknown to most by actual sight and presence? . . .

Even of his fellow-linguists how many have read his great poem through? One of themselves has said it—few have gone beyond the Inferno; nay, most have stopped short at two passages of the Inferno—*Francesca da Rimini* and *il Conte Ugolino*. And of his fellow-cosmopolitans how many have read even so much? . . .

Any acquaintance with a work so sublime must needs be better than none. A shadow may win the gaze of some who never looked upon the substance, never

---

* Longfellow wrote her a letter of praise about the book.

tasted the entrancement of this Poet's music, never entered into the depths of this Philosopher's cogitations. My plan is very simple. After in some degree setting forth what Dante's Universe is as a whole, and what autobiography and history show his life-experience to have been, I proceed to expound in greater detail—here and there unavoidably with slight repetition—the physical and moral theories on which his Three Worlds are constructed; and to narrate, now in his own words, now in a prose summary, the course of his stupendous pilgrimage. . . .

Ambitious as Maria's undertaking was, it appeared to succeed on her own terms, with a thousand copies sold in England and America, and she was soon consulting with Gabriel about improving the frontispiece and lithographs for another printing, and communicating her satisfaction to Richard Garnett, British Museum director, that even Dante specialists—for whom the book was not planned—had found it worthwhile. But she had no interest in writing another book, nor even in reading anything in the English language. Contemporary fiction was "morbid," and she resorted instead to old Italian books, which were "soothingly unsensational."

Christina's critical success followed Maria's. *Sing-Song*, with over a hundred evocative illustrations by Arthur Hughes, had been cryptically dedicated "without permission" to "The Baby" whose existence suggested the nursery rhymes—Cayley's young nephew in Cambridge—her vicarious way, perhaps, of having a Cayley baby of her own.

Publication came at a peak of Victorian interest in children's literature and illustration, made most notable by "Lewis Carroll," Robert Louis Stevenson and Kate Greenaway, and like much writing for juveniles seemed intended for grave, precocious children tended by overeducated governesses. The personified small animals ("When fishes set umbrellas up . . ."), the quaint enumerations ("A pin has a head, but has no hair . . ."), the rhetorical questions ("Who has ever seen the wind?"), the metaphorical definitions ("Hope is like a harebell trembling from its birth . . .") appealed to the tastes of adult readers *to* children, and the *Sunday Times*, in January, 1872, seeing "imaginative power" united with "supreme delicacy and tenderness," declared her the finest female poet of her day, while the *Academy* called *Sing-Song* "one of the most exquisite in its class ever seen." It would take six years, nevertheless, before it would go into a second printing; but in the few months before her malady would enter a dangerous new portion of its cycle, she took pleasure in her success, and even picked up her pencil again. By March she was bedridden, Sir William reassuring the family (although he had seen only two cases before) that the disease was neither contagious nor fatal. But Christina had little appetite, vomited frequently, and had to be fed every two hours. Outwardly she looked improved, and when she could hold a book, read history. In mid-April Maria saw her sister's throat uncovered for the first time in months, and was "agreeably surprised" at how much the swelling had diminished, and how much less obvious was Christina's skin discoloration. Yet a month later the family remained as concerned as ever, for Jenner had noted that the patient's most serious problems would come from exhaustion. To William she was in "a terriby low condition," and it appeared that the process was advancing "with fatal and frightful steadiness."

While Christina had been declining, and writing nothing, Gabriel appeared to be in the best condition of his life. When he had reluctantly packed to leave Kelmscott he had written Bell Scott that had he the opportunity to remain longer—three months would have been enough—he would have had another volume of poetry ready. At Cheyne Walk he painted with renewed vigor. He even laughed off an anonymous attack on his poetry in the October (1871) *Contemporary Review*, "The Fleshly School of Poetry," although the choice of adjective went to the heart of mid-Victorian sexual repression and its hypocrisies which protected "respectability." Puritan consciences had diverted the painting of the nude into mythical and classical subjects, and Rossetti himself rarely drew any more flesh than appeared on face, neck and arms. Still, even his friendly critics had for years (like Stephens in 1865) praised "the marvellous fleshiness of the flesh" on Gabriel's canvases, and the pseudonymous "Thomas Maitland" perceived similarities in the diction Rossetti employed in his love poetry. Gabriel's real or assumed indifference stood up until he heard that Robert Buchanan had been identified as the enemy. Expected at Scott's for dinner that evening, Gabriel arrived late, bursting in with the name of Buchanan. "He was too excited to observe or care who were present, and all the evening he continued unable to contain himself, or to avoid shouting out the name of his enemy. I was glad when the sitting came to an end, and one after another left with a private word of inquiry regarding Rossetti. From this time he occupied himself in composing a long reply, which he read over a hundred times, till the lives of his friends became too heavy to bear."

William warned Gabriel that "it were best left undone," but Gabriel went ahead anyway, publishing "The Stealthy School of Criticism" in the *Athenaeum* in December. All it did was encourage other attacks, Buchanan himself preparing the most detailed rejoinder, searching microscopically through Gabriel's sonnets, with the perverse glee of the private pornographer, for allegedly "spicy" passages, and concluding that "The House of Life" was very likely the identical house where the writer found "Jenny"—a brothel. Rossetti's poetry, he concluded, recorded "the most secret mysteries of sexual connection and with so sickening a desire to reproduce the sensual mood, so careful a choice of epithet to convey mere animal sensations, that we merely shudder at the shameless nakedness."

Gabriel had been pretending to be undisturbed, writing Hake early in 1872 about another review which accused him of "emasculate obscenity" in attempting to "attach a spiritual meaning to the animal passions," that he "laughed on reading it and laugh in thinking of it." But the support he saw Buchanan picking up renewed his paranoid fears of a conspiracy to blacken his reputation. It also inspired new concern that his relationship with Jane Morris would be exposed and the exhumation of his wife's grave revealed. Two additions not in Buchanan's original attack but in his enlarged pamphlet would further disturb Gabriel's nights. Both were veiled references to his marriage, and suggested that Buchanan knew more than he really did:

The truth appears to be, that writing, however nasty, will be perfectly sanctified to English readers if it be moral in the legal sense; and thus a poet who describes sensual details may do so with impunity if he labels his poems—"Take notice! These sensations are strictly *nuptial;* these delights have been sanctioned by English law, and registered at Doctors' Commons!" We have here the reason that Mr. Rossetti has almost escaped censure . . . for Mr. Rossetti, in his worst poems, explains that he is speaking dramatically in the character of *husband* addressing his *wife*. Animalism is animalism, nevertheless, whether licensed or not; and, indeed, one might tolerate the language of lust more readily on the lips of a lover addressing a mistress than on the lips of a husband virtually (in these so-called "Nuptial" Sonnets) wheeling his nuptial couch out into the public streets.

It was no secret that his wife had been dead for ten years, and it was not claimed by Gabriel that all, or even most, of his published poems were written about, during, or prior to his luckless marriage. What nuptial couch, then, was he wheeling out into the streets of London? Did Janey's face and figure emerge too conspicuously in his poetry, despite the cosmetic alterations? Whatever his actual lifestyle, Gabriel had not acquired a public reputation for bohemianism, or worse, and in fact needed the respect of respectable people in order to elicit purchasers for his paintings. His way of life, he thought, was being threatened. Through the spring of 1872, according to William, "His fancies . . . ran away with him, and he thought that the pamphlet was a first symptom in a widespread conspiracy for crushing his fair fame and hounding him out of honest society."

Few letters of his survive from these months, almost as if his family and friends discreetly did away with the wild ones. "I write this late from Wm's," goes one to Madox Brown. ". . . His calmness induces me to think that I probably have been making too much of the matter." Certainly the aura of scandal Gabriel sensed swirling about him seldom came then to Euston Square, and the matter was not discussed by the brothers in the presence of the pious Rossetti women, particularly the gravely ill Christina.

Ironically, then, just as the accusations of lewdness were being leveled at one Rossetti, another—Maria—had responded to an advertisement from that most respectable of organizations, the Society for the Promotion of Christian Knowledge, which was seeking material for new publications. From her drawer she dredged a series of religious lessons in letter form which she had written for a Bible class for young women in her parish a dozen years before. William thought them "up to a high standard in their kind," and Maria sent them off. Later in the year *Letters to my Bible Class on 37 Sundays* was published by the S.P.C.K. It was not a major literary event, but Maria, more and more withdrawn into her contemplative world, was satisfied.

Other, more authentic, literary events had more impact upon the Rossettis. A month before, Gabriel had called at Euston Square and discussed with William his perplexity at discovering that his household expenses were now exceeding £1,000 a year. Reeling now from criticism, Gabriel found that the butcher and baker mattered much less. In "Lewis Carroll's" *Hunting of the Snark*, for example—despite Charles Dodgson's friendship of a decade's standing—Gabriel "found" a veiled personal attack. Toward the end of May his emotional state began alarming William, who nevertheless had other things on his mind and could not take wild talk of secret conspiracies seriously when Christina was "exceptionally low," and again confined to bed. She had nearly choked to death when a piece of potato had lodged in her swollen throat, and she had been horribly frightened. Neuralgia had made her a quivering mass of pain, and heart palpitations and vomiting left her exhausted. Out of bed for a few minutes one day in mid-May, she fell, unconscious, to the floor, and William had carried her back to bed. Gabriel had to be left to his delusions. On Sunday, June 2, when William was again able to go to Chelsea, he found his brother so agitated that it was unsafe to leave. Bell Scott came by to help. The day should have been further improved by the arrival of a representative of the firm of Pilgeram and Lefevre, who was to pick up, and pay for, the just-completed *The Bower Meadow*, the background for which Gabriel had painted at Sevenoaks (as *The Meeting of Dante and Beatrice in Garden of Eden*) twenty-two years before. Obsessed with treachery, he took the high price he was willingly paid—£735—as evidence that he was being cheated, and that night was wracked by paranoiac delusions. The next day, "so far as office attendance allowed," William noted in his diary, he remained with Gabriel: "Scott, Dunn, F[anny] also about him: & in the evg. he & I went rd. to Brown's. Some table-turning the evg. rather earlier at Chelsea: the table moved very consider[abl]y, but not violently, & some messages came, purporting to be from Lizzie. Nothing very marked in these, unless one can so consider the answers that she is happy, & still loves G.—Initials for her young brother, H.S., given correctly. G. was, I fancy the only person at the table who knew of the "H": I did not—or rather had wholly forgotten."

That Gabriel had to again "summon" Lizzy indicated the extent of his anxiety, and that "H"—the subject of her suicide note—was again alluded to, could only have reinforced a guilty conscience which had been, at least since the exhumation, happily dormant. On Wednesday June 5 the postman arrived at Cheyne Walk with a parcel. It was a presentation copy of Browning's new *Fifine at the Fair*, with a personal inscription: "To Dante Gabriel Rossetti from his old admirer and affectionate friend. R.B." "This is very handsome of Browning, very handsome!" he commented to Madox Brown, and rushed off an acknowledgment. "My dear Browning. Thanks once more for a new book bearing your name loved as of old. And even before I read it, let me say, Thanks. . . ."

Walking up and down in the studio after posting his letter, Gabriel began leafing through *Fifine*, first becoming startled, and then horrified, by what he began imagining as a sly undermining of his reputation. "Why, this is an attack on Bohemians!" he told Madox Brown; and after reading further he added, "This is an attack on me!" Since Gabriel's senses were at times confused by sleeplessness, whiskey and chloral, Brown assured him that no personal allusion was possible, but Gabriel's anger only increased, and he threw the offending book into the fire. Madox Brown quickly rescued it, but Gabriel would not take it back, and it remained in Brown's possession the rest of his life.

As William remembered it, "My brother looked into the book: and to the astonishment of bystanders, he at once fastened on some lines at its close as being intended as an attack on him." Very likely he saw his "Jenny" and "The Blessed Damozel" lampooned, his guilty conscience about his dead wife ridiculed, and himself alluded to as a sensual seeker-out of lewd women. The Epilogue—which Rossetti may have glanced at first, if he thumbed the pages back-to-front, confronted him, in the ghost-haunted widower, with a mirror-image of himself:

> "What, and is it really you again?" quoth I:
> "I again, what else did you expect?" quoth She.

> "Never mind, hie away from this old house—
> Every crumbling brick embrowned with sin and shame!"
> Quick, in its corners ere certain shapes arouse!

> Let them—every devil of the night—lay claim,
> Make and mend, or rap and rend, for me! . . ."

Browning probably did have, at the least, "Jenny" in mind when he wrote *Fifine*, and was far less enthusiastic about Gabriel's "scented" poetry when apart from the poet than he was in person; but he could not have imagined the result, especially since two decades of widespread turning and rapping had left the Epilogue allusion a personal reference only to paranoiacs who fit the description.*

From William, who "no doubt . . . knew more than we did," Bell Scott learned some details which he wrote to Alice Boyd. Browning, Gabriel was sure, "was his greatest enemy, determined to hunt him to death." In the process, he decided, the walls of Tudor House were "mined," as well as "perforated by spies," and everything he did and said "was known to the conspirators." While in the literary journals London critics confessed bafflement at *Fifine*, at an old brick house in Cheyne Walk where a rapping session had evoked a dead wife two nights before, one reader, at least, understood every dark passage. Conspiracies closed in darkly about Gabriel, and from Euston Square William hurried to Chelsea. That night, shaken, he closed his diary with the concern that it might be his last entry. "This diary work," he confided, "is becoming too painful now if important matters are to be recorded, & too futile & irritating if the unimportant are made to take their place. I shall therefore drop it. Perhaps a great change may have come over the face of things when—or if—I next resume it: or there will have been, as Swinburne says, 'An end, an end, an end of all,' & no resumption of it."

---

* Nevertheless Browning knew of Gabriel's attempts at Tudor House to summon Lizzy, and there is further evidence that he had encouraged Buchanan, perhaps because Gabriel had once banteringly referred to the obscure and complicated *Balaustion's Adventure* as "Exhaustion's Imposture." Yet Browning certainly would not have sent Gabriel *Fifine* had he thought the Rossettian element was as unsubtle as it seemed, in effect, to be.

XII

Lost Summer

1872

abriel's paranoid delusions impelled Marshall and Hake to send for an eminent specialist in nervous disorders, Dr. Henry Maudsley, but on his arrival at Cheyne Walk, Gabriel accused him of falsely posing as a doctor in order to further the conspiracy, and Maudsley hastily bowed out. Since Hake had been a literary friend, his words were more persuasive. He sent for a cab, urging Gabriel to go home with him to Roehampton. Again Gabriel argued about conspiracies, but when the cab came he agreed to climb into it with Brown and William.

Summer darkness came late on a London June, but it was already night when the cab arrived at Hake's house overlooking Richmond Park. It had been a harrowing journey. Gabriel kept insisting that a bell was being rung on the roof of the cab to annoy him, and he even berated the cabman, as they alighted at Hake's house, with "Why did you ring that bell?" The cabman looked blank. Gabriel's auditory delusions, present earlier in Cheyne Walk, would continue.

Wearily, Brown went back to London in the cab and the others went to bed, Gabriel having happily announced that he had found what he had so long ceased to feel, "and that was peace." But the next morning was again strange. It was the Saturday before Whitsunday (June 8), and the roads were filled with holidayers in their vehicles, as well as a group of gypsy vans which crowded the highroad, and which Hake and his party encountered when they went out for a walk. For Gabriel the gypsy vans were suspicious. He fancied, William remembered, that what he saw was "a demonstration got up in his disparagement; and he was with difficulty restrained from running after some of the conveyances, and interchanging a wordy war with their drivers. Our walk was abridged." Then followed an incident involving a party of merrymakers going to Richmond Park, two of whom carried poles between which a banner was stretched. Gabriel identified it as a gibbet and declared that it was intended for him—that they were on their way to set up a gallows for him in the park. He rushed out of the house shaking his fists at the crowd, and William and Hake had to follow to restrain him.

Although the rest of the day passed without incident, seeking something harmless to pass the time after dinner, Hake suggested reading aloud, and a history of Rome was handed to William, opened to a page at random. "As ill luck would have it, this passage detailed some of the tiger-monkey pranks, played by Caligula or Domitian, to drive his submissive senators half out of their senses. The scenes depicted bore a perilous analogy to the grotesque encumbrances of my brother's brain. I came to a full stop, though greatly urged by him to proceed, as he wanted to know the too-appetizing details." William changed the subject—to "family matters," Hake recalled—and all then retired for the night.

Gabriel may have taken his nightly dosage of chloral before going to bed, but if so it had no useful effect, for he lay awake and heard (he later told William) "a voice which twice called out at him a term of gross and unbearable obloquy." What voice, and what term, William would not repeat, but what followed may be the clue, for feeling unable to escape his persecutor Gabriel "laid his hand upon a bottle of laudanum which, unknown to us all, he had brought with him, swallowed its contents, and dropped the empty bottle into a drawer."

No one awakened Gabriel on Sunday morning. He always slept late. When morning turned to afternoon, and Hake looked in and saw his guest sleeping with unusual placidity, he decided it was a turn for the better. Toward four o'clock he changed his mind. Gabriel's appearance seemed "no longer satisfying to a medical eye." William rushed out for a neighboring doctor to confirm Hake's worst fears, and the two physicians agreed that the cause was probably "an effusion of serum on the brain," and that Gabriel was "already past all hope." It was William's grim duty to inform his mother and sisters, to whom Hake extended the hospitality of his home. Accompanied by young George Hake, William went off to Euston Square, stopping first at Madox Brown's in Fitzroy Square, for his good friend was a combination of surrogate elder brother and father-figure. Refusing to consider the case as hopeless, Brown rushed off to locate John Marshall, who had been Gabriel's doctor for years. William went on to Euston Square, seeking first his tough old aunt Eliza, who had an apartment in the house.

Someone would have to take care of Christina, who was bedridden; and William also wanted assistance with him when he broke the news to his mother and Maria. Aunt Eliza, who had served in the Crimea with Florence Nightingale, was an indomitable and useful lady.

It appears that Christina was told, for a sonnet of hers suggests that Sunday night, when she would have no information for a day or more other than what seemed to be her brother's imminent death:

> . . . My brother's blood, my brother's soul, doth cry:
> And I find no defence, find no reply,
> No courage more to run this race I run,
> Not knowing what I have done, have left undone;
> Ah me, these awful unknown hours that fly,
> Fruitless it may be, fleeting fruitless by,
> Rank with death-savour underneath the sun! . . .

Long after dark Mrs. Rossetti and Maria arrived with William at Roehampton, followed closely by Brown and Marshall. Gabriel, they found, was still alive, Hake desperately holding a large bottle of ammonia to his patient's nostrils. Taking William aside, Hake produced the empty bottle he had found, clearly labeled "Laudanum—Poison." * Marshall ordered strong coffee force-fed to Gabriel as antidote, and directed that he be massaged to keep his circulation and respiration active, not leaving until he saw some signs of returning consciousness.

The next day Gabriel gradually revived. He was passive and despondent, and suffered from partial paralysis, from the hip, in one leg, brought on, Dr. Marshall suggested, "by his remaining so long in a recumbent position, under the benumbing influence of the laudanum." A colloquy of friends and relatives was necessary. Planning a funeral would have been easy. Planning for Gabriel's convalescence was more difficult. He could not be left in Cheyne Walk, with its attendant memories, and Marshall flatly rejected that possibility. The Rossettis felt unwilling to impose upon Hake any longer than necessary, but the other alternatives, including a private asylum, were few. "In my own house," William noted, "with Christina on a bed of sickness, perhaps of death, three other female inmates (not to speak of servants), and myself daily called away to a Government office, Dante would just then have caused the most wearying anxiety." The anxiety was felt most by William, who realized that if word got out of Gabriel's incapacity, or—worse yet—of his removal to an asylum, creditors would descend upon

---

* Mrs. Rossetti and her daughters were never told of the laudanum, nor that the illness was the aftermath of a suicide attempt. "They finished their days," according to William, "in ignorance of the facts."

Cheyne Walk in hordes. His brother's finances at the best of times were chaotic and debt-burdened. Now everything might be seized, and sold at a fraction of its value, with Gabriel's further emotional collapse assured. Brown and Scott suggested moving all of Gabriel's pictures, finished or in progress, including the huge *Dante's Dream*, to Scott's house nearby. With Dunn's help the transfer was hurriedly accomplished, and the collection of blue china removed as well. Then the asylum plan fell through.

While Maria and Mrs. Rossetti were concurring that an asylum would be best, and Hake and Marshall were pondering one, Gabriel took matters into his own hands. Despite William's entreaties, he insisted on returning to his own house. Realizing that he had lost control of the situation, William was perilously near breaking down himself. The responsibilities pressing upon him, with Christina possibly dying, and Gabriel worse than dead, were more than he could bear any longer. Seeing as much, Madox Brown proposed the experiment of taking charge of Gabriel himself at Cheyne Walk. Gratefully, William agreed, and that Thursday Gabriel, leaning on a stick, hobbled to a cab and went off with Brown to a house stripped of all his working canvases.

Passive and despondent, and still subject to delusions, Gabriel seemed not to notice that his occupation was gone, and William was kept away by Brown with assurances that there was "improvement" and "the most perfect quiet & reasonable behaviour," and that a joint checking account was being set up so that William could handle Gabriel's finances. All the principals, William Fredeman writes in his exhaustive study of the summer of 1872, seemed "determined to send optimistic reports to William," whom Scott described to Alice on the 14th as "getting into a more composed state," and no longer looking upon his responsibilities as "overwhelming." On the 15th Scott wrote again, reporting that he had been to Tudor House until one in the morning, and had played whist with George Hake, Dunn and Brown, with Gabriel joining in for a time, stopping to listen carefully for something at one point and then announcing, "Now don't you all acknowledge how much stiller it is tonight than it has been for many days?" If the stillness were merely the absence of his conspirators, he had not yet shaken free from his delusions.

Brown decided to move Gabriel to Fitzroy Square. At least then Brown could return in part to his own family and professional life. On the evening of the 17th the removal took place, William having been informed the day before that Dr. Marshall thought there was now "not the slightest objection" to his visiting Gabriel. What the doctor thought about Gabriel's seeing Jane Morris as well is unknown, but before Gabriel left Cheyne Walk Jane had prevailed upon her husband to take her there, leaving Gabriel afterwards more depressed than before. But despite his continued delusions he had carefully refrained from alluding to Jane, asking instead for his plump and ancient Fanny, who was in and out of the house as often as in earlier days. Fanny would see nothing of Gabriel for many months thereafter as the transfer to Fitzroy Square sufficed only to provide time to solve a few of the more pressing financial problems, and to decide where Gabriel should be sent out of London.

Acting for William, who had finally returned to daily business at the Excise Office, Brown made arrangements to sell Gabriel's china and to settle the matter of what to do with the Cheyne Walk servants. He also opened all of Gabriel's mail, and found an offer from William Graham of one of his country places in Scotland. Arrangements were made quickly. George Hake, then between terms at Oxford, would stay with Gabriel, and he, Brown, and Gabriel's manservant Allan, left for Urrard House, Perthshire on June 20. There Gabriel turned to matters of immediate concern, as the walls at Urrard House could not be expected to conceal conspirators. To his mother went a letter assuring her that the only one in the party not in the best of health was Allan, who had not yet adjusted to Scotland;* and to William went two letters, one asking him to secure in his name the furniture and goods in Fanny's house at 36 Royal Avenue, to put off prying creditors, and the other a formal one in which he consigned all the goods in Fanny's house to William in payment for loans made over the years, and asked that an appropriate legal stamp be affixed to the document. The "Elephant" had to be taken care of.

Within a week Gabriel had moved to another Graham country seat, Stobhall, overlooking the Firth of Tay, which two centuries before had been the home of the Jacobite Drummonds. The change of house changed little else. He was still subject to his delusions, but discussed them rarely, George Hake wrote William, because of "our want of faith" in them. He slept better, but only with the aid of whiskey and chloral, and limped or drove through the countryside for want of anything else to do. "We find it hard to get through the day," Hake confessed. When Bell Scott replaced Brown at Stobhall he looked hopefully for signs of a restoration in vigor sufficient that Gabriel would not ask to go to Penkill, where, Scott feared, in his incapacity he would make slaves of everyone. Physically he was indeed improving, but the country quiet only changed the appurtenances of the conspiracy. Even the birds in the trees were mocking him. He slept five or six hours a night,

---

* Allan, a tubercular as well as an alcoholic, was returned to London on July 5, although Gabriel, the delusive conspiracy still in mind, objected to Hake that Allan was "the only friend we had here and that he acted as a check upon the servants in their designs."

but only when self-drugged, and when appealed to about reducing his whiskey intake he became excited and threatened to throw himself out the window if his sleep were taken from him.

Even one of the Cheyne Walk delusions returned, as he confided that the walls were hollowed and contained people who listened through holes made for curtain-hooks no longer used. Some sounds Hake attributed to wrens and sand-larks clearly visible to Gabriel were not that at all, he told Hake, but small boys hidden from them who were taunting him. When William suggested a sea voyage, or a therapeutic trip abroad, Hake wrote him, "You have no idea how he invests with undue importance the most trivial circumstances. If we start[le] a rabbit (you know how they lie in the grass) or if a passing countryman civilly bids us a 'good night' or even a watch dog barking as we pass—all are studied insults. What then would it be if he was travelling?" His enemies, he told Scott and Hake, would decoy them away and then murder him or cause him to disappear, and when they were out of sight for a time he would grow greatly agitated. Watching seine fishermen draw in their nets, he told Hake, "You see that? It is an allegory of my state. My persecutors are gradually narrowing the net round me until at last it will be drawn tight."

Reports on Gabriel's condition went largely to Brown, who wrote to Scott on July 6 that he and Hake "did quite right *not* to send your letters to William [as] he is not in a state to bear them." At least one other agony was spared William as Christina, able again to travel, went first to Hampstead with her mother, then to Glottenham in Sussex, where, languid and listless, she had little to do but sit and watch the robins and the emmets. At least the birds did not berate her, and she wrote William of her hope to return in September "to keep house with you, as in old days, in much harmony."

However depressed by family circumstances, William had its business to attend to. "Not a day passes," he wrote Scott, still then at Stobhall, "—& sometimes not an hour or two consecutively—without my being called off to write some letter, run some errand, receive some visit, offer some information . . . regarding Gabriel or his affairs, so that the pull upon my working faculties & my spirits continues not small. . . ." Having his brother in a remote place in Scotland made matters worse, for diagnoses of his condition were made by nonmedical companions to physicians hundreds of miles removed from the scene, and the remedies suggested applied the same way. Added to Gabriel's discomforts was the swelling of his chronic hydrocele, which made sitting uncomfortable and at least stimulated his desire to walk. Dr. Hake thought the hydrocele "a useful reality among his fancies," but in the end it was relieved by a local doctor. Still, Stobhall had proven no solution to the basic problem, and Marshall suggested that as an alternative to what was considered the most drastic step—the asylum—a young doctor with a new practice might be induced to take Gabriel in. But William was not being consulted. Despite William's continuing activities on Gabriel's behalf, Brown was still writing to Scott that William was "rather more composed but by no means fit to hear discouraging reports as yet."

Although William, while conducting Gabriel's London business, slept some nights at Cheyne Walk, it was Treffry Dunn's responsibility to maintain the house, put off Fanny, and refer problems he could not handle to Madox Brown or to William. Was Alexa Wilding to be kept on retainer although Gabriel could not use her? What should be done to exterminate the rats and mice in the studio ceiling? * What should be done with the garden zoo? Should replicas underway be completed? How much instruction in managing the household should be tolerated from Fanny? What was the Italian or Latin lettering on a picture to be restored, which had "all run into one confused mass"?

On July 13 Scott was replaced at Stobhall by Dr. Hake, who had been away from Gabriel long enough to observe some change, and who seemed better able to induce his charge to do what was necessary. He began by treating Gabriel as a sane human being, and Gabriel responded well to the professional presence about the house. His conversation remained free of the usual conspiracies, but Hake realistically wrote to William that Gabriel very likely "has his secret delusions but he says less & less about them and it is easy to change the subject as he is not now excited about them." A complication in their situation was that Stobhall had to be vacated at the end of July. William had sent out strong hints to Scott that Penkill was desirable, but Gabriel on the 23rd declined the invitation, telling Miss Boyd that he would be unfit company. The Hakes, then, began searching the countryside for suitable accommodations, finding them at Trowan Farm, near Crieff, where a Mrs. Stewart had a house available.

Since Gabriel had to be put up, with the younger Hake, at a hotel in Perth for two days while the transfer was accomplished, it was taken as a sign of continued improvement that he was not made unduly anxious by the noise and bustle. Yet to keep Gabriel from further insomnia, which Hake believed was a major factor in his patient's delusions, he felt compelled to add morphine to the chloral and alcohol Gabriel was already taking to induce sleep. More chloral might have been dangerous, and the amount already in nightly use was losing its effect. The idea of the addictive morphine sent panic through William, and Hake lectured him that "moral matters appear magnified with distance." The next day, after still further

---

* Which may have contributed to Gabriel's sense of conspirators literally within his walls.

entreaties from Euston Square, Hake was at pains to allay any concern. Gabriel had improved more in less than two months than might have been expected in six, he thought. "A stranger looking at him now would say he was a valetudinarian, or perhaps a *malade imaginaire*. We notice improvement every week. . . . He initiates subjects of conversation, and will listen to almost anything save his own works. . . ." But one subject which never came up was Jane Morris, who pressed William for information. "I . . . know well how completely you must sympathise with me at this juncture," she wrote, "and so hope you will excuse me."

Janey was being handled carefully by all of those involved with Gabriel. Without mentioning the lady in question, William wrote Howell that Gabriel had been so "madly in love" that almost any extreme of hypochondria could have evolved from the effect of the affair on his mind. Since everyone in Gabriel's circle assumed that the relationship with Jane was at the least a contributing factor to Gabriel's breakdown, no one wanted to see the relationship, whatever it was, resumed. But no one in the circle could broach the subject to Jane, and Gabriel, apart from her, seemed content enough in Trowan's jewel-like setting near rivers, lakes, waterfalls and pine-covered hills, in which he walked, although lame, six miles a day. George Hake thought the area was "the second place in the world in point of solitude—the desert of Sahara being the first," but somehow it was ideal for his patient, who ate lustily, sent for wine (which Mrs. Stewart did not furnish), and trudged all the local paths with the help of a stick. He was being kept as remote from the cares of his former world as he was distant from it physically. He had reluctantly approved the sale of his china for £650, but was told nothing of Howell's exertions to sell some of his pictures, was kept from receiving most letters, and through a strategy of advancing the clocks was put to bed—on watered chloral and watered whiskey—at earlier times than he knew.

Sending his accounts to William on August 11, George Hake emphasized the progress that had been made, but did not suggest that William visit. The brothers had not seen each other for nearly two months, but William had earlier noted that he could not leave Somerset House for any extended period during August and September. He had been referring to the possibility of his being needed to accompany Gabriel abroad, and it was the excuse to keep him away altogether until it was certain that his own emotional state was sound. Perhaps the least of William's anxieties would come from George Hake's accounts. For the period from June 29 to August 10 the costs to Gabriel were £34 ls. lld. Apparently the Hakes as well as the others who had accompanied Gabriel at various times were paying their own expenses, Dr. Hake having also sacrificed his practice in London. The elder

Hake—perhaps only second to Madox Brown in his selfless devotion to Gabriel—followed up his son's letter to William the same day with one of his own in which he frankly told William that although there was comparatively little reason for further anxiety, he did not doubt that Gabriel still had "something on his mind." But "this is now *borne lightly.*" What it was, the Hakes surmised, was Jane Morris.

For Dr. Hake the dreaded day arrived on August 12. Several letters had arrived from Janey earlier, asking for information about Gabriel and even hinting that she might be in Scotland and could visit. None of the inquiries were mentioned to Gabriel. The subject came up, finally, from Gabriel himself. First he announced that he felt prepared, henceforth, to open his own mail. Then he wrote a long letter to Janey, the effort—or the contents—upsetting him sufficiently to disturb his sleep. "On waking this morning," Dr. Hake wrote to William, his brother "spoke unpleasantly about the conspiracy for the first time this fortnight."

Hake was in a quandary about how to handle the letter to Mrs. Morris. Finally he decided that it had to be mailed, but sent at the same time his own tactful letter to Janey, with a copy to William:

You will receive a letter with this from Rossetti and as this is the first instance of his resuming correspondence with his nearest friends I feel naturally very anxious concerning it and about any answer you may feel it necessary to make especially as this morning on awaking he referred to his old delusion for the first time after a long silence on the subject, and a great apparent improvement in many other respects.

As a medical man, and viewing you and Mr. Morris as among Rossetti's dearest friends, an anxiety arises in my mind to learn whether his letter exhibits any sign of delusion. If so it must be inferred that there are still remains of his disorder; if happily it does not, a more favourable view may be entertained—for there is a certain wilfulness about our dear friend in his present state which may even make him say certain things for the sake of consistency partly, and in part to attain some indulgence as to whisky &c, when it is advisable to oppose him—

May I further take the liberty of asking you to be very guarded in your reply to him—telling him only amusing and cheering facts, not noticing in the slightest degree his delusion if he has manifested any to you—

I am sure you will appreciate my motive in thus writing and I should take it as a kindness if you would send your answer to me under cover to Mr. [William] Rossetti that he may receive early intelligence at this rather important juncture.

To William she responded that Gabriel's letter "showed no sign of his late distressing illness," and to Hake she reported the same thing, the discreet doctor writing to William that he burned the letter "together with all yours and all other letters on the subject of this illness." Since Gabriel was beginning again to direct his own affairs, Hake was already making cautious plans to withdraw, his confidence bolstered by Gabriel's writing to Treffry Dunn for painting supplies, and renewing correspondence with William and Christina. Since Trowan had been taken for September as well as August, Hake suggested his own release from captivity—that it would be useful for Gabriel's rehabilitation "to have an exchange of prisoners by substituting Dunn for me. . . ."

Three letters from Gabriel to Dunn detailed the materials he wanted shipped, including the canvas for the long-delayed copy of the *Beatrice* for Graham; and another to Christina followed one from her which drew from Gabriel his happiness at the restored "firmness of her handwriting." For the first time, on August 29, Hake even hinted that a visit from William—and Brown—would be in order, to discuss Gabriel's future plans. "I shall not go [back] to London," he had told Hake—and the doctor had logically, and unhappily, interpreted that to mean a move to Kelmscott. Other matters had to be settled as well. The Cheyne Walk house had its advantages ("the scene of his success"), but Hake pointed out to William the disadvantages of its high cost of maintenance. If its expenses exceeded Gabriel's means the result "might . . . be serious as engendering depression."

Dunn's leaving Cheyne Walk for Trowan first alarmed Gabriel. It meant abandoning the house to the servants. He wrote Fanny to lock the studio and keep the key. He was also sufficiently worried about "poor Fanny" to ask William to look in on her and to have her call at Somerset House if he had no objection. (The picture it raises, of the florid, buxom "Elephant" calling, in her best cockney, upon the staid, grey-bearded Assistant Secretary, defies description.) Now that he was somewhat improved Gabriel thought better of William's zeal in paying off the most pressing creditors with funds realized by the sale of the Cheyne Walk china and some of the pictures, and in cutting costs by disposing of the garden menagerie. With the implied reproof came instructions to "pay away as little as possible"—that it was not necessary "to have made payments at midsummer to those who received good instalments at Xmas. . . ." The old Gabriel was indeed reviving.

To Dunn, a Cornishman who loved London's fumes and fogs, the Scottish climate was "of the most melancholy description," a "continual downpour" which kept him indoors and thus in more close attendance upon Gabriel than he preferred, after his months of independence. To William he reported that Gabriel's appetite, self-described as delicate, was nothing of the sort. "You would alter your opinion if you saw how he tucks into his meals. We get a most liberal supply of game from Graham so that our·

meals, in a savage sort of way, are eatable, but there is an entire absence of vegetables whi[ch] makes them somewhat monotonous." He was kept up hours later than he liked, forced, in the absence of Gabriel's cronies, to make conversation, and to listen, in the absence of Gabriel's doctor, to tales of persecution at Cheyne Walk and to Gabriel's plans to have part of the studio wall pulled down to locate "the whole paraphernalia of machinery which has been erected for his special annoyance." (What Gabriel did not know was that part of the house had indeed been torn down—thieves in the night had stripped large quantities of lead from the roof.) But Dunn was surprised to discover how good a copy Gabriel had quickly made of the *Beatrice*, which was nearly finished. In London, Dunn had written to, or been visited by, William nearly every day, and from Scotland he continued to fill him in on Gabriel's business affairs as well as upon Gabriel, and was grateful that it was George Hake, rather than he, who slept in Gabriel's room.

To his mother on September 12 Gabriel wrote that the interruption to his work had been "a heavy evil," and that it remained to be seen whether he could resume it. But he was already planning, as a result of a flurry of correspondence with Janey, to do his painting at Kelmscott, where he had lived the happiest months of his life. Once the good Dr. Hake had left Trowan, Gabriel found no compensations for the remoteness, and with the replica delivered to Graham, he was ready to leave. Rejecting William's offer to provide companionship at Kelmscott he wrote that what he needed most of all was to be left to himself. "Wherever I can be at peace," he wrote, "there I shall assuredly work. But all, I now find by experience, depends primarily on my not being deprived of the society of the one necessary person." * He was aware of his "somewhat morbid state of mind," and still limited by his lameness, but late in September he left Dunn to settle his affairs in Scotland, and accompanied by George Hake boarded a third-class carriage for London, en route to "the one necessary person."

Gabriel arrived in London on September 24, and visited for a few hours at Euston Square before changing trains at Paddington Station. William had been forbidden to tell Fanny of the brief London stopover. Christina had warned William on returning from Sussex, "*Pro* you will find me fatter; *contra* of a fearful brownness." Withered by illness, she was nevertheless at Euston Square when Gabriel arrived, and she seemed better to him, he wrote William the next day, "than I had ventured to hope." As for himself, he was "determined now to make every effort not to go under again."

---

* When William published Gabriel's letter he discreetly omitted the second sentence.

XIII

Break-Up
1872-1876

It is difficult to describe an idyll. Such evocations are best left to the poets, of which Gabriel was surely one; and he celebrated what would be nearly two years at Kelmscott in his sonnets. Yet it was one of the most curious of idylls, in that Gabriel's partner in felicity was—and remained—the beautiful wife of the man who had once been his best friend, and who now abandoned the country house he loved to let someone else usurp his marriage. Left alone in Kelmscott at the close of the secluded summer of 1871 the year before, Gabriel had written a sonnet describing his desolation with intense physical imagery:

> What of her glass without her? The blank grey
> There where the pool is blind of the moon's face.
> Her dress without her? The tossed empty space
> Of cloud-rack whence the moon has passed away.
> Her paths without her? Day's appointed sway
> Usurped by desolate night. Her pillowed place
> Without her? . . .

"I cannot tell you," Rossetti explained to Hall Caine ten years later, in a voice choked with sobs, "at what terrible moment it was wrung from me."

Reunited with Janey four hours after he had left London, Gabriel counted his blessings. "Here all is happiness again," he wrote William the next day, "and I feel completely myself. I know well how much you must have suffered on my account, indeed, perhaps your suffering may have been more acute than my own dull, nerveless state during the past months. Your love, dear William, is not less returned by me than it is sweet to me, and that is saying all."

He began a new brooding *Proserpine* with Janey, had his brother for a visit in October, William sleeping in Morris's vacated bedroom, and—when Janey was to be away—Gabriel invited his mother and sisters, explaining that another visiting model was likely to be about, but that Miss Wilding was "quite ladylike." After a silence of nearly five months, on his return from Kelmscott William noted in his journal for November 3, 1872, "I resume this diary under much less gloomy circumstances than when I left it off, altho' all causes of distress & anxiety are by no means removed. . . ." William had found his brother "in very good trim, although occasionally something showed in his mind some trace of lurking suspicion. . . ."

At Kelmscott, with George Hake remaining with him as factotum, he felt removed from conspiracies against his reputation, yet his living there at all while Morris conducted The Firm at Queen Square was enough to set tongues in London as well as in Lechlade wagging. Dunn reported to William that passersby would stop to gaze at Tudor House, and that Gabriel's own friends gossiped about him loudly at Solferino's Restaurant. Even Bell Scott, writing to Alice Boyd, would refer nastily to "the hollow chested (hearted?) matron" of Kelmscott, and to her "more than amiable husband." Had any of them understood the symbolism of his *Proserpine*, even more scandal might have been raised, for few of the myths were more applicable to Gabriel's own situation. In his painting Janey stands holding the bitten pomegranate which bound the legendary Proserpine to remain with her husband Pluto in the netherworld, from which she was permitted release for half the year—if she dutifully came back.

Gabriel often attached sonnets to his paintings, later integrating them into his *House of Life* cycle, and to Maria he sent his lines on the *Proserpine*. If she knew of their implicit meaning, she was silent about it, writing him instead, "Graceful and melodious as is your English sonnet, I agree with you in preferring the Italian. But no wonder; for, as it is thought and character that create language, thoughts that would more naturally take birth in an Italian than in an English character will of course find the most fitting expression in Italian." If she had meant that Gabriel's passionate sensuousness had little trace of repressed respectability, she went to the core of her brother's Italianate qualities—and possibly, too, to the sources of his sexual appeal. Yet Maria, very likely, was only indulging in her own loyalties to her Italian origins, and recognizing that Gabriel was the closest, among the other Rossettis, to herself in Italianate instincts, despite his outward

Englishness. He would, in fact, live out his life without ever visiting the land of his second language.

There was much painting to be done to restore Gabriel's finances, and he set about doing it, requesting materials through Dunn, arranging deals for his work through Howell, and even asking Maria to find in her minute Dantesque chronology, for background for a picture, "the exact year, month, and day, of Dante's meeting with Beatrice" at the end of the *Purgatorio*. He was now, he assured William, "paying new debts strictly on the nail," and by early 1873 had accumulated £1,000 in the bank.

Discreetly, Jane made periodic visits to Queen Square with her daughters, and Gabriel either then sent for visitors, or entrained for London on business or to have dinner with his family. Morris, Gabriel had long known, divided his affections unevenly between his daughters, being always more devoted to the pathetic, epileptic Jenny than to the pretty, vivacious May, whose normality he seemed to resent. Gabriel offered to adopt her, as he had once tried, with Lizzy, to adopt Nellie Farren. May was willing, and even resented her father's hardly unanticipated refusal. Yet Morris could not have been expected to give up to Gabriel more than he had already done, even if his estranged friend had been likely to make a good parent. May remained Gabriel's Kelmscott child.

When the river at Kelmscott flooded, and Jane and her girls were gone, Gabriel tramped the higher meadows alone, or with George Hake, or collaborated by mail with William, who agreed to do most of the work "in order to get it off," on Ellis's proofs of a new edition of the *Italian Poets*, to be retitled *Dante and His Circle*. Although Gabriel worked with great energy—the 46″ x 22″ *Proserpine* was painted seven times on seven different canvases in little more than a year, because one or another was unsatisfactory, damaged in transit, or even lost in shipment—it was with diminished powers. Something had gone out of him in the summer of 1872, although his projects were numerous and fewer abandoned than before.

In 1873 Gabriel seldom left Kelmscott. Fanny saw him at least once at Cheyne Walk, but he communicated with her mainly by mail, often indirectly through William, whom he had informed earlier* that Fanny had become a widow, her "incubus" of a husband having finally died. The letters to Fanny, which William excluded altogether when he published his brother's correspondence, were an anthology of excuses or apologies for not seeing her, bribes of small checks to appease her, and playful exhortations to her to give up to Dunn or Howell or William some item she had filched which he wanted for background in a picture. "Hullo Elephant!" he would

---

* November 25, 1872.

write, "Just you find that pot for I can't do without it!" But he urged her to "take care of your funny old self," forbade her to come to Kelmscott, and tried to arrange for her (through Howell's sales of paintings she had acquired from Gabriel) to purchase her rented house in Royal Avenue.

Alexa Wilding, who—with Jane Morris—had superseded Fanny as model years before, made trips to Kelmscott in Janey's absence, usually accompanied by Dunn, to sit again, and the first result, *La Ghirlandata*, was sold to Graham, "the only buyer I have who is worth a damn," according to Gabriel. And Dunn also found "a singular housemaid of advanced ideas"—as Gabriel described her to Brown—who sat nude, except for the lute in her hands. Howell quickly sold the picture (*Ligeia Siren*) for £210, after Gabriel, in deference to Victorian decorum, added drapery to mask "the unpopular central detail." New sonnets enigmatically described his dark night of the soul, and evoked, often interchangeably, both Lizzy and Janey, the deliberately fuzzy autobiographical elements often further blurred not only by self-censorship but by poetic sensibility.

To Aglaia Coronio, Morris, in a stream of letters, poured out his bitterness at being kept from his "harbour of refuge," while mired in his London house, where Jane's sister Bessy got on his nerves. Rossetti's presence at Kelmscott, he complained, was "quite selfish business," and "a kind of slur on it: this is very reasonable though when one thinks why one took the place, and how this year it has really answered that purpose [of Gabriel's]." His meeting Gabriel when necessary had become "really a farce," but Janey was back again: "her company is always pleasant and she is very kind and good to me." Like Proserpine, Mrs. Morris at intervals returned to her husband, Gabriel filling the void—because no one since William's lone visit had been invited to Kelmscott while he and Janey were together—with new and old friends, the new ones including a lawyer with literary ambitions, Theodore Watts, and *The Time*'s music critic, Franz Hueffer, who had just married Brown's younger daughter Cathy, leaving the artistic Lucy, at twenty-eight, still husbandless at Fitzroy Square.

Christina had remained ill through the first months of 1873, subject to what William described as recurrent "hysterical attacks" when one cause of discomfort was only replaced by another. Sir William Jenner cautioned the family to attach no particular importance to her emotional problems. Christina was slowly recovering, and even going through batches of old poems to see whether any were worth offering to magazines—under a pseudonym, she insisted, because they were not up to her best quality. With Gabriel even farther along toward rehabilitation, William was ready for a vacation, and receptive to Bell Scott's invitation to join Scott, Letitia and Alice Boyd on a trip to Italy. But rather than become the chaperon for his friend's *ménage à trois*, he invited Lucy Brown to join the party, using the Scott threesome for purposes of decorum. "Old Scotus seems quite sulky about it," Gabriel told William, adding that he did not want the remark to get back to Scott. But William was determined to have her along. "For several years . . . I had had a warmly affectionate feeling for Lucy Brown," he wrote in his memoirs. "She was the mainstay of her father's house; I always saw her [as] sweet, gentle, and sensible; she had developed ability of no common order as a painter." Also, like William, she was freethinking in religion, despite her having been brought up for several years in his own household, largely by Maria; and was far more attractive than one might have expected of a woman of twenty-nine who had yet to elicit an offer of marriage.

During their travels in Italy, William wrote later, "I decided that I would not again part with Lucy, if I could help. I proposed marriage to her, and was accepted." At their ages—William was forty-three—they had no need to consult their parents, but in any case secured the cordial approval of Mrs. Rossetti and Madox Brown. He had told Lucy from the moment that they began considering marriage, William assured his mother, that he would continue living with her and his sisters, and that his wife would have to accommodate herself to that arrangement. But as a modest gesture in the direction of Lucy's need for a room of her own, William offered her "one room or other" to be turned into her studio. It seemed—to him—an adequate compromise.

At Kelmscott, where she was visiting Gabriel (while Janey was at Queen Square), Christina heard the news. "My dear Lucy," she wrote, "I should like to be a dozen years younger, and worthier in every way of becoming your sister; but such as I am, be sure of my loving welcome to you as my dear sister and friend." To William she wrote similarly, that he had brought "a fresh spring of happiness and interest into our family." The engagement, uniting two families that long had been close, appeared marred only by new illness. Maria, in quiet agony from a painful stomach complaint, had been hospitalized, at her request, at the All Saints Hospital at Eastbourne, a convalescent home established by the Anglican Sisterhood to which Maria and Christina had long been close. In London, however, as the Rossettis and Browns visited and dined back and forth, there was nothing on the horizon but imminent happiness.

The house at Euston Square underwent, at William's direction, drastic renovations to prepare it for Lucy's arrival, and was, he reported, "pretty nearly topsy-turvy, as there are painters and plasterers about the house, and various interchanges of rooms going on—books turned out into passages in a desolate condition, etc." Many of William's surplus volumes collected over decades as a reviewer and as a browser in secondhand bookshops were set aside to be given to a "Friendly Society" run by local clergymen. One of the books accidentally placed on the pile was a treatise on Swedenborg he had been lent by the Sunderland sage, Thomas Dixon. While packing the discards, Christina and her mother lighted upon the frightening work of religious unorthodoxy, removed it and fed it to the fireplace. William was less than phlegmatic about the episode. Lives long settled into placid patterns were being disrupted by the belated ending of his bachelorhood, and there were episodes which anticipated scenes in Chekhov's *Three Sisters*. Evicted from her room and sleeping temporarily in the dismantled library, Christina discovered that her coughing (her throat was still swollen) could be overheard by guests in the adjoining dining room. It was degrading for her, she decided, and exploded hysterically in what she called afterwards an "ebullition of temper." Later in the day, before William returned from Somerset House, she laid a written apology for him to find:

. . . *You* I do not mention, so completely have you accommodated yourself to the trying circumstances of my health: but, when a 'love paramount' reigns amongst us, even you may find such toleration an impossibility. I must tell you that not merely am I labouring under a serious relapse into heart-complaint and consequent throat-enlargement (for which I am again under Sir William Jenner's care), but even that what appeared the source of my first illness has formed again, and may for aught I can warrant once more have serious issues.

The drift of all this is that (through no preference for me over you as you may well believe, but because of my frail state which lays me open to emergencies requiring help from which may you long be exempt) our Mother, if I am reduced to forego all your brotherly bounty provides for me, will of her own unhesitating choice remove with me. We believe that from all sources we shall have enough between us, and you know that our standard of comfort does not include all the show demanded by modern luxury. I have very little doubt that an arrangement may be entered into which shall lodge us under one roof with my Aunts; thus securing to us no despicable amount of cheerful companionship, and of ready aid in sickness. . . .

I do not know whether any possible modification (compatible with all our interests, and not least with Lucy's) may occur to you as to arrangements: to me, I confess, there scarcely seems any way out of the difficulty short of a separation. Perhaps in a day or so you will let Mamma or me know what you judge best.

Of course Mamma is in grief and anxiety; her tender heart receives all stabs from every side.—If you wonder at my writing instead of speaking, please remember my nerves and other weak points.

The threatened immediate separation of the family did not occur, but the outburst foreshadowed the problems Lucy would have as youthful interloper in a household of ailing and aging females. Blinded by adoration of his younger sister and by affection for his family, William could not yet see the friction which lay ahead.

Maria's decision to leave the household was advanced less by what she called "Lucy's enthronement as bride" at Euston Square than by her illness. She was more seriously ill than she permitted her mother and sister at first to know, and through the Anglican Sisterhood of All Saints, Margaret Street, lay expert medical care as well as the path to heaven. Even Dr. Jenner had been associated with the Margaret Street Sisterhood, a nursing order, and for twenty years Florence Nightingale's combination of piety and medical care had been a stirring example, with aunt Eliza Polidori—who lived under the Euston Square roof—one of her Crimean veterans. If her illness were not so grim as to prevent it, Maria could look forward to more active years than her dwindling tutorial work in Italian suggested would be the case if she remained in the Rossetti domestic circle. The Anglican sisterhoods had liberated many women from stultifying domestic spinster-hood by making it socially acceptable for them to involve themselves in teaching, nursing and social work, and both Christina and Maria had been, as "outer sisters," on the fringes of the movement.

Early in September, when there were signs of renewed illness, Maria announced what Gabriel called "her very serious step." Seeing Maria—still moon-faced—for the first time in her broad, ballooning nun's habit, with the black scapular and veil, and the stiff white collar and wimple, Christina thought her "a decided lark," and Gabriel wrote Fanny from Kelmscott that Maria had become "what is called Sister of Mercy,—one of those old things whom you see going about in a sort of coal-scuttle and umbrella costume."

Lucy offered to paint a portrait of Maria in her "map of black," Maria accepting the description good-naturedly; and while some professed concern at her disappearing within the fortress of the All Saints House, Maria assured prospective visitors that they were permitted inside from 3:30 to 4:45 on Thursdays and Saturdays (except during Lent), as well as Sundays and festival days. But she discouraged Saturdays, as she intended to be home then as often as possible, and even on other days "might be in the world when visitors called." Still, the reason for the novitiate was to chart her departure from the world. Despite her talents as a scholar, Maria's piety had always been as simple as that of her Vastese forebears. She was afraid to look at Blake's designs for the book of Job because of the second commandment, for her eyes might light upon the figure of Yahweh, and in *Time Flies*, years later, Christina wrote of Maria that she "shrank from entering the Mummy Room at the British Museum under a vivid realisation of how the general resurrection might occur even as one stood among those solemn corpses turned into a sight for sightseers." But as a Sister she was neither morbid nor inactive, and for her order translated the *Day Hours of the Roman Breviary*, which became, with later revisions, the standard work, reissued in 1923 as *A Book of Day Hours for the Use of Religious Societies.*

Despite his "coal-scuttle and umbrella" levity, Gabriel was genuinely concerned about Maria at Margaret Street. William had written him that there were no fires permitted in the establishment, and Gabriel answered, "I simply could not exist on such terms—it would be a noviciate for another world; and I view the matter as most serious for her." It turned out that the strict rule was relaxed in Maria's case, as Gabriel's prediction would have been only too accurate.

Maria's last opportunity to dine at home before donning her Sister's garb was on October 30. Gabriel remained at Kelmscott, painting his debts away, and William was to be late, having gone to fetch Lucy, Bell Scott becoming surrogate second brother for the occasion. They discussed how curious it was that Maria's new vocation was within a protestant tradition, and then, with both brothers away, brought up another family matter. "We touched upon William," Scott wrote Alice Boyd, "and they . . . , but especially Christina, confided in me how very much alarmed they had been for William ever since Gabriel's illness, and that they were truly glad of the Lucy advent, as they wd. of anything else that might break the spell that seemed to hold him. For weeks they said he never uttered a word to any of them, and now he talked [of] 'When Lucy is here'; this and a good deal more made me entirely relent towards poor Billy Waggles." Yet when William arrived with Lucy, he was, Scott thought, still morose. Impending marriage was no antidote for the problems he knew he would still be facing with a family of near-invalids.

Gabriel was less better than he seemed. From Kelmscott that September he described his failures to his old friend Frederick Sandys in terms of an Italian proverb his father used to quote:

> If you don't know at twenty,
>   You never will know:
> If you don't do at thirty,
>   You never will do:
> If you're owing at forty,
>   You will always owe.

And, Gabriel mourned, he was forty-five. Still, when Janey was at Kelmscott he painted for long hours, although many of them were wasted in false starts and abandoned canvases and drawings. As unreliable as ever, he still sought out commissions, writing his mother about his lack of renewed interest in poetry that "the Crust of Bread has to be secured, and that can only be done by painting." Yet his unhealthy regimen cut into his hours of working daylight. As in Cheyne Walk days, he dined at ten in the evening, then often stayed up until the first light of dawn, dosing himself at five in the morning with chloral and whiskey. It would be afternoon before he would be steady on his legs again, affably chatting with his visitors from London—if Janey were away with Morris—or sequestered in the drawing-room studio with the one necessary person.

At Christmas Janey rejoined Morris at Queen Square, and Gabriel paid two visits to Euston Square, finding Christina still ill and Maria "in canonicals" and uncomplaining. William, he thought, was "looking far from well" as the day of the marriage approached, and new responsibilities loomed. There had even been tiffs with Lucy, relayed to Gabriel by nineteen-year-old Nolly Brown, who regularly sought Gabriel's advice about his own writing and painting. One spat had originated when Lucy had asked William, in the manner of most lovers seeking reassurance, whether he loved her more than anyone else; and he had hesitated, then stubbornly refused to say that he loved Lucy more than he loved his mother. There was a quarrel, especially foolish for a prospective groom past forty and a bride now thirty, but it passed over.

Nolly had also sought advice from Maria, feeling that an immersion in Dante would be good for his writing, but he was put off. Her educational efforts now, she pointed out from Margaret Street, were for the benefit of the poor; all her spare moments were crowded with community work; and her few visits home were brief and impractical for reading Dante with him. Maria had made her decision to live and work within the Sisterhood, and was keeping it utterly.

Without a scrap of Maria's faith, William and Lucy were married as agnostics on the last day of March, 1874, minus a church ceremony—and thus without Maria—and with a minimum of guests, Gabriel predicating his attendance on "a few real intimates," since after two years' absence from the social gatherings he used to love, and often staged himself, he confessed, "I am not equal to it, now that solitude is the habit of my life." At the wedding breakfast were, other than William and Lucy, only old Mrs. Rossetti, Christina, Gabriel, the Madox Browns and the Morrises. "I have to go to a wedding next Tuesday," Morris had grumbled to "Louie" Baldwin, sister of Georgie Jones, "and it enrages me to think that I lack the courage to say, I don't care for either of you, and you neither of you care for me, and I won't waste a day of my precious life in grinning a company grin at you two."

It was unusually ungenerous of Morris, but the outburst was very likely because he was forced to bring himself—and Janey—into Gabriel's company. He had been unequal to the task of extricating his wife from Gabriel without losing Janey in the process,* but two weeks after the marriage employed a new tactic, writing his former friend that he would not continue to share the lease of Kelmscott once it expired "since you have fairly taken to living at Kelmscott, which neither of us thought the other would do when we first began the joint possession of the house; for the rest I am too poor and, by compulsion of poverty, too busy to use it much in any case, and am very glad if you find it useful and pleasant to use."

The strategy may have been to induce Gabriel to relinquish *his* share, but no sign of such a move appeared during the spring and summer of 1874, as he stubbornly settled in at Kelmscott, while his brother was moving Lucy—after their wedding trip to France and Italy—into Euston Square, and their mother and Christina were staying as "paying visitors" at the All Saints Hospital at Eastbourne, by the sea, to be with Maria. At Kelmscott an increasingly brooding and suspicious Gabriel had replaced the poet-painter of the earlier idyll. Inertia as well as insomnia often gripped him, and even his once-trim beard grew unkempt as well as grey. The notebook he kept always in his waistcoat pocket, for quick access when a poetic image insinuated itself, was seldom opened. He was increasingly brusque and even cruel to his closest friends, refusing to see Swinburne, who had battled Buchanan for him; becoming meanly inconsiderate to innocent young Nolly Brown, who had visited to ease Gabriel's loneliness; often treating George Hake as demandingly as a low servant, although Hake had completed his Oxford education with difficulty in order to be at Gabriel's service, even postponing the beginnings of a career to stay at Gabriel's side. Even his old crony Jimmy Whistler seemed to be a conspirator when, in May, he arranged an independent show of his own work which would include paintings of both Frederick Leyland and Mrs. Leyland. "I have no doubt at this juncture," Gabriel wrote Madox Brown, "it will send Whistler sky-high, and Leyland will probably buy no one else any more!" His suspicions of everyone but his closest confidants had alarmed William and Lucy when they had visited in the spring, and even Janey began feeling uneasy about him, perhaps accounting for her willingness to go with her husband on a holiday to Belgium at the end of July, where at Bruges Morris

---

* The sly Howell, rebuffed when he and his wife attempted to intrude into Kelmscott while Janey was there that March, not only apologized but commiserated righteously with Gabriel about the problems he was having with Janey's husband and friends who were trying to "cripple her pleasure." The "Portugee" even confided to Gabriel that William as well as Madox Brown were mean to Fanny, and that he and Gabriel were her only real friends. But the devious Howell was selling Gabriel's pictures and wanted to continue pocketing the fees.

arranged for the same room they had on their honeymoon fifteen years before.

At just about the same time, walking with George Hake by the Thames near Kelmscott, Gabriel passed a group of fishermen. Fancying in his renewed persecution mania that they had called out some insult to him, he turned on them and spat out abuse, Hake rushing to calm the astonished anglers, and to hurry Gabriel away. But quickly the incident became a choice piece of local gossip, augmenting rumors of the curious *ménage* at the manor house. Suddenly Kelmscott was impossible for Gabriel. Abandoning everything for Hake to pack, he left forever what had been his favorite place in the world.

With the tenancy of the manor house reverting ironically to Morris after all, the break was nearly complete; but it did not become final until late in the year, when Morris reconstituted the firm under his sole management, buying out the inactive partners. Gabriel set aside his share for Jane when the legal formalities were completed in March, 1875. The costly gesture— £1,000 was involved *—may have been calculated to infuriate her bitter husband, and very likely did. Morris never saw Rossetti again, although his waning spell continued to magnetize Janey.

Conspiracy and suspicion still hung over Cheyne Walk for the returned householder, but although he still heard, he told Stillman, "the voices of those who had combined to ruin his reputation discussing the measures they were going to take," he was temporarily shocked out of his insomniac self-pity by the illness and death of young Nolly Brown, whom, he wrote Madox Brown in grief, might have proved a great artist as well as "the first imaginative writer of his time." † In Nolly's memory Gabriel composed a mediocre sonnet, "Untimely Lost," as well as a mediocre study for a proposed memorial painting he never began, "The Question." Then he returned to painting lush women in luxurious settings under fanciful, usually Italian, titles, his chloralized senses exaggerating facial features and warping color values; and after dark, with Dizzy, the Kelmscott dog, by his side, he paced the Chelsea streets with Dunn, or Hake, or Watts, before he would consent to climb behind the heavy curtains of his four-poster bed and draw the Genoese velvet hangings at his windows which further closed him off from the onset of dawn.

---

* Eating his cake while having it, Rossetti often borrowed from the amount he had settled on Janey, promising to pay interest, but his loans were never repaid in full.

† Knowing Gabriel's fear of meeting old and estranged friends, Brown cautiously asked Gabriel whether it would be all right if Holman Hunt and Swinburne came to the funeral. Gabriel consented and was present at Finchley Cemetery on November 12, 1874.

Soon he was restricting his walks to a narrower and narrower compass, because he assumed paranoiacally that anyone else who happened to be in the street was scrutinizing him. As William later described his brother's strategy, defending him from stories of pathological reclusiveness, while indirectly corroborating them, Gabriel "did not go to and fro in the streets, in a casual sort of way, to any extent worth mentioning; but he went out constantly—I believe only occasionally missing a day—in the late evening. His habit was to enter a fly* from his own door with George Hake, and drive to some airy spot, very often the Circles of Regent's Park. There he got out, took a longish walk with this companion, and then reentered the fly, and drove home. I am far from saying that this was a wholly rational proceeding, or that it did not bespeak a certain exaggerated craving for seclusion; but it is a very different thing from [Bell Scott's allegation of] 'living within the house, and never going even into the street.' "

At Euston Square the two months' nursing of Nolly had left Lucy exhausted, and Gabriel, who had worried earlier about Lucy's susceptibility to "colds and such-like," confided to Dr. Hake what he could not have told William—that her health seemed to him "destined to be a permanent cause of anxiety." After the marriage he began, as a wedding gift, a portrait of her in which she appeared in the full bloom of health, but it was completed before Nolly's illness and death. Also, in its full-lipped exaggeration, William conceded, it hewed "somewhat too much to the known [late] Rossettian type to be an absolute likeness." A more accurate likeness, he thought, was done two years later by Madox Brown, showing Lucy and her firstborn daughter, Olivia. Named for Nolly Brown, she was born on September 20, 1875, and to the anguish of the other inhabitants of the Euston Square house she was not baptized.

Younger by more than a dozen years than Christina, Lucy seemed rather to be generations removed from her sister-in-law's world. Each was more correct than tolerant of the other's outlook, and earlier effusions of sisterly affection were forgotten when narrow piety and broad liberalism collided, as when the second wife of Holman Hunt paid a call upon Lucy at Euston Square. An old friend of Madox Brown, Hunt had married his deceased wife's sister abroad, since canon law forbade such a connection, and the marriage was not recognized as legal in England, although few cared. When Edith Holman Hunt, personally a lady of impeccable rectitude, was announced by the maid, Christina (who was also in the drawing room, with her mother) arose and walked out without greeting the sinful woman. Lucy was quietly outraged.

---

* A light one-horse carriage; a hackney cab.

Not yet fully weaned from his family, William would attempt to reconcile antagonisms which Gabriel, remote from the scene, never knew existed. For his brother, Gabriel innocently told Dr. Hake, marriage had been "a great boon to his somewhat fossilized habit of life for years past, and all at Euston Square is most pleasant." For a rare visit from Gabriel, all of the inhabitants had trotted out their best smiles, and Christina, now shaking off her malady, was visibly better; but life became decidedly more complicated for the Rossetti ladies, all of them far more fossilized than the hyperactive (although bland) William, once the baby arrived, with nurse and noise and new demands on space in the house. Christina, gradually regaining her strength, found distractions at first in traveling with her mother to visit Maria at the Mission Home in Clifton, near Bristol, or at the All Saints Hospital at Eastbourne, where they remained for lengthy stays. Euston Square seemed no longer to be home.

For Christina, whose face and figure had shrunk under her bonnet and black shawl, her willingness to leave Euston Square at all, whatever the new threat to her settled existence, suggested her satisfaction with the restoration, as much as could be expected, of her former appearance, although she would write, to put off some visits and visitors, "I am now disposed to ask rather that some who kindly recollect me should continue their remembrance than that they should re-admit me to their acquaintance."

Christina was also writing again, and having mended her relations with Macmillan, had published—again with Arthur Hughes's illustrations—*Speaking Likenesses* in time for the Christmas season of 1874. A series of fanciful yet moralistic stories told to several girls by their aunt to pass the time as they sewed, it was a minor effort, only too realistically described by its original title, *Nowhere*. Gabriel had suggested changing it because it might embarrass his sister to be inadvertently connected to "that free-thinking book called *Erewhon*, which is 'Nowhere' inverted." Quickly, Christina agreed, finding that "My small heroines perpetually encounter 'speaking (literally *speaking*) likenesses' or embodiments or caricatures of themselves or their faults." The book sold well—over a thousand copies in two months—but did nothing to advance her art. When Macmillan published her collected poems in 1875, to which she had added verses excluded from her first two books of poetry, her place as one of the first poets of the day was reinforced; but she had written little since her long illness.

Christmas of 1875 was spent with Gabriel at Aldwick Lodge, by the sea near Bognor, but Maria was absent. The previous month her novitiate had ended, and Gabriel had written Bell Scott, "Poor Maggie is parting with her grayish hair next Sunday, and annexing the kingdom of heaven for good."

But he remained worried about her, and worried about more than her Yuletide loneliness. On Christmas Eve Maria wrote him a long letter about peace and love, explaining the austere joy which self-denial brought into a nun's life, but neither austerity nor self-denial had ever been part of Gabriel's experience. "Would you believe it," he wrote his mother in April, 1876, "that my Bank passbook shows my receipts from April '75 to the same month this year to have amounted to £3,725? and I believe this is somewhere about my average income. Yet I am always hard up for £50." Prior to the Christmas of Maria's letter he had ordered a sealskin coat for his mother from Farmer and Rogers in Regent Street, asking the shop to send several for choice, and instructing Mrs. Rossetti to select "the *largest, best and warmest.*" If any self-denial were practiced it was on the part of the proprietors with whom Gabriel dealt: he demanded advance payments from his patrons; his own bills were seldom paid within the year.

He had "returned from Kelmscott for the winter," Gabriel had lied to Dr. Hake, because it had become increasingly necessary to make trips to London. But in October, 1875, he once more fled the city, his unpaid bills, and the portly Fanny, taking with him unfinished canvases commissioned by Graham and by fashionable London photographer Clarence Fry, the loyal George Hake, and their dog.

Aldwick Lodge, on the Sussex coast, was a large, old house so secluded and sea-lashed that Gabriel frantically rushed letters to his relatives and friends urging visits to provide him with company, especially in the late hours, and to Alexa Wilding instructing her to entrain for Bognor with Dunn to sit for Graham's *Blessed Damozel.* Janey, too, was to sit—for the *Venus Astarte*—but her visits were rare, and brief, as she pleaded renewed delicacy of health, and Gabriel would write, dejectedly, to Fanny, "I wish I had a good elephant to talk to."

Hungry for Janey's presence, and jealous of the hours he had with her, he always made sure other guests were gone when she and her children arrived and that no interloper broke the spell of his idyll. He would put off visitors with such circumlocutions as that "a lady's kind consent to sit to me [has] forced me to put a veto beforehand on all other visits," or explain to an authentic confidant such as Watts that "Mrs. M. . . . is still in so delicate a state (though improving) that . . . she would not be equal to any but the most intimate circle." * Few of his verses date from his months of

---

* Aware of Gabriel's sensitivity in such respects, William once (September 1876) arrived at Cheyne Walk to discover Mrs. Holme Sumner staying to dinner after she had sat to Gabriel (who was awed by her statuesque beauty). Rather than intrude, he left without announcing himself.

increasing despair and separation from Jane, but one sonnet dated 1875 suggests his frustration in such lines as

> To-day your lips are afar,
> Yet draw my lips to them, love. . . .

Recalling the Christmas of 1875, Dr. Hake described Gabriel as "much unstrung," silent on his walks with Watts and himself along the boulders fringing Selsey Bay. It would be a long winter, with Janey not returning until March and then only for a fortnight. With solitude and anxiety his consumption of chloral increased, and he berated George Hake for giving him short measure. His paranoia grew worse, and on reading passages in a posthumous collection of Nolly Brown's writings, sent to him by Nolly's father—and Gabriel's oldest and best friend—Gabriel wrote a pained letter to Madox Brown that he could not read the rest. He suspected that he had been satirized, reading attacks on himself where only a sick mind could have seen them. Only his old commercial shrewdness remained intact. His dealings with agents and clients, as before, were models of tactful screwing-up of prices, excuses for nondelivery and requests for additional advance payments.

Anxiety about the long-quiescent shade of Lizzy returned, and, fearing that his health was failing for the last time, Gabriel left a memorandum for George Hake with instructions for his cremation and a prohibition against his being buried at Highgate, the final resting place of his father—and Lizzy. Also the letters in his black portmanteau—clearly from Janey—were to be burned, and William was to inform the writer of those letters that it had been done. With his insomnia worse, he was now breakfasting at one in the afternoon, and writing Fanny that the sea air was no longer benefiting him, and that he was planning to go home. But he would not leave until a libel suit which Buchanan had brought against the publisher of Swinburne's attack on him, "The Devil's Due," was over, frightened that he might be subpoenaed as a witness in the action.

On June 30, 1876, the jury found for Buchanan and directed the *Examiner* to pay £150 damages. Rossetti then packed a traveling bag for his return to Chelsea, as usual leaving everything else to George Hake. The anxiety-ridden months at Bognor had left Gabriel exhausted—tired, even of life. The little poetry he wrote in 1876 expressed nothing but spiritual weariness, and the painting he accomplished repeated, usually more crudely than before, the familiar settings and symbols. "As for poetry," he confessed to Miss Boyd, "it seems to have fled afar from me; and indeed it has no such nourishing savour about it as painting can boast, but is rather a hungry affair to follow. Nevertheless I mean to write some more poems yet, and good ones too."

At Cheyne Walk he was, he told Dr. Hake, "shaky and inert." But his sister Maria was much worse. He visited her at Margaret Street and found her condition "alarming." It was even worse a few days later, and Miss Brownlow, the Mother Superior, had her moved first to Clifton and then to the hospital at Eastbourne at the same time as the inevitable domestic crisis finally erupted at Euston Square. The joint household had had a prolonged trial, and the two aunts had already left to take part of a house in Bloomsbury Square. "No two persons," William wrote, "could be less encroaching or less interfering, or more observant of the rightful rule that the wife is the mistress of the house, than my mother and sister; and yet the harmony in the household was not unflawed, and was sometimes rather jarringly interrupted. It was obviously a great grief to my relatives to find that Lucy, to whom they had been looking as a possible corrective of my heterodox opinions, was just as far from orthodoxy as myself. Not that they either badgered or slighted her on this account; but the feeling existed on their side, and on the other side the cognizance of the feeling. After giving a fair, or indeed a prolonged, trial to the experiment of a joint household, we decided to separate."

"Our Euston Sq. home-party is broken up!!" Christina announced to Gabriel, adding that she and her mother would look for a place to move that autumn. "I suppose it may be best to regroup ourselves, and of course we part friends. William is cut up, I think, at losing our dearest Mother; but I am evidently unpleasing to Lucy, and could we exchange personalities, I have no doubt I should then feel with her feelings." It was a difficult time for a break, with Maria clearly sinking, and the family put the best gloss on the tensions at Euston Square. From Eastbourne Christina sent a diplomatic letter to Lucy, hoping, she wrote, "that when two roofs shelter us and when faults which I regret are no longer your daily trial, that we may regain some of that liking which we had as friends, and which I should wish to be only the more tender and warm now that we are sisters. Don't, please, despair of my doing better."

While Maria was again returned to London for urgent medical consultation the family continued exchanging cautious messages. William suggested that his strong-minded wife might not be entirely innocent, and his mother wrote Gabriel that the avoidance of "mutual annoyances . . . will promote the comfort of most generous and affectionate William." The most drastic solution was the only effective one. Christina and her mother found a new place to live at 30 Torrington Square, a short walk below Euston Road and near the rooms of Charles Cayley, whose devotion to Christina had outlasted all the horrors of her illness. Denuding 36 Euston Road of their furniture, which left the dining room nearly bare and several bedrooms empty, Christina and Mrs. Rossetti, again joined by the two aunts, moved in October.

It was a time of sorrow as well as a time of change for the family. In October, after exploratory abdominal surgery, Maria was given no chance to survive. A malignant uterine tumor proved inoperable. She was not told, but she understood, and with her unswerving piety she faced the fact of death with serenity. "She is heavenly-minded, brave and calm; indeed the grief is ours, and the dread ours, rather than hers," Christina reported, and warned William to be prepared for what she could not write. A second operation to drain fluid was temporary in its relief, but—despite fever and pain—Maria remained lucid, chatty and serene, although her voice was a whisper. One of her motives for joining the Sisterhood, she confided to William, was to obtain from God for him and for Gabriel "the grace of conversion." William was at first surprised into silence; then he told Maria frankly that if his convictions changed, the outward signs would also. When Gabriel last saw her she was still alert. On her last day, before she fell asleep for the last time, she told her aunt Eliza that she had seen angels. Maria was forty-nine.

Even Gabriel—attended by George Hake—braved the funeral at Brompton Cemetery. The oak coffin was inscribed with words she had wished to appear: "Maria Francesca, a Sister of the Poor, fell asleep in Jesus 24 Nov 1876. Jesu Mercy." To Thomas Dixon, William wrote of her intellectual qualities, and then added, "Whatever the true solution of the world's mysteries may be, assuredly all has been & is well with her." The four Rossettis were now three.

XIV
Three Rossettis
1876-1882

For the unhappy Christmas of 1876 the family gathered at William's house, and on an even unhappier New Year's Day the Rossettis met at Cheyne Walk, forcing Gabriel to be up at the unusually early hour of 11:30 A.M. For a New Year's gift, Cayley, who loved sending odd tokens to Christina, sent her from Sussex a sea mouse with brightly colored scales, noting, "I did not see my way to dry it; so I put it in spirits of wine—not without fears for my carpet-bag's contents." Cayley, the only regular gentleman caller at Torrington Square other than William, would come to tea, and remain for the evening ritual of whist. Life had passed Cayley by, and when at Madox Brown's for dinner William urged him, as a Dante scholar and translator, to apply for a new Dante lectureship at University College, London, he was noncommittal. It was too late for that, and he returned to his latest project, a new translation of Petrarch, and visits to Torrington Square, where his preserved sea mouse was on display.

In her poetic code the diffident Cayley had been a mole, and when the *Athenaeum* for March 17, 1877, published Christina's "Mirrors of Life and Death," it was full of animal symbolism, from the eagle and the dove to the mole and the mouse. When she asked Gabriel to use his good offices to have the poem accepted, he objected to the imagery, and Christina realized that she should act for herself "now that I am old enough and tough enough." She made some small changes, but kept her mouse and mole, writing Gabriel, "I have thickened my skin and toughened the glass of my house sufficiently to bear some fraternal stone-throwing."

By the time the poem appeared, Gabriel had been distracted from it and in the process had created new concerns for Christina and William. He had new causes for depression and was drowning them in chloral. The one necessary person was unavailable to him. Some months before, Jane's elder daughter, Jenny, had suffered a nervous breakdown from which she would never fully recover, and Jane had removed her to the country to convalesce. It meant that Jane, too, was removed, and inevitably Fanny filled the vacuum: even more than filled it, as the only outsider who had any control over Fanny was William, then preoccupied with his growing young family, and seldom seen at Cheyne Walk. There was a quarrel with George Hake, whom Gabriel had called a "torpid boy." Remaining awake far into the night to read to, or chat with, Gabriel would have left anyone torpid, and the unselfish Hake—officially Gabriel's "Secretary"—decided that he had finally had enough and planned to leave, hoping to part friends. But when Gabriel discovered through Fanny that young Hake would be going, he shouted him out of the house. Hake never returned.

"That woman Fanny has been planning the whole thing for the last month or two," he wrote his father on January 13, "& has gained such an ascendancy over D.G.R. that he is not really accountable for his action." Treffry Dunn, coming calling at Euston Square about another matter, told William, who wrote Hake of his regret—but not his surprise—at the news, despite Hake's "brotherly devotion" over the years. "I am sure you have had to bear, & have good humouredly borne a good deal of unpleasant and capricious demeanour . . . ." Gabriel's temper had been strained, William knew, not only by the absence of Janey, but by the pain and discomfort of his hydrocele, which urgently needed surgical repair but which Gabriel was refusing to consider. As far as Gabriel was concerned, it was, as he carefully phrased it to Watts, "getting no news from the anxious quarter" that was making him "quite ill and unable to work." Unquestionably he was quite ill.

In February, 1877, William's second child, named Gabriel Arthur Madox Rossetti, was born. Again Lucy used the cradle they had borrowed from Anne Gilchrist, William writing Mrs. Gilchrist some months later, "I religiously hope . . . there will not be a[nother] new baby to put into it. Our two children are a great pleasure and interest to us both: but at my present age, 48, & with income dependent on my continuing to be alive in this world, we both think two of them enough, if only Destiny will so permit." Despite such pious organizations as the British Union for the Discouragement of Vicious Advertising, antidotes to Destiny were available in many forms; but William and Lucy would have three more children, including twins. The cradle would continue to be rocked.

Spring, Gabriel complained, from his seclusion, was chilly and stormy.

He could not use his garden, and had grown to actively dislike his house; but Watts had been unable to locate a suitable replacement. Fortunately, the replica business had not fallen off, for the dearth of new commissions would have concerned Gabriel more if he had been in better health to accomplish them. He was, he confessed to John Schott, Fanny's lodger and Gabriel's substitute factotum, in a very weak state. His insomnia was reduced very little by massive doses of whiskey-diluted chloral, and when there was kidney involvement to aggravate his bulky hydrocele, Dr. Marshall insisted on surgery.

Technically the operation was a success. The cause of immediate complaint was alleviated. But Gabriel, although warned that he could measure his life in months rather than years if he could not reduce his chloral intake, could not bring himself to cut it enough and failed to rally. Christina and Mrs. Rossetti came to Cheyne Walk to see Gabriel and confer with his doctor; and William, who had been vacationing in the country with Lucy and the children, rushed to London, prepared to offer to stay indefinitely at Cheyne Walk, although he confided to his wife that his presence would neither be good for him nor useful to Gabriel—an admission of the change in their relations since the marriage.

Having his mother and sister in frequent attendance was less than helpful as far as Gabriel was concerned, yet he was too weak to protest. It meant keeping the Elephant away, and devising subterfuges to get at his whiskey and his chloral. Even worse, Brown reported to his daughter Lucy, "Gabriel tells me his mother and Christina are [working on] converting him to Xtianity—and in *his* state as to the philosophy I see no harm in that . . . , though from his general conduct he seems more fitted to turn Turk . . . ." The result was chaos at Cheyne Walk, as Dunn, Watts, Brown, and Gabriel's mother and sister combined their efforts and threatened to kill Gabriel with kindness where chloral had so far failed. To Lucy, Brown suggested that "nothing short of my being placed in authority by the commissioner of Lunacy" would put a stop to it.

William found his brother depressed, weak and wheezing, and told him as strongly as he could without being unkind that a new pattern of living was necessary if he were to return to a useful existence. He had to stop hiding away from people in Cheyne Walk, and cease his dependence on chloral. And William suggested immediate removal to the seaside or to Penkill. Gabriel argued that he was too ill to endure a journey, and returned to his old delusions about people insulting him in the streets and everywhere else he went. William dropped the subject, and proposed sleeping at Cheyne Walk, but Gabriel saw little practical value in it since William would have to go to work in any case and they would see little of each other in waking hours. Mustering the courage to ask about Fanny, William wondered where she was, and when Gabriel confessed that she had left after a tiff (almost certainly about money) and that he had no idea where she had gone, it seemed appropriate to insist on Gabriel's recuperating elsewhere.

Marshall ordered Gabriel out of the gloom of Cheyne Walk, and prescribed sea air. Brown then arranged for departure from his house, as Gabriel could keep postponing the trip if still at his own. On August 17, to William's relief, Gabriel, accompanied by Madox Brown, a day-nurse and a manservant, Albert, to help enforce, as Christina put it to William, "that moderation which his very life requires," went, on unsteady legs, to Herne Bay, near Margate.

Gabriel's nights, on reduced chloral, were restless, and although his hands trembled too much for him to take up a brush, he was able to write his mother that it was "the absolute want of occupation" that was "rotting my life away hour by hour." Brown was a kindly companion, "but such a life is almost unbearable." Life became even less tolerable when Christina and Mrs. Rossetti arrived at Herne Bay. Gabriel had invited them because he could not evade doing so, but grumbled to Madox Brown (as Brown wrote to Lucy—and thus, indirectly, to William) that "their company will be exceedingly dull and that when they come he ought to have *someone* besides to modify their extreme quietude." Yet Brown thought their presence was useful—"because with his mother 77 and Christina scarcely yet restored from her illness he is forced in some degree to restrain his lamentable ways and speeches."

How Gabriel's finances withstood such drains upon his shrinking income as the maintenance of Tudor House while he was away for long periods of convalescence is no mystery. Dunn, for months at a time, received no salary, and the merchants who supplied Rossetti no money. His doctors were often close friends who did not bill him, and those of his friends who stayed with him at Herne Bay paid their own expenses, while his brother and sister and mother quietly paid some of Gabriel's as well.* After some importuning letters from Fanny reached him at Herne Bay he decided, although the act of writing was painful, to write to Fanny "to take the best step in life that you can for your own advantage, and quite forget about me." He might have to cease painting altogether he explained, and live, with his mother and sister, as cheaply as possible.

Furious, Fanny wrote again, and Gabriel reminded her that she was

---

* Christina's professional income in 1876 was only £37.9.0 and in 1877 £53.10.4, but her mother collected dividends on inherited investments which brought in several times that sum, and which would go eventually to Christina herself.

writing to "a helpless cripple, with no means of judging as to future livelihood." If he were able to work again she would be his first care: if not, he would himself be existing on charity. By mid-September, however, he saw improvement in his trembling hands, and wrote further, putting her off, but this time not altogether. He might need her. Dunn was threatening to leave for his native Cornwall to look for remunerative artistic employment, as he could no longer live on unpaid arrears in salary. Gabriel's Cheyne Walk world was crumbling and there was only the loyal Watts, whom he asked to try to locate Fanny. If Gabriel could somehow recover enough to not need to accept the offer of his mother and sister to move to Cheyne Walk, he wanted the Elephant available to resume her old roles. But on not having her rent at Royal Avenue paid, as usual, by Gabriel, she had left without leaving a forwarding address, although Gabriel knew that what Schott paid her was practically enough to cover the rent.

Toward the end of September a letter addressed from 96 Jermyn Street arrived for Gabriel. It was from Fanny, who announced herself as part-proprietress of a "hotel," which Dunn tracked down as The Rose Tavern, in which she had purchased a ninety-five year lease. The Elephant had carefully hoarded her money and put it to use in the service of herself. "You surely cannot be angry with me for doing what I have done," she explained. Gabriel had urged her to look after herself, and Dunn, she added, had been hostile and sneering. "I keep three servants and an accountant," she announced proudly, "and Mr. Schott still interests himself for me." (He had in fact moved in with her and would eventually make her Mrs. Schott.) For Fanny it was the climax of a success story, and she added, in case it were a matter of concern to Gabriel that her clientele could be lifting mugs of beer which might sully a framed Rossetti, "I have NONE *of your* pictures in any part of the house excepting my bedroom and private sitting room." Gabriel managed a response which combined surprise and relief. She would not embarrass him, nor be a drain upon him; and he expected to see her again. "You will perceive by the writing of this letter," he closed, "that I am improving in the use of my hands."

He was improving, as Christina devised all sorts of soporifics, including buttermilk, as folk remedies for insomnia; and to get through his days with the women Gabriel was willing to play chess or whist. By the end of the month he had even begun a drawing of his mother, to which he later added a second head—Christina's. It was one of the most successful efforts in portraiture he had accomplished in years, with none of the mannerisms of commercial canvases—"quite up to mark," as he wrote William. Having taken his holiday with his family, William had been unable to again leave Somerset House, to visit Gabriel, and was grateful for the opportunity for literary work. Two days after Gabriel's departure for Herne Bay, in fact, William had spent his Sunday writing an *Encyclopaedia Britannica* article on A. W. Kinglake, author of the travel classic *Eöthen*, and the next week spent his evenings revising the lectures on Shelley he had delivered in March at the Birmingham Institute* for publication in the *Gentleman's Magazine*. He was also working on his *Lives of Famous Poets*, and a three-volume Shelley. Gabriel may have been the great genius among the four Rossettis, but he was also a great inconvenience.

For Christina the months at Herne Bay were recuperative to her own poetic powers as well as to her health. To Gabriel her state at her arrival was a surprise, for she was, he told Brown, "in a weaker and more disabled condition" than he had realized, and yet had left London to be housekeeper for him. Her mood that autumn fit the season, although Watts, on a visit, persuaded her to see her first sunrise in the country, which she found awesome and splendid. She found no words to put it into verse, but writings from nature did emerge from her experience, notably the thirty-seven stanzas of "An Old World Thicket" and the meditative "The Thread of Life," as well as "An October Garden," which figuratively described the life she had chosen, or at least accepted:

> In my autumn garden I was fain
>   To mourn among my scattered roses;
>   Alas for that last rosebud which uncloses
> To autumn's languid sun and rain
>   When all the world is on the wane. . . .

The *Athenaeum* received the poem through Watts, and sent Christina a check for £5. Happily she wrote William that "all [was] cheery in the way of business," but Gabriel himself provided little cheer. He needed larger quantities of his drug again, and Christina and her mother gave in rather than risk hysteria.

He wrote William himself, in explanation, that when he was back at his work again, he had to "take means to procure a continuance of proper sleep, or work will go to the wall altogether." And to Frederick Shields he defended his work of the previous five years—since the terrible summer of 1872—as having resulted in "at least a dozen works . . . which are unquestionably the best I ever did." Yet he worried that "an opinion would get abroad that my works were subject to a derogatory influence which reduced their beauty and value." The "drug," he insisted, had not injured his work, while rumor about it "would be most injuring to me."

---

* Where he accepted twelve guineas per lecture rather than demand more, because it would not have been right to accept significantly more than the ten guineas his father-in-law, Madox Brown, had received.

"In general health he is wonderfully recovered," Christina wrote William, "but this sleeplessness saps hope and spirits." Besides, Gabriel was restless to return home, and thought of giving in to his sister's suggestion that they come live with him. He could give them the whole first floor, he mused to Watts, yet he had misgivings about his habits, which "might . . . scare them; and then there is the difficulty of Fanny, who, although she need not of course be always there, is at times almost necessary to me." He still expected her to share his bed when he needed her, and his loneliness at other times as well, and there would have been no way to insulate his nocturnal and amoral existence from the devout and dull daily lives of his mother and sister. Finally, a combination of factors ended his indecision over an appropriate solution. His bank account was down to what he described as an "evanescent" £400. Rain and further omens of winter had come; and Janey, whom he had not seen in many months, was leaving for Italy on November 15. He planned to return to Cheyne Walk and the life as before, while assuring his friends, not without hints of annoyance, that he was taking only a third of the quantity of chloral he had needed before his most recent calamity. Less would be useless, he told Brown testily. "Any man in my case must either do as I do, or cease from necessary occupation. . . ."

On November 9 he was back at Cheyne Walk, having first asked Watts to see to it that Fanny had a latchkey returned to her. Then he bade the other "necessary person" farewell, and sought for a way to paint without her.

Emotionally Gabriel was on the edge of breakdown. Even his favorite alternate model, Marie Spartali Stillman, was about to leave for Florence, after sitting for *Fiammetta*; and while patrons were clamoring for their long-delayed works, Dunn made good his threat and left for long periods of painting on his own. Gabriel was already shaky from renewed overdosages of his drug, and almost his only hold on the world outside was the resourceful Theodore Watts, who shared with Shields—who again was living in London—the chore of looking in at Cheyne Walk. Watts took care of paying bills, providing legal advice and putting off creditors, as well as pressing Gabriel to work by day and go to bed at night. Often, too, there was the matter of what to do about Fanny, who found it to her interest to be accommodating to Gabriel, while Watts and William worried about how to reduce her influence now that she was in business for herself. And Fanny sensed their coolness and returned it. At Christmas there was also a family crisis because Lucy invited her mother-in-law to Christmas dinner with her grandchildren. Gabriel would not leave Cheyne Walk, let alone be present at "so extended a party." It would be, he told his mother, "a serious incubus" to him and "a bad omen for the coming year" not to have her break bread at Christmas at his home, and he stood petulantly on his rights as eldest son. The others gave way. The tantrum reflected Gabriel's instability, and was itself the worst omen for the new year.

Jane Morris remained away in Italy, Gabriel writing her many more letters than the many which have survived, for one from Jane notes, "To wade through a drawerful of your letters would be the work of a day for me." On grounds of her health and that of her children she remained under an Italian sun, but almost certainly she was being wary of renewed intimacy with him, and Gabriel mused unrealistically about making a trip to Italy if he could find a friend to accompany him. He was short on friends. His quarrel with Madox Brown had still left them estranged, and he seemed to look for ways to damage his relationship with his brother even while continuing their exchanges of so many years. A few months after the Christmas uproar he noted to William on receiving a presentation copy of William's *Lives* that he was sorry to see the name of William's revered Walt Whitman "winding up a summary of great poets: he is really out of court in comparison with any one who writes what is not sublimated [Martin] Tupper. . . ." It was a perverse thank-you.

Gabriel was in his fiftieth year, and William in his forty-ninth, a curious time for William to think about throwing over the only full-time job he had ever held in his life. He had worked in Somerset House since he had been fifteen, and saw himself as rising no higher than his Assistant Secretaryship. Even with his seemingly infinite patience, he was mired in monotony, and jumped at the chance offered by the death of the Secretary and Keeper of the National Gallery to apply to the Prime Minister, Lord Beaconsfield,* for the post. He did not expect to get it, and if he had, it would have meant a salary loss. Nothing happened, and he continued at Somerset House as before.

It was, for the Rossettis, a surprisingly uneventful year. Christina wrote little, summered at Walton-on-the-Naze, accepted calls from Cayley, and refused to accept, from William, a gift of a mummified head and hand an acquaintance had brought back from Egypt. He had offered it because she "used to have a penchant for such lively objects," but she wrote him in August, 1878, that she "could not feel easy at keeping bits of fellow-human-creatures as curiosities; my preference would be to give them reverent burial." William gave the objects to a medical friend, William Gill. They would not have harmonized with Gabriel's collection of exotic objects, and he might have taken the gift amiss, although he was working with nearly his

* Disraeli had been raised to an earldom by the Queen in 1876.

old zeal to reduce his debts, and trying in every way he could without actually emerging from 16 Cheyne Walk to discourage speculation that he was too ill to paint. At the end of December it even required a letter to *The Times* to rebut the allegation that "a neighbour of Mr. Whistler's, whose works are not exhibited to the vulgar herd," had turned away the Princess Louise by having a servant tell her when she called to see his paintings that he was "Not at home." Not so, Gabriel wrote. "It is true enough that I do not run after great people on account of their mere social position, but I am, I hope, never rude to them; and the man who could rebuff the Princess Louise must be a curmudgeon indeed." Gabriel was no curmudgeon, and in his letters as well as in conversation with his few close friends he could suggest the Rossetti of old, but few were encouraged to penetrate his self-isolation. Anne Gilchrist's son Herbert recalled hearing a stranger arrive at Tudor House with introduction in hand, and Gabriel's leaning over the banister of the staircase above to call down to the servant at the door, "Tell the gentleman that I am not at home."

Early in 1879 Jane Morris began sitting for Gabriel again, although more in a token fashion than anything else, and Gabriel frugally began versions in oil of studies of her he made nearly a decade before, her face on the canvas now idealized to resemble neither the past nor the present Janey. It was important to do them quickly. He owed Leyland, and Valpy, and Graham and others, pictures and, receiving little for finished work long paid for, he was reduced to further replicas, for which he was grateful for Dunn's return. The amount of work Gabriel turned out belied his bad health, yet would bring him through the year only £1,030, a third of his usual income. Bills accumulated, and he had to work even more hurriedly, repeating his old themes even when not copying them directly. Still, his ability to paint unflaggingly was itself a restorative, and he declared that he was not dead yet. He even advised Lucy Rossetti on her painting, suggesting to her a way to lay on a white ground "more crisply and brightly," and even sending her a tube of his favorite paint. Lucy until her marriage had considered herself a professional painter, but had been hampered by ill-health and child-raising.* Gabriel's willingness to interest himself in her work was another sign of restored equilibrium.

For William it was a year of disappointment. He conceded himself as trapped in the Inland Revenue, once the National Gallery trial balloon failed to fly, and he found new solace in the work he had been doing since 1874 as art critic for the *Academy*. As a young man he had brought zest to his criticism because it had been possible "to strike a stroke or two for the

---

* Helen Maria Rossetti, her third child, was born in November, 1879.

'Praeraphaelite' painters in the days when they were ringed round with foes, and to carry the battle into the enemy's camp." But nearly twenty-five years later, even though he had accepted the assignment, "it was stale to me, and to a great extent monotonous, and moreover it often diverted me at inconvenient moments from my regular work at Somerset House. I had to run out to an exhibition when I had more than enough employ at my office-desk." In an unguarded moment he had said as much to Charles Appleton, the *Academy* proprietor, and had quickly added the equally hazardous comment that "as I was now a family-man, and not justified in throwing up any source of regular income, I was fully minded to continue my function as art-critic." Appleton bided his time, but one evening in 1878 William received a message from him that the duties of art critic had been transferred, effective immediately, to a young journalist, James Comyns Carr. William was shocked, but was able to keep his hand in artistic and literary matters by using Gabriel's friend Watts as intermediary with Norman MacColl, editor of the *Athenaeum*. Soon William was reviewing books there occasionally, but in one notice he used the term "literary vampires" in referring to the practice of Richard Herne Shepherd of reprinting juvenile poems by writers who had preferred to see their early work forgotten. To William the phrase was harmless "chaff," but Shepherd sued for libel.

Only seven months before, William had been involved in a libel case but only as a witness, and then with great reluctance. And he was not proud of his part in the proceedings, putting down almost nothing about it in his diary, and omitting the episode from his later memoirs. Whistler had sued Ruskin for having called him, among other things, a "cockney coxcomb" (at the least the Massachusetts-born Whistler was no cockney), and having long before alienated the artistic establishment, could find almost no one to take the stand in his support. Gabriel, with paranoid attachment to his privacy, was unavailable, but there was another Rossetti. William as an art critic had admired Ruskin's writings and as a P.R.B. brother owed Ruskin something for his early support. But he had often praised Whistler's work, and regarded Whistler as a friend. In the end William testified "in opposition to Ruskin's interest," while not being overly helpful to the embattled Whistler. Instead, he squirmed under cross-examination by Sir John Holker, Ruskin's attorney:

ROSSETTI: I consider the *Blue and Silver* an artistic and beautiful representation of a pale but bright moonlight. I admire Whistler's pictures, but not without exception. *The Falling Rocket* is not one of the pictures I admire.

SIR JOHN: Is it a gem? [Laughter]

ROSSETTI: No.

SIR JOHN: Is it an exquisite painting?

ROSSETTI: No.

SIR JOHN: Is it very beautiful?

ROSSETTI: No.

SIR JOHN: Is it eccentric?

ROSSETTI: It is unlike the work of most other painters.

SIR JOHN: Is it a work of art?

ROSSETTI: Yes, it is.

SIR JOHN: Is two hundred guineas a stiffish price for a picture like that?

ROSSETTI: [after a long pause, while laughter bubbled up in the courtroom] I think it is the full value of the picture.

Uneasily, William stepped down, having encouraged, in his careful choice of words, the suggestion that Ruskin was correct in deriding the prices Whistler asked for "flinging a pot of paint in the public's face." William had tried to satisfy both sides. Although the verdict went to Whistler, he was awarded only a token farthing, and went into bankruptcy.

In June, 1879, the Shepherd case was heard, and William was not called in the matter. Shepherd was awarded £150, which Sir Charles Dilke, publisher of the *Athenaeum*, paid without accepting William's offer to share the costs. Although William continued to receive books to review, they were few and infrequently received. At fifty he was nearly finished as a general critic, and it was a void in his life.

Christina filled her own literary void—for her poetic facility had flagged—with devotional prose works which seemed the result of her near-fatal illnesses. First there was *Seek and Find* (1879) which she sold outright, as Maria had done before her, to the S.P.C.K. for £40, carefully inserting "one solitary footnote," for which the unnamed source, she wrote Gabriel, was "our dear good Maria." The next year she sold to the S.P.C.K. *Called to Be Saints*, in which she had unsuccessfully and predictably failed to interest Macmillan in 1876; and there would be later volumes, *Letter and Spirit* (1883), *Time Flies* (1885), and *The Face of the Deep* (1892). When, after the second one, Gabriel protested about how little she must care about her fame, Christina answered quietly, "I don't think harm will accrue to me from my SPCK books, even to my standing; if it did, I should still be glad to throw my grain of dust in the religious scale." Besides, she had to write, and when her creative impulses in verse faded ("Just because poetry *is* a gift . . . I am not surprised to find myself unable to summon it at will and use it according to my choice"), her instinctive piety provided a creative outlet.

Eventually she did manage to put together sufficient new poems for a small volume, and with some fear that they were not up to her standard offered them to Macmillan. Before he even saw them he accepted the book, which belied her brother's concern, "I am quite pleased about Macmillan," she wrote Gabriel, "because he said *yes* without asking to see the M.S. or making a single inquiry as to either bulk or subject." The book would be *A Pageant and Other Poems* (1881). "I am somewhat in a quake," she confessed to William, "a fresh volume being a formidable upset of nerves,—but at any rate, it cannot turn out TWINS!"

Destiny had indeed revisited Lucy and William in April 1881, presenting them with more than Mrs. Gilchrist's much-used cradle could contain—Mary Elizabeth *and* Michael Ford. Gabriel's long months of renewed decline again took second place to William's own problems, as Lucy weathered her final pregnancy only with difficulty, and the infant twins were themselves sickly. Gabriel was low too, his consumption of chloral increasing so alarmingly that Marshall, his doctor, told him that if he were put into a Turkish bath he would sweat chloral at every pore. As a depressant which lingered in the body it should have left him as listless on arising as he was agitated on retiring, but he could still be animated by Janey's presence, and towards the close of 1879 began from her a picture (based on an earlier drawing) he first called *Monna Primavera*, and afterwards renamed *The Daydream*.

Janey had posed for it, a book on her knee, in the fork of a sycamore tree in Gabriel's garden, which by late summer of 1879 would have been impossible. No more did the lavish tent go up each May, and no more did peacocks rustle through the tall grass; and Gabriel, who now never used the garden he once loved, was even facing the prospect of having his ground landlord build homes on the furthermost portion. The thought of losing the space was as nothing to Gabriel compared to the inevitable loss of privacy. Arriving to dine with his brother on one traditional Monday night, William found him painting the background of a picture and, rather than disturb him, walked out into the garden for the first time in three years, finding it an expanse of "rankness and tangle." Janey as well as everything else on the canvas evoked an earlier and seemingly less troubled day.

With amazing resilience, Gabriel had come through another chloral crisis before Janey's series of quiet visits began, and during the worst period, with Fanny more to be seen as Gabriel needed someone nearby, there had been new difficulties with his brother, who had necessarily been more than attentive, bringing Lucy with him on many of his visits. But this meant rushing Fanny out the back door as Lucy entered the front door, prompting a sharp note from the recuperating Gabriel that such a "joint visit" needed advance notice, as it might not be possible "to dislodge anyone who might happen to be here." The next time, he warned, he might not be "at home" if Lucy turned up suddenly at his door. Fanny obviously was often staying the night. It was not easy for either William or Lucy to be understanding, although they persevered.

To Lucy, Gabriel once confessed, "I must seem as bad an uncle as the one in the *Children in the Wood* almost," and William recalled that Gabriel's almost complete seclusion self-limited him after 1877 to rare visits to Torrington Square to see his mother and sister. "He saw our eldest child Olivia twice or thrice in her earliest infancy; the other four he never saw at all. And yet he took an interest in all of them, and was pleased to hear any little details of how they were going on. This was assuredly a rather curious state of things, as affecting two brothers who had always been and always continued to be extremely fond of one another." But there was one day in 1880 William did not recall (perhaps he was never told of it) when Lucy decided on her own to take her children, including Gabriel's young namesake, to Cheyne Walk to brighten her brother-in-law's day with their high spirits. From the poet as he sat in the studio in his shabby painting coat there was a reluctant, momentary effort at welcome, and the elder children responded dutifully. After that he ignored them, and unaware of any snub they romped happily up and down the stairs and through the corridors until they mother took them home. Gabriel never saw his nieces and nephews again.

For William alone, Gabriel was always at home. Among other things, to his brother he was eager to talk of his renewed interest in spiritualism, although without any further desire to experiment with it himself, and of his conviction, after years of skepticism, in the immortality of the soul. He needed William to share such confidences. With Dunn away, and the handful of intimates not always available, there was otherwise only Fanny, to whom such conversation would have been absurd. And Fanny, Gabriel realized, was even unreliable as a provider of a more vulgar but still vital accommodation, for she understood that her future would be in Jermyn Street. One pathetic appeal to William (who had just visited) was, "I am so low and lonely that it would be a great boon if you could come up for an hour or two this evening. I know it is a tax on you, but tell Lucy, with my love, that I hope she will not mind." Very likely William followed soon behind the servant who brought the note.

Despite his difficulties Gabriel kept up a large correspondence, was jovial to his intimate circle of callers, wrote verse again, worked with Watts on clarifying Christina's publishing arrangements with Macmillan, and was contemplating a successor to Dunn, who appeared likely to strike out professionally for himself, either in his native Cornwall or back in London. No longer did Gabriel want a purely artistic helper: he now had so little concern for his earlier work except as material to copy for coin himself that he would refer to the "Blessed Dam" or "Blasted Damozel," and thought in terms of a "secretary" who might be a more loyal incarnation of the ubiquitous Howell. (Although barred from Tudor House, the Portugee seemed to be marketing his own copies of Gabriel's work, usually turned out by his tough and talented mistress, Rosa Corder.) The young man Gabriel had in mind was a Liverpool building contractor's clerk with literary aspirations, Thomas Hall Caine, who had sent Gabriel a lecture he had delivered on Gabriel's poetry, and was rewarded with lengthy letters in which the poet brought solace to his loneliness. Before they had even met, Gabriel had hopefully hinted to Caine, "I have often thought I should enjoy the presence of a congenial and an intellectual house-fellow and board-fellow in this big barn of mine, which is actually going to rack and ruin for want of use." In the offer Caine saw his entrée into London literary life, and kept up the correspondence until he could break free for London.

The gradual withdrawal of Janey Morris from Gabriel's life may have helped occasion his next chloral crisis, yet it also spurred the writing of new poetry. "Dearest Janey," one letter began, "Long absence and many disappointments have inured me to missing the sight of you." Yet despite his words he was not reconciled to the longer and longer intervals between visits. He wrote often to inquire about her health (which was better than she indicated), and penned new sonnets for "The House of Life" in poignant recall of his sensations of "ardour." Curiously, Jane at one point aggravated Gabriel's frustrated desire when acknowledging a gift of his drawings, writing that she had insisted on unpacking the box herself and had decided to hang his pictures by her bed "so that I may always have the pleasure of feeling them near me in bed, and seeing them when dressing and undressing . . . ." It was a strange way to lower the sexual temperature of their relationship.

When deprived of the presence of the beloved, Gabriel had only the consolation of memory. Although

> . . . through dark forest-boughs in flight
> The wind swoops onward brandishing the light,
> Even yet the rose tree's verdure left alone
> Will flush all ruddy though the rose be gone;
> With ditties and with dirges infinite.

By September 1880 the canvas of *The Daydream* was done and sold to Gabriel's friend Constantine Ionides for £735, and Janey had slipped in and out of Tudor House several more times. Also by then young Caine had finally been to Cheyne Walk, Gabriel writing Madox Brown shrewdly that his visitor seemed "modest, yet not likely to miss a chance that can be duly seized." To Caine, both Rossetti and his house seemed to be falling into desuetude. He noted, as might a builder's clerk, "the brick work falling into decay, the paint in need of renewal, the windows dull with the dust of months, the sills bearing more than the suspicion of cobwebs, the angles of the steps . . . and the untrodden flags[tones] of the little court . . . overgrown with moss and weed, while round the walls and up the . . . door and windows were creeping the tangled branches of the wildest ivy . . . ."

Rossetti had appeared in his knee-length painting coat (which he wore all day, even to meals), looking older than his fifty-two years, as his abundant beard and mustache were streaked with grey and his thinning hair curled round his ears. Prepared for disciplehood, Caine thought Gabriel's face was "singularly noble," and his resonant voice magnetic, both of which made it easier to recognize the poet of their correspondence. But Caine was not yet free to move in, and Gabriel had to continue to rely on his small band of friends who, usually by arrangement, came at least one each evening, William taking the Monday evenings, staying to dinner and often overnight. Shields added the enthusiasm the increasingly careworn William lacked, and Watts supplied efficiency and vigor. His wig looking increasingly too large for his face as age shrunk him, the tall, dour Bell Scott still made regular calls, but Madox Brown, dignified in old age by a long white beard, lived now in Manchester, where he was painting frescoes for the town hall, and could only look in when in London.

Isolation had its compensations, for in solitude Gabriel plodded on with both pictures and poems, reading new lines to his visitors and unveiling the evidence that his painter's hand had not lost its cunning. But as he wrote to Christina early in 1881, "With me, Sonnets mean Insomnia." Whatever the restless agonies of his nights, he still managed, most days, some brush-strokes worthy of his better years, and his friends usually found him genial in the evening, coiled on a sofa and ready to talk spellbindingly about writers and writing, or to declaim, from memory, long stretches of poetry in a voice as deep and rich as ever. But at Christmas 1880 his health was again undermined by the toxic effect of the chloral he craved, and he was too ill to go to Torrington Square. The weather was too foul for his mother; despite her long sealskin coat, to travel instead to Cheyne Walk; but William and Lucy, sensing his need, left their children long enough to see that Gabriel was not alone on the day that meant much to him.

William's earlier lecturing experiment had led to other invitations, and before he left London he had talked over with Gabriel his unsuppressed desire to write poetry, although he knew he did not have the creative powers of his brother and sister. The traditional sources of poetic inspiration,

Gabriel knew, had not moved William to verse, and he suggested instead a series of "Democratic Sonnets," which would give his brother an opportunity to versify the political events of his own lifetime. The idea intrigued William, for in better days he had argued happily for hours with Swinburne on such subjects, and although Gabriel for years had put Swinburne off, William had kept up their friendship and often came to his aid when Swinburne needed it. Nearly dead from drink in 1879, Swinburne had been rescued by the indefatigable Watts, who cared for him at Watts's pretentiously named "The Pines" in Putney and limited him to a daily glass of ale. Swinburne had become very deaf, making exchange of conversation difficult, and William's visits to Putney Hill usually resulted in his politely suffering to have read to him Swinburne's newest effusions, which became increasingly mediocre as his distance from whiskey increased. But his letters to William were filled with the old political fire, including Swinburne's unceasing regicidal fervor, and may have pushed William's sonneteering into more radical channels.

More businesslike than inspired, William had mulled over Gabriel's idea and decided that a hundred sonnets were "a proper number; fewer than this would not make a batch producible as a small volume." From January 28 to February 8, 1881, when he was away lecturing in Newcastle and Glasgow, William produced at least a sonnet a day, sending one on Garibaldi to Gabriel. "I rejoice to see so fine a sonnet," he wrote William, "and shall await the others with great interest. You may be the family bard yet." Encouraged, William sent more, on Mazzini, the Corn Laws, the French Republic, and Louis-Philippe, and Gabriel expressed concern that William was "doing them rather fast." A veteran of *boutes-rimés* competitions with Christina as well as Gabriel, William could turn out lines that scanned properly whether or not they were poetic in feeling, and as someone who lived a systematic life he had begun by making a chronological list of a hundred subjects for sonnets and crossed out the subjects he had versified. Gabriel criticized each one he received, recommending changes, and on March 6, after William's forty-fifth sonnet, warned Lucy, "I should think that sore throat must have resulted in two sonnets instead of one daily on William's part. I hope the ailment does not make his political poetics quite inexorable."

Swinburne had helped keep William engrossed in the project, writing him after the assassination of Czar Alexander II on March 13, "At last! 'One more unfortunate' has joined *'quel cattivo coro' di re** who would not

---

* Swinburne was quoting from Thomas Hood's "The Bridge of Sighs" and (in "that caitiff choir of kings") from Dante's *Inferno*.

have been tyrants but that they could not bring themselves to be less or more than kings. It is in a spirit of Christian hilarity, not of inhuman exultation, that I call upon you . . . ." Soon after, William produced a sonnet, "Tyrannicide," in which he argued that "An instinct in the world proclaims it just," and another "Fenians," which declared,

> An Irish patriot we have called a felon:
> No matter . . . .
> Melon termed pumpkin still will taste of melon.
> An Irish felon-patriot is a man
> Who loves his country splotched with alien shames,
> And dares a halter. . . .

After seeing others titled "The Red Flag," "The Commune," "The Red Shirt," and "John Brown," Gabriel was roused to protest, feeling like Dr. Frankenstein, that he had created a monster beyond his power to control. The family might be embarrassed by the radical slant of the sonnets. Gabriel himself might have unwanted attention called to himself, and his own forthcoming *Ballads and Sonnets* might be hurt. William's government job might itself be put in jeopardy. Pressing the latter motive, Gabriel decided to confront William indirectly, through Lucy. On April 12, 1881 he wrote her:

. . . Several of William's truest friends, no less than myself are greatly alarmed at the tone taken in some of his Sonnets respecting 'Tyrannicide,' Fenianism, and other incendiary subjects. It seems to me and to others that the consequences are absolutely and very perilously uncertain when an official (as William is) of a monarchical government allows himself such unbridled license of public speech. . . . The least evil I should apprehend, were William to persist in including such subjects, would be the certainty of his never attaining the final step of the Secretaryship in his office which he so well deserves. But very much worse consequences than this seem to all of us but too likely; and my object in writing this letter is to awaken your mind to the clear possibility of absolute ruin, in such a case, for my dear brother, and his family whom he loves so well. The very title, Democratic Sonnets, seems to me most objectionable when coming from one who depends on the Government for his bread. . . .

It is extremely painful to me to trouble you on this subject, while in your present delicate state;* but I really can keep silence no longer, the series being so far advanced; also I do not venture to speak to William direct, lest his first impulse should be to resent it as an encroachment, and so frustrate all attempt to avert what I and others view as a great danger. . . .

---

* Lucy was in her final month of pregnancy. The twins Michael Ford and Mary Elizabeth were born on April 22.

The same day, thinking better of his approach through Lucy, Gabriel wrote "a short propitiatory note" (as he described it to his mother) to William, in which he explained what he had done, ascribing his reaction to "the absolute call of brotherly love," and hoping that it would cause "no kind of division" between them. Quickly Mrs. Rossetti came to Gabriel's support, as did Christina, who announced, "I anxiously join in the hope that poor dear William will listen to prudent counsels." It was an irony that prudence of some kind should come at last from Gabriel, but Lucy was a lady of pronounced liberal opinions, and apparently took Gabriel's letter to William without taking Gabriel's side in the matter.

For the "brotherly letters," William sent his thanks, while tactfully upbraiding Gabriel for any anxiety he may have caused Lucy. Then he set out his own position. As a government official he would be likely to draw attention to himself if "Democratic Sonnets" were not "absolutely stillborn," but he was "prepared to encounter criticism" and to "brush [it] aside with equanimity." He realized, too, that if he were in line for the Secretaryship at what was by then the Inland Revenue Office of the Treasury, his published radical opinions might be held against him, but he regarded his chances of succession as "not a little" dubious. Beyond that, he thought, there was little cause for alarm. Democracy coexisted with monarchy in England, and freedom of expression was his right, and although he was "not wedded" to his title, he saw none better. But he intended to be his own man:

Any idea of my undertaking to write verse about the public events of my own time, & yet failing to show that I sympathize with foreign republics, & detest oppression, retrogression, & obscurantism, whether abroad or at home, must be nugatory. To set me going is to set me going on my own path.

I don't think that the other persons who agree in your anxieties on the subject can count for much. I suppose Watts is the principal person, & he can have read very little of the sonnets. Perhaps Mamma & Christina also: but Mamma's great age & Christina's isolated devoteeism diminish the *practical* importance of their view.

As you evidently don't agree with the tone of the sonnets, I shall drop my idea of dedicating them to you—unless you revive the proposal; & shall abstain from reading [to] you new items of the series, if you don't ask for them. . . .

Rejecting Gabriel's concern about the subversive nature of his verses, he nevertheless accepted his "affectionate solicitude," and there was no acrimony. Gabriel even offered to continue to read and criticize any new sonnets, while insisting that it had been his duty to warn William of the implications of the project. "Of course," he added, "much as I should prize the dedication to me of a work of yours, I think now that I will ask you for some other than this one." And to their mother Gabriel wrote later in the month that he had made his point as strongly as he could, "but I can trace no results either in his mind or in his wife's. . . . I . . . do think that Lucy must, in spite of appearances, be sufficiently aroused to prevent William from running any real risk." Yet it never became necessary. William persevered with his project into the autumn, completing seventy-two of his hundred. "Some of them," he thought later, "which I wrote with real interest for the subject, and an inclination to have my say about it, show a sufficient measure of force and ardour, both in thought and in diction— somewhat less in poetic accomplishment. Several others, which I produced merely as being germane in theme to the series, are the reverse of good. This therefore was my essential reason for leaving off."

Long afterward they were published, with a dedication sonnet "To the Memory of Dante Gabriel Rossetti." By then the radicalism had little but historical interest; but even so "The Red Flag," "Chartism" and "Tyrannicide"—to which Gabriel had particularly objected in 1881—were excluded.*

Part of Gabriel's apprehension had concerned the possible impact of William's verse upon press reaction to his own new volume of verse, which, through the spring, he was preparing. *Ballads and Sonnets* would contain forty-seven sonnets written since the 1870 collection, which nearly doubled the group constituting "The House of Life," † and narrative poems he labeled as ballads, although the pseudo-ballads were not up to the standard of his earlier work. With the new book he "reissued" his *Poems* of 1870, which was so thin once he removed the "House of Life" sonnets that he had to fill it out with an unfinished work begun in 1848, "The Bride's Prelude." The poem, he confessed, was "unelevated and repulsive," but to make two books of little more than one he had to make compromises. "Its picturesqueness," he decided, "is sufficient to make it pass muster, though it has no other quality to recommend it. Besides, I don't see how it can be spared as the space must be filled."

Asked to go through the proofs, William made voluminous notes on his objections and recommendations, Gabriel acknowledging on May 20, "I read all your notes with interest and some with advantage." Translated, it meant that he incorporated some of the suggestions, and rejected others. Watts, too, had the honor of criticizing the text, but his own mediocrity as a poet could contribute little that was useful to Gabriel's revisions, and in fact

---

* See further on the publication of "Democratic Sonnets" in Chapter 16.

† From which he removed "Nuptial Sleep," because of Buchanan's notorious objections.

gave Gabriel a higher opinion of his later productions than they deserved, Watts even planting in the "Literary Gossip" column of the *Athenaeum* an announcement that the three new ballads, "one romantic and two historical," were "no doubt the most ambitious and the most important poems Mr. Rossetti has produced."

By the time the volumes were in press Gabriel's physical condition and his financial condition had both worsened. Having promised himself never to sell drawings of Janey, he nevertheless offered Fry (through Watts) several of them, needing the hundreds of pounds each would bring. Finally, his huge *Dante's Dream at the Time of the Death of Beatrice*, returned first by Graham and then by Valpy, because it was too big for any wall in a private home (Graham had tried the staircase), was sold through Hall Caine's efforts, but again Rossetti had to break a personal rule out of financial need. He had refused to exhibit publicly all his life, and certainly would not have risked exhibiting prior to a sale, but the municipal art gallery in Liverpool had to abide by the rules of the Liverpool Corporation, which required that no picture could be purchased for the city except out of the annual exhibition. Hard up as he was, Rossetti remained unyielding, although the sale would then only be a matter of form. Finally Caine came up with a compromise. "Rossetti," he appealed, "give the picture to *me* and *I* will exhibit it and sell it to Liverpool." It was exhibition nevertheless, but Gabriel could at least claim that he had not shown it for sale, nor even shown it himself. The picture became technically Caine's property, and Caine sold it for the agreed-upon £1,550.

Not for two months would Gabriel get his money, however, for he could only be paid out of the receipts of the Exhibition, which was open until November. Finally the check came, and Caine flung it to his host, who was in bed. "There you are, Gabriel!" he crowed. "We've done the trick, you see!" But by then there was little to cheer Rossetti, who was ill enough to have to dictate letters to Caine, his handwriting having become at times pitifully tremulous.

On August 7, four weeks before the sale to Liverpool had been arranged, Caine had moved in with Rossetti as "Secretary" for bed and board—and literary connections, and when Gabriel was certain that Caine was coming, he rebuffed Dunn, then about to return to London, sending him £50, a promise of £3 a week until his arrears in salary were paid, and his dismissal notice. Gabriel in any case was no longer in need of an artistic assistant. Although his earlier eye trouble had been, very likely, neurotic, one of the toxic effects of chloral hydrate was to affect the nervous system and sense organs, and Gabriel's eyesight was failing again, perhaps due to chloral-induced congestion of the optic nerve. For more than a year, in order to read, he had to wear a second pair of spectacles over his now-usual pair. Deafness also troubled him, but he could not give up his drug. The chloral crises—actually breaks in tolerance—were now coming closer together than before, as his whiskey and chloral intake (still a phenomenon marked in medical texts) overwhelmed the detoxification powers of his liver and kidneys. The only solution was to limit his intake, which often exceeded twelve grams nightly, but the device only succeeded while he was too ill to filch or cadge additional dosages. Again country air was recommended, and on September 19 Gabriel, accompanied not only by Caine but by Fanny, left for the Lake Country in a reserved railway car crowded with books and artists' materials.

At lodgings at the foot of Fisher Ghyll, near Keswick, Gabriel made another of his seemingly impossible recoveries. To William he wrote that letters admiring the landscape so revered by the Romantic poets were not in his mode, but that the region beloved by Wordsworth was indeed "very beautiful and an absolute solitude." He had lived intermittently among such scenic grandeur, but only when recuperating from illness, and little of the environment ever touched his art. For his poems and pictures, Cheyne Walk and its garden had been sufficient, but he owed a canvas to Valpy, and set up his easel in the country "to drudge a little at an easy replica" for him, a *Proserpine.* And he wrote, in a spidery hand, a few wan letters, some to Janey. At Fisher Ghyll, too, he waited out the reviews of his *Ballads and Sonnets,* which appeared in mid-October, and notices of his Liverpool picture, Watts and Caine doing their best in the press to set an adulatory tone.

Weak and easily exhausted, Gabriel had expected to remain away from London indefinitely, but Caine had to leave for brief periods to deliver lectures, and during one of his absences Fanny—carefully identified by Caine only as Gabriel's "nurse"—unwisely revealed to Gabriel that his secretary had been giving him nightly doses of the drug which were little more than water. To Gabriel it explained his lethargy and melancholy, and he became greatly agitated. When Caine returned, he found Fanny gone, and Gabriel eager to flee the oppressive solitude. On October 17—they had only been away four weeks—Gabriel boarded the express from Scotland at Penrith, and sat up all night in coat, hat and gloves, as if London were the next station a few minutes away.

First Caine tried to distract him during the dreary journey by chattering brightly, but the ride was long and Caine wore down, whereupon Gabriel, not yet stupefied by chloral, but his tongue loosened by depression and fatigue, unburdened himself to his young companion in the jolting compartment. Gabriel had never so done to anyone else. Earlier he had told

Caine, sadly, that "an organized conspiracy existed, having for its object to annoy and injure him, and to hold him up to the public execration as an evil influence on his time. So tyrannical . . . had the conspiracy become, that it had altered the habits of his life, and practically confined him for years to the limits of his own home." * Now he told of returning to Chatham Place to find Lizzy's letter—and body. He confessed to "never [having] forgiven himself for the weakness of yielding to the importunity of friends, and the impulse of literary ambition, which had led him to violate the sanctity of a wife's grave . . . ." And he represented himself as a man who had destroyed his happiness "after engaging himself to one woman in all honour and good faith," because he "had fallen in love with another, and then gone on to marry the first out of a mistaken sense of loyalty and a fear of giving pain, instead of stopping . . . at the door of the church itself." He was guilty, then, of his wife's death, he suggested, not from any "act of infidelity on his part," but "because the good woman he had married was reading his secret in spite of all his efforts to conceal it, and thereby losing all joy and interest in life." The revelations of remorse and of unrequited passion, however they were triggered, were at least in part a calculated strategy to win future sympathy and understanding, as he knew without asking that Caine would tell the story, however many pieces of Gabriel's personal puzzle he reshaped or omitted entirely.

Caine thought he understood, although during his months at Cheyne Walk Jane Morris had been the only intimate friend of Gabriel's whom he did not meet. When she was expected Gabriel would send a note to Caine, who would be elsewhere in the house: "The lady I spoke about has arrived and will stay with me to dinner. In these circumstances I will ask you to be good enough to dine in your own room to-night." Having already lived so close to the evidences of Gabriel's heartbreak, the young writer was profoundly moved, and regretted the arrival in London which ended the reminiscences at dawn. Gabriel needed help up the stairs at Cheyne Walk. "Thank God!" he said, "Home at last and never shall I leave it again."

---

* Another writer (and onetime artist) to suffer from the Rossetti syndrome was Evelyn Waugh, whose paranoia and hallucinations about overheard conspiracies (novelized by him in *The Ordeal of Gilbert Pinfold*, 1957) was attributed by his psychiatrist, Eric Strauss, to a combination of sleep-inducing drugs (Waugh suffered from chronic insomnia and took phenobarbital) and alcohol. In 1962–63 Waugh again suffered from persecution mania which involved, as in Rossetti's case, "overheard" and imagined events, and again he had been ingesting abnormal quantities of both soporifics and alcohol—this time gin. Neither the insomnia nor the paranoia ever left him completely, and the internal damage contributed to his relatively premature death at sixty-two. Ironically, Waugh's first major book—before he became famous as a novelist—had been a biography of Rossetti.

He confessed to being "very ill," and his few letters suggested little desire to hang on to an existence where his only pleasure was the nightly blotting of consciousness. The "calm presence of William" helped, but he could see few of his old friends who wanted to congratulate him on his *Poems* and *Ballads* as a way of seeing him for perhaps a last time. Even Fanny was seldom available, although she was again willing to come, for the Rossetti women might be visiting, and Gabriel could not keep them away. He brooded over his imminent inability to provide even for himself, and William assured him that his brother's home would always be his own. A nurse, Mrs. Abrey, was called in to oversee his needs, and as the obvious signs around him gathered he surprised his rationalist brother by asking to see a priest for confession and absolution. The request had probably been triggered by a letter from Christina, who had confided on December 2,

I want to assure you that, however harassed by memory or anxiety you may be, I have (more or less) heretofore gone through the same ordeal. I have borne myself till I became unbearable to myself, and then I have found help in confession and absolution and spiritual counsel, and relief inexpressible. Twice in my life I tried to suffice myself with measures short of this, but nothing would do; the first time was of course in my youth before my general confession, the second time was when circumstances had led me (rightly or wrongly) to break off the practice. But now for years past I have resumed the habit, and I hope not to continue it profitlessly.

> 'Tis like frail man to love to walk on high
> But to be lowly is to be like God,'

is a couplet (Isaac Williams) I thoroughly assent to.

I ease my own heart by telling you all this, and I hope I do not weary yours. Don't think of me merely as the younger sister whose glaring faults are known to you, but as a devoted friend also.

Canon Burrows called at Christina's suggestion, but Gabriel only insisted to Bell Scott, "I can make nothing of Christianity, but I only want a confessor to give me absolution for my sins." None was sent for. Gabriel spent most of his days prostrate on a sofa, where with friends around on Sunday December 11, he suddenly exclaimed that his left side felt paralyzed. Hall Caine and Westland Marston carried him to bed and summoned Dr. Marshall, who placed a newly qualified young doctor in the house and tried to wean Gabriel from chloral by substituting morphine and diluted chloral, and a week later the chloral was stopped altogether, and only a token amount of whiskey permitted. By Christmas the paralysis was restricted to Gabriel's left hand and arm, but he was too ill for visitors, and only William left his Christmas dinner to come to Cheyne Walk.

Early in the new year Gabriel was able to complete another copy for Valpy, a *Joan of Arc*, but the strain was too much. He could barely keep his depression about his failing powers out of his letters to his mother and sister. Late in January, 1882, Gabriel's old friend, the architect John Seddon, offered a cottage near Margate to remove the patient from the gloom of Tudor House, and despite Gabriel's vow uttered only two months earlier, he left via Victoria Station for Birchington-on-Sea on February 4, with only Mrs. Abrey, Caine, and Caine's twelve-year-old sister Lily as companions. Christina and Mrs. Rossetti wanted to join Gabriel there, but were forbidden by their doctor to stay near the sea during the winter. When Gabriel wrote to them of his "sore disappointment" in not having their company he was, perhaps for the first time, being more than merely diplomatic.

Birchington was dreary, even stormy, with brief intervals of sunshine. Too feeble to walk about outdoors much, he lounged about in his old, nearly threadbare, painting coat, paid tender attentions to Lily, and complained of cold and discomfort, often removing a black glove he now wore on his paralyzed hand to warm it at the fire. His easel had been set up to continue work on the *Joan of Arc*, but he could apply himself to it barely long enough to set up brushes and paints, and looked forward to such visitors as Watts and young William Sharp, who would write for *The Yellow Book* a decade later as "Fiona Macleod." Because of Gabriel's shifting moods, William unreasonably interpreted to Christina a letter of February 17 in which Gabriel apologized for not being able to help the town fathers of Vasto with a design for a memorial to their father; and Christina replied, "It is trying to have to do with him at times, but what must it be TO BE himself?"

For William it was difficult to keep his mind on the bureaucratic routine at Somerset House, since by almost every post came news of Gabriel's further deterioration. One letter, at least, was unexpected. He was invited to act as the junior examiner for Italian literature and language for a scholarship in the Taylorian Institute at Oxford. The academic distinction felt good to a bald greybeard who had left school at fifteen to become a clerk. William accepted.

At a time when Gabriel was nearly past caring, plaudits were becoming commonplace. Laudatory articles about him were appearing in journals formerly hostile, or even vicious, and twelve thousand copies of *Ballads and Sonnets* had been sold within a month of publication. Even the cranky Buchanan—perhaps looking for publicity—had dedicated his newest book to "An Old Enemy," with apologetic verses in which he confessed having wronged "an honoured head," and now offered "peace and charity":

> Pure as thy purpose, blameless as thy song,
> Sweet as thy spirit, may this offering be:

Forget the bitter blame that did thee wrong,
And take the gift from me!

Visiting Gabriel just before the retreat to Birchington, William had seen Buchanan's bathetic apology, the verses copied out for Gabriel by William Sharp; and William had observed that they were "a handsome retraction of past invidious attacks." Gabriel was more cynical, suggesting instead that the verses may really have been intended for Swinburne. Twenty years later, Buchanan died, and the *Morning Leader* inquired whether William would write an obituary notice, assuming that he would have nursed his brother's grievance through the intervening years and might now be expected to affix an eye-catching diatribe onto Buchanan's grave. William declined. It was not his style.

Free from chloral in the raw, final weeks of winter, Gabriel's mind was clear but his body ravaged, and he surrendered to pain by taking to his bed, remaining chatty and animated when friends called—as did Leyland and Watts and Sharp—but giving in to depression about his condition when Christina arrived with her mother. Only Howell brought Gabriel back, briefly to the happier old days, visiting once—although they had been estranged after bitter disagreements about money due from sales of Gabriel's paintings. "And what are you doing now, Charles?" asked Gabriel.

"Buying horses for the King of Portugal," said the irrepressible Howell, and, Hall Caine, who was there, added, "Rossetti laughed until he nearly rolled out of his seat." And Howell "stayed all day, telling stories, veracious and apocryphal, of nearly everybody known to us in the world. . . ." The visit of "this unaccountable being," Caine wrote, did Gabriel good, "and he laughed all evening after the man had gone, talking of his adventures of various kinds, as well as telling his familiar stories all over again." Yet this "was but the flickering of the lamp that was slowly dying out."

To William on March 24, Christina reported that Gabriel was "going back apparently rather than going forward, and is so comfortless and sinking and so wasted away that at last this morning I urged him to see a local Dr . . . ." Diplomatically, Dr. Harris concluded that Gabriel's state was "*not* irremediable," but it was, and on April 5 Christina delivered to William his revised opinion, that Gabriel's kidneys were seriously diseased. Nephritis had been almost inevitable once his liver and kidneys had finally been overwhelmed by chloral abuse, and the uremia was irreversible. William had traveled to Birchington the previous weekend, finding Gabriel "barely capable of tottering a few steps, half-blind and suffering a great deal of pain," but he was rational and had even managed to dictate two weak sonnets to Caine, who dutifully set them down. William planned to return the following weekend, which would begin with Good Friday, but he was recalled a day early by telegram, and when Caine told Gabriel that Watts and William were coming the next day, Gabriel sat up and commented in his now-slurred speech, "Then you really think that I am dying? At *last* you think so; but *I* was right from the first."

Although drowsy most of the time, he was able to make his will with the assistance of Watts, a necessary precaution as William realized that the testament still in force left everything to Lizzy, and that her brothers would be the beneficiaries. She had urged Gabriel with her dying words to take care of Harry Siddall, and had he died before making a new will that object would have been achieved with a vengeance. Signed on April 8, the new one left a choice of small drawing or personal memento to his mother, sister, brother, Madox Brown, Bell Scott, Burne-Jones, Watts, Swinburne, Leyland, Shields, Graham, Valpy, and Caine; and to Jane Morris "three of the largest and best of the chalk drawings for the subjects of which she sat that are now hanging in my studio . . . [and] also the profile head of her in chalk now hanging over the mantelpiece in the studio." As in the case of Maria, Christina had again refused to be a beneficiary as long as her mother was alive. The residue of the estate after payment of debts and testamentary expenses was to be divided equally between Mrs. Rossetti and William, while William, of "five Endsleigh Gardens"—he had not moved but the name of his street had been changed—was declared sole executor. Following that, Gabriel's desire to live failed altogether. He permitted the rector of Birchington, who had been denied admittance weeks before, to see him and pray at his bedside with Watts and Mrs. Rossetti. Throughout the night as Saturday passed into Easter Sunday, April 9, Christina and Mrs. Abrey kept vigil beside the barely conscious figure, and twice during the day, in a calm voice much clearer than his usual indistinct speech, Gabriel said, "I believe I shall die tonight. Yesterday I wished to die, but today I must confess that I do not." Although a rigid unbeliever, William tried, perhaps thinking about staging a dignified end, to read to his brother sections of Ecclesiastes. Gabriel objected. That evening, as preparations were being made for another night of waiting for the end, Gabriel cried out twice, writhed convulsively and then lay still. It was 9:31 P.M.

XV

Two Rossettis
1882-1894

Although William recorded in his diary late on Easter Sunday, 1882, that "the pride and glory of our family" had died, that was all the time he had for sentiment. He had to try to keep the death secret long enough to permit the last check Gabriel signed—for £300—to be cashed, so that local funeral expenses could be met, and so that creditors, and Fanny, could be held off. Watts was to delay the obituary notice in the *Athenaeum* until the day of the funeral, and William wrote to his wife's brother-in-law, Franz Hueffer, *The Times*'s music critic, to postpone the appearance of a death notice in *The Times*. In tiny Birchington the news was too big to be suppressed, and it leaked quickly to London. F. S. Ellis, Gabriel's publisher, advanced the money instead, and the burial took place on Friday afternoon, April 14, at Birchington churchyard. Two days earlier Fanny had read the death notice in *The Times*, and rushed a letter to William, who prevented her mourning in person by not replying until it was too late. "Your letter of the 12th only reached me this morning about 9," he wrote coldly on the day of the funeral. "The coffin had been closed last evening, and the funeral takes place early this afternoon—there is nothing further to be done."

At half-past three the cortege, consisting of a hearse and five mourning coaches, left the seaside cottage. At the graveside, where the small company included Gabriel's patrons Heaton, Graham and Leyland, old Mrs. Rossetti, now eighty-two, was supported on one side by William and on the other by Christina. Somehow loyal Aunt Charlotte managed to be there, as well as

Boyce and Stephens. The local vicar read the service; flowers were thrown into the grave after the coffin was lowered; the men shook hands with William, and the group scattered, most of them heading back to London. The *Standard* reported the next day that a "public funeral at Highgate, where the wife and father of the deceased are interred," had been thought of, "but for family reasons . . . was abandoned." It had never been a possibility, Gabriel fearing to the end the posthumous wrath of Lizzy.

Despite the secluded burial spot, interest in Gabriel's death was intense, and *The Times* marveled that a painter who almost never exhibited his work, and avoided press publicity to an extent unprecedented in the modern history of art, "should on this principle have achieved a reputation scarcely inferior to that of the most popular favourites of the day." Newspapers and magazines snapped up sentimental effusions about Gabriel, from Christina's "Birchington Churchyard," to verses from William Sharp, Theodore Watts and the estranged Algernon Swinburne. William's own writing was restricted to the prosaic but more important business of beginning to settle his brother's chaotic and debt-ridden estate. He employed Dunn at a pound a day (for nearly four months) to make watercolor sketches of the familiar rooms in Cheyne Walk before everything was inventoried and dispersed (and to complete some of Gabriel's unfinished replicas), invited the friends and relatives named in Gabriel's will to choose as directed from drawings and books and personal effects, and began fending off claims against the estate, one of the earliest of them a bill for £52 from a pharmacy in New Bond Street for chloral Gabriel had furtively acquired in addition to his open purchases from another firm.

There were even offers of help which William had to fend off. Fanny, for example, tied her useful knowledge of Gabriel's affairs to payment of promissory notes she had extracted from Gabriel. Howell, who could have been even more useful, and whom William could not help liking, could not be trusted. "I will—however awkward for myself and perhaps not kindly taken by you," William wrote to him firmly, "—say that I had rather not renew any visiting or family intimacy between your house and mine. Our intimacy was severed some years ago by circumstances in which I was not personally concerned, and I think we had better leave it on that footing—mutual helpfulness in any business relations which may be advantageous to both of us, without renewal of familiar visiting, &c."

Bargaining adroitly, William sold what he could from Gabriel's effects—including seven Elizabeth Siddal drawings to Howell for £55—before a two-day auction was held at Cheyne Walk on July 5 and July 6. According to the Liverpool *Mercury* the attendance was "enormous," while in London the *World* carped that the sale of Gabriel's belongings "must be

considered a high festival of the relic *cultus.* One understands the interest
attached to the easel of a distinguished painter, or the writing-table of an
eminent poet; but an ordinary-minded person finds it difficult to understand
an enthusiasm which runs up window-curtains and occasional chairs to four
times their value." William may have been especially pleased that four
unbound issues of *The Germ* went for six guineas, and that the Blake
sketchbook for which he had lent Gabriel ten shillings, very likely never
repaid, was sold for one hundred and five guineas. The sale raised nearly
£3,000, but—as expected—several lots knocked down to Howell at the
auction were still unremoved and unpaid for weeks later. Although William
thought that the amount was about equal to Gabriel's debts, and that the
deliberately delayed sale of Gabriel's own paintings would bring in a
handsome inheritance, there were many more debts still to be claimed,
especially resulting from undelivered commissions for which advances had
been paid. Still, prospects appeared good that Gabriel's estate could cover its
obligations, especially when Watts, who was handling Gabriel's posthumous
legal affairs, was able to surrender the Cheyne Walk lease advantageously.

Not everything went well in the disposition of Gabriel's affairs. There
was a dispute with Madox Brown about how to market the unfinished
Rossetti canvases Brown had agreed—in William's words—to "overhaul."
Elderly and sensitive about his own diminishing reputation, he returned
huffily to his own Manchester frescoes, leaving William to write a check to
reimburse him for his London expenses. What William had been planning
was a sale of the stock of Gabriel's pictures, some needing completion or
restoration, once an exhibition at the Royal Academy (which had requested
a show) had helped to enhance Gabriel's public reputation and to improve
the subsequent prices at Christie's sale. Brown wanted credit for his
finishing touches, not a private unloading of the canvases he would quietly
complete. Dunn was called in, and was paid, according to Watts's entry in
the estate accounts, "for assistance in preparing pictures &c for the sale."
William was unhappy even at that evidence of another hand, for he wanted
the works sold as Rossettis, and although he had his way, and the exhibition
had a good press, the sale took place in a depressed art market. Only about
£2,500 remained after expenses.

William was now deep into the business of guarding and enhancing his
brother's reputation. Watts called often at Somerset House, where William
now freely conducted his family's business as well as the Queen's, and
proposed a memoir, which William agreed would have more credibility
coming from a non-relative. He began to collect Gabriel's letters to his
family to fill out the volume, Christina copying out for her mother those
passages their "monitory blue pencil" left as fit for print, rather than

furnishing William with the originals. Even before the family was at work there was another memoirist in the field, Hall Caine, who wanted to do a book of his recollections and Gabriel's long letters to him. The proofs William and Watts read—books were printed from manuscript and ready for sale more rapidly then—were largely innocuous. Caine, however, claimed more intimacy than his few months with Gabriel suggested were possible, put the story of the exhumation of the poems into print, and quoted voluminously from Gabriel's purported conversations with him, including a passage about Nolly Brown which caused Lucy to write him an angry letter. On second thought she sent it to Watts rather than directly to Caine, and William and Watts agreed to predicate permission to publish Gabriel's letters on excision of the derogatory remarks about Nolly Brown alone, Caine having insisted about the exhumation, rebutting William's plea, "I should be grieved to give pain to your mother, but my first duty is to truth as I know it." By mid-autumn the book was out, and Christina pronounced it "neither unkind nor unfriendly," understanding "the circumstances under which his experiences occurred."

Handling Gabriel's posthumous business required hard bargaining by William. It was rumored that Fanny was offering for sale letters addressed to Gabriel from Swinburne and Ruskin, which might be embarrassing. And Fanny had an undated IOU for £300 from Gabriel which she brought for payment once the Christie sale was over. Pressed for the alleged date, she named one which William observed preceded recorded payments to her by Gabriel of more than £1,000. Still, Watts suggested a conciliatory check, as she was capable of making trouble, and William gave in—but, stubbornly, only to a £25 "free gift" for which she was to surrender the promissory note. Fanny took the money.

From Fanny and Schott there was still further awkwardness, as they had opened at 1A Old Bond Street a "Rossetti Gallery," where for a fee one could view thirty oils, drawings and watercolors Fanny possessed, as well as photographs of others. There was no proof that she did not own them, and William could do nothing. (Besides, he realized that some of the pictures exhibited were fine enough to enhance Gabriel's reputation, although he was further rankled that the ubiquitous Howell was reported to have produced Fanny's catalog.)

Some problems were small, such as the dozens of requests for Gabriel's autograph. William sent old canceled checks. A more serious dilemma involved Gabriel's unpaid and now impatient patrons. Valpy and Graham and Leyland were owed considerable sums. They had to be settled with out of the earnings of the estate, as long as enough remained in the estate to pay the death duties. Even settlement with Dunn was protracted, for Gabriel's onetime assistant had not been able to make a career of his own, and had taken to whiskey and quarrelsomeness. The matter of a gravestone at Birchington was also a focus of discontent, although everyone who counted agreed on employing Madox Brown to do the design. The problem was that Christina, and the eighty-three-year-old Mrs. Rossetti, insisted on a cross, while William preferred a "neutral" symbol, and had Lucy as ally. Eventually William gave in, explaining to his tougher-minded wife that it was not unreasonable that a man buried in a churchyard should have a headstone appropriate to the location. But he insisted that the monument not suggest in its wording that he approved of the cross.

Assembling Gabriel's manuscripts and letters, William saw editorial projects looming once Watts completed his memoir, but Watts gave no sign of even working on it, and William restively approached Gabriel's publisher, Ellis, about a collected edition of the works. Something had to be thrown into the breach to keep Gabriel's reputation alive. Skeptically, Ellis pointed to the many copies of *Ballads and Sonnets* he had remaining. He would not permit himself to be left with unsaleable stock. A few months later, however, he impulsively retired from business in favor of his nephew Gilbert Ellis, who first wanted to jettison his Rossetti list and then reconsidered in favor of a collected edition of the poems, to be followed within a year—he hoped—by Watts's and William's joint volume.

Hearing that William was contemplating a study of Gabriel, and an edition of his letters, Bell Scott wrote to urge reasonable candor. "The personality of Gabriel with all its weaknesses and delusions was a perfect individuality, and the most fascinating I have met. . . . The place he must take . . . makes it certain that a true picture of his nature as exhibited in his life, is necessary to avoid the lies and revelations that have been poured out by half-enlightened writers about Shelley, Byron, and others and warrant[s] such a treatment. If your dear mother wd. dissent from this, delay your work. But to give only one side of him by letters to his family [alone] you must see is only like Mrs, Stow's *Sunny Memoirs* with alas! the infernal unrevealed story beneath. . . ." But William was not about to let loose infernal unrevealed stories, and counted upon Watts's dilatory biographical muse to be equally discreet. In the meantime, there were the unpublished poems.

Not concerned about textual variants, William came home from Somerset House each evening to work on reordering Gabriel's published pieces and sorting through unpublished material for additional writings worthy of the ones Gabriel had passed for publication himself. The unpublished matter was to be the project's chief claim to attention, and William had to be less than fastidious in order to find enough new copy, selecting, he confessed in a preface, "only such examples as I suppose that he would himself have approved for the purpose, or would, at any rate, not gravely have objected to." Uncollected, out of Victorian timidity, was the sonnet "Nuptial Sleep," because Buchanan had found in it "merely animal sensations," and "After the French Liberation of Italy," which used the imagery of a prostitute's embrace. And there were more problems, William worrying about giving precise dates of composition of individual sonnets in "The House of Life" because—he noted in his diary—there were "considerations" to dissuade him. He knew which poems were prompted by a passion which *followed* the death of Lizzy Siddal, and wanted to inhibit any biographical reading of the sonnets.

Cautiously, William blurred the chronology by omitting dates, and in a preface he carefully blended fact and reticence. Lizzy's death, and the retreats to Kelmscott, were unavoidable realities, but William saw no reason to do more than acknowledge them. Yet he also conceded that his brother had found himself in difficulties by "loving, if not always practising, the good." When the edition finally emerged into print in 1887 the notices were favorable. Those of William's (and Gabriel's) friends who supplied a number of them were very likely relieved by William's skillful combination of fairness and propriety. For a time the preface stood as the major biographical source about Gabriel, for Watts's promised memoir remained only a promise.

Less than a year after Gabriel's death, another Rossetti was buried, William's son Michael, one of the twins. Not quite two, he had been sickly since birth, and one night late in January, 1883, Christina was called to Endsleigh Gardens, where she found William and Lucy already grieving, as there was no hope. Without asking her nonbelieving brother and sister-in-law, who stood by without protesting, Christina baptized the dying baby with her own hands, explaining to Lucy afterward that "baptism (where attainable) is the sole door I know of whereby entrance is promised into the happiness which eye has not seen nor ear heard nor heart of man conceived." Later she wrote a poem to Michael Ford Madox Rossetti, "a Bud not to blossom," and

> A Holy Innocent gone home
>   Without so much as one sharp wounding word;
> A blessed Michael in heaven's lofty dome
>   Without a sword.

For Lucy and William it was as much a relief as a sorrow, and William, at least, could put aside grief in the press of work. By the summer of 1883 he had settled with Valpy, paying him nearly £1,600 out of the proceeds of

Gabriel's estate, and had compromised with Graham for an additional £400, rushing out a check to settle the inheritance tax when Watts was as dilatory as usual, and the Controller of Legacy Duties, in a division of William's own department, began threatening William with legal proceedings. Still, Watts would regularly turn up at Somerset House to go over the estate's accounts and legal affairs, and William in his free hours would pore over his brother's papers and pictures, now piled high at 5 Endsleigh Gardens. At home he encouraged his eldest daughter's literary interests by reading Shakespeare to her on evenings he could spend at home, Lucy during the day tutoring her as well as young Arthur in Latin and French. Next door, at Miss Smith's School, the children learned the rudiments of dancing, and from Cathy Brown Hueffer the children received voice lessons. Once a respectable mourning period was over, the Rossettis had also returned to entertaining literary and artistic friends and acquaintances in their memorabilia-filled home, novelist "Vernon Lee" sniffing after her first visit to Endsleigh Gardens, "Oh, what a grimy, dingy, filthy aesthetic house!"

Pre-Raphaelitism was Vernon Lee's bane, and in her *Miss Brown* she produced a melodramatic three-decker populated by posturing poets and painters, some of them deep in drug addiction, alcoholism and unnameable debaucheries. Even worse, to her taste, was what she described as "the cheap-and-shop shoddy aestheticism" of Pre-Raphaelitism, the phony "medieval sort of thing—no stays and no petticoats, and slashings, and tags and bootlaces in the sleeves, and a yard of bedraggled train," aesthetic houses cluttered with "weird furniture, partly Japanese, partly Queen Anne, partly medieval," in which poets wrote "of the kisses of cruel, blossom-mouthed women, who sucked out their lovers' hearts, bit their lips, and strewed their apartments with coral-like drops of blood." No wonder that Vernon Lee, on her annual visit (from Italy) to England, reported to her mother that Watts and the Rossettis "seem to sulk," and that Wilde, Gosse, and the Morrises openly avoided her. But Lucy Rossetti relented a year later, and invited her to tea, Vernon Lee interpreting the gesture as a "rapprochement." Still *Miss Brown* affected her reputation for years. Some Victorian critics found the book "too repulsive" to review, while other critics were of the society whose hospitality she had breached.

One of the poets castigated by implication in Vernon Lee's fiction had been Swinburne, who, however innocuous now, dedicated—to Christina's embarrassment—one of his books to her, his harmless *Century of Roundels*. He wrote to her more, now that Gabriel was dead, although Gabriel had not been available as addressee for years past. When Swinburne had sent his *Tristram of Lyonesse*, she had responded that it was "a valued gift," but it was an awkward one as well, for it was the fourth of his books he had presented to her, and "I not one hitherto to him." In return she sent him her edifying *Called to Be Saints*, which he accepted graciously, praising her verses to the Holy Innocents and to St. Barnabas and other worthies. As he knew from William, she had once been horrified by one of his gifts, the scandalous *Atalanta in Calydon*, and had pasted strips of paper over lines in the atheistic chorus in her copy.

Helping William put Gabriel's letters into discreetly censored shape had been one of Christina's few literary activities following Gabriel's death. After initial uneasiness over the blue-penciling, and Mrs. Rossetti's temporary retirement from the task on grounds that the pain was too great, both women went at the task with vigor, Christina copying out the unobjectionable passages, in the process finding segments of the past restored to her and wishing—she admitted in *Time Flies*—that "a certain occupation at once sad and pleasant and dear to me, and that moment inevitably drawing toward a close, could have lasted out the remainder of my lifetime."

Soon there was another life to relive through the sorting-through of papers and letters. Charles Cayley was still making his regular visits to Christina for tea and whist, and for talk of her poetry and his new translation projects. Seemingly unchanged in his sixtieth year, he wore his usual neat but out-of-fashion clothes and his abstracted, otherworldly air. He was wearing both when Lucy Rossetti and her children discovered Cayley at the British Museum looking at the huge bones of the ichthyosaurus which had not yet been pieced together and mounted. For security—since the bones made tempting souvenirs—an attendant kept the door locked, but they were admitted to gaze, perhaps because Richard Garnett, a senior official of the Museum, was a close friend. Walking down the corridor after the guard had let them out and re-locked the door, Olive stopped suddenly and wondered aloud, "But Mamma, where is Mr. Cayley?" They hurried back; the door was unlocked, and Cayley was discovered in a hollow made by the stacked bones, hands behind his back, deep in a daydream.

In February, 1883, he wrote to Christina and asked that she become his heir and literary executrix. To her "dear old Friend" she answered that she foresaw "the apparently at least equal probability" that she would die first, but she valued the proof of his affection. Although she would cherish "some trifle that you had been fond of . . . ," she would be his executrix but not his legatee. The offer touched her, and she felt it necessary to explain her own plans, which assumed that she would outlive her mother and two aged aunts, and would not need any estate Cayley might leave. If William survived her, she confided, she owed him much. "William made me a home for so many years that . . . I am inclined to rate the money-portion of my debt to him at (say) £100 a year for 20 years: here at once is £2,000! and far enough am I [yet] from possessing such a sum. . . . I dare say you will trace, though I certainly have not stated, what sort of train of thought set me upon saying all this." Should she have anything further to bequeath, beyond her estimated indebtedness to William, she implied, it would go to Cayley himself.

Satisfied of her regard, Cayley made his will on May 3, 1883, declaring that in the event of his dying before his "dear and kind friend Miss Christina Georgiana Rossetti," he bequeathed all his unsold stock of published books which Longmans & Co. "are in the habit of selling on commission for me, and all sums actually payable to me on account of such sales. . . . And the said Christina Rossetti is also to have my best writing desk, and any packet that may be lying therein addressed to her, and she shall be entitled to reclaim or order to be destroyed any letters of hers which may be found among my papers. . . ."

The morbid minuet over, they returned to their usual relationship of superannuated never-were lovers, a gift of a book from Cayley arriving on November 30, in advance of Christina's fifty-third birthday on December 5. It was a *Francesca da Rimini*, the story of the torrid love affair also told by Dante (who romanticized the facts), and as far removed—whatever the version—from the course of Cayley's and Christina's life as it was possible to conceive. On the day of her birthday Cayley failed to arrive as expected at Torrington Square; nor was he there the next day. On the morning of December 7, when Christina came home from church, she found Cayley's brother Arthur waiting in her drawing room. He had come down from Cambridge on hearing the news of Charles's death. Cayley had apparently had a fatal heart attack on her birthday.

Christina went to his house to see him for the last time, and laid a white wreath on his bed. Then, William recalled, "She . . . came round to me at Somerset House, to tell me of it. I shall not easily forget the look of her face, and the strain of self-command in her voice; she did not break down." There was a large packet of letters Sophie Cayley wrote to her the next day. Did she want them returned? "You were I know the friend he valued most. . . ." Although Christina asked the family to destroy the letters, some came back into her own hands, including the letter she had written about their wills. For the *Athenaeum* William wrote an affectionate obituary notice, concluding, "We shall not look again upon his like." Friends wrote letters of sympathy to Christina as if she were a bereaved widow. In a sense she was. She accepted the writing desk.

For a few years there was some tiny income from Cayley's legacy of translations from Homer and Petrarch. In 1884 Christina realized

£4.15.10; in 1885 only £1.7.1. As late as 1890 she noted income of £0.8.1. Strangely, even Maria's *Shadow of Dante* still brought in a trickle of pounds every year. But Christina's own earned income now came very little from writing, instead resulting from modest dividends. William tried to get her to write something other than religious prose for the S.P.C.K., and even procured a contract for her to do a biography in John H. Ingram's *Eminent Women* series, in which Lucy was also doing a book. The first subject suggested, Adelaide Procter, she rejected on grounds that she had "for so long dropped out of literary society" that she was unable to deal with it. Next, she turned down a Mrs. Browning because she assumed that Browning would not cooperate, and because she had no desire in any case to probe into the marital relation. Then came Mrs. Radcliffe, whose Gothic romances she had enjoyed when young. A summer of desultory "Radcliffiz-ing" at the British Museum in 1883 turned up insufficient data, she determined, and Christina forewent the £50 due on completion. "Someone else, I daresay, will gladly attempt the memoir," she apologized to Ingram. "But I despair and withdraw." The experience reinforced the conclusion to which she had come while expurgating Gabriel's letters: one's life had best remain private. To a correspondent who, in 1883, asked for data about herself, Christina replied, "Pardon me as to the biographical details. If there are any, I am in favour of keeping them back at any rate till the *whole* (in my case quiet) life can be summed up with the final date."

For William, biography had become the central fact of his existence, with Somerset House mainly a place he went to perform his official duties in the interstices of his preoccupations with Gabriel's life and works. He even dreamed of his brother—that he was "in converse with Gabriel," noting in his diary on March 31, 1884 that they discussed Chaucer, William particularly recalling a reference he had made to Gabriel to the puzzling term "Shippes hoffestere," which he tried defining in his diary but gave up and wrote himself a futile reminder to look it up. If he had, he would have discovered that his dream-conversation was reasonably accurate: "shippes hoppesteres" appeared in the "Knight's Tale." It was almost as odd an occurrence as some of the results of his table-rapping sessions with Gabriel after Lizzy's death.

Perhaps it was no less odd that William should be writing to the President of the United States. Long a zealous missionary for Walt Whitman, whom he had never met but considered a great and good friend, William had concluded his Whitman edition for his English publisher with the words that Whitman, not Longfellow, was the national poet of the United States. When in 1878 his English publisher sought an American house to issue a transatlantic edition, no American publisher would consider the book so long as that sentence stood in print. Consulted in the matter, William thought that he retained his integrity by writing that "so far as I am concerned with the book, the sentence must remain as it stands: but that, if their own trade-interests in America required an alteration, they cd. act as they chose (the money-property in the book being the Publishers', not mine). . . ." The line was dropped. In 1885 William was instrumental in an English effort to secure an American pension for Whitman, and (as treasurer of an informal organization) in soliciting English funds for Whitman's support. To President Grover Cleveland on June 13, 1885, William explained that although in Europe Whitman was regarded as, "since the death of Victor Hugo, . . . the poet of the largest scope, strongest initiative, & widest future, alive in the world," many Americans still "denounced and derided" him. To "leave Whitman to die, old, paralyzed, & poor," * would be "an indelible stain upon the star-spangled banner," and a "national shame." Nothing happened. Whitman was not only persona non grata to the government bureaucracy, but despite his meager royalties in no great need. The London *Daily News* the next year had an editorial, "Poet in Penury," which quoted the American consul in Glasgow to the effect that Whitman, ailing at his home in New Jersey, was desperately poor, but the issue for the following day (December 17, 1886) included a cable from New York with the news that a reporter for the New York *Evening Post* had been sent to Camden to investigate, and discovered the poet in good health and comfortable circumstances. The efforts to raise money in England wound down.

If one believes William's diary, the first thought he had that the entries he had made over the decades might be publishable was early in 1885, although even then he conceded that what he had written—however worthy—was "dry & meagre." The realization resulted in no change in the nature of his entries, yet eventually his compilations of diary-jottings, letters and documents provided for him a veritable cottage industry. But first came the *Collected Works*, and after it, still in the absence of Watts's memoir, he began what he confessed was a work of "shreds and patches," *Dante Gabriel Rossetti as Designer and Writer*, an attempt to record and analyze the work without excessive intrusion upon the still-promised biography. In the midst of his busy life the hours he could spare for the new book were few. He was still reviewing books, visited by and visiting literary friends, handling estate matters, finding time to be with his young family, worrying over Lucy, who ailed and took to her bed more often, and discovering new distractions at

---

* A paraphrase of a line in Whitman's "A Carol Closing Sixty-Nine" and also in "Prayer of Columbus." The allusion very likely would have been lost on the President.

Somerset House, where fear of anarchist bombings—there had already been several attempts on government buildings—had caused the dark, narrow stairwell which ran by his office to be sealed.

Early in 1886 there was a new, and inevitable, concern. The winter was severe, and the eighty-five-year-old Mrs. Rossetti too frail to confront it. If she left her bedroom at Torrington Square, it was only to pace, with effort, the adjacent drawing room. In February she fell, and took to her bed. Early in April, her daughter wrote in the family diary she kept for her mother, "I, Christina Rossetti, happy and unhappy daughter of so dear a saint, write the last words. Not till nearly a half hour after noon on April 8 . . . did my dearest mother cease from suffering. . . ." William was present at the bedside, but Lucy was in Italy, to spare her the gusts of early spring. On April 12 Mrs. Rossetti was buried in the same plot as her husband—and Lizzy. Christina was left in the old house in the square with her aged aunts and two servants. In her mother's will she was left about £4,000. William was left only a token £100. He thought it was just, but Christina set aside half of her legacy for him. William would agree only to accept the promise of it in her own will, and it was left that way.

By autumn Christina was willing to forego mourning, and helped celebrate Olive's eleventh birthday by accompanying William and the children to the Zoo in Regent's Park. To the children she was an exotic figure, bundled and bonneted in black, who strained with great sincerity for a wit which might amuse young minds, yet was full of curious religious exhortations. One must never use the word *eternal,* and no book must ever be placed atop a Bible. Neither idea ever occurred to a young Rossetti. Usually the children found Christina, as their cousin Juliet,* who often tagged along, remembered, in "a black dress and a white lace cap, . . . in the back room of her house with her hands folded, thinking and waiting for the kettle to boil." The three Rossetti girls, and Juliet, liked to visit Christina, who would greet them with "Welcome, merry little maidens," and sit them down to tea and sweets, or let them watch her goldfish, or supply them with little presents. Once she made for Juliet a tiny table and chairs out of chestnuts and pins and red string, and putting them in a box for her to take home she exhorted, "When you look at them, remember Aunt Christina." Yet what the children most remembered were the two wasted and wrinkled old aunts "who lay in beds on the opposite sides of a room, with a strip of carpet in the middle. They were so old that they couldn't stand up, and they could hardly talk. They always seemed to me to

---

* Juliet Hueffer (later Soskice), daughter of Francis (Franz) Hueffer and Cathy Madox Brown, and sister of Ford Madox Hueffer (Ford).

be waving their long skinny hands. They wore big nightcaps with frills round the edges and flowered bed jackets." After tea, the children would be sent up to them to be looked at, as great-aunts Charlotte and Eliza were starved for affection; and they would stretch out their gaunt arms to the frightened children who stood warily on the strip of carpet.

For Christina it was almost a dereliction of duty to leave Charlotte and Eliza to themselves, and she seldom left Torrington Square for long. In the mid-eighties, when she once went to dine with her brother's family, William noted that it was the first time in four years. Yet at bad times, which came now more frequently, Lucy Rossetti was herself shut indoors for long periods, and her chronic bronchitis seemed a euphemism for what neither she nor her doctor were willing to name. Instead, he first prohibited her from going out—and being exposed to "draughts"—except between noon and two, and then only if conditions were favorable. Then her doctor sent her, with the children and their governess, to Ventnor, and finally suggested Mediterranean locations in France or Italy as having more salubrious air. In mid-November 1886 Lucy and the two elder children left for San Remo, while the two younger ones were housed with the Browns and the Hueffers. When William could take a holiday he followed his family to Italy.

William's commitment to Gabriel's reputation continued to be the fixed star in his firmament. With Watts back-pedaling from his promise about a life of Gabriel, William predicated his willingness to do a Keats monograph in Eric Robertson's "Great Writers" series on the inclusion of his brother, his ultimatum that "if Gabriel were omitted, greatly postponed, or treated contrary to my feelings, I am at liberty to resign Keats entirely." Joseph Knight was commissioned to do a *Rossetti*, and William agreed to make materials available to him if Knight would submit the manuscript for examination. He did, and William—especially concerned about the Lizzy Siddal section—found "the spirit in which the facts are treated" satisfactory.

Well into the year of the Golden Jubilee of Queen Victoria—1887—Lucy returned to England, seemingly improved. Not until June 15, when Mary, who had been living with the Browns in Manchester, was returned, was the whole family reunited in London. William had worried over the doctor's bills, and the away-from-home expenses, which were absorbing much of his income, although Lucy had the safety-valve of the Ravensbourne Wharf, near Greenwich, which—through her father—she owned, and rented. June 21 was Jubilee Day—a public holiday—and everything was forgotten in parades and displays of thousands of Japanese lanterns, fifteen hundred of them in Torrington Square, where Christina and her ailing aunts could see the illuminations from their windows. William took young Arthur along Regent Street, Piccadilly, Bond Street and Oxford

Street to see the blaze of lights and to mingle with the throngs, arriving home at the unprecedentedly late hour of ten-thirty. The next morning William was back at Somerset House, writing a review of a biography of Shelley for the *Athenaeum*.

A few months later he was himself the victim of a review of a biography, and in it was no trace of William's own characteristic critical good manners. He should have expected it, because in April 1887, his caution in supplying Joseph Knight with materials for a life of Gabriel, and in seeing to it that what was written was safe, had resulted in a review of the book by Oscar Wilde which oozed with faint praise. The best that could be said of Knight's *Dante Gabriel Rossetti*, Wilde had observed in the *Pall Mall Gazette*, "is that it is just the sort of biography Guildenstern might have written of Hamlet. Nor does its unsatisfactory character come merely from the ludicrous inadequacy of the materials at Mr. Knight's disposal. . . . Rossetti's was a great personality, and personalities such as his do not easily survive shilling primers."

That September, again in the *Pall Mall Gazette*, Wilde bluntly labeled William's life of Keats "a great failure." Rossetti, Wilde charged, isolated the man from the work, and then misunderstood the work. "Even where Mr. Rossetti seeks to praise, he spoils what he praises. To speak of *Hyperion* as 'a monument of Cyclopean architecture in verse' is bad enough, but to call it 'a Stonehenge of reverberance' is absolutely detestable. . . ." Before Wilde was through citing chapter and verse he had demolished William as a critic. "There is no necessity to follow Mr. Rossetti any further as he flounders about the quagmire that he had made for his own feet. A critic who can say that 'not many of Keats's poems are highly admirable' need not be too seriously treated. Mr. Rossetti is an industrious man and a painstaking writer, but he entirely lacks the temper necessary for the interpretation of such poetry as was written by John Keats." Not yet done, Wilde in 1889, unaware of William's long battle to have Whitman published legitimately, referred to "poor Mr. William Rossetti's attempt to Bowdlerize and expurgate [Whitman's] song." No wonder that Richard Curle, who knew William for nearly twenty years, and often was put up for the night on Shelley's sofa in the book-lined study, found that his elderly and courtly friend spoke "of only one person . . . with real bitterness. That one person was Oscar Wilde. . . ."

In 1888 William took on a new assignment at the Inland Revenue, above his usual duties, which had become monotonous and easily reassigned. Lord Iddesleigh asked him to undertake, for the Board of the Inland Revenue, the reviewing of lists of art works received in probate matters in order to provide an opinion of the prices estimated. It would become one of the happiest of his occupations, as it took him to stately homes to view the works themselves, and brought him anew into an art world not encompassed on four sides by Gabriel's pictures. Christina's reclusive world continued to shrink. Her invalid aunts Charlotte and Eliza circumscribed her own life, while William's work at Somerset House, his reviewing books and dining-out among literary people, his goings and comings at such literary gatherings as the Shelley Society, where he even chaired a session, and his being called upon by such French radical politicians as Sarrazin, seemed to her to be a life crowded with excitement. Yet William wrote, disconsolately, on March 19, 1888, that his diary was "dreary work," with little to record but Lucy's increasingly pain-wracked health, which sent him to bed earlier and earlier so that he could compensate for his broken sleep at night. Only on rare occasions were the old days relived, as when William returned to editing his brother's papers, or had Hunt, or Brown, or Swinburne (with the ever-present Watts) to dinner.

When Lucy had periods of better health she was an indefatigable hostess, eager to bring what seemed now to be old Victorians together with the new literary and artistic generation. Among the new were the lively, expatriate Americans Aline and Henry Harland, who wrote books under their own as well as exotic names. Harland in 1894 would be the editor of that notorious phenomenon, *The Yellow Book*. Remaining with her invalids, Christina never appeared among the literati in William's and Lucy's drawing rooms, even after, at eighty-seven, in 1890, Charlotte Polidori died. There was still another aunt, who would live on until 1893. Only one major event unconnected with mortality would yet occur at Torrington Square, and it would involve William and Lucy. Reluctantly, William had succumbed to his wife's pressure and had agreed to move to 3 St. Edmund's Terrace, in his description "a line of street raised well above the level of Regent's Park, and not far below the summit of the closely adjoining Primrose Hill . . . not a cloud-capt summit, but in London it counts as the nearest approach to a hill that we have to show." Lucy had been bent on finding purer and less foggy air for her ailing lungs, while settling near her now-aged father, who had just relocated in London only two houses away, at 1 St. Edmund's Terrace. Charlotte Polidori had owned the lease of their former house, and had bequeathed it to William, making it possible to live there rent-free. Nevertheless, when Richard Garnett vacated No. 3, moving to the British Museum premises on becoming Keeper of Printed Books, Lucy bought his leasehold, which despite its address looked out on the unsightly sheds and pipes of the West Middlesex Water Works and doubled her husband's walking distance to Somerset House.

The move meant repacking all his books and memorabilia—for the last time, William hoped. But in the late summer and early autumn of 1890 there was an interim between residences, which the family first spent in the boredom of Bruges, and then with Christina. "I have just lately been having my brother and his family (6 in number) staying here," she wrote her friend Ellen Proctor on October 30; "this made a great change and *stir up* in my quiet habits." Only Aunt Eliza, "confined to her bed weak in body and not less so in mind," shared the house, and when the Rossettis moved out Christina returned to the shadows.

William loved his new library, despite the view, and so did his children. The young Yeats called on him there to discuss Blake and George Moore called to discuss an Independent Theatre production of Shelley's *Cenci*; but the library had to be shared with the children, who were writing and hectographing a subversive, monthly Anarchist propaganda journal christened *The Torch*. The children included an additional girl, a year older than Mary. Juliet Hueffer had joined the family in 1889 when her own was split by the death of her father. (Cathy left Hammersmith, taking Ford * and Oliver with her to Madox Brown's house, and Juliet was taken in by the Rossettis, two houses away.) Juliet and Mary were in awe of the older girls, and of Arthur, who loved to make chemical experiments at home, and once burned off his eyebrows and hair when he heated a tin of gunpowder over a gas jet in the day nursery. The three precocious older children, Olive, Arthur and Helen, not only composed the paper but took the younger ones out with them on Sundays to that perennial safety-valve of free speech, Hyde Park, to wave red paper banners and hawk copies of *The Torch*. "I think it must have been interesting and uncommon," Juliet remembered, "because whenever anybody bought a copy they would first stand for some time staring at the cover, and as soon as they got to the title of the first article they would to an absolute certainty (we knew because we used to watch) turn round suddenly and stare after us."

Despite the chaos in his library, William would screw up his thick white eyebrows and pore over the material the children were preparing for *The Torch*, making suggestions by saying in a soft voice, "Don't you think so?" But Lucy, despite her political radicalism, deplored the fact, Juliet remembered, "that on the day on which the paper went to press we were all quite black with the part that comes off on your hands and face, and Olive and Arthur were hot and irritable. Besides, she said, it was not right for my uncle, who was employed by the Government, to have a paper of that kind printed in his house." Down the street, her brother Ford, although a contemporary of the older children, was not as deeply involved as Juliet with

---

* Afterwards Ford Madox Ford.

The Torch, although he became sufficiently friendly with the anarchist leader Prince Peter Kropotkin to take his awed young sister to Kropotkin's to tea. His aunt Lucy, Ford thought, "no doubt would have approved of any activities of her children, so long as they were active in a spirited and precocious way. But I imagine she would have preferred their energies to continue to be devoted to the productions of the Greek plays which caused me so much suffering.* In any case the world was presented with the extraordinary spectacle of the abode of Her Majesty's [Assistant] Secretary to the Inland Revenue, so beset with English detectives, French police spies, and [Czarist] Russian *agents provocateurs* that to go along the sidewalk of that respectable terrace was to feel that one ran the gauntlet of innumerable gimlets."

On April 21, 1892, William—under pressure from Lucy—banished his brood and their nefarious publication to the basement, and he missed the excitement of their activity† but was able again to write and talk to literary colleagues. But for their basement pressroom the children now acquired a real but ancient printing apparatus, setting the type and running the pages themselves, the creaking and groaning adding new distractions to their father's more legitimate activities. But at the least, there was the comfort of immunity for St. Edmund's Terrace from anarchist bomb outrages, which had been frightening London for half a dozen years.

Lucy was less and less well, gradually giving up the children's education to the governess. On good days she would still sweep into the room used for lessons and sometimes take them over herself, ejecting the governess from her chair. She knew the difficult questions to ask, was not sparing of a spanking, preached a variety of thrift that was closer to frugality, and declared, Juliet recalled, "that no one had the right to spend one idle moment on this globe. If she couldn't write or teach and lecture she would scrub, or sweep the streets, or clean drains rather than be idle." Enforced inactivity exasperated Lucy, but by 1891 she was usually too exhausted for anything else. When, in April, 1892, she got up from her bed to attend, with William, the funeral of Tennyson at Westminster Abbey, her appearances in public had become rare. Now forty-nine, she was weak and wasted from "congestion of the lungs," and her tension during the long,

---

* Arthur and Olive were encouraged by their mother to write Greek-style plays which the Hueffer and Rossetti children performed at home, in white muslin robes Lucy concocted, and behind backdrops she painted.

† Olive, seventeen and the most militant, had already lectured on "The Children of the French Revolution" at Manchester. In 1903 she and Helen would publish their account of their radical activity as a novel, *A Girl Among the Anarchists*, under the pseudonym "Isobel Meredith." In the book *The Torch* became *The Tocsin*.

wearing illness had developed into quiet hysteria. The previous November her behavior had developed into active and unexplained hostility toward William. Possibly she thought that he was, immersed in his own work, insufficiently concerned with her own condition (which she dreaded to define although she was bringing up blood). Perhaps, too, although William was past sixty—and aware of her frailty—he was still sexually importunate. Whatever the reasons, Lucy ejected her husband from their bedroom and moved in the teenage Olive, which guaranteed that he would no longer share the conjugal bed. He was profoundly hurt, but stoical, and counted the blessings of his growing children, who, despite their devotion to *The Torch*, and to radical politics, were sources of pride.

By the summer of 1893 it was obvious that the disease was inexorable. Dr. William Gill no longer shied away from calling it *tuberculosis,* advising Lucy that her days would only be lengthened in a milder climate, and she prepared to return to Italy. On September 29 William drew a check to Lucy to pay the next month's rent, and another to Christina to pay her the half-share due on Gabriel's royalties. Drained by medical bills, and down to £67 in his account, he planned to sell some of his few investments in order to finance Lucy's stay abroad, when Christina sent her a check for £100 as a going-away gift. It initiated Christina's last effort at reconciliation with Lucy, with whom she had been at odds, but for formal demonstrations of good will, since the difficult months preceding the marriage. Her later overtures to Lucy had been met by fears that she would proselytize the children, and her well-meant words of religious comfort to Lucy in her suffering were resented, for Lucy remained a steadfast unbeliever. "If ever it would give her the slightest pleasure to see me, pray let me know," Christina had urged William the previous April. "I should be afraid of startling her were I to present myself unexpectedly, as I am such an occasional phenomenon." But Lucy had not been interested, although by then she knew that Christina was herself in what was probably her last illness.

In the last days of September, while Lucy's departure for Italy was delayed by her low condition, the two dying women confronted each other. "I did not like her to leave England without my at least trying to see her once more," Christina wrote William on October 4, "and when I got to your house she consented to admit me." At best it had to have been an awkward scene. At seven in the morning on October 3, with Olive, Helen and Mary accompanying her—*The Torch* went into temporary suspension —Lucy had finally left St. Edmund's Terrace en route to Lake Maggiore. Arthur saw them off on the boat-train to Calais from Charing Cross Station, and went on to his physics and chemistry classes at the Polytechnic Institute.

In the crisp October weather, William—having said his farewells at home—walked, more melancholy than usual, to Somerset House.

Three days later Madox Brown suddenly died. He was seventy-two. To spare Lucy the sudden shock, William wrote her a series of letters intimating her father's serious illness before sending her one announcing Madox Brown's death. In any event, she could not return. Instead, she fled the winter chill at Lake Maggiore, first going to Genoa and then to the Hotel Victoria at San Remo, Olive remaining with her. After settling Madox Brown's affairs and securing leave from his post, William prepared to follow Lucy to Italy but, he wrote in his memoirs, "she preferred that I should not do so." But on March 19, 1894, he received a telegram that Lucy was sinking rapidly, and he and Arthur rushed to San Remo. She rallied, but there was no hope. William was at her bedside when, in the early morning of April 12, Lucy died. They had been married twenty years. She was buried at San Remo.

By a will drawn in the last year of her life Lucy left everything, from her share of the wharf in Greenwich to the St. Edmund's Terrace leasehold, equally to her four children—including money, William noted, ruefully, "of my own giving." To himself her sole bequest was her portrait by Gabriel. Lucy's late-blooming animus toward her husband had persisted beyond the grave.

When William returned to London a widower in April, he had little desire to return to the routine of Somerset House. Under Civil Service rules he was due to retire at the beginning of the month of his sixty-fifth birthday, September 25, 1894. He was only a few months from that date. To the Board of the Inland Revenue he applied for leave until the date of his official retirement, August 31. It was granted. He had given forty-nine and a half years of service to his department.

There was no lack of occupation for the retiree. "To get up in the morning not knowing 'what to be at,' " he wrote, "to dribble through the lagging hours, and then retire to bed without any sense of anything enacted, seems to be a very wretched fate, and one, in the case of a man who retires old from a long career of regular work, far from unlikely to lead to an early collapse of the vital energies, with the coffin closing the scanty perspective." Although he might have found it welcome to dispose of the days as he chose, the novelty was not yet to be. There was too much to do. Madox Brown's estate had to be settled, then Lucy's; and Christina, he knew, was "past cure." And then there were his children.

Despite William's being all but excluded from his wife's will, his children were still minors, and he was trustee. He descended into the basement at St. Edmund's Terrace, Ford Madox Ford wrote, "and ordered the press and all its belonging to be removed from his house . . . *The Torch* . . . removed itself to Goodge Street, Tottenham Court Road, a locality as grim as its name. There it became a sort of club where the hangers-on of the extreme Left idled away an immense amount of time while their infant hosts and hostesses were extremely active over their [printing] forms." Why William finally carried out what Lucy in her lifetime had failed to force him to do is difficult to explain other than that he was reacting to his exclusion from her will in favor of his children. Yet the children understood the fitness of *The Torch*'s being removed from the home—if not the house—of a servant of the Crown. Because of the timing of the expulsion of *The Torch*, Ford Madox Ford always felt that it had been Lucy who had protected it, and William who in his new freedom had accomplished a long-standing desire. Yet it was probably not that way at all.

By the time of William's bereavement Christina had withdrawn almost totally into her drawing room overlooking the darkly shaded square. She corresponded with old friends who still survived, such as Henrietta Rintoul, whose name was never mentioned to William; and at fifty-eight she now needed reading spectacles to pierce through the haze of words. In 1888 a signal event had been to visit Maria's grave, and then her mother's; and at Christmas she again emerged to view, at St. Edmund's Terrace, Olive's new pseudo-Greek play, *Theseus*. In 1889 she went over William's proofs of *Dante Gabriel Rossetti as Designer and Writer*, making meticulous annotations. In 1890, when she reached sixty, she lived like a recluse of eighty, although permitting—between ten and one—such old acquaintances as George Hake, and such new ones as Katherine Tynan to visit. By mail she still promoted Gabriel's posthumous reputation, arranging in 1891 to sell to the National Gallery, for a modest sum, the self-portrait of the young, long-haired Gabriel she had acquired from Eliza Polidori. The money meant little to her, as she had gradually accumulated the modest bank accounts and investments of her sister and mother, and her Polidori aunts and uncles, as well as a half-portion of Gabriel's estate. By 1891 her income was over £600 a year and two years later was over £700 a year, but she never had use of that much money because she had long been an easy mark for unscrupulous begging letters.

When he was asked, William advised her on business matters, and when he could, he visited, always arranging to have dinner with Christina on the evenings when the Shelley Society met at University College, and she looked forward to the second Wednesday of each month. She could not conceal from him the obvious fact that her health was more and more precarious. If she failed to mention her condition, she remarked in a letter to William, he could be sure that it was worse. She seldom dwelt upon it, but in May, 1892, after persistent pain, she underwent surgery for cancer in the left shoulder and chest, cautious Victorian terminology, perhaps, for a radical mastectomy, then a relatively new procedure. Afterwards only self-drugging with sedatives kept her going, and she knew she was involved in what might be a long ordeal of dying.

Despite—perhaps, even, because of her intimations of mortality Christina worked with greater intensity than before on her last productions for print, two books for the S.P.C.K. *The Face of the Deep* (1892), ostensibly a study of the Book of Revelation, was, as well, a collection of essays, observations and poems, while *Verses* (1893) was an assemblage of poetry from earlier devotional works. Once, when William visited, she proposed dedicating the book to him, and he hesitated, explaining his doubts as to whether devotional Christian poems should be dedicated to anyone who did not share those beliefs. Christina thought about it, and then wrote her brother, "Since we talked about it I have come to the conclusion that very likely you were right. . . . But, if so, I shall leave it undedicated; and you and I will know that in my heart thus it stands:—

> To my dearest Brother
> William Michael Rossetti
> I commend these verses."

To William, who worried about her isolation, she explained, "Beautiful, delightful, noble, memorable as is the world you and yours frequent,—I yet am well content in my shady crevice: which crevice enjoys the unique advantage of being to my certain knowledge the place assigned me." She lived, she told Watts serenely, "in a circle of the absent," and to Miss Tynan she insisted, unconvincingly, that though she had been "a very melancholy girl," she was now "a very cheerful old woman." With her black garb, "spiritual face" and "heavily-lidded eyes," she reminded Katherine Tynan of an Italian nun, but Olive Rossetti, who perceived her less romantically, saw "a short, stout, elderly woman with prominent eyes and heavy leaden complexion . . . dowdily dressed in black and with an unbecoming bonnet set on her greying hair, making her way to and from the Church in Woburn Square where she was the regular occupant of a pew." Her other side was rarely seen, Olive remembering Christina's "affectionate stroke for old Muff," the cat, and the "odd snatch of nursery rhyme or playful memory [which] would bring a smile to her lips summoning up from the dead past a pale shadow of the sprightly Christina of far off days."

Verses was a great popular success. "Mrs. Garnett called one day," she wrote William late in December, 1893, "and told me that by Christmas there was no meeting the demand for *Verses*: at one considerable shop she was at she heard that twenty or thirty applications had to be negatived for the moment." In April 1894 a third printing was called for. By then she was writing only for herself, and her letters were her major contact with the world outside, which had become less and less attractive. A once-major part of that world had intruded when Alice Boyd asked permission to include in the *Autobiographical Notes* of the now-dead W. B. Scott a poem Christina had addressed to him, and she replied warmly. Then the memoir was published, releasing skeletons from Gabriel's closet which William found sensational and scurrilous. At least the former was true, Scott having become exasperated in his last years about the anemic versions of Rossetti's life. William told Christina about the book, which he had castigated in a letter to the editor of the *Academy* as "unkind, unhandsome, inaccurate, and practically incorrect and misleading." Christina refused to read it.

The previous June her aunt, Eliza Polidori, had died after a long, agonizing illness, and Christina saw herself as next (although Lucy preceded her). Her cancer had recurred, but heart trouble—a legacy of her exophthalmia—made further surgery impossible. She was just as glad "to escape the heavy expense of an operation and its context," and endured the "mischief." At just about the time that Lucy was living out her last days in Italy, Cayley's shade reappeared in Christina's midst via a visit from Mary and Henry Cayley, her old friend's niece and nephew. When Henry fetched his sister, Christina found the young architecture student straight and tall. "Dream children," both were a reminder of the gentle, abstracted scholar with whom she had shared so many days of her life, and a suggestion of what might have been.

With her key to the fenced-off Torrington Square gardens, on sunny days Christina was able to sit outdoors. In all but the worst weather she attended church, and in any event held household services twice a day with the maid, cook, and servant-nurse, Harriet Read. By June she could no longer climb stairs, and had been forced to move her bed into the drawing room, with its tall windows facing the square. Around her she had placed the objects for which she had the most affection—a chalk drawing Gabriel had made of her, a portrait of her mother's favorite brother, Byron's physician friend John Polidori, a reproduction of Frederick Shields' homiletic *The Good Shepherd*, a small bookcase of religious works and her favorite novels. And there were always flowers, sent by friends, or brought in person.

Visitors found her serene but admittedly in great discomfort. By August she needed heavy doses of opiates for the pain. Her mind became clouded, and she became subject to hysteria, William in his honesty specifically directing Mackenzie Bell, one of Christina's last regular visitors and her first biographer, to note the hysteria which manifested itself in her final months, "particularly during semi-consciousness, [the symptoms] chiefly manifesting themselves in cries." A literary lady in the next house, disturbed by the sounds from Christina's drawing room, even wrote to William to urge him to have his sister moved to the back room, as the "distressing screams . . . , *especially* at the hours I have hitherto devoted to writing, between 8 and 11 P.M.," left her "perfectly unable to work." She would move to another room if she could, the writer offered, "but there is no gas in the back," and "the mental strain is killing me. . . . I am trying to support myself by literature, so you may understand and forgive the reason of my troubling you."

The strain was telling on William also. Trying to be father and mother at once, he had more of his children's affairs to look after than ever before, from fulfilling his promise to take young Mary to the Tower of London (and the just-completed Tower Bridge) if she scored high on her botany examination, to—despite Olive's failing shorthand—taking all the children to the Zoological Gardens, his favorite oasis for forgetting his troubles. To be with his ill wife most evenings he had given up dining out a year earlier, and now to be with his children he steadfastly continued to decline invitations, however attractive the guest list.

During the hours the children were away at school he worked at editing Gabriel's letters, which he now intended to accompany the biography of Gabriel he finally managed to get Watts to confess he would never write himself, although Watts insisted that he had "a large assemblage of notes" which apparently did not exist. On September 4 William began the memoir. Still, he managed to be at Torrington Square to see the sinking Christina almost daily—until Arthur injured himself in a chemical fire at the Polytechnic. His left eye was scorched, and at University Hospital he was treated and his head bandaged. Summoned from home, William took his son back to St. Edmund's Terrace. That night he used his own bed for Arthur, sharing it so that he could be watchful through the night. Then the routine of visits to Christina continued, Arthur recovering without permanent damage.

By then William had employed a professional nurse at Torrington Square, so that Christina would not be left alone. On good days he found her cheerful and able to discuss his writing projects, even offering annotations for Gabriel's letters and reciting from memory a poem she had written when she was twelve. But when left alone—and it was not always possible to have someone with her—her self-discipline gave way. William heard again from Christina's neighbor. "It is because I feel so much for Miss Rossetti, that her screams overwhelm me so much . . . ; to sit alone and listen to cries one cannot soothe is distracting. That was the reason why I had to give notice to leave. . . . I trust you will pardon my letter, and receive my sympathy." Was Christina overwhelmed, in the fashion of the fanatically pious, with remorse over minuscule sins, or about her unworthiness for the hereafter? After several days when her talks with William were earnestly about matters of religion, and musings about heaven, she burst out, as he was leaving, "I should like to see you there." Through the shortening autumn days, as she weakened, William continued to note "hysterical touches," including fancies of animals, "like pussy-cats," nearby, "looking for sleep."

When Christina was lucid, William wrote, Charles Cayley "continued to be a living personality" in her heart. "More than once, when she lay on her bed awaiting the manifest end in suffering and in patience, she spoke to me of him, and of her love for him, in terms of almost passionate intensity." She had saved with great care all his writings, and any small belongings of his that had come into her hands. Near the end William heard her say of Cayley, "I was so fond of him." On Friday afternoon, December 28, 1894, William visited, and stood over her bed silently. She did not recognize him. But in weeks past she had come out of similar relapses, and could again. Before he left, he kissed her forehead, and at the door turned back for a last look. Her eyes were closed, but her lips were moving silently—perhaps, so often before, in prayer. Early the next morning the housemaid came in to relieve Harriet Read, but this time Mrs. Read refused to go. At six she noticed Christina's lips again moving, but an hour later there was no sign of life. A note was rushed to William: "Dear Miss Rossetti has passed peacefully away after Seven. Please Come." At eleven he arrived, with Olive. The small, narrow bed on which Christina lay had been moved directly under the picture of *The Good Shepherd.*

The funeral was at Christ Church, Woburn Square, on January 2. Snow had fallen during the night, but had not deterred a large number of uninvited mourners who joined William and his children, and a few friends. The hymns sung were settings of Christina's poems.

One Rossetti

1895-1919

n the first days of 1895 William poked around in the hushed house in Torrington Square, pondering how to make the accumulations of three generations of Polidoris and two generations of Rossettis intelligible to the inheritance tax appraiser. Then he had to decide what he wanted to retain and what would go to the auctioneer, although some articles were disposed of by sale or gift to Christina's friends, and William unwisely let some of her poetical manuscripts go for small sums as well. For a while, too, his memoir of Gabriel occupied his days, until on April 28 he noted its completion "with a sense of thankfulness and relief."

The companion volume of family letters had first been planned to have only a few letters from Gabriel to other persons than himself, but Christina's death brought William all of the surviving letters from Gabriel to their mother, to Christina, and to the Polidori aunts. With so much material, he could choose the most attractive and the most significant letters, discreetly excising references—and even allusions—to Fanny Cornforth or Jane Morris; indiscreet or unreasonable remarks about Gabriel's long-suffering and impatient patrons, friends and relatives; and even most of the paragraphs about the borrowing of money. What would be printed would be scrupulously dated and annotated, but the result was a duller and more high minded Dante Gabriel Rossetti than the facts might have shown. "A brother neither is nor can be the best biographer," he admitted in his preface, and added frankly, "Some readers of the Memoir may be inclined to ask me—'Have you told everything, of a substantial kind, that you know about your deceased brother?'—My answer shall be given . . . without disguise: 'No; I have told what I choose to tell; if you want more, be pleased to consult some other informant.' " His reticence would be accepted as exactly that, rather than as whitewash. When the volumes appeared late in 1895 William was rewarded by the assumption of his biographical integrity, for which he was willing to take the criticism that his prose was stuffy and inelegant.

When actress Lena Ashwell read the *Memoirs* late in 1895 she inferred from them that William no longer knew what had happened to Henry Treffry Dunn, Gabriel's assistant, and wrote William, "It struck me that you might possibly care to know where to find him. It is very sad that a man with such talent should have sunk so low, but some three years ago I came across him in a second-hand shop in King's Road, Chelsea. He was painting tables and corner cupboards . . . ." Dunn had been in the workhouse, and had been rescued for painting chores far removed from his former responsibilities at Cheyne Walk. If William would take an interest in Dunn, Miss Ashwell concluded, "perhaps he might still do good work." But William never located him, although there was every reason, as guardian of the Rossetti reputation, for William to feel some guilt at Dunn's plight. Years before Dunn had brought his recollections of life at Cheyne Walk to William to clear with him references to, and quotations from, Gabriel and his family. William had gone through the manuscript removing references which reflected badly on Gabriel's lifestyle, or that even mentioned Fanny or Janey, and recommended that Dunn, instead, fill the gaps by telling more of his own intimacy with Gabriel. The drastic surgery was too much for Dunn. His most commercial material amputated, he could never get the manuscript into saleable condition.

When William heard next of Dunn, he had been rescued by Watts (who had become Watts-Dunton), at whose home in Putney the white-haired derelict had appeared. Watts-Dunton fitted up a room at The Pines as a studio for him, fed him, and gave him funds for a bedroom a short walk away. There was, of course, the inevitable condition (which had also brought serenity to Swinburne's life): no more whiskey, and only a single glass of ale to be taken at the Green Man, nearby. But privation had undermined Dunn's health. One day at his easel in The Pines he collapsed, and was rushed to St. George's Hospital, where he died, a few days later, in February, 1899. Watts-Dunton paid for the funeral. Among Dunn's possessions was his *Recollections of Dante Gabriel and His Circle.* When it was published, expurgated, in 1904, it was with a prefatory note by W. M. Rossetti.

For relaxation William spent hours each week at the Zoological

Gardens, a short walk from St. Edmund's Terrace; and for years his journal was peppered with notes of his progress from the pelicans to the gibbons to the zebras, and notes of new births and new construction. (The retired civil servant needed his tours of inspection, and assigned them to himself.) Early in June the actual removal of effects from Torrington Square to Sotheby's began, resulting in chaos at St. Edmund's Terrace, where William had piled what he intended to keep. Eventually he cataloged his acquisitions, including the books, and began to work on the major portion of his inheritance from Christina—her manuscripts.

Within a fortnight of Christina's death, William had received an offer from the Rev. Edmund McClure of the S.P.C.K. to publish Christina's unprinted devotional verses. Few people could have been more unsympathetic to the goals of the S.P.C.K. than William, who parried the question by declaring that his sister left no "collection" of unprinted religious verse. But she had indeed left more unpublished poetry than even he then anticipated, and in the autumn he put together a substantial volume, *New Poems*, which justified itself by his pointing out that even the verses which were not up to her best work showed "the growth of her mind." Notes to the poems, and his adding dates of composition, added to the book's interest, especially his cautious account—explaining the passionate lines—of "an unhappy love-passage in my sister's life" and of her having been twice offered marriage by suitors to whom she was "well disposed," but whom she rejected out of "religious considerations." But he was not above substituting words in the texts which altered the nuances of poems where the writer's passion appeared too physical. He wanted his version of the saintly Christina to stand; but he was too scrupulous—or too much aware of the future value of her manuscripts—to destroy the evidence. Yet his biases bent in the opposite direction as well. He realized that as her brother, and as a person totally out of sympathy with her religion, he was the wrong person to write her life. Besides, he persisted in thinking, by careful control of the information furnished to another biographer (he had learned nothing from his experience of spoon-feeding Knight material for the life of Gabriel), he could keep back details of Christina's life he preferred not to have in print.

The obvious choice was the pious Mackenzie Bell, who had visited Christina almost daily as she lay dying, and almost before her coffin had been lowered in the grave had proposed himself to William as biographer. Once the *New Poems* were out, William agreed to him, while guardedly providing only a minimum of biographical data, some of it in letters by Christina. To Bell these were holy relics, and he afterwards offered to buy eighteen of them. Foolishly, William not only sold them for the token price of £15, but included the copyright as well. Later he paid a heavy price for his assumption that the letters would always be available to him. When he wanted to use them himself in a volume of Christina's correspondence, Bell refused.

As High Church as Christina, Bell had been her fervent admirer, and would hardly have violated her sanctity in his pages; but he had consulted Hunt and Shields, who told him of the unhappy and unconsummated love affairs. Even the most cautious references to them outraged William, who nevertheless had already mentioned them in the *New Poems*. Bell was called in and instructed—William noted in his diary for September 14, 1896—to "modify his book . . . in various respects." When the book finally appeared, more than a year later, William found it of little value beyond being "admiring and kindly," and including "most of the few facts which were available for being stated." Bell was a pedestrian writer, but even a more stylish biographer could have done little with the Victorian saint image to which William had limited him. "He has hung over Mr. Bell," the *Times*'s "Literature" supplement condemned, "like a kite over a mouse. . . . A note about a 'knobbed bodkin' is as precious, neither more nor less, than the most characteristic revelation of the soul of a mystic. If Mr. Bell had been a stronger man, he would have accepted all the jejune material supplied him by Mr. William Rossetti, and would have silently rejected whatever did not suit his purpose. But he visibly shudders under the eye of that ancient mariner, and down goes the whole material, knobbed bodkin and elaborate glass chandelier and all."

Grand schemes for producing, in five volumes, a compilation of letters and documents that would combine the history of the Rossettis in England with the history of Pre-Raphaelitism filled William's days in the later nineties. First he methodically bundled all his raw material into segments representing each projected book, then put everything into chronological order. Even five months spent in Switzerland were no handicap as he took the appropriate bundle with him, finishing the first volume of 1,368 manuscript pages (which would become *Pre-Raphaelite Diaries and Letters*) late in 1896. The children were now little burden. Olive and Helen, both trying to become writers, often traveled with him, and Arthur was working in Manchester, and would soon be manager of the Lancashire Stoker Works. Mary was the only problem. She was sickly, and often away for rest cures. William worried about her.

Early in 1897 Olive, packing for a prolonged stay in Florence, rummaged about her room for her belongings and turned up what was in effect the shade of Janey Morris which her father had been so careful to ignore in his books. Long before, Gabriel had browbeat young Nolly Brown into parting with a William Morris canvas of Jane Burden as a youthful and regal Queen Guinevere, the only portrait in oils Morris had ever done. For Gabriel it was a constant reminder of the young woman whom, but for his duty to Lizzy Siddal, he might have married. The portrait went unmentioned in his will, and William had meant to "return" it to the Morrises when he discovered it at Cheyne Walk. Then it disappeared and was forgotten. Apparently Olive, in 1882, had quietly walked off with it, and left it for Mary, fifteen years later, to announce the rediscovery. Morris had recently died, but despite the price which the rarity might have brought, William turned the picture over to Sydney Cockerell, the estate's executor, for delivery to Janey.

For a man in retirement William remained as busy as before, although he had more opportunity for travel than ever before, even going to Australia. Yet, although he was in England at the time of the Diamond Jubilee in June 1897, he "paid no attention to it" on the great day itself, June 22, "crossing the doorstep only to post a letter." The stubborn old regicide of the still unpublished "Democratic Sonnets" was not interested, except to note that a celebratory bonfire on Primrose Hill "produced no noticeable effect."

What treasures and memorabilia had been accumulated by William only became clear to him as through 1898 and 1899 he cataloged the museum which the muffled rooms at St. Edmund's Terrace had become. The hoard was awesome in quantity. There were "834 drawings &c by Gabriel or connected with him; 1015 by the Family (Lucy, Lizzie, &c) or connected; 4358 miscellaneous; 159 Japanese . . . ." He was amazed at the total.

Examining pictures remained William's only gainful employment other than writing, as he continued his post-retirement tax appraisal work, traveling to Brighton or Wigan or Newcastle to examine collections. In 1899 he added the Duke of Hamilton's pictures, in Edinburgh, to his itinerary, but was beginning to feel that since he knew few of the new generation of painters, he was becoming obsolete in yet another way. The Duke of Hamilton, at least, did not collect anything of the sort.

Early in 1898 Olive had renewed the Rossetti family's ties with Italy by marrying journalist Antonio Agresti, and settling down in a house overlooking the hills of Fiesole. It gave William further reason to travel in Italy, and relieved his anxieties about trying to publish his projected mammoth series of family documents, only one segment of which had found a publisher. Interest in the Pre-Raphaelites, and in the Rossettis in particular, had already been thoroughly mined by William and by the friends of Gabriel's last years. William Sharp had gone on to write Scotch tales for *The Yellow Book* under the transvestite pseudonym of Fiona McLeod. Joseph Knight, the biographer of Gabriel whose book William had emasculated as it was being written, was editor of *Notes and Queries*. Hall Caine had discovered a remunerative career as a novelist, writing such Isle of Man thrillers as *The Deemster* and *The Manxman*. Nearly seventy, William's other careers were behind him, but only one of his compilations, for the years 1854–62, found a publisher—and that because of the interest in Ruskin. It was released in 1899 by George Allen as *Ruskin, Rossetti, Preraphaelitism*. The remainder evoked massive disinterest, and William enlisted William M. Colles of the Authors' Syndicate, one of the earliest literary agencies, to try to locate a publisher for the formidable overflow. For years afterward their generally unfruitful correspondence kept both of them busy.

The English reading audience was glutted with cautious compilations of Rossetti papers. Mackenzie Bell's earnest biography of Christina, for example, brought its author only £34 in its first year of publication. William was disappointed, but continued on his family projects, editing and translating, between attacks of rheumatism and gout, his father's versified autobiography, editing Madox Brown's diary, his own P.R.B. diary, John Polidori's diary about the Byron-Shelley circle, and Rossetti papers bringing the story beyond Lizzy's death. His typist, Ethel Dickens, granddaughter of the novelist and one of the innovators of the secretarial service concept which the typewriter made practical, was earning more from William's projects than was William himself.

Living in his family's past was not always of William's own doing. Correspondents were constantly asking him to sell or give away memorabilia of Gabriel or of Christina, evidence to him that there was an audience for Rossetti books. Readers wanted notes, autographs, scraps of manuscripts and letters, even locks of hair; and some shrewdly asked also for a memento associated with William. Where the object was available and of no great commercial value, he generally offered it without charge, making up his postage deficit by charging overly modest prices for books or letters, in the process scattering Rossettiana around the world. In some cases the exchanges with collectors took up vast quantities of his time, one not-untypical series, to Frank W. Burgess in Lewes, ending, after at least sixty letters from William, only with Burgess's death. And midway through the two-year correspondence William even suggested that since the writers were on such familiar epistolary terms they drop the *Mr.* from their letters and refer to each other only as "Dear Burgess" and "Dear Rossetti"!

Not all his reminders of the glorious past were so pleasant as to enable him to pass the emptying hours in the study at St. Edmund's Terrace in blissful nostalgia. In 1899 James and Henry (Harry) Siddall, William learned, had gone into the poorhouse. The brothers had remained close, James looking after "his rather half-witted brother" who had "never been able to take up any definite occupation," and carrying on a cutlery business—the trade long in their family—in the Old Kent Road, until both were too enfeebled and indigent to remain out of the Kennington Workhouse. When William discovered their plight, he extricated them and gave them a regular allowance, but they found the workhouse easier than maintaining themselves, and returned. Once out again, they turned to William, once offering him a faded watercolor of Lizzy by Gabriel. He bought it for eighteen pounds, sold it to Fairfax Murray for more, and gave Siddall the extra money.

Some pictures by Gabriel were worth much more. Through a dealer, Croal Thomson (of the Goupil Gallery), a South African diamond millionaire on New Year's Day, 1900, offered £1,000 for a crayon portrait of Christina, chin on hands, a pencil drawing of Lizzy in an armchair, and another of Janey Morris dozing. Two days later he had raised his offer to £1,100, but William would not give up the portrait of Christina. It was a choice that Swinburne, William's most distinguished surviving friend, would have applauded, as his letters to William were regularly filled with adoration for Lizzy and veneration for Christina. "I cannot say how much I wish you would come and see me some day," the quiescent old revolutionary and reformed alcoholic wrote him in 1902. "It is so very long since we met. I should like to show you my almost daily walk along the side of a lovely little lake . . . with a woody though not 'lawny' islet in it, and through an evergreen avenue of some length and exceptional variety of beauty." The fervid young poet who would slide naked down the banisters of Tudor House seemed invisible in the elderly permanent guest at The Pines, Putney Hill.

On February 17, 1902, William put down the manuscript of his latest project, his own *Some Reminiscences*, having written 174 pages and brought his narrative up to 1860, and traveled across Putney Bridge to visit Swinburne. Gouty and stiff in the piercing cold, William marveled at his friend's splendid health (he wore no coat outdoors, on the ice), and listened to Swinburne read the first act of a verse play about the Borgias, in which, moved by his subject, the old poet was as anti-clerical as ever. The renewal of the friendship on the personal level pleased William, and there were further visits, although William's tolerance was tried at least once more.

After he sent Swinburne a copy of Christina's *Poetical Works* (a new edition, with William's memoir) early in 1904, Swinburne answered tactlessly, "The book, in the monumental phrase of Blessed Sarah Gamp, is indeed 'rich in beauty': but, good Satan! what a fearful warning against the criminal lunacy of theolatry! It is horrible to think of such a woman—and so many otherwise noble and beautiful natures—spiritually infected and

envenomed by the infernal and putrefying virus of the Galilean serpent—
'and thinkin' in their innocence that it's all werry capital'—as Saint Anthony
Weller has it.* Had I been your sister's brother . . . ." And he went on,
even more violently, about the bestial degradation of God-worship. But
William knew that Swinburne, despite the tirade, thought that Christina as a
poet was second only to Sappho—and possibly Mrs. Browning.

Despite his age, and some persistent infirmities, he was keeping up with
the literary world around him better than with the art world, which required
going out into the studios and galleries to view the new. A matter of pride
entered into his decision to rest his gouty foot on a pillow at home, and to
resign his post as Professional Assistant to the Inland Revenue for Estate
Duty on Pictures and Drawings. There was, he thought, a seeming lack of
self-respect in a bald, hoary bearded and "so old a man" who rushed about
to strangers' homes to earn a fee assessing their inheritance taxes.

At his own home strangers were always welcome, especially if they
painted or wrote; but they needed no talent whatever if they came from
Italy. One contemporary recalled realizing that he had settled somewhere in
William's neighborhood when he was stopped on Primrose Hill by a
dark-eyed, olive-skinned foreigner of whose inquiries he could only make
out the words "Signor Rossetti." Soon he became used to such incidents.
"Whenever there was an Italian in London who needed help, whether he
was [an] oboe-player in an orchestra, or organ grinder with a monkey
buttoned up under his coat, or a hokey-pokey man in search of the capital to
set up his nomad shop on wheels—wherever there was an Italian in distress,
he seemed inevitably to find his way to the house of 'Signor Rossetti,' who
was a sort of consul general for all Italians in London. . . ." Sometimes
William was victimized, and he knew it, but the next needy *paisano* would
again be taken up to William's bedroom "and rigged up with a new set of
underclothing and a new suit with half a crown in the pocket of it."

Many of the strangers were neither scruffy nor unknown outside St.
Edmund's Terrace. William Rothenstein, the artist who had married Alice
Knewstub, daughter of Gabriel's first painting assistant, visited, and like
writer Richard Curle, became a good friend. Ford Madox Hueffer came,
bringing Joseph Conrad. To Rothenstein, William was "the only one of the
[surviving] Pre-Raphaelites who was sympathetic towards the work of
younger writers and painters. He even thought that we youngsters were
better draughtsmen and more skillful painters than was his brother."
Rothenstein thought it was absurd—for Gabriel's early drawings were
"among the great drawings of the world"—but he appreciated the

---

* Swinburne was quoting first from Dickens's *Martin Chuzzlewit* and then from the
Posthumous Papers of the Pickwick Club.

encouragement, which William would supplement by saying, often, after a remark by his young visitor, "I am so glad to hear this from you. That was Gabriel's opinion too."

"If William Rossetti had a sweet and modest nature," Rothenstein wrote long afterwards, "he was by no means the 'fool for a brother' that Morris proclaimed him to be; on the contrary, he was an admirable critic of literature and art; he had kept his faith in the power of art bright and clean; and his outlook on life was broad and humane. He didn't like the clatter the younger generation made in the press, and in the social world, so he lived in retirement. But to any who went to see him, he gave himself generously."

Japanese poet Isaumu Noguchi sent some of his verses ahead, and then spent an afternoon with William, as did lesser figures, who also mailed their poems in advance, one of them a Birmingham accountant who proposed founding a P.R.B. "cult." Only William's leaving London for long periods stopped the flow of visitors; and the house was often quiet for months at a time, as he visited Arthur and Dora Rossetti—and Geoffrey William, his first grandson—in Bolton, or Olive in Italy.

Late in November, 1903, William received from Miss Dickens the completed typescript of his *Reminiscences*, and took it with him to proofread en route with Helen and Mary to Naples, where Helen—in a civil ceremony—was to marry Gastone Angeli. It would be a short-lived and tragic marriage. On July 18, 1904 Gastone Angeli died in a hospital in Rome. Two months later his posthumous child was born.* Helen returned with her daughter to live at St. Edmund's Terrace.

With his memoirs completed in 416 ms. pages, none of them, William safely ventured, "likely to violate confidence or create scandal," he turned over the typescript to Colles to find a publisher, and returned to his Rossetti papers, intending to bring the documentation to 1882, the year of his brother's death. He would never find a publisher willing to carry the narrative that far, yet he had a mass of material going well beyond that, some of it, he thought, "not uninteresting."

Still, he continued arranging the material, even returning to the long-dormant and incomplete *Democratic Sonnets*, which Ford Madox Hueffer, now a publisher's reader, offered to print. William cut some sonnets as being dated, and permitted the remainder to make up a small book. When they came out in 1907 he was embroiled in some minor controversies with London newspapers not over their radical content but over the allegation, which he denied, that they were not published when written because he had considered them too "outspoken." Yet even then he did not publish all he had written, some undoubtedly because they were

---

* Imogen Angeli (Mrs. Dennis).

mediocre. But others may well have been too outspoken, even for 1907.

In large part what William was producing was make-work: he needed an occupation to keep himself going, and inevitably it had to be a literary one, although inevitably, too, he knew, he would exhaust the vein of familial record. On September 25, 1905, he had written in his diary, without any sense of unhappiness, "Today I am 76. Must be not very far from my finale." As he drew closer to eighty, and the untapped Rossetti archives grew thinner, he had even more reason to regret his Polidori longevity. Publishers were politely deaf to ideas he elaborated for new Rossetti books, and it was a small triumph each time a publication of his appeared which, although it earned no money, required no author's outlay.

As the first decade of the new century drew to a close, two friends of William's earliest days still remained. Swinburne survived quietly in Putney, visited by admirers carefully screened in advance by Watts-Dunton. His seventieth birthday in 1907 had brought him empty honors he rejected, such as an honorary doctorate from Oxford forty-eight years after his expulsion from Balliol without a degree. William even read a report in *The Times* that the 1908 Nobel Prize for Literature might go to his old friend, and on inquiring to Algernon, was told, snappily, "Let me . . . assure you that I have not been offered the honour of taking a back seat behind Mr. Rudyard Kipling." The award for 1907 had just gone to the author of "Gunga Din," none of whose melodies sounded harmonious to Swinburne. At the Rose and Crown, where he went for his pint, whatever the weather, nothing had changed. No one there seemed to have read the rumor from the *Svenska Dagblad* in *The Times*.

The next year William noted Swinburne's death as "a great grief." The poet, during the treacherously chill early spring of 1909, had gone for his daily pint as coatless as usual, and came down with influenza. It became pneumonia. At ten o'clock on Saturday morning, April 10, Swinburne died. The day before the end, Watts-Dunton, bedridden himself with influenza, had tottered to a desk and written a note to William. That Saturday afternoon William, accompanied by Helen and little Imogen, hurried to Putney to find Swinburne already dead. William put his arm around Watts-Dunton's shoulders to comfort him, and the two literary survivors looked lingeringly at Gabriel's drawing meant to memorialize Nolly Brown, "The Question," which lay on Watts's bed. Watts had acquired it, long before, from the Rossetti estate. It was a Blakean vision of a young man gazing into the impenetrable face of the Sphinx, a winged creature half-woman, half-beast. In the foreground a stricken youth has fallen to his knees, while an old, bearded man, leaning on his staff, approaches from the right and stares at the scene. Watts had brought the drawing out of storage not because the death of William's promising young brother-in-law had any relationship to the passing of an aged poet who had thrown all his thunderbolts, but because the picture pondered death.

Clara Watts-Dunton, who at twenty-one—four years before—had married the walrus-mustached, seventy-three-year-old Watts, took William into Swinburne's room to look upon "dear glorious S's dead body" for the last time, and then led him back to her husband's bed, where Watts asked William to consider going to the funeral at Bonchurch, Swinburne's birthplace on the Isle of Wight. Watts had promised his militantly freethinking companion of nearly thirty years that the burial service of the Church of England should never be read over his grave, but Swinburne's sister (and co-executor) Isabel, like Watts bedridden with influenza, insisted upon an Anglican funeral. Watts at first had yielded but William sent him a note to stiffen his resolve, and Watts telegraphed the vicar at Bonchurch that the burial service must not be used. Then he telegraphed William to ask him to be an observer, in hopes that Swinburne's wishes would be carried out. William assumed the inevitable, answering, "No: I wd. have gone but for the service, wh. I think absolutely wrong." In his place he sent Helen, an ardent Swinburnian, who watched the vicar read the opening lines of the Anglican ceremony as soon as the coffin emerged from the hearse, and while professing to submit to Watts's injunction, stopped short only of reading the entire Established Church service. Once they realized what he was going to do, Helen and several others registered their dissent by walking away.

There was no such problem with William's last surviving P.R.B. companion, William Holman Hunt, who only became more respectable as he grew older, despite his unsanctioned marriage.* For years the two men had not been close because of the mutual hostility between Hunt and Gabriel, but as Gabriel became reclusive, Hunt resumed contacts with William. Still, in the 1890s William refused to consult Hunt on biographical matters relating to the P.R.B. for Hunt claimed for himself what William intended proposing as Gabriel's contributions. Again relations cooled, but Hunt was satisfied that he had made his own case once he published his own recollections in 1905. William had predicted that some of Hunt's "notions" would be "entirely fanciful," and Hunt indeed claimed almost perfect recall, even of conversations a half-century old, or more. And what he recalled, William noted sadly in his diary, often "construed harshly" Gabriel's motives. Making detailed notes as he read, William planned on publishing a lengthy refutation; but in the final pages he came upon lines his former P.R.B. crony wrote in comparing the Rossetti brothers. "Who shall say,"

---

* The Deceased Wife's Sister's Marriage Act became law in 1907, legitimatizing Hunt's union *ex post facto*.

Hunt concluded, "that to write out sonorous, well thought out, and perfectly adjusted verse is nobler than to live and walk through life with sincerity and generous unselfishness?" William remembered, too, the undignified controversy in the press when he had replied to William Bell Scott's posthumous crotchets about Gabriel, and decided instead to offer Hunt personally his contrary versions of their prentice years.

The result was an invitation to lunch a month later, early in 1906, where Hunt and William renewed their fractured friendship. At Hunt's William very likely saw the daguerrotype of *The Girlhood of Mary Virgin*, which Gabriel had presented to his P.R.B. crony as a parting gift when Hunt left on his first painting expedition to the East more than a half-century before. Gabriel had written on it lines from Tom Taylor's *Philip van Artevelde*:

> There's that betwixt us been, which men remember
> Till they forget themselves, till all's forgot,
> Till the deep sleep falls on them in that bed
> From which no morrow's mischief knocks them up.
>   from D.G.R.

Despite his break with Gabriel, Holman Hunt had kept the picture on his table (or carried it with him) through the years. The bittersweet memory of the Brotherhood had lingered.

Nothing was said for hours about the points of dispute in Hunt's book until Mrs. Hunt mentioned the notes. William produced them from a pocket and handed them to her, "to be examd. at leisure." The afternoon ended cordially, William noting in his diary, "It is truly a great satisfn. to me to have seen old H. once more & with undiminished good-will, after so long an interval. I shall try to look him up again from time to time." Hunt visited at St. Edmund's Terrace as well, although the crusty old painter with the patriarchal white beard was wispily frail and nearly blind. William would lead him about by the hand, murmuring, "My dear old friend."

As late as 1908 the old P.R.B.'s were still seeing each other, William having dinner with Hunt on Hunt's eighty-first birthday, and noting that it was "nearly the only time" he had dined out since 1893. Two years later Hunt was dead, and William, now eighty, was a pallbearer when Hunt's ashes were interred in the crypt of the Painters' Corner at St. Paul's Cathedral. In the evening, following the ceremony, he finished an article for the *Contemporary Review* on his memories of Hunt.

The day after, April 3, there was a knock at the door at St. Edmund's Terrace. It was another figure from the past, James Siddall. Harry was dead. William no longer would have to carry out Lizzy's deathbed entreaty. Yet at seventy James Siddall could not survive outside the workhouse without help, and William agreed to pay him £25 a year in quarterly installments. Later Siddall managed to secure an old age pension, but since it was too small to live on, William cut back his payments while continuing a portion of the old allowance as a supplement. A long life was expensive. He had inherited what remained of the Rossetti and Polidori estates, but also their obligations. And Mary, long ailing with arthritis and sent to Germany for doctoring, proved incurable, and William was resigned to caring for a chronically ill daughter who needed expensive treatment, a widowed daughter and a granddaughter, and the various supplicants who came to the door, from newly arrived Italian immigrants to the ubiquitous James Siddall.

The past, in other ways, refused to disappear. Rummaging in a cupboard in what had been Arthur's bedroom, Helen turned up a quantity of unfinished canvases by Gabriel, Dunn and Lucy. William had forgotten that they existed. Some were put aside as worth preserving. The rest were finally declared rubbish. Two days later Helen found what appeared to be the beginning of Gabriel's "Desdemona picture," which in his last years he had begun to paint in oils from Marie Spartali Stillman. Only the head and arms had been painted in. William gave it to Helen, who salvaged it by trimming away the blank outer sections of the canvas.

There was now little literary activity which William aspired to do. Ford Madox Hueffer had become editor of a new magazine, the *English Review*, and asked him to put together some Rossetti-Madox Brown correspondence for it. Other magazine editors came to him when a contemporary died, seeking a memoir-article. To get some of his work published he could no longer wait to be asked, and paid the firm of Elkin Mathews £40 to publish his translation of Dante's *Purgatorio*, and additional pounds to publish his edition of Dr. John Polidori's diary. Now and then he wrote letters to the editor, correcting biographers and memoirists who alleged things about Gabriel or Christina or Madox Brown which William felt were erroneous, even correcting, in painstaking detail, his nephew Ford, in the *Outlook*, when Hueffer published his *Ancient Lights and Certain New Reflections*. The future Ford Madox Ford had faint regard for accuracy, and was usually satisfied that what should have been so actually was so.

For the most part William's work, at eighty, was done, except to continue to be the watchdog of the Rossetti reputation, and he was under no illusions about his own fame when writers came to call, or—as William Rothenstein did—to draw his portrait. He knew what his current literary worth was, for when he made out his annual income tax return on May 4, 1910 he discovered that only one percent of his income of nearly £2,000) (including his pension) was earned by his own writings. He had collected £19.5.1. by his pen.

Two days later the morning papers brought the unexpected news of the grave illness of the King, and on the morning of May 7 William read of the death of Edward VII the previous night. It was, the now-mellowed old socialist and onetime advocate of regicide thought, "a national loss, but one must wait to see what comes of King George." Moved by the King's passing, the author of *Democratic Sonnets* "adopted mourning," and mused upon mortality. Most of his old acquaintances were gone, and when he went to a luncheon at the National Liberal Club he sat with representatives of a younger generation, some of whom he did not know at all. John Burns, a workingman who had achieved cabinet status, recognized him and came up to shake his hand. William, a white-bearded patriarch of no political significance, was pleased.

Troubled by rheumatism and gout, as well as by continuing publishing frustrations—for no publisher wanted his three later volumes of Rossetti papers*—he confessed early in 1912, "I feel of late very aged and feeble, but am not *ill*: my literary career is no doubt closed." As the executor for Gabriel and Christina he was still consulted regularly on matters concerning them, and on visiting his failing old friend Watts-Dunton in Putney he talked as usual about literary matters; but his chief consolations had become his pipe and his first phonograph, with its huge horn of a loudspeaker. His life remained orderly and benign. William's days, Richard Curle remembered, "went by like clockwork, and he was as methodical as a machine. One could tell to a minute when he would be down every morning, when he would enter his study—the most fascinating little book-lined room, whose window opened on to a neglected garden where cats were always prowling and scratching—, when he would have his first pipe, when he would settle to work and when he would stop, when he would go out in his slouch hat and poet's cloak, a real figure of the past, for his afternoon walk across Primrose Hill, and when he would retire for the night." He methodically docketed his papers and letters, preserved book catalogs he received, attached labels to everything in the house connected with Christina or Gabriel in order to validate its provenance, and managed the sale of photographs of his brother's pictures. In 1911, on receiving the new eleventh edition of the *Encyclopaedia Britannica*, he patiently began reading it through from A to Z, omitting only the mathematical articles. In good weather he often strolled to the Regent's Park Zoo, where life had constant interest for him, but one fine spring day in 1911, while he was waiting in the crowd which had gathered to see the lions fed, his gold watch, which had once been his Polidori grandfather's, was stolen. It had been lifted from him once before—in Switzerland in 1896. This time it was not recovered. Another piece of his past was gone.

---

* 1870–76, 1876–82 and 1882–94.

Rossetti "had the most amazing memory," Curle discovered, "and not only for great events for things long since forgotten by everybody else. . . . One would ask him, for example, whether he remembered anything about some obscure murder which happened in 1858. In answer he would first say, 'Let me reflect,' and then presently he would begin like this: 'On the tenth day of October, 1858, a servant girl, named Harriet Welbore, employed by a family at Twickenham, opened the front door at seven thirty-five in order to take in, as usual, the morning supply of milk, when she perceived, lying in a pool of blood,' and so on. . . . It was astonishing, and sounded all the more astonishing because of the resonant modulations of his voice." Yet William's leisurely sense of the past irritated his younger contemporary, Henry James. Despite the circumlocutions of his own mandarin style, which had even made a labyrinth of his conversation in his later years, James was exasperated by William's alleged inadequacies at anecdote. One of the former Inland Revenue official's favorite stories was of observing philosopher Herbert Spencer proposing marriage to "George Eliot" on the back terrace of Somerset House overlooking the Thames. "You would think that a man would make something out of a story like *that*," he protested to William's nephew Ford, "but the way he told it was like this." And in a falsetto meant to reproduce William's voice as it appeared to him, James squeaked, "I have as a matter of fact frequently meditated on the motives which induced the lady's refusal of one so distinguished; and after mature consideration I have arrived at the conclusion that, although Mr. Spencer with correctness went down upon one knee and grasped the lady's hand, he completely omitted the ceremony of removing his high hat, a proceeding which her sense of the occasion may have demanded."

The absurdity of the situation appealed to James, and the failure of William Rossetti's literary imagination to rise to it seemed to him outrageous. "Is that the way to tell *that* story?" he demanded. But when William discussed his own role in the past it was as much without ornamentation as without vanity, as he recognized his limitations and understood his role. Reading William's long and unsuccessful poem "Mrs. Holmes Grey," Curle noted aloud that two lines in it appeared superior to the rest. Undisturbed, William said simply, "These were the only lines in the poem written by Gabriel."

At St. Edmund's Terrace he puttered in his study, wrote letters daily, and worried over dwindling royalty income and increasing prospects of a European war, which he felt the Germans would win. Early in 1914 he received a telegram from May Morris: "Mother died suddenly here yesterday." He had not been in touch with her in many years, and had even hesitated sending her Gabriel's *Collected Works* a quarter century earlier, fearing to remind anyone—even Janey—of the relationship he would barely mention in his books about Gabriel. His eyesight was failing badly, and even with new spectacles William found it difficult to read the small print of the newspapers at just the time that war news was filling so many columns. Olive still lived in Rome, and her father worried about the war reaching Italy. He could do little about it, but sent her a £5 note in each letter, and felt better for it.

Years before, Mackenzie Bell had refused permission to include letters from Christina he had purchased in William's collection of her correspondence. In 1916 he suddenly tried a Rossetti publishing proposal out on William, who answered acerbically that he was too old and infirm and had no desire to see Bell. He *was* too infirm, with shaky legs and fading vision, but he was also repaying Bell.

By 1917 he was living entirely downstairs, where, to spare his feeble legs, his bed had been moved. The war deprived him of small comforts, and the old age he hated deprived him of other small pleasures. The dragging on of the carnage had left him "downcast," and £5 notes to Olive remained all he could do. He characterized his eighty-eighth birthday as "that dismal anniversary," for, he scrawled in his diary, he was now "half-seeing," and could only write "a wretched scrap." The memorabilia on the study walls had grown hazy. The last letter he wrote was dated October 13, 1918.

To Curle he had once said, "I should regard it as a disaster if I were to live to be ninety." During the winter of 1918–19, just after he was cheered by the end of the war, he suffered a severe chill, and took to his bed. With none of the painful melodrama which had accompanied the end of his brother and sisters, William Michael Rossetti died at three o'clock in the afternoon on February 5, 1919. He was eighty-nine.

Afterword

On February 8, 1919, Highgate Cemetery was covered with a heavy blanket of recent snow except where a grave had been opened for William's ashes. Only a few mourners—William's four children, and Alice Rothenstein, Edith Holman Hunt and two representatives from the Italian Embassy—clustered about the family plot which already held his mother and father, and Lizzy and Christina. The last of the four Rossettis, he had lived long enough to be nearly forgotten. And he was, J. C. Squire wrote in his weekly book column, "not the kind of man about whom anecdotes clustered." He had been the chronicler of the Pre-Raphaelite movement for nearly seventy years, and had been involved in its origin. He had been instrumental in rescuing Blake from neglect, Whitman from opprobrium, Shelley from textual emasculation. Posterity has looked kindly on men for much less.

Buried at Brompton Cemetery with her other departed Sisters of the Poor, Maria—like Gabriel—had been separated in death from her family. It had been her ill fortune to be first born and least attractive. The unhappy combination in a brilliant intellectual of the lower middle class meant only spinsterhood and the need to earn a livelihood. Similar gifts in a family of blood or means—or both—might have meant a salon in which to manipulate men and women of an upper bohemia. Maria could only fulfill her family obligation by producing a work on Dante, and then attempt to escape into the shadows of a nunnery.

Christina's tragedy, unlike Maria's, had become her triumph. In repression and religion were the stuff of her art, and although Virginia Woolf put it cruelly (while considering Christina "about as good as poetesses are made, since Sappho . . ."), there was something to her remark that "Christina Rossetti positively liked being ill," and that "it reminded her of her narrow bed, and of the chance of hell fire, and the probability of eternal torment. And to a Christian this is about the most cheerful thought in the world." The horrors she embraced were the price of her song.

Logically, Gabriel should not have been the most influential painter and poet of the Pre-Raphaelites, although he supplied what are considered the movement's most characteristic elements, from its romantic medievalism to its lush color and almost palpable detail. By standards of his contemporaries, he was unschooled and unskilled, and—paradoxically—a commercial artist who refused to advertise his art through public exhibition. As Roger Fry once put it, "the ordinary world of vision scarcely supplied any inspiration" to Rossetti, for he was the poet as well as the painter, of images of passionate desire which elevated his models into mythic beings. As he explained himself,

> Under the arch of Life, where love and death,
> Terror and mystery, guard her shrine, I saw
> Beauty enthroned; and though her gaze struck awe,
> I drew it in as simply as my breath.

Although Gabriel was the victim as well as the limner of that vision, Whistler protested, from his own deathbed, "You must not say anything against Rossetti. Rossetti was a king." Earlier a disciple during the *annis mirabilis* at Oxford had cried out, "Why is he not some great exiled king, that we might give him our lives to try to restore him to his kingdom!" And Burne-Jones, preparing a young friend to meet the Master, cautioned, "We shall see the greatest man in Europe."

The author of "Hand and Soul," Gabriel was hand and soul of both flowerings of Pre-Raphaelitism, and monarch of all the Rossettis. Grandparents, parents, aunts, uncles, brother and sisters were, one way or another, lieges at his court or historians of his reign. It became difficult, even though one sister had been a poetic genius, for the world to remember that there were other Rossettis. Yet no playwright could have invented the four Rossettis, in all their reality, without being charged with melodrama. The stuffy rooms of their surviving houses, their pictures and papers, the pages of their books, are alive with their shades.

Sources

All PRB-related sources dated 1963 or earlier utilized in this study are described in W. E. Fredeman's *Pre-Raphaelitism. A Bibliocritical Study* (Harvard, 1965). Because of the easy accessibility of this major bibliographical tool, not all of these pre-1964 sources are cited below, although many of particular significance will be referred to where appropriate. Other than the published sources cited below chapter-by-chapter, the major documentation for *Four Rossettis* has come from manuscript materials in the British Library, the Princeton University Library, the Humanities Research Center of the University of Texas and the Angeli and Penkill Collections of the University of British Columbia. Some of the texts of poems quoted from diverge from the W. M. Rossetti versions slightly as they are taken from versions which preceded his editing and/or tinkering. Except where clarity requires expansion, after Chapter I, the four Rossettis will be referred to below by their initials.

I

The major published sources for the children's early years are, except where otherwise noted, William Michael Rossetti, *Some Reminiscences* (New York, 1906); Gabriele Rossetti, *A Versified Autobiography*, trans. W. M. Rossetti (London, 1901); R. D. Waller, *The Rossetti Family, 1824–1854* (Manchester, 1932); Oswald Doughty, *A Victorian Romantic: Dante Gabriel Rossetti* (Oxford, 1960); Lona Mosk Packer, *Christina Rossetti* (Berkeley, California, 1963); and Rosalie Glynn Grylls, *Portrait of Rossetti* (London, 1964). A copy of Maria's "Princesse Borghese" is in the collection of the late Lafayette L. Butler, Hazelton, Pa. The "Rome" translation by MFR is in the Angeli Collection, UBC. DGR's reference to *Anselemo the Accursed* in an autograph letter (May 2, n.y.) to C. F. Murray at the HRC, Texas, as is WMR's reference (15 May, n.y.) in a letter to Thomas Dixon on being since boyhood, an avowed nonbeliever.

II

WMR's and DGR's prentice years and the teen-age years of CGR and MFR are set forth in WMR's *Reminiscences* as well as in his memoir of DGR, in the DGR *Letters,* in Doughty, Packer and Waller, W. B. Scott's *Autobiographical Notes* (New York, 1892), and W. H. Hunt's *Preraphaelitism and the Preraphaelite Brotherhood* (London, 1905–06). These sources continue to be vital to succeeding chapters. The "G.C.D.R." drawing appears in V. Surtees, *Rossetti: The Paintings and Drawings* (Oxford, 2 vols., 1971). Many of the *bouts-rimés* are in ms. at Princeton.

III

The surviving mss. of the *P.R.B. Journal* have been edited, annotated and published by W. F. Fredeman (Oxford, 1975). A copy of the "Free Exhibition" catalog is at Texas. The excisions by WMR of references to Collinson in CGR's letters can be seen in mss. at Princeton, where, also, is CGR's ms. letter to WMR, 28 April 1849, asking William not to copy for Woolner any of her poems which appear to be too personal, the Collinson affair clearly implied.

IV

CGR's poems unpublished in her lifetime were printed, slightly expurgated, by WMR in *New Poems* (London, 1896); many of the expurgations are restored in Packer. The breach of DGR's confidence about "PRB" by Reach via Munro, is described by G. H. Fleming in *Rossetti and the Pre-Raphaelite Brotherhood* (London, 1967). The most authoritative source for the identities of DGR's models, picture-by-picture, is in Surtees, often based on unpublished letters or letters published there for the first time.

V

Lucy Brown's "education" at the Rossettis is described in a letter from CGR to WMR, 4 July 1853, a typed copy of which is at UBC. CGR's novella, *Maude*, was published posthumously by WMR. Madox Brown's diary is published in part by WMR in *Ruskin, Rossetti, Preraphaelitism* (New

York, 1899). Holman Hunt's description of his painting the head of Jesus in *The Light of the World* from Christina appears in a letter from him to Edward Clodd, 11 January 1898, published in Clodd's *Memories* (London, 1916).

VI

Barbara Bodichon's letters to Bessie Parkes about Lizzy Siddal are at Princeton. DGR's undated letter to F. J. Furnivall about the cesspoollike state of the Thames at Blackfriars is at Texas. CGR's *bouts-rimés* sonnet-endings mailed from Frome to WMR 23 February 1854 are at UBC.

VII

Ruskin's letters to DGR were first published in *RRP*, as were most of Lizzy Siddal's few poems. The biographer who links "The Cup of Cold Water" to DGR and Morris is Doughty. The CGR biographer who applies the Eucharist concept to the theme of "Goblin Market" is Packer. Violet Hunt's allegation about Collinson comes from her unreliable *The Wife of Rossetti* (New York, 1932). The drawing for "The Ballad of Fair Annie" is at the Birmingham City Museum and Art Gallery. The quoted recollections of Burne-Jones are from Frances Horner's *Time Remembered* (London, 1933). Lizzy's undated plea to DGR to return to help her is at Princeton. Arthur Hughes's recollection of Gabriel's behaving at Oxford "like a prince" in his painting coat is from a letter quoted by Fredeman in "A Pre-Raphaelite Gazette: The Penkill Letters of Arthur Hughes to William Bell Scott and Alice Boyd, 1886–97," *Bulletin of the John Rylands Library*, 49:2 (Manchester, 1967).

VIII

The medicinal uses of laudanum for tuberculosis of various types in the nineteenth century are discussed in R. and J. Dubos, *The White Plague: Tuberculosis, Man and Society* (London, 1953). Georgiana Jones's memories of Lizzy are from her *Memorials of Edward Burne-Jones* (London, 1904). Gabriel's acknowledgment of half a £50 note on 27 July 1861 is at UBC. The abortive adoption of Nellie Farren is taken from an interview with her by W. Graham Robertson in his *Life Was Worth Living* (New York & London, 1931). The reaction of Henrietta Rintoul is taken from CGR's description in her letter to William, 30 November 1860, at UBC. Miss Rintoul's age is based upon her death certificate at the General Register

Office. (She is likely to have been even older than her declared age, which was 79 in 1904.) WMR wrote about Lizzy at length both in his *Reminiscences* and in the *Burlington Magazine*, May 1903. Maria's relationship with Cayley is based upon her letters to him at Princeton. The retrieval of Lizzy's pet bullfinch is noted from Frances Rossetti's diary for 17 February 1862, at Princeton.

IX

The disfiguring of DGR's model Ellen Smith is noted in the ms. of Treffry Dunn's memoir of DGR at Princeton. Swinburne's letters to WMR here and hereafter are from the Cecil Lang edition *The Swinburne Letters* (New Haven, 1959). WMR's tobacco box is referred to in Dunn. Gabriel's interest in purchasing a lion for his Cheyne Walk menagerie is from Georgiana Jones, *Memorials.* The snowy New Year's night at Cheyne Walk is described by DGR in a letter to C. A. Howell, 2 January 1867, at Texas. DGR's technique of painting a model in the nude and adding the clothing afterwards is described in *The Times*, 18 April 1882. The correspondence of DGR, CGR and WMR with Macmillan is from Packer, *The Rossetti-Macmillan Letters* (Berkeley, Calif., 1963), except where textual corrections have been made from ms. DGR's confession that he must spend his Sundays with Fanny is from a letter to Howell, 20 October 1867, at Texas. The plans for Maria's Italian exercise book, and word of its initial success are from CGR to DGR, January 1865, Princeton, and WMR's diary, 2 October 1868, in *Rossetti Papers, 1862–1870* ed. WMR (London, 1903). Maria's contract for the book with Williams and Norgate, dated 27 February 1867, is at UBC. Letters from CGR about *The Prince's Progress* are from Janet Camp Troxell, *Three Rossettis: Unpublished Letters to and from Dante Gabriel Rossetti, Christina, William* (Harvard, 1937). Later chapters, through to CGR's death, are also indebted to Troxell.

X

The mutual Whistler-Rossetti interest in séances is described in S. Weintraub, *Whistler* (New York & London, 1973). WMR's descriptions of the séances he attended are in his ms. journals at UBC, and in the "Spiritualism" chapter of Helen Rossetti Angeli's *Dante Gabriel Rossetti: his friends and enemies* (London, 1949). Christina's letter on the subject is in the *Family Letters*, and dated 23 December 1864. WMR's letters to Mrs. Gilchrist are published in C. E. Gohdes and P. F. Baum, eds., *Letters of William Michael Rossetti to Anne Gilchrist and her son Herbert Gilchrist* (Durham, N.C., 1934). Subsequent chapters are also indebted to this volume. Other letters from WMR and to WMR are in his *Rossetti Papers.* Bell Scott's reports of the séances are from his *Autobiographical Notes* as well as from his letters as edited by W. E. Fredeman in the article "Prelude to the Last Decade: Dante Gabriel Rossetti in the Summer of 1872" in the *Bulletin of the John Rylands Library*, 53 (Manchester, 1970–71). Cayley's letter to DGR on the peacocks is at Texas. DGR's reference to "dead stock" is in an undated letter to an unidentified correspondent at Texas. The DGR correspondence with Howell about the exhumation is in Troxell. Entries from Allingham's diary here and elsewhere are from *William Allingham's Diary* (Fontwell, Sussex, 1967). William Morris's letters are quoted in the biography *William Morris: His Life, Work & Friends* by Philip Henderson (New York, 1967). W. D. Paden's *La Pia de' Tolomei* monograph is printed as *The Register of the Museum of Art,* The University of Kansas, II (November 1958). The Munby diary entry is from Derek Hudson's *Munby: Man of Two Worlds* (Boston, 1972). The letters from Jane Morris to DGR (Princeton) and DGR to Jane Morris (BL) are now published in John Bryson, ed., *Dante Gabriel Rossetti and Jane Morris: Their Correspondence* (Oxford, 1976).

XI

DGR on the unpleasantness of the exhumed ms. is from Fredeman, "Summer of 1872." Bell Scott on the ms. is quoted in Packer. WMR on DGR's "supernatural visitation" is from the journals at UBC; Dunn's version is from his *Life with Rossetti.* MFR's correspondence with her publisher is at UBC. The gloom of the interior in Gabriel's Cheyne Walk house is described in lines WMR excised from Dunn's *Life* and visible in the ms. at Princeton. Stillman's version of DGR's introduction to chloral is from W. J. Stillman, *The Autobiography of a Journalist* (New York and Boston, 1901). The comment by John Butler Yeats is from his unpublished memoir in the Yeats Papers, Dublin. WMR to Dixon on the Franco-Prussian War is from a letter at Texas dated 28 August 1870. James Russell Lowell on MFR's *Shadow of Dante* is an 1872 review collected in *Among My Books*, III (Boston and New York, 1904). CGR's letters to F. S. Ellis are in Packer, *Rossetti-Macmillan Letters.* Rossetti's reaction to Browning's *Fifine* is described, quoting both WMR and Brown, in Rosalie Grylls, "Rossetti and Browning," *Princeton Library Chronicle*, 33 (1972).

XII

The basic documentary source is W. E. Fredeman's "Summer of 1872," which quotes from or refers to 206 letters or other documents relevant to the months of DGR's breakdown and recuperation. Other material comes from WMR's memoir of DGR, which is detailed about incidents WMR chooses to relate, and memoirs of such friends and associates as Hake, Scott, and Dunn, and Helen Rossetti Angeli's *Dante Gabriel Rossetti* (particularly her chapter, "Rossetti's Health and Decline"). Material on DGR's chloral addiction and its aftermath, here and in succeeding chapters, is medically based upon David I. Macht and Nellie L. Gessford, "The Unfortunate Drug Experiences of Dante Gabriel Rossetti," *Bulletin of the Institute of the History of Medicine*, IV (1938); S. C. Dyke, "Some Medical Aspects of the Life of Dante Gabriel Rossetti," *Royal Society of Medicine, London Proceedings*, LVI (1963); and on toxicological data in Louis Sanford Goodman and Alfred Gilman, *Pharmalogical Basis of Therapeutics* (New York, 1965).

XIII

The Hall Caine material here and in XIV is from his two memoirs of DGR, notably the less reticent 1928 version. WMR's diary entries are from UBC. Maria's letter to Nolly Brown is at UBC. The Italian proverb DGR quotes from his father is in a letter to Frederick Sandys, 4 September 1873, at Texas. Data on the Eastbourne Hospital is from Packer, ed., *The Rossetti-Macmillan Letters*. Maria's nun's habit is self-described in an undated letter to Lucy Madox Brown, at UBC. The Euston Square dinner WBS attends is described in his letter to Alice Boyd, 31 October 1873, in Fredeman, "Summer of 1872." The scandal about DGR and Mrs. Morris is also related by WBS in two letters to AB, both extracted in "The Summer of 1872." WMR relates the loss of his Swedenborg books to Dixon in a letter, 7 March [prob. 1874], at Texas. WMR's marriage and its domestic aftermath at Euston Square is told in WMR's *Reminiscences* and the *Family Letters* as well as WMR's unpublished diaries. WMR's letter to Dixon on Maria's death is at Texas. Christina's published notes to WMR on Maria's last illness are in the *Family Letters*; the unpublished ones are at UBC. W. B. Scott's obituary notice on MRF is from an unidentified newspaper cutting at Princeton.

XIV

DGR's letters to WMR and Lucy on "Democratic Sonnets" are in the *Letters*. Other material relating to the "Sonnets" appears in Roger Peattie's unpublished PhD dissertation, "William Michael Rossetti as Critic and Editor, together with a Consideration of His Life and Character" (University College, London, 1966), and in Leonid M. Arinshtein and

W. E. Fredeman, "William Michael Rossetti's 'Democratic Sonnets,'" *Victorian Studies*, XIV (1971). Cayley's letters to CGR are at Princeton. Swinburne's letters to WMR are in Lang. CGR's letters to Macmillan are in Packer, ed. WMR on his family is from his *Reminiscences* and his diary. Christina's 2 December 1881 letter to DGR is from the *Family Letters*. The medical evaluation of DGR's detoxification failure and subsequent death is based upon consultation with physicians specializing in drug-related cases and on the publications referred to under XII.

XV

A file of letters, newspaper cuttings and documents relating to the settling of DGR's estate and disposition of his effects is at Texas. CGR's letters to WMR not in her published letters are at both UBC and Texas. (She refers to the "monitory blue pencil" in a letter to WMR, 7 November 1882, at Princeton.) "Isobel Meredith's" *A Girl Among the Anarchists* was published by Duckworth in 1903. CGR's and WMR's account books are at UBC. Juliet Hueffer Soskice's memoir of her childhood at St. Edmund's Terrace is *Chapters from Childhood* (London, 1922); Ford Madox [Hueffer] Ford's less trustworthy memoirs, in part encompassing the same time and place, are *Memories and Impressions* (New York, 1911), published in England as *Ancient Lights and Certain New Reflections* (London, 1911); and *Return to Yesterday* (New York, 1932). Swinburne's letters to CGR are in Lang. References to Vernon Lee are from Peter Gunn, *Vernon Lee* (London, 1964) and Vineta Colby, *The Singular Anomaly* (New York, 1971). Sophie Cayley's letter to CGR on the death of her brother, 8 December 1883, is at UBC. WMR's accounts of the deaths of his close relatives are in his diaries, *Reminiscences* and notes to CGR's published letters. The letters of the "literary lady" neighbor in Torrington Square are in Packer. WMR's chronicle of CGR's last days, more detailed than his usual diary entries, is at UBC. The program of CGR's burial service is at the Pattee Library, Pa. State Univ.

XVI

WMR's letters to Mackenzie Bell are at Princeton. His letters to W. M. Colles of the Authors' Syndicate are at Texas. Details of WMR's day-by-day existence is drawn from the UBC diaries (also the major source for this period in Roger Peattie's dissertation on WMR) and from the *Reminiscences*. WMR's last encounters with the Siddalls are described in the diaries and in an unpublished letter of 22 September 1911 to an unknown correspondent, Rutgers Univ., quoted by Peattie. WMR's letters to Burgess are from the collection of LaFayette Butler. Richard Curle's memories of St. Edmund's Terrace are from *Caravansary and Conversation* (New York, 1927) and William Rothenstein's are from *Men and Memories* (London, 1931). WMR's last months of frailty are described in a letter from Helen R. Angeli, 28 January 1919, to Richard Curle; and one from WMR himself to Curle, 20 June 1913, describes the limitations of old age. Both are at the Pattee Library, Pa. State Univ.

Afterword

The list of mourners at the funeral is from Peattie. J. C. Squire's comments are reprinted in *Books in General* (London, n.d.), under the pseudonym of "Solomon Eagle." The "exiled king" utterance was Philip Marston's. The comments by Virginia Woolf are quoted from the first volume of her *Letters*, ed. Nigel Nicolson and Joanne Trautmann (London and New York, 1975). Roger Fry's comment appears in "The New Rossettis at the National Gallery," *Burlington Magazine*, XXIX (1916).

Acknowledgments

I am grateful for assistance to members of the Rossetti family, especially to the late Helen Rossetti Angeli (who began responding to my queries as early as the early 1960s), Mrs. Imogen Dennis, Mrs. R. A. O'Conor and Mr. T. R. O'Conor. Rossetti scholars have been more than helpful, in particular PRB bibliographer (and editor of the forthcoming Dante Gabriel Rossetti letters) W. E. Fredeman, DGR scholar C. L. Cline, iconographer Virginia Surtees, and biographer Rosalie Glynn Grylls (Lady Mander). Many libraries, museums, art galleries and their staffs have assisted, especially the Ashmolean Museum, Oxford; City of Birmingham Museum and Art Gallery; University of British Columbia Library; British Museum (British Library); Firestone Library, Princeton University; Fitzwilliam Museum, Cambridge; Houghton Library, Harvard University; Humanities Research Center, University of Texas at Austin; Pattee Library, The Pennsylvania State University; and Tate Gallery. I am indebted, too, to Charles T. Butler, the late LaFayette Butler, Alexander Clark, Maurice Cramer, Fred D. Crawford, Phyllis Dolich, David Farmer, Robert W. Frank, Robert S. Fraser, Stephen R. Grecco, John A. Hargleroad, M.D., Albert L. Ingram, M.D., Philip Klass, Cecil Lang, Dan H. Laurence, Charles W. Mann, Bernard S. Oldsey, Ralph E. Pilgram, M.D., Shirley Rader, Warren Roberts, Frank Swinnerton, Janet Camp Troxell, Michael Yeats, Philip Young, and to my wife (and companion in research), Rodelle.

Acknowledgments regarding particular manuscripts utilized are noted under Sources, and regarding illustrations as part of each caption.

S.W.

Index